OFF THE BEATEN PATH® SE

British Columbia

THIRD EDITION

Off the Beaten Path®

by Tricia Timmermans

The Globe Pequot Press

Guilford, Connecticut

For Luke, Mary-Louise, and Daniel

917.11
OFF
2002

Text design by Laura Augustine
Maps created by Equator Graphics © The Globe Pequot Press
Text illustrations by Carole Drong

ISBN 0-7627-1025-X
ISSN 1536–6154

Manufactured in the United States of America
Third Edition/First Printing

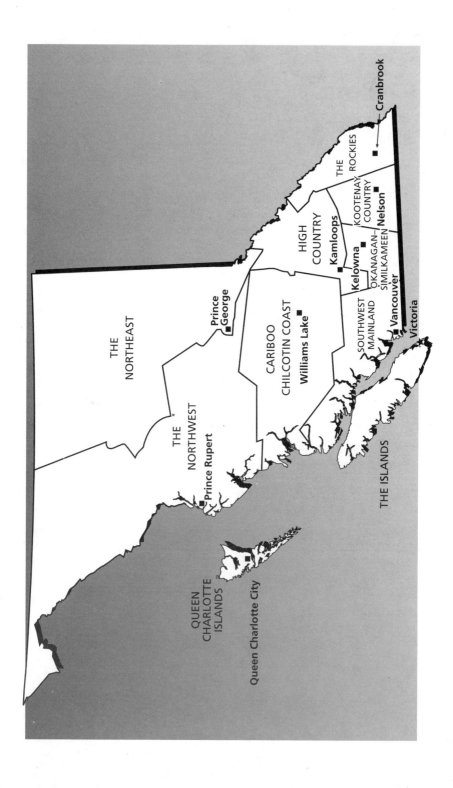

THE NORTHEAST

THE NORTHWEST

Prince Rupert

Prince George

CARIBOO CHILCOTIN COAST

Williams Lake

HIGH COUNTRY

Kamloops

Kelowna

KOOTENAY COUNTRY

OKANAGAN–SIMILKAMEEN

Nelson

THE ROCKIES

Cranbrook

SOUTHWEST MAINLAND

Vancouver

Victoria

QUEEN CHARLOTTE ISLANDS

Queen Charlotte City

THE ISLANDS

Contents

Acknowledgments

Thanks to all the proud British Columbians who have enthusiastically provided new information for this edition. Regional and local tourism staff have been helpful with corrections and suggestions, often enlightening me with tales and trivia pertinent to their areas. Loving thanks again to my ever-supportive family and friends. Their assistance, encouragement, and humor have helped make the researching and writing process a pleasant experience.

Introduction

Canadian humorist Stephen Leacock once quipped about British Columbia: "If I had known what it was like, I wouldn't have been content with a mere visit—I'd have been born here." No doubt he was referring to the extraordinary beauty of BC's postcard-perfect, snow-covered mountains and blue lakes, the exciting history of this wild province, and the courage and friendliness of its people. This book is intended to help you discover what Leacock was enthusing about, while introducing you to some of the best of BC's lesser-known attractions—your fun will be in tripping over a few more on the way. I hope that as you continue to explore BC, my adopted province, with *British Columbia Off the Beaten Path®* in hand, you might soon be wishing you'd been "born here," too.

Contact Information

For general information and bookings write Tourism BC, Box 9830, Station Provincial Government, Victoria, V8W 9W5; or phone **Super, Natural BC** at (800) HELLOBC (435–5622) in North America including Mexico. Outside North America phone (250) 387–1642. In England visit Tourism British Columbia, Third Floor, 3 Regent Street, London, England, SW1Y 4NS. Visit www.hellobc.com for free reservations and information service.

The Islands

Tourism Vancouver Island, 203-335 Wesley Street, Nanaimo V9R 2T5; (250) 754–3500; fax: (250) 754–3599; info@islands.bc.ca; www.islands.bc.ca

The Southwestern Mainland

Vancouver, Coast and Mountains Tourism Region, 250–1508 West Second Avenue, Vancouver, V6J 1H2; (800) 667–3306 or (604) 739–9011; fax: (604) 739–0153; info@coastandmountains.bc.ca; www. coastandmountains.bc.ca

Thomson Okanagan and High Country

Thomson Okanagan Tourism Association, 1332 Water Street, Kelowna, V1Y 9P4; (800) 567–2275 or (250) 860–5999; fax: (250) 860–9993; info@thompsonokanagan.com; www.thompsonokanagan.com

Cariboo Chilcotin Coast

Cariboo Chilcotin Coast Tourism Association, 1188 North First
Avenue, V2G 1Y8; (250) 392–2226; fax: (250) 392–2838;
cta@landwithout limits.com; www.landwithoutlimits.com

Kootenay Country and the Rockies

Tourism Rockies, P.O. Box 10, Kimberley, V1A 2Y5; (250) 427–4838;
fax: (250) 427–3344; for brochure requests: (800) 661–6603;
info@bcrockies.com; www.bcrockies.com

The Northeast, the Northwest, and Queen Charlotte Islands

Northern British Columbia Tourism Association, P.O. Box 2373,
Prince George, V2N 2S6; (800) 663–8843; (250) 561–0432; fax: (250)
561–0450; info@NBCtourism.com; www.NBCtourism.com

BC Ferries, 1112 Fort Street, Victoria, V8V 4V2; (250) 386–3431 or
(888) 223–3779 (in BC) for information and reservations.
Call (604) 444–2980 or (888) 724–5223 (in BC) for automated vehicle
reservations between Vancouver and Vancouver Island using Visa or
Mastercard. fax: (250) 381–5452; www.bcferries.bc.ca

BC Museums Association, Suite 516, 409 Granville Street, Vancouver,
V6C 1T2; (604) 660–0840; fax: (604) 660–5043; BCMA@Museums
Assn.bc.ca; www.museumsassn.bc.ca/~bcma/

BC Parks, Second Floor, 800 Johnson Street, Victoria, V8V 1X4; (250)
387–5002; www.elp.gov.bc.ca/bc parks. Information on *all* BC Parks
can be accessed from this site.
(For camping reservations telephone the Discover Camping Campground Reservation Service at 800–689–9025 or 604–689–9025 in
Vancouver, or visit their Web site at www.discovercamping.ca.)

Fishing regulations and licenses: Available at most local fishing
outlets and government agent offices. For information phone the
Ministry of Fisheries in Victoria at (250) 387–9589.

Forest Recreation (1,430 recreation sites with approximately
12,000 no-service campsites): Ministry of Forests, Forest Practices
Branch, Box 9513, Station Provincial Government, Victoria, V8W
9C2; (250) 387–6656; fax: (250) 356–5909;
www.for.gov.bc.ca/hfp/hfp.htm

Hunting Regulations: Ministry of Environment, Lands and Parks,
Wildlife Branch, P.O. Box 9374, Station Provincial Government,
Victoria, V8W 9M4; (250) 387–9739; www.elp.gov.bc.ca/wld

BC Highway Condition Information: Communications Branch, Ministry of Transportation and Highways, 5B 940 Blanshard Street, Victoria (P.O. Box 9850 Station Provincial Government) V8W 9T5; (250) 387–7788; fax: (250) 356–7706; www.th.gov.bc.ca/bchighways/ roadreports/roadreports.htm

The best on-line general information for travelers to BC can be found on-line at www.BritishColumbia.com. Here you'll find extensive travel, sports and recreation, entertainment, tourism, and real estate information.

BC Facts

Where *is* BC?

BC lies between 114°03'12" and 139°03'40" W longitude and between 48°17'34" and 60°N latitude. Canada's most westerly province is bordered on the west by the Pacific Ocean and Alaska; Alberta is to the east, the Yukon and Northwest Territories to the north, and Washington, Idaho, and Montana to the south.

How many of us are there?

BC's population, as of July 1, 2000, was 4,064,000—11.09 people per square mile (4.28 per square km).

Capital stuff!

Victoria, located on Vancouver Island and named for Queen Victoria of England, is British Columbia's capital city.

Canadian dollar conversion to the U.S. dollar:

May 2001—$1.53 Canadian for one U.S. dollar (0.65 U.S. cents for one Canadian dollar)

BC is BIG!

Only thirty *countries* in the world are larger than British Columbia, which takes up a whopping 366,282 square miles (948,596 sq km). It is larger than France and Germany combined. As well, it is larger than the combined area of Washington, Oregon, California, and Tennessee and is two and a half times larger than Japan. Comprising 9.5 percent of the Canadian land surface, it runs 780 miles (1,250 km) north/south and 650 miles (1,050 km) east/west. British Columbia ranks number three in Canada in both population and land mass, behind Ontario and Quebec.

Where *is* everybody?

British Columbia has forty-four cities, fifteen towns, forty villages, twenty-eight regional districts, and fifty-three district municipalities. Sixty-five percent of the population lives on the lower mainland and southern Vancouver Island.

The long and the short of it!

British Columbia's highest **mountain** is Fairweather Mountain, at 15,298 feet (4,663 m), in the northwestern corner of the province. The longest **river** is the Fraser—850 miles (1,368 km)—which drains one-quarter of the province. The longest natural **lake** is Babine Lake—110 miles (177 km). The longest **valley** (which is also the longest in North America) is the Rocky Mountain Trench—870 miles (1,400 km). The highest **waterfall** is Takakkaw Falls—1,650 feet (503 m)—in Yoho National Park. It is also Canada's highest waterfall—almost ten times the height of Niagara Falls—and when measured by vertical drop, the highest in North America.

How many islands did you say?

Approximately 6,500 islands and islets lie off British Columbia's coast.

It's Official!

Flower: Pacific dogwood *(Cornus nuttallii)*

Bird: Steller's jay *(Cyanacitta stelleri),* the cheeky fellow you'll meet in campgrounds

Gemstone: the lovely, dark-green British Columbian jade

Tree: Western red cedar *(Thuja plicata donn),* which has been known to grow to about 200 feet (60 m)

Tartan: The provincial tartan has five colors (blue, white, green, red, and gold), each with its own significance.

Time out!

Special holidays in British Columbia are **Victoria Day** (Monday preceding May 24), **Canada Day** (July 1), and **BC Day** (first Monday in August).

INTRODUCTION

Wave the flag!

The BC emblem, designed and adopted in 1960 and based on the crest within the coat of arms, consists of a Union Jack (symbolizing British Columbia's origin as a British colony) on the upper third and a gold half-sun (symbolizing its position as Canada's most westerly province) superimposed on three wavy blue bars (the Pacific) on the bottom. The motto is *Splendor Sine Occasu* ("splendor without diminishment").

What time is it?

There are two time zones in British Columbia. Most of the province is on Pacific Time, but near the Rockies, east of Kootenay Lake, the time moves one hour ahead to Mountain Time. Daylight Saving Time for most of British Columbia (yes, there are a few holdouts!) starts on the first Sunday in April and ends on the last Sunday in October.

So, are you saving any?

The average weekly earnings for a British Columbian in March 2001 were $644.64 ($US 420.85), compared with $627.73 ($US 409.81), for the average Canadian.

It's the law!

British Columbia's legal drinking age is nineteen.

You don't like the weather? Wait fifteen minutes!

Because of BC's diverse climates, average temperatures and annual precipitation rates are wide-ranging. In Vancouver January average high and low temperatures range between 42°F and 33°F (5°C and 0°C), and July high and low averages are between 74°F and 55°F (23°C and 12°C). In Prince George (in the northeast), the January ranges are between 24°F and 5°F (-4°C and -15°C), whereas the July ranges are closer to those of Vancouver at 74°F and 45°F (23°C and 7°C).

Vancouver's annual precipitation average is 42 inches (1,069 mm); the average annual snowfall is 21 inches (534 mm); and the average number of days with precipitation is 161. Prince George, on the other hand, averages 24 inches (610 mm) of precipitation, 92 inches (2,341 mm) of snow, and 162 days of precipitation.

In the Beginning: A Peek at British Columbia's History

10,000–13,000 years ago: Carbon dating has confirmed occupation of some BC sites to this period. It is believed that the first people came across the Bering Strait from Asia.

1774: Juan Pérez Hernández saw the coast of British Columbia, did not land, but claimed the region for Spain. (Many of the islands in the Strait of Georgia—Galiano, Valdés, Quadra, for example—bear Spanish explorers' names.)

1778: Captain James Cook, leading two British ships, dropped anchor in Nootka Sound on the West Coast of Vancouver Island.

1789: Spain and Britain disputed ownership of the west coast of North America.

1790–92: The Nootka Sound controversy was settled by the Nootka Conventions, which gave equal trading rights to both Britain and Spain but did not establish ownership.

1792–94: Captain George Vancouver mapped the west coast from Oregon to Alaska, naming Vancouver Island "Quadra and Vancouver's Island" and northern Washington and southern British Columbia "New Georgia." The northern coast was called "New Hanover."

1793: Alexander Mackenzie entered the eastern part of British Columbia via the Peace and Upper Fraser Rivers. He reached the Pacific at the mouth of the Bella Coola River.

Early 1800s: Trading posts were established along the Fraser and Columbia Rivers by members of the North West Company and the Hudson's Bay Company.

1849: Vancouver Island was declared the first crown colony, with Fort Victoria as its capital.

1851: James Douglas, an official with the Hudson's Bay Company, became the first governor of the new crown colony of Vancouver Island.

1852: The Queen Charlotte Islands became a dependency of the colony.

1857: Gold was discovered on the lower Fraser River, resulting in an explosion of gold seekers in Victoria (where they went to obtain permits).

1858: A crown colony was declared on the mainland and given the name British Columbia. James Douglas became the first governor.

1861: The Cariboo Road (from Yale to Barkerville) was completed.

1866: The crown colonies of British Columbia and Vancouver Island were made one, with New Westminster as the capital. The eastern boundary was defined by the Rocky Mountains, between the 49th and 60th parallels.

1868: The seat of government was moved to Victoria.

1871: British Columbia became the sixth province to be admitted to the Dominion of Canada.

Some famous British Columbians who either live or have lived in BC

Artists Emily Carr, Mary Pratt, Bill Reid, and Jack Shadbolt; *astronaut* Dr. Bob Thirsk; *environmentalist* Dr. David Suzuki; *first female Canadian prime minister* Kim Campbell; *National Hockey League stars* Gordie Howe, Joe Sakic, Paul Kariya, Mark Recchi, Greg Adams, and Russ and Geoff Courtnall; *championship auto-racing-teams driver* Greg Moore; *golfer* Dawn Coe Jones; *figure skater* Elizabeth Manley; *baseball's* Larry Walker; *basketball's* Steve Nash; *Olympic medalists* Ross Rebagliati (snowboarding); Nancy Greene Raine, Steve Podborski, and Kerrin Lee Gartner (skiing); Silken Laumann and member of parliament David Anderson (rowing); *actors* Michael J. Fox and Jason Priestly; *actresses* Pamela Anderson of *Baywatch,* Meg and Jennifer Tilly, and Alicia Silverstone; *pianist and singer* Diana Krall; *composer and producer* David Foster; *singers* k. d. lang, Colin James, Long John Baldry, Joni Mitchell, Bryan Adams, Burton Cummings, and Sarah MacLachlan; *opera singers* Richard Margison and Benjamin Butterfield; *film director* Atom Egoyan; *authors* Alice Munro, Nick Bantock, Joy Kogawa, Douglas Coupland, Carol Shields, and Wade Davis.

Recommended Reading

Adventuring in British Columbia by Isabel Nanton and Mary Simpson (1998 Douglas and McIntyre, Canada; Sierra Club Books, USA). An excellent guide for the outdoor adventurer; this book is packed with practical information, well-researched, and well-written.

A Traveller's Guide to Aboriginal BC by Cheryl Coull (1996 Whitecap Books, Vancouver). A comprehensive guide to BC's First Nations' locations, history, and culture.

Ravens and Prophets by George Woodcock (1993 Sono Nis Press, Victoria). First published in 1952, this book describes the BC of postwar days; written by one of Canada's most prolific authors and editors.

The West Beyond the West—A History of British Columbia by Jean Barman (1996 University of Toronto Press). A thorough treatment of all aspects that shaped the British Columbia of today.

Nature BC—An Illustrated Guide to Common Plants and Animals by James Kavanagh (1993 Lone Pine Publishing, Vancouver). An excellent layman's guide, beautifully illustrated and simply described.

British Columbia Wildlife Viewing Guide by Bill Wareham (1991 Lone Pine Publishing, Edmonton). Maps show where you'll find what. Tiny, but loaded with information.

The B.C. Fact Book—Everything You Ever Wanted to Know about British Columbia by Mark Zuehlke (1995 Whitecap Books, Vancouver). The consummate fact book on BC.

British Columbia: A Natural History by Richard and Sydney Cannings (1996 Greystone Books, Douglas and McIntyre, Vancouver). A coffee table book, written by the experts in the field and graced with excellent photographs.

B.C. for Free (and Almost Free) by Pat Kramer (1992 Whitecap Books, Vancouver). Loaded with "freebie" information!

The Encyclopedia of British Columbia (2000, Harbour Publishing). Full-color, 824-page print edition and a companion CD-ROM. The publisher, with the help of hundreds of knowledgeable British Columbians, has produced the quintessential work on BC—ten years in the making.

Geology of British Columbia: A Journey Through Time by Richard J. Cannings and Sydney G. Cannings (1999 Greystone).

Safety Tips

When traveling on any of BC's logging roads, it's a good idea to visit the local logging company office to find out about activity on the road. Evenings and weekends are the best times to travel. Logging trucks **always** have right of way, so drive slowly, keep well to the right, and pull over if unsure of your safety.

OFF THE BEATEN PATH

About hiking: Always be prepared to stay overnight! You just never know.
Always carry a rain jacket. (Hypothermia can kill even in summer.) Carry
a first-aid kit and water-purifying tablets. (Giardiasis, an intestinal infec-
tion often referred to as Beaver Fever, is not unheard of.) Carry a compass
and a map and tell someone of your intended time and route plan. Be
aware that bears and cougars are wild animals and should be treated with
utmost respect. Always keep to marked trails, make plenty of noise, and
keep your food in airtight containers. And **be polite.** Never go onto First
Nations reserves or other private property without permission.

Tips for Spending

Unless otherwise stated, prices and rates do not include the 7 percent
Provincial Sales Tax (PST) or the 7 percent Federal Goods and Services Tax (GST). British Columbia does not offer a PST visitor rebate
program, but the federal government does offer a GST rebate program
for visitors from outside Canada. For more information on GST
refunds, write Canadian Tax Refund, Box 42090, Vancouver, V6P 6S6
or claimsdept@canadiantaxrefund.com. To find out what is eligible
and to print a Tax Refund Application Form, go to www.canadian
taxrefund.com.

*The prices and rates listed in this guidebook are quoted in Cana-
dian dollars and were confirmed at press time. We recommend,
however, that you call establishments before traveling to obtain
current information.*

The Islands

Whether it's for the warm Pacific air or the billions of blossoms counted each February in Victoria's **Flower Count,** many Canadians are moving west to the islands. I had lived in three provinces and two territories before I discovered that this 282-mile-long (453-km) island, with its Gulf Island neighbors, is the pièce de résistance of this country I now call home.

Separated from mainland British Columbia by Queen Charlotte, Johnstone, and Georgia Straits and from Washington's Olympic Peninsula by the 100-mile-long (160-km) Juan de Fuca Strait, Vancouver Island, with more than 2,100 miles (3,400 km) of coastline, is North America's largest island, occupying an area about the size of Maryland. A mountainous spine runs its length, and long fjords on its Pacific west coast cut deeply into the island. Lush forests of large Douglas fir and cedar thrive in the moderate, ocean climate. Victoria, on the southern tip of Vancouver Island, is the province's capital, with a population of approximately 320,000.

After exploring Victoria's Inner Harbor and suburbs, we'll head out to explore the colorful tidepools of Botanical Beach, meet the artists of Salt Spring Island, camp among the giant, old-growth trees at Carmanah Walbran Park, and watch killer whales from aboard a converted mission boat. On an island off the far north, we'll learn of the aboriginal past in a unique cultural center. This is but the tip of the overflowing cornucopia of adventures in store.

Victoria

Rated in *Condé Nast Traveler*'s 1998 Readers' Choice Awards as Canada's number-one tourist destination and number six in the world, Victoria is jokingly called the land of the newlywed and the nearly dead. Perhaps this is but a reflection that younger people, like their grandparents, are now seeing the light and choosing to settle in Canada's Garden of Eden.

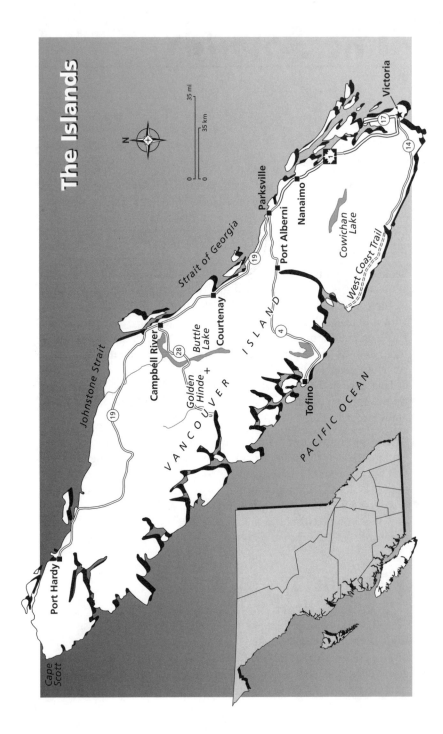

The Islands

THE ISLANDS

AUTHOR'S TOP TEN PICKS
ON THE ISLANDS

Caving in Horne Lakes Provincial Park

Frisbee golf at Pender Island Disc Park

Kayaking in the Gulf Islands

Logging sports in Sooke

Camping in Carmanah Walbran Provincial Park

Exploring the tidepools of Botanical Beach

Whale watching in Robson Bight

Scuba diving on Hornby Island

Skiing at Mount Washington

Bungy jumping in Nanaimo. NOT!

On any warm spring or summer day, the downtown core of Victoria hums with activity as both locals and tourists alike head to the *Inner Harbor,* where dozens of mime artists, balloon twisters, didgeridoo players, face painters, bagpipers, fiddlers, and Japanese calligraphers all vie for a spot along the waterfront promenade. Above them, beside baskets of brilliantly colored blooms hanging from nineteenth-century-style street lamps, frightfully English, red double-decker buses, horse-drawn carriages, and kabuki cab pedalers carry tourists from one end of town to the other, giving the city a festive feel.

Victoria is equally exciting at water level. You'll discover this during a three-hour kayak lesson and pleasure paddle ($55) with *Ocean River Sports* (1437 Store Street, Market Square, V8W 3J6; 800–909–4233; 250–381–4233; fax: 250–361–3536; info@oceanriver.com; www.oceanriver.com). If you don't need the lesson, rental rates are: singles $14 per hour and $42 for the day; doubles $17 per hour and $50 for the day. For groups of ten or more wishing to learn more about the island's marine life, its old-growth rain forest ecology, or its native peoples' plant use, contact *Coastal Connections Nature Adventures Inc.* (1027 Roslyn Road, V8S 4R4; 250–480–9560 or 800–840–4453; coastcon@islandnet.com; www. islandnet.com/~coast.com). Experienced naturalist guides run fascinating trips ranging from three-hour walks ($49) to ten-hour instructional, sail-kayak-hike Gulf Islands explorations that include gourmet picnic lunches ($199).

IMAX/Museum

*I*f the weather isn't enticing you outdoors, drop into the **National Geographic Theatre** (250–953–IMAX) at the **Royal British Columbia Museum** (675 Belleville Street, 250–356–7226; 888–447–7977; www.royalbcmuseum.bc.ca) and surround yourself with amazing imagery on a six-story-high IMAX screen. Shows are every hour from 10:00 A.M. to 9:00 P.M. daily. Then step into one of Canada's top museums, where woodblock paved streets bring you back to the late 1800s, and woolly mammoths take you back even further.

Trivia

Contrary to popular belief, Vancouver Island did not break off from the mainland but had its geological birth in the South Pacific. It "docked" with the North American continent about 100 million years ago, somewhere near Oregon or California, and worked its way north along faults similar to the present-day San Andreas fault.

With the sea so close, try a tasty seafood lunch. One of my favorites is right downtown across from the ***Victoria Visitor Info Center. Sam's Deli*** (805 Government Street; 250–382–8424; www.samsdeli.com) piles the shrimp high to produce delicious shrimp-and-avocado sandwiches. Their date squares are made fresh daily from owner Barb Housser's grandma's recipe. Thick clam chowder, freshly squeezed orange juice, and tasty spinach salad are what keeps clients returning. It's open from 7:30 A.M. till 11:00 P.M. in summer (shorter hours in winter) and is a great spot to sit outside and watch the passing crowds while enjoying a cappuccino or a frosty beer. Tell your friends back home to visit www.samsdeli.com/

Supernatural Sleuth

*M*y late grandmother instilled in me a healthy respect for ghosts. Her tingling tales are imprinted in my psyche, so it was with some apprehension that I set out early one evening in search of Victoria's specters. I'd heard that in Bastion Square the "White Lady" had been seen gliding along Chancery Lane behind the Maritime Museum. But no luck. She'd flown. Night was falling, so I crossed over to the Spirit of Christmas store on Government Street, hoping to catch a glimpse of the dark-haired man sometimes seen in a top-floor window. Whether I was too late and he'd evanesced, I don't know, but while there I did hear a chilling tale.

You see, the building once housed the Bank of British Columbia. One morning, a clerk of Chinese descent, while getting cash from the dark, deep vault, bounded out, hysterically screaming that she'd seen "something down

there." It turns out that before it was a bank, a Chinese crematorium operated in the building's depths. The clerk's assistant saw nothing. Nor did I. The only "spirit" I could find was a fluffy white angel atop a Christmas tree.

I slipped over to Tod House. That's western Canada's oldest dwelling, out in Oak Bay. The story goes that a woman wearing leg chains had been seen inside pleading for help. I peered through the windows, desperate to see at least a suggestion of a shadow. Nothing. Not even a meowing black cat. It was quite dark by now, and I was feeling cheated. Victoria Golf Course was on the way home. I skulked across the fairway in search of Doris Gravlin. She'd been murdered there in 1936, and . . . suddenly, a ghostly figure in a wedding dress drifted by the rocky shore. Seagulls in the mist, you say. No way! Oh YES, Grandma would have been proud.

samcam.htm for a view of Victoria with you in it! You could perhaps arrange a time to be on the corner of Government and Humboldt Streets (near the stately and luxurious *Fairmont Empress Hotel* (250–384–8111; www.fairmont. com) to wave to them. See if you can spot the spying live-cam server located at Sam's!

Shoppers looking for the offbeat will enjoy *Market Square* (www.marketsquare.victoria.bc.ca) on the waterfront between Johnson and Pandora Streets. This funky shopping center borders Canada's oldest *Chinatown.* The entrance is marked dramatically by the intricate and colorful *Gate of Harmonious Interest.* (Don't try to drive down Chinatown's Fan Tan Alley. It's Canada's narrowest street and is but 4 feet wide in places.) Often the site of festivals and concerts, Market Square is home to about forty-five stores with such curious names as *Fat Phege's Fudge Factory* (250–383–3435), famous for its fudges and brittles; the *Royal Holographic Art Gallery* (250– 384–0123; www.holograms.bc.ca), where $14.95 will buy a matted rose that *holographically* blooms before your eyes (perhaps an appropriate souvenir to take home from Victoria); the *Green Cuisine Restaurant* (250–385–1809; www.greencuisine.com), a vegan restaurant with a self-serve salad bar, dessert bar, and hot buffet, open daily from 10:00 A.M. to 8:00 P.M. (you can download coupons and recipes from the Web site); and the *Rubber Rainbow Condom Company* (250–388–3532; 888–423–7193 toll free), where you might be surprised what $3.99 will buy. They glow in the dark!

After dark enjoy a meal at *John's Place* (723 Pandora; 250–389–0711), where my favorite is the Thai Chicken. Laced with crunchy cashews, it's awfully addictive, and there's an endless supply of hot, herby bread. But spare some room for an enormous piece of apple pie. Breakfasts are huge, too. A Wurlitzer and great photos give it a fifties feel.

Over in *Oak Bay* (head east along Fort or Johnson Street), just ten minutes from the city, million-dollar Tudor-style waterfront homes with perfectly manicured gardens reinforce the more-English-than-England-itself reputation Victoria has acquired.

But this suburb, with the added color of billowing spinnakers, has its own particular charm.

And none more charming than **Chocolate,** an eleven-year-old harbor seal who spent his first year at Sealand after his mother abandoned him. When Sealand closed in 1990, Chocolate stayed around. If you want to feed him (and his mates), the Marine Store at the top of the ramp at Oak Bay Marina sells a bag of fish nummies for $2.00. You'll find Chocolate and pals salivating at the bottom of the ramp. If they're not around, run the tap in the fish-cleaning sink.

For more scuttlebutt on Chocolate, phone **Oak Bay Marina** (250–598–3369; 800–663–7090 toll free; obm@obmg.com; www.obmg.com) and talk to Steve, the local marine-life expert. If you've never tried fishing before, Steve can direct you to proven fishing grounds, just fifteen minutes offshore. Private fishing charters offer complimentary tea or coffee and come fully equipped with tackle, bait, and rods.

While at the marina, there's fine dining at the **Marina Restaurant** (250–598–8555; www. marinarestaurant.com). Ask about their early-bird specials served daily between 5:00 and 6:00 P.M. For more casual dining, the **Café Deli** is right below. Sit out on the sunny deck and watch yachts gently rock, while a great blue heron fishes nearby. Stroll along Beach Drive to Willows Beach, an inviting spot for a family day in the sun, then head up one block to Estevan Village for hot and yummy fish and chips (wrapped traditionally in newspaper) at **Willows Galley** (250–598–2711; open Wednesday to Sunday 11:00 A.M. to 7:00 P.M.), then cross the road to the licensed **Willow Tree Cafe & Bakery Shop** (250–592–8311; open daily from 7:30 A.M. to 5:00 P.M.) for dessert—my favorite is a piece of their apple pie accompanied by Australian ginger ice cream.

Trivia

Victoria can lay claim to Canada's longest frost-free period, which stretched over 685 days in 1925–26; so, too, it can claim BC's highest annual amount of sunshine: 2,426 hours in 1970. It must also claim, however, Canada's longest wet spell, beginning on April 19, 1986, when it rained for thirty-three days.

On the way back down Estevan to the beach, turn left on Heron Street and walk a block to number 2564. You'll be looking at the **John Tod House,** western Canada's oldest house still standing today and reputedly haunted. Construction finished in 1851, some twenty years before British Columbia was brought into the Canadian Confederation.

Up in the village of **Oak Bay,** there's a kaleidoscope of shops, teahouses, and galleries. The **Blethering Place Tearoom** (2250 Oak Bay Avenue,

250–598–1413; open from 8:00 A.M. to 9:00 P.M. daily) is a fine place to meet the locals and enjoy British high tea ($15.95). There's more: Irish music will have you crooning on Fridays, British comedy and music is a charmer on Saturdays, and on Sundays, New Orleans spiritual jazz will set you tapping. It's on the corner of *The Avenue* and Monterey. Further down *The Avenue* toward the city, a local favorite, **Blighty's Bistro** (2006 Oak Bay Avenue; 250–592–5111), serves a delicious bowl of Christina & Michelle's mulligatawny soup. For a main item try Richelle's Roast, pork roast stuffed with apples, carrots, parsley, and prunes, complete with gravy, twice baked potatoes, and vegetables of the day. This dish is so popular that it sells out every night. Each menu item is named for staff or regular clients—very young Oak Bay fry get a huge kick when they see their names on the menu. Reservations are recommended. Alternatively, the **Penny Farthing Pub** (2228 Oak Bay Avenue; 250–370–9008) is an exquisitely decorated establishment featuring daily specials and live Celtic music Thursday to Saturday evenings.

Down from the village, at the corner of Newport and Windsor, is the **Windsor House Tea Room and Restaurant** (2540 Windsor Road; 250–595–3135). It sounds British, and if that's what you want, you won't be disappointed! Pick up a London *Weekly Telegraph* at **Windsor Park Place** (250–592–5315) next door and settle in to enjoy your hot buttered crumpets, classic cream scones, butter tarts, finger sandwiches, and a pot of steaming English tea. A full-lunch menu features delicious homemade soups (including ginger carrot soup), plus chicken potpies and spinach feta cheese crepes. It's open Monday to Saturday from 11:00 A.M. to 6:00 P.M. If you're lucky, you'll catch a game of cricket being played on the pitch across the road in Windsor Park. Only in Victoria!

The British theme continues at the **Oak Bay Guest House** (1052 Newport Avenue, V8S 5E3; 800–575–3812 or 250–598–3812; fax: 250–598–0369; oakbay@beds-breakfasts.com; www.beds-breakfasts.com), a 1912-built bed-and-breakfast inn with claw-foot bathtubs, period furniture, and lots of charm. You may even be greeted by a fully dressed butler. Breakfast is a four-course, genteel feast. Rates are from $60 for a single room in off-season to $180 for a double studio suite in high season. If it's a pub-style meal you're after, or just a pleasant waterfront spot for a beer, *The Snug* at the *Oak Bay Beach Hotel* (1175 Beach Drive, Victoria, V8S 2N2; 250–598–4556; 800–668–7758; fax: 250–598–6180; www. oakbaybeachhotel.bc.ca) serves light meals in a warm atmosphere, with incredible views of snow-covered Mount Baker from the outdoor deck.

It's not all Old World charm in this municipality, though. Kids will love the tropical decor at the *Oak Bay Recreation Center* (near Fort and Foul Bay Roads at 1975 Bee Street; 250–595–7946). With an ozone-purified pool, sauna, hot whirlpool, and waterslide, you'll leave imagining you've had a trip to Hawaii. View a complete list of their programs at www.district.oak-bay.bc.ca. For cyclists, Oak Bay offers splendid roads with brilliant scenery—mountains, oceans, gardens, parks—with just the right mix of hills and flat stretches. You can rent a bicycle ($19 per day) downtown at *Cycle Victoria Rentals* (250–885–2453; 877–869–0039 toll free; fax: 250–477–9660; info@cyclevictoria rentals.com; www. cyclevictoriarentals.com) in the Victoria Marine Adventure Center at 950 Wharf Street; a second location is at 747 Douglas Street opposite the convention center. Scooters and motorcycles are also available for rent. Before leaving home, check some of the local cycling Web sites to help plan your trip: www.cyclingvictoria.com and www.simbs.com (South Island Mountain Biking Society).

To return to the city by the most scenic route, take Beach Drive past the gloriously posh *Victoria Golf Course* (250–598–4224; $150 for a cool eighteen holes for nonmembers) to *Clover Point,* where huge ships, paragliders, and high-flying kites are often in view; then continue past *Mile Zero* of the Trans-Canada Highway near *Beacon Hill Park.* Keep to the water. At the breakwater at 199 Dallas Road, join locals at the *Ogden Point Cafe* (250–386–8080; fax: 250–386–8087). It's very popular for its tasty soups, sandwiches, bakery, desserts—and more. It's open daily 8:00 A.M. to 10:00 P.M. (till 8:00 P.M. in winter). There's a full-service dive center below. *Ogden Point Dive Center* (199 Dallas Road, Victoria, V8V 1A1, 250–380–9119; fax: 250–385–9110; info@divevictoria.com; www.dive victoria.com) offers weekend dive charters, daily trips, and scuba diving holidays. If you're looking for somewhere close to downtown for an excellent meal and delightful accommodation, it's easy walking distance to *Spinnakers Brew Pub and Guest House* (308 Catherine Street; 250–386–2739; spinnakers@spinnakers.com; www.spinnakers.com). From the Johnson Street Bridge (the blue bridge) downtown, it's a short walk

Trivia

Western Canada's oldest school (still standing) is Craigflower School in Victoria. It was built in 1855 and is now a museum.

past Songhees (all those apartments!) to Lime Bay. Spinnakers is a well-known establishment on the waterfront. Noted for their beer, you'll also find luxury bed-and-breakfast accommodation, where double Jacuzzis and fireplaces are but two of the delightful features. Double rates in high season range from $159 to $249; from $129 to $209 in low season.

For more information on Victoria area attractions, contact the ***Victoria Visitor Info Centre*** (812 Wharf Street V8W 1T3; 250–953–2033; fax: 250–382–6539; info@tourismvictoria.com; www.tourismvictoria. com.; for accommodation reservations only, phone 800–663–3883 or 250–953–2022).

Outdoor enthusiasts can hike, cycle, skate, even ride a horse (anything not motorized) in the Victoria area along the ***Galloping Goose Trail,*** a 35-mile (57-km) former railway line. Maps and information are available from the Capital Regional District Web site at www.crd.bc.ca/parks/pdf/galgose3.pdf.

From Victoria, a turn south off the Trans-Canada onto Highway 14 brings you to the village of ***Sooke,*** a haven for fabulous bed-and-breakfasts. Find one listed on a comprehensive photo-board at the ***Sooke Region Museum*** (Box 774, Sooke, V0S 1N0; 250–642–6351; info@ sooke. museum.bc.ca; www.island. net/~srm_chin). It's located at 2070 Phillips Road on the corner of Highway 14, about forty minutes from downtown Victoria. While at the museum, take a peek in tiny ***Moss Cottage,*** one of Sooke's oldest buildings. And don't leave Sooke without try-

All Sooke Day Logging Sports

*I*f you're in Sooke the third Saturday in July, don't miss the **All Sooke Day Logging Sports** *championships. Competition is fierce at events such as log birling, ax throwing, log rolling, high rigging, and speed tree-climbing. Experts from all over the world compete for cash prizes and trophies. But there's much more than logger sports. The day starts at 7:00 A.M. with a pancake* *breakfast and ends at 1:00 A.M. with a good old-fashioned dance at the Community Hall. There's bingo for any age, and kids can try their skills in a greasy-pole climb, a hockey slapshot event, and a wall climb. Food is an event in itself, with the highlight being a barbecue salmon meal. There's even something for the tiny ones at what the Sooke folks say is the best Baby Show on the island.*

ing the area's best halibut burgers at **Mom's Café** (2036 Shields Road; 250–642–3314)—when traveling west from Victoria, take the first turn right after Sooke's only set of traffic lights. If you decide to stay overnight here, a popular accommadations in the area is on the beach at Billings Spit. Reservations for the **Billings Spit Beach House** can be made on-line or by phone (toll free 877–642–1910, information@billingsspitbeach house. com; www.billingsspitbeachhouse.com). For detailed information on Sooke's attractions and accommodations, visit www.sookenet.com.

Continue west past driftwood-strewn beaches through Jordan River and Port Renfrew to the colorful tidepools at **Botanical Beach.** In all it's about a two-hour journey from Victoria, but don't miss a low-tide visit to this virtual aquarium, with its brilliant red gumboot chitons, giant green sea anemones, purple sea urchins, and blood stars. With the completion of the Juan de Fuca Marine Trail, hikers now have access (four separate entry points off Highway 14 from China Beach to Botanical Beach) to superb wilderness day- and multiday hiking within easy driving from Victoria.

Sidney

Highway 17 (locals call it the Pat Bay) runs the length of the pastoral Saanich Peninsula, linking Victoria with Sidney and Swartz Bay, where BC ferries connect to the mainland and the Gulf Islands. **Sidney by the Sea** is to many people merely a town you pass when traveling to or from the ferry, but it's worth a closer look.

To see the area from a nautical perspective, be sure to try a **Sidney Harbor Cruise** with **Barbara and the Starships** (250–655–5211; starship@ pacificcoast.net; www.pacificcoast.net/~starship). A one- or two-hour cruise in a glass-enclosed boat is in effect a mini-wildlife tour. Tickets for the one-hour tour are $13.50 for adults, $12 for seniors, and $7 for children. There's an optional lunch stop at Canoe Cove's **Stonehouse Pub** (250–656–3498), where they offer a 25 percent discount if you come off the cruise, (the $3.95 thick clam chowder is a meal in itself), or Shoal Harbor's **Blue Peter Pub & Restaurant** (2270 Harbour Road; 250–656–4551; chrisw@islandnet.com; www.islandnet.com/~blue pete/), after which you can hop on the next ferry back past Sidney's waterfront homes. At the Blue Peter, you can enjoy a hearty meal any time of day—it's open daily from 7:00 A.M. to 11:00 P.M.—and seafood is their specialty. Every Tuesday in summer is Crab Night, when you'll feast on freshly boiled crab served on the deck overlooking Tsehum

Harbour. Inquire here about the ***Blue Peter Yacht Charters***. Step aboard a ship-shape, 40-foot (12-m) sloop (which leaves from directly in front of the pub) and sail through glorious island waterways. A typical half-day charter is $200, which for six people is a mere $35 each.

While you're in Sidney, visit the ***Sidney Museum*** (9801 Seaport Place; 250–656–2140/1322; fax: 250–656–2847; smchin@island.net). It has an echolocation chamber, demonstrating how marine mammals orient themselves, and the skeleton of Scar, a 23-foot (7-m) killer whale. Drive to the end of Beacon Avenue and turn left into Seaport Place. In summer it's open daily from 10:00 A.M. to 5:00 P.M.; admission is by donation. Another museum worth visiting in Sidney is the ***British Columbia Aviation Museum*** (1910 Norseman Road, Sidney, V8L 5V5; 250–655–3300; fax: 250–655–1611; bcam@ bcam.net; www.bcam.net). It's by the southeast corner of the Victoria International Airport. Some of the many planes on display include the Eastman E2 Sea Rover (the only one left in the world), the Noorduyn Norseman (presently being restored to airworthy standards by museum volunteers), and an exact replica of the 1897 Chanute Glider, whose design influenced the Wright brothers.

Over on the waterfront, the ***Sidney Spit Ferry*** (250–474–5145) runs a foot-passenger ferry to ***Sidney Spit Marine Park,*** 3 miles (5 km) across on Sidney Island. Here you'll see seabird nesting colonies, fallow deer, and even a few exotic birds. Contact BC Parks South Vancouver Island District (250–391–2300) for more information. The ferry leaves on the hour from the pier at the foot of Beacon Avenue from May 15 till September 30, 9:00 A.M. to 6:00 P.M. daily. Round-trip fares are $10.75 for adults, $8.75 for seniors, and $7.75 for children. Then return to the Beacon Avenue beat and discover some of the unique gift shops and bookstores for which Sidney is renowned.

TOP ANNUAL EVENTS ON THE ISLANDS

Trumpeter Swan Festival, *Comox Valley; early February; (250) 335–1419*

Pacific Rim Whale Festival, *Tofino; late March; (250) 725–3414 or (250) 726–7742; whalefest@island.net*

Brant Wildlife Festival, *Parksville/Qualicum; April; (250) 752–9171; fax: (250) 752–9883*

Victoria Harbor Festival, *Victoria; late May; (250) 953–2033*

Nanaimo Marine Festival, *Nanaimo; late July; (250) 753–7223*

Sooke Fine Arts Show, *Sooke Arena; early August; (250) 642–6351*

Classic Boat Festival, *Victoria; early September; (250) 385–7766; fax: (250) 385–8773; msampson@vreb.org*

Festival of Lights, *Ladysmith; December; (250) 245–5888*

Salt Spring and Pender Islands

North of Sidney, island-hop by BC Ferry to **Salt Spring Island,** home to many of Canada's best-known artists and writers, and **Pender Island**, where beaches, markets, galleries, hiking, and the Gulf Islands only disc golf course (a free-eighteen-poler!) make for a quiet but active retreat.

The largest of the Gulf Islands, Salt Spring has a year-round population of approximately ten thousand.

From the ferry terminal at Fulford Harbor, Beaver Point Road leads off the Fulford-Ganges Road for 6 miles (9.5 km) to **Ruckle Provincial Park,** with walk-in (not far!) beachfront campsites. There's also a new twenty-site group campsite available. Phone (250) 539–2115 for group campsite bookings. The area is still a working sheep farm, with the original 1870 Ruckle homestead at the park entrance.

The Fulford-Ganges Road runs north for 9 miles (14.5 km) to **Ganges,** through what was once BC's largest fruit-growing area. **Mount Maxwell Provincial Park** (day use only), 5.5 miles (9 km) up a steep, rough road, has spectacular views. Take Cranberry Road, about a mile south of Ganges, and follow the signs. You'll bump your way up to Baynes Peak, at 1,932 feet (589 m) the highest point on Salt Spring Island. An observation point at the edge of a vertigo-inducing precipice provides breathtaking views south over the Fulford Valley toward Fulford Harbour and the Gulf Islands and west to Sansum Narrows and Maple Bay. It's worth the wear on your vehicle (or your boots).

On Saturdays you'll find the ferries and highways are full of folks heading

Lives of the Rich and Famous

When exploring Salt Spring Island, you might bump into one or two famous personalities who either live on the island or who find this gem of a hideaway the perfect escape. Such well-knowns as Robert Bateman (conservationist, naturalist, and artist), Arthur Black (well-known Canadian radio personality and humorist), Randy Bachmann of Bachmann Turner Overdrive and The Who, and Valdy (one of Canada's favorite folk singers) all call Salt Spring Island home. Others who have visited on occasion are Barbara Streisand, Gary "Radar O'Reilly" Burghoff of M*A*S*H fame, Robert DeNiro, Al Pacino, Tom Hanks, Candice Bergen, Steven Spielberg, Tom Cruise, and Robin Williams (no introductions needed).

to the *Salt Spring Island Saturday Market* (www.saltspringmarket.com), which runs from the first Saturday in April to October at the head of Ganges Harbor in Centennial Park. Locals sell flowers, jewelry, and pottery—anything from a slice of watermelon to a sequined frog.

South Africans Ruth Opperman and Phillip Du Preez recently became island transplants after pulling up roots at Gibsons on the mainland. They've reopened *Ruphi Fabrics and Ceramics* in a "sixty-five-year-old beaut of a house" at the foot of Ganges Hill in the village at 163 Fulford-Ganges Road, SSI, V8K 2T9; (250) 537–1337; ruphi@saltspring.com; www.ruphi.com. Bright hand-painted wall hangings, tablecloths, and checkered or polka-dot ceramic pieces give their factory a colorful, eccentric look. They'll ship pieces home for you, too. Look for the huge ART FACTORY sign in the village.

If you missed the Saturday market, the *Naikai Gallery* (3102 Grace Point Square, 115 Fulford-Ganges Road, Salt Spring Island, V8K 2T9; 888–643–9320; toll free; 250–537–4400; naikai@saltspring.com; www.islandnet.com/~naikai/) has a huge variety of locals' works. It's open from 10:00 A.M. to 5:00 P.M. seven days a week, from Easter to Thanksgiving, with varying hours during winter. One local artist of note is Carol Haigh. Her acrylic originals and lithographic marine scenes grace the Naikai's walls.

Grace Point Square has more than lovely galleries. The *Bouzouki Greek Café* (250–537–4181) looks down Ganges Harbour to the Sisters Islands. Its hosts, Greg and Shirley Keith, serve traditional Greek fare. The Bouzouki is open for lunches and dinners from 10:00 A.M. to 9:00 P.M. six days a week (closed Sunday).

A fun spot to enjoy a glass of local Whale Tale Ale is *Moby's Marina Pub* (124 Upper Ganges Road, Salt Spring Island, V8K 2S2; 250–537–5559; 800–334–MOBY; mobyspub@saltspring.com; www.mobyspub.com), on the Ganges Harbour waterfront. Live entertainment and an active, pretty harbor, plus first-class pub food, make it a popular haunt.

From Ganges, Lower and Upper Ganges Roads lead northwest to Vesuvius Bay Road and the twenty-minute ferry to Crofton on Vancouver Island. Sunset Drive, running to the northwest tip of Salt Spring, is a pleasant drive hiding a couple of high-end bed-and-breakfasts, including the *Beach House on Sunset* (930 Sunset, SSI, V8K 1E6; 250–537–2879; fax: 250–537–4747; beachhouse@saltspring.com;

www.saltspring.com/beachhouse) and *Anne's Oceanfront Hideaway* (168 Simson Road, SSI, V8K 1E2; 888–474–2663 or 250–537–0851; fax: 250–537–0861; annes@saltspring.com; www.annesoceanfront.com), where you wake to coffee on the deck looking across Stuart Channel, followed by a four-course island breakfast in the dining room. Spend a day canoeing, biking, or shopping, then soak in the hydromassage hot tub before bed. Prices range from $160 to $205 off-season and $190 to $250 high season.

Contact the *Salt Spring Island Visitor Info Centre* (121 Lower Ganges Road, Ganges, SSI, V8K 2T1; 250–537–5252/4223; fax: 250–537–4276; chamber@saltspring. com; www.saltspringisland.bc.ca) for more information about this attractive island, so aptly named in earlier days by its native Cowichan people: *Chu-an,* or "facing the sea."

South Central Vancouver Island

From Crofton, a 6-mile (10-km) drive north along the coast road (43 miles [70 km] north of Victoria) leads to *Chemainus* (the Little Town That Did). When faced with a severe economic downturn, the townspeople didn't say "die" but instead came up with an idea that managed to turn Chemainus into the world's largest outdoor art gallery. The *Chemainus Visitor Info Centre* (9796 Willow Street, Box 575 Chemainus, V0R 1K0; 250–246–3944; fax: 250–246–3251; ccoc@ tourismchemainus.bc.ca; www.chemainus.com) is open year-round and has maps to help you find the first-class murals that depict the town's history, including native culture, Japanese and Chinese heritage, the building of the railroads, and the town's logging beginnings. You could even get a chance to stay in a restored mill house.

The *Olde Mill House* (9712 Chemainus Road, Box 1046, Chemainus, V0R 1K0; 250–416–0049; 877–770–6060 toll free; fax: 250–246–4457; stay@oldemillhouse.ca; www.oldemillhouse.ca) is a century-old historical home constructed for mill employees and is now run as a bed-and-breakfast inn. It is centrally located across from the *Chemainus Theatre,* one of British Columbia's favorite professional theaters (800–565–7738 or 250–246–9820; ctheatre@cow-net.com; www. ctheatre.bc.ca), and near the murals. You'll be invited to sample the Olde Mill House's own fruit wine and to use the barbecue area for dinner.

Just south of Chemainus is Duncan, famous not only as the home of the *World's Largest Hockey Stick* (seen outside the Cowichan Community Center at 2687 James Street) but also for its totem poles, about eighty of which decorate the city. Visit the **Quw'utsun' Cultural and Conference Centre** (200 Cowichan Way, Duncan, V9L 6P4; 877–746–8119; 250–746–8119; fax: 250–746–4143; askme@quwutsun.ca; to see them being carved. Here you'll find yourself immersed in the culture of the Coast Salish Natives. Their heritage is depicted in an excellent audiovisual presentation called *Great Deeds.* In the *Big House,* built in the style of a longhouse with huge cedar beams and planks, you'll be treated to a presentation of dancing, native drumming, and singing, while feasting on traditional native dishes. Duncan is 37 miles (60 km) north of Victoria on the Trans-Canada over the scenic Malahat Range. From the Nanaimo Ferry terminal, it's 32 miles (52 km) south. For more information contact the **Duncan Visitor Info Centre** (April 15–October 15) at 381A Trans-Canada Highway, Duncan, V9L 3R5; (250) 746–4636 or 748–1111; fax: (250) 746–8222; duncancc@islandnet.com; www.duncan cc.bc.ca.

Just 5 miles (8 km) south of Duncan (and 31 miles [50 km] north of Victoria) is the pretty coastal village of **Cowichan Bay.** Here you'll find art galleries, marinas, and a quaint farmhouse bed-and-breakfast called the **Old Farm Bed and Breakfast** (2075 Cowichan Bay Road, Cowichan Bay, V0R 1N0; phone/fax: 250–748–6410; 888–240–1482 toll free; stay@ oldfarminncowichan.com; www.oldfarminncowichan.com). This recently renovated, stately, three-story country home was designed by Samuel Maclure of Empress Hotel fame in the early 1900s for a retired English sea captain. Breakfast is a wonderful event and is served elegantly at a large table. All rooms (starting at $85 for a double) have views of evergreens and fruit trees, delightful gardens, and an estuary formed by the Cowichan and Koksilah Rivers, which flow into Cowichan Bay. The high-ceilinged rooms are exquisitely decorated, and all have en-suite bath. Relaxation comes easy in the chaises, gazebo, and hot tub outside, and when you're ready for

A Ban on Gift-Giving

*T*he Potlatch is a traditional feast or ceremony common among the Indians of the Pacific Northwest, especially the Kwakiutl. The word is Chinook jargon derived from the Nootka word patschmati, *meaning* gift. *Its traditional purpose was to validate the status of the chief or clan,* *although individuals also used it to try to enhance their social ranking. Gifts were exchanged, and property was destroyed in a competitive display of affluence. It was prohibited by the government in 1884, but the practice continued in secret. The ban was lifted in 1951.*

some exercise, enjoy badminton, horseshoes, a stroll down to the waterfront, or perhaps a game of tennis on one of the oldest grass tennis courts in the world (second only to Wimbledon) at the **South Cowichah Lawn Tennis Club**.

Wild West Side Trip From Duncan

About 3 miles (5 km) north of Duncan, Highway 18 starts its 95-mile (153-km) cut across southern Vancouver Island to **Bamfield**, a town where the main street is the sea—shades of Venice—and half the community is accessible only by water taxi. To get there take Highway 18 west to **Lake Cowichan Village,** a distance of about 19 miles (30 km). The Visitor Info Centre (125C South Shore Road, Box 824, Lake Cowichan, V0R 2G0; 250–749–3244; fax: 250–749–0187; chamber@cowichanlake.ca; www.cowichanlake.ca), open May 24 to September 2, may have maps. You'll find the office in the log cabin at Saywell Park. Wind past Cowichan Lake, either north through Youbou named for lumber mill owners Mr. Yount and Mr. Bouton!) or south through Honeymoon Bay (March Meadows Golf Course here is the home course of LPGA tour player Dawn Coe-Jones), to the Nitinat Main junction. Twelve miles (19 km) on, turn left onto South Main for 3.5 miles (5.6 km) to the Nitinat General Store, where you can eat a cafe meal, fuel up, and find a bed next door in the **Nitinat Lake Motel** (250–745–3844). Open year-round; rooms (some with kitchenettes) range from $45 to $65. Cross the Caycuse River Bridge and turn right onto Rosander Main. You're now but 18 scenic miles (29 km) from **Carmanah Walbran Provincial Park,** site of Canada's tallest tree and the

The Nuu-chah-nulth

The Nuu-chah-nulth ("along the mountains") people on the west coast used to whale in open seas in cedar canoes—not a very safe occupation. As part of their intensive training program (sexual abstinence, fasting, bathing, and learning how to capture the huge mammals), the whalers also visited sacred shrines made up of skulls and images of whales and deceased whalers. As a further *aid, the whaler's wife would lie completely still while her husband was on the kill, to ensure that the whale, too, would be docile. Captain Cook, when he came to the coast in 1778, was seen drifting too close to a reef. The Nuu-chah-nulth called out to him, "Nootka, nootka," meaning "Circle round." His misunderstanding resulted in these people being misnamed as the Nootka.*

tallest Sitka spruce in the world, the **Carmanah Giant.**

A Carmanah holiday with my teenage kids, despite rain and rough roads, is one of my best camping holiday memories. For public safety and environmental protection, the trail to the 312-foot (95-m) **Carmanah Giant** is out of bounds. But the 2.3-mile (3.8-km) trail upstream along Carmanah Creek to the **Three Sisters,** and the 2.9-mile (4.6-km) downstream trail to the **Fallen Giant** are both awesome. For information contact BC Parks, South Vancouver Island District, RR 6, 2930 Trans-Canada Highway, Victoria, V9E 1K3; (250) 391–2300; fax: (250) 478–9211; parkinfo@victoria1.gov.bc.ca; www.env.gov.bc.ca/bcparks.

When traveling in this area, be aware that that you will be sharing the road with huge logging trucks—safety checkpoints are often set up—and the operator's directions must be followed; and if continuing on to Bamfield Inlet, keep a close watch for the signs to the village, which can easily be missed. Bamfield is also accessible via a 63-mile (102-km) unpaved logging road south from Port Alberni or via the MV *Lady Rose* (see Port Alberni section). The Port Alberni route has less unpaved road, is wider, has fewer logging trucks, and is usually in better shape than the road from Lake Cowichan, but from Victoria it's approximately an hour longer. If you're worried about wear on your vehicle (or don't have a good map), take the Port Alberni route. Another option for getting there is to call **West Coast Trail Express**

Hiking the West Coast Trail

*A*t one time considered the world's most difficult hiking trail, the 47-mile (75-km) **West Coast Trail** stretches from Pachena Bay (near Bamfield) in the north to the mouth of the Gordon River (near Port Renfrew) in the south. Boardwalks and ladders have reduced its category now to "one of the most difficult." Needless to say, careful planning, including knowledge of how to read a tide table and possession of good-quality wet-weather gear, is essential. A maximum of sixty hikers are allowed daily on the trail, broken down into forty-eight reserved spaces and twelve (six at each end of the trail) "first-come-first-served" spaces. There is a $25 reservation fee, payable at the time of booking, plus a $70 hiking fee and a $25 ferry fee. Yes, there are a couple of rivers to cross! You can expect to be hiking for about six days, during which time you'll possibly see sea lions, bears, whales, countless seabirds, and incredible Pacific vistas. Check www.sookenet.com and follow the hiking link to a "Hiker Preparation Guide" to the trail, plus several useful links such as a tide graph.

(250–477–8700; fax: 250–477–8774; bus@trail bus.com; www.trailbus.com) to find out about daily buses from Victoria and Nanaimo.

Once you have reached Bamfield, you have a few comfortable accommodations to choose from, including **Woods End Landing** (380 Lombard Street, Box 108, Bamfield, V0R 1B0; phone/fax: 250–728–3383; 877–828–3383 toll free; woods end@island.net; www.woodsend.bc.ca). Here you'll find first-class cabin or duplex accommodations in a rustic, beachy setting—a short hike to Brady's Beach or the Cape Beale lighthouse. For the adventurous, experience a kayak trip through the Broken Group Islands with fascinating shoreline caves and abundant marine life. To learn more about what you've seen, the **Bamfield Marine Station** (Bamfield, V0R 1B0; 250–728–3301; fax: 250–728–3452; info@bms. bc.ca; www.bms.bc.ca), near the mouth of the inlet, offers guided field trips.

Hiking the reservations-only **West Coast Trail** (Box 280, Ucluelet, V0R 3A0; 800–663–6000 or 250–726–7721)—or camping beside the world's largest spruce trees in Carmanah Walbran Provincial Park or windsurfing on **Nitinat Lake** are but three of the activities the outdoor adventurer should put on a list of "west coast things to do."

Rub-a-Dub Tubbers

*I*n one Vancouver Island city, "taking a bath" does not necessarily have the traditional connotations. One of BC's craziest annual events started in 1967 as a wild publicity stunt for the city of Nanaimo. **The Great International World Championship Bathtub Race and Marine Festival,** *or more succinctly the Nanaimo Bathtub Race, has grown as fast as its mother city. In the beginning forty-seven "tubbers," kept afloat (or not!) by whatever means possible, made their way from Nanaimo, 36 miles (58 kms) across Georgia Strait to Vancou-* ver's Fisherman's Cove. Today tubs are high-tech, and the course is much altered, but the spirit of the original "tubbers" lives on, as can be attested to by Paul Johnson, whose family has raced since 1967: "Insanity is definitely a part of it," says Paul. Further attestation to this dementia can be seen the evening before the race at the traditional **Sacrifice to the Bathtub Gods** *boat-burning ceremony in Swy-A-Lana lagoon. So if you're in Nanaimo in July, join the crazy crowds, and perhaps pack along your own bathtub!*

North to Nanaimo

The Trans-Canada leads north from Duncan to Nanaimo, a city enjoying Canada's mildest climate, and home of the **Bungy Zone Adrenalin Center** (888–668–7874 or 800–668–7771; local numbers: 250–716–RUSH or 250–753–JUMP; jump@bungyzone.com; www.bungy zone.com). The center uses the only legal bungy bridge in North America. Legal or not, whatever you do, don't look down—the drop over the Nanaimo River Canyon is 140 feet (42 m). In February you might try a free Valentine's Naked Love Plunge—definitely one of the more unusual ways to celebrate Valentine's Day. Alternatively, choose between an Ultimate Swing or a Flying Fox (both $50). If you're up for it, a bungy jump costs $95 (or $100 for a lifetime membership, with each jump thereafter $35). To date, 100,000 incident-free plunges have been made into the Nanaimo River Canyon.

The food at Nanaimo's **Dinghy Dock Pub** (250–753–2373) will also give you a rush. Take a ten-minute ($4.75) Protection Connection ferry (250–753–8244) from the dock on Front Street to Protection Island and try Sex in a Dinghy! Relax, it's but a heavenly dessert. For an entree try the Louisiana Blackened Halibut Burger. The burger plus the dreamy dessert will set you back a whole $13. The pub is open 11:30 A.M. to 11:00 P.M. (midnight on weekends) from the end of March to Thanksgiving.

Nanaimo's Famous Bar

*I*n 1854 miners from the United Kingdom arrived to work Nanaimo's coal fields. As a comfort, their worried mothers sent this delicious treat, which became known as the Nanaimo Bar. This is the original decadent recipe:

Bottom layer: $1/2$ c. unsalted butter; $1/4$ c. sugar; 5 tbsp. cocoa; 1 egg, beaten; $1^3/4$ c. graham wafer crumbs; $1/2$ c. finely chopped almonds; 1 c. coconut. Melt butter, sugar, and cocoa in top of a double boiler. Add egg and stir to cook and thicken. Remove from heat. Stir in crumbs, coconut, and nuts. Press firmly into an ungreased 8 x 8 pan.

Middle layer: $1/2$ c. unsalted butter; 2 tbsp. plus 2 tsp. cream; 2 tbsp. vanilla custard powder; 2 c. icing sugar. Cream butter, cream, custard powder, and icing sugar together well. Beat until light. Spread over bottom layer.

Third layer: 4 squares semisweet chocolate (1 oz. each); 2 tbsp. unsalted butter. Melt chocolate and butter over low heat. Cool. When cool, but still liquid, pour over second layer and chill in refrigerator.

Trivia

- *There are nineteen golf courses within an hour's drive of Nanaimo.*

- *You'll never guess where the word* Nanaimo *comes from. It originated when the first non-native settlers tried to pronounce the local Coast Salish people's name for themselves:* Sneneymexw. *The word means "great and mighty people."*

For further information on the Nanaimo area, contact the **Nanaimo Visitor Info Centre,** Beban House, 2290 Bowen Road, Nanaimo, V9T 3K7; (250) 756–0106 or (800) 663–7337; fax: (250) 756–0075; info@tourismnanaimo.com; www. tourismnanaimo.com.

From Nanaimo's downtown harbor the MV *Quinsam* car/passenger ferry runs hourly (approximately) between 6:00 A.M. and 11:00 P.M., taking twenty minutes to reach **Gabriola Island,** famous for its beaches, artists, and prehistoric rock carvings (petroglyphs). You'll see reproductions of these petroglyphs on the museum grounds. Then head southeast for about 8 miles (13 km) down a sometimes very steep South Road to the United Church to see the real thing. Dozens of petroglyphs have been uncovered here. Follow a short marked trail to the site, being mindful not to damage these sacred images. If you visit in the early evening when the shadows are long, you're in for some interesting photography. If you head north after the ferry dock, you'll come to **Malaspina Galleries,** sandstone formations that provide hours of fun for the adventurous wishing to dive into the deep waters below. The **Gabriola Visitor Info Centre**—open mid-May to Thanksgiving—in Folklife Village (575 North Road, Box 249, Gabriola Island, V0R 1X0; phone/fax: 250–247–9332; info@GabriolaIsland.org; www.gabriolais land.org) has more information on these attractions, as well as on the ten-day Dancing Man Music Festival held in the spring. Although the perimeter roads measure less than 20 miles (32 km), Gabriola has more than four dozen art and craft studios, three provincial waterfront parks, and a campground (250–247–2079) by the beach. It also has a number of moderately priced bed-and-breakfasts. For one with spectacular views across to the Coast Mountains, contact **Sunset Bed & Breakfast** (RR 1, Site 1, C-7, Gabriola Island, V0R 1X0; toll free: 877–247–2032; 250–247–2032; sunset@sunsetcl. com; www.sunsetcl. com). It's about seven minutes north from the ferry. Ask about Sunset's Constructive Living workshops held during the off-season. Another B&B (with great views across the Gulf Islands) is **Green Gates Bed and Breakfast** (2345 South Road, RR 1, Site 23, C-33, Gabriola Island, V0R 1X0; 250–247–9870 or 604–680–0673; greengates@ gabriolaisland.org; www.gabriolais land.org/greengates). Both B&Bs have rooms starting in the $80 range.

Parksville/Qualicum and West

Parksville and Qualicum are renowned for having some of the best beaches in Canada, all easily accessible. Add to these beaches the newly designated **UNESCO Mount Arrowsmith Biosphere Reserve** (which encompasses Mount Arrowsmith, Mount Cokely, Mount Moriarty, and all the watersheds that flow from them into the Strait of Georgia), plus a multitude of exciting activities for all ages, and you have one of the world's top recreational areas.

Entering Parksville on Highway 19A from the south, turn right after the railway tracks and stop off at the excellent **Parksville Visitor Info Centre,** 1275 East Island Highway, Box 99, Parksville, V9P 2G3; (250) 248–3613; fax: (250) 248–5210; info@chamber.parksville.bc.ca; www.chamber.parksville.bc.ca, to find out about accommodations, attractions, and restaurants; then visit **Craig Heritage Park and Museum** (250–248–6966; open in summer only) next door to find out about the area's beginnings. If it's the beach you're after, it's right downtown! Fishing, swimming, hiking, and camping (103 sites) are available at **Englishman River Falls Provincial Park** southwest of Parksville. Take Highway 4A 3 miles (5 km) west, then drive south on Errington Road for 5 miles (8 km). Here you'll find a spectacular canyon situated between two cascades, plus excellent hiking trails that meander through old-growth forest. If you visit in autumn, look for spawning salmon in the Englishman River. Phone (800) 689–9025 or (604) 689–9025 for Discover Camping reservations.

Just north of Parksville the village of **Qualicum Beach** is often bypassed,

Can't Top This Diner!

As you pass Qualicum Bay, you may find yourself doing a double take at the Marilyn Monroe/James Dean mural painted on the Cola Diner (6060 Island Highway, Qualicum Beach, V9K 2E1; 250–757–2029; fax: 250–757–9789). You see, Marilyn is missing her top. A hot debate on www.colaland.com is being waged to determine whether she should wear a towel or not. Car buffs may be more interested in the '57 Chevy hanging off the front of the building. Inside, you'll find more cola memorabilia and excellent diner-style eating. Modern log cabin accommodations are also available here, set in the woods just steps from the beach. E-mail reservations@colaland.com or phone/fax the above numbers to reserve. Interestingly enough, one of the mural artists, John F. Mortenson, is Marilyn's cousin.

but its pretty gardens and interesting stores warrant a stop. Turn off Highway 19A, head up Memorial, and turn right onto West Second Avenue to get to the shopping area. If it's an eclectic restaurant you're after, try **Lefty's** (by Qualicum's only traffic light; 250–752–7530). Also located in Parksville (250–954–3886) next to Thrifty's grocery store, Lefty's offers imported organic coffee, "LeftCoast Cuisine," and Italian sodas.

For more information on the area contact the **Qualicum Beach Visitor Info Centre** (2711 West Island Highway, Qualicum Beach, V9K 2C4; 250–752–9532; fax: 250–752–2923; info@qualicum.bc.ca; www. qualicum.bc.ca). For comprehensive tourism information on the area stretching from **Nanoose Bay** (south of Parksville) to **Deep Bay** (south of Courtenay), contact the **Oceanside Tourism Association** at Box 374, Qualicum Beach, V9K 1S9; (250) 752–2388; fax: (250) 752–2392; toll free: 888–799–3222 or visit www.oceansidetourism.com.

Back on the highway, about 5 miles (8 km) north, is an exquisitely decorated, four-and-a-half-star bed-and-breakfast called **Bahari** (5101 Island Highway West, Qualicum Beach, V9K 1Z1; 250–752–9278; 877–752–9278 toll free; fax: 250–752–9038; relax@baharibandb.com; www. baharibandb.com). The views are outstanding, especially from the hot tub, sitting at eagle-height above basking seals in Georgia Strait. It's a stopover you won't forget in a hurry. Rates, including gourmet breakfast, range from $85 for a queen bed in low season to $250 for a two-bedroom apartment operated as a deluxe bed-and-breakfast in high season. The apartment is also available as a self-cater at $180 ($120 in low season).

From Bahari it's only a few miles north to the turnoff to the **Horne Lake Caves Provincial Park.** Look for the Horne Lake Store and Café and follow the signs for about 12 miles (20 km). The caves are open year-round for self-guided exploration. Guided tours are also available. Check out the Web site at www.hornelake.com for information. Choose from a one-and-a-half-hour family tour to a seven-hour "Underground Extreme" expedition, where rappelling down a seven-story underground waterfall is part of the adventure. Write: Box 3531, Station Main, Courtenay, V9N 6Z8; phone/fax: (250) 339–0555; e-mail: adventure@hornelake.com. Anyone planning to "self-explore" the caves should be familiar with caving safety. Expect tight entrances with some rugged climbing inside. Helmets and lights can be rented for $5.00. These caves are some of the most accessible and beautiful of the thousand-known caves on Vancouver Island. One in particular, **Riverbend** (a locked cave), is loaded with crystal formations and ancient fossils.

If you've never slept in a teepee, you'll have the chance at the **Horne Lake**

Teepee Adventure Camp (contact previously mentioned information). Here you can canoe, ride horses, try some rock climbing, and take part in the fun family adventures that run daily in summer.

To unearth more treasures along this bottom third of Vancouver Island, take Highway 4 to Tofino, 107 miles (173 km) west of Parksville. On the way keep an eye out for *Bill Gruff* and friends or grazing goats on the sod roof at the *Coombs Old Country Market* (Box 219, Coombs, V0R 1M0; 250–248–3343; fax: 248–250–9593; ocm@ bcsupernet.com; www.oldcountrymarket.com), walk along jungle paths at *Butterfly World* (250–248–7026), camp at *Little Qualicum Falls Provincial Park,* and stand in awe in *Cathedral Grove* (MacMillan Provincial Park), where some of the largest Douglas fir trees left on Vancouver Island still stand. Despite the 800-year-old trees misted in moss and sword ferns, you'll quickly realize you're in the heart of logging country as you approach *Port Alberni.*

Trivia
Tofino, *nominated for a UNESCO Biosphere designation, gets twice as many inches of rain, but only half the hours of rain, as Vancouver.*

Although industry dominates here, outdoor activities are top-rate in the Port Alberni area. One for the very fit (and well-prepared) is a hike to *Della Falls,* at 1,444 feet (440 meters) Canada's second-highest free-falling waterfall (and the sixth highest in the world). It's in Strathcona Provincial Park and can be reached via paved road (look for signs just west of Port Alberni) to Sproat Lake Park and by boating the length of Great Central Lake (northwest of Port Alberni), followed by a 10-mile (16-km) hike beside Drinkwater Creek. Another activity is to join kayakers and hikers heading south to Bamfield, Ucluelet, or the West Coast Trail on the *MV Lady Rose* or *MV Frances Barkley.* If you join them, expect to see sea lions, whales, eagles, and spectacular scenery. Return trips cost $45–$50, and if you want to stay a while, you can rent kayaks or stay in the newly decorated *Sechart Whaling Station* lodge accommodation (nineteen rooms from $45 per person) near the *Broken Group Islands,* one of the three physically separated units that make up the *Pacific Rim National Park Reserve* in Barkley Sound. (The other two are *Long Beach* and the *West Coast Trail.*) Contact *Lady Rose Marine Services* at Alberni Harbor Quay (250–723–8313 or 800–663–7192 April through September; fax: 250–723–8314; www. ladyrosemarine.com) for information on the Alberni Inlet trip as well as for kayak rentals and lodge information. While there, try the schnitzel at the *Little Bavaria Restaurant* (3035 Fourth Avenue, 250–724–4242 or 800–704–2744). It's tasty and substantial.

Tofino, 21 miles (34 km) to the north, and *Ucluelet,* 5 miles (8 km) to the south, lie at the end of Highway 4, with glorious **Long Beach** between. *The Pacific Rim National Park Reserve Information Centre* (P.O. Box 280, Ucluelet, V0R 3A0; 250–726–4212, or 726–7721 off-season; pacrim_info@pch.gc.ca), a mile north of the Ucluelet-Tofino junction on Highway 4, is open daily from June to September. Short films and exhibits of marine biology of the Pacific west coast and the culture of the Nuu-chah-nulth make the **Wickaninnish Interpretive Center,** a short distance north of the park Info Centre, worth a stop. While there, enjoy a seafood dinner at the **Wickaninnish Restaurant** (open mid-March to mid-October 11:00 A.M. to 9:30 P.M.; 250–726–7706) and maybe catch a glimpse of Ukee, Ucluelet's gray whale mascot, some-where in the pounding waves outside. Start your west coast adventure in Ucluelet with an easy walk along the **Wild Pacific Trail.** Accessible to the physically challenged, it starts (or ends) at a parking lot on the corner of Peninsula Road and Coast Guard Road, passes **Amphitrite Lighthouse,** then links to a twenty-minute boardwalk loop through old-growth forest in **He-Tin-Kis Park** just south of Terrace Beach. The Pacific Ocean views from this trail are nothing short of spectacular.

Accommodations are fairly spectacular too. A stay at *A Snug Harbour Inn* (Box 318, 460 Marine Drive, Ucluelet, V0R 3A0; 250–726–2686; toll free: 888–936–5222; fax: 250–726–2685; asnughbr@island.net; www.asnugharbourinn.com) will be a stay to remember. Set into woods along a dramatic coastline, every room has a jetted tub, a fireplace, and a private deck for viewing this wild and wonderful west coast.

Tofino's Eagle Aerie Gallery

*O*ne of Canada's best-known artists is Roy Henry Vickers of the Tsimshian eagle clan. You may be lucky enough to meet him at the **Eagle Aerie Gallery** (350 Campbell Street, Tofino; V0R 2Z0; 250–725–3235; fax: 250–725–4466; 800–663–0669; eagleaerie@tofino-bc.com; www.royhenryvickers.com) in his self-designed, longhouse-style show-room. Splendid, tall totems support the huge beams of this ethereal building. As you enter through the beaten-copper front doors, you'll notice a strong smell of cedar and be struck by the peaceful feeling inside—what Vickers himself has described as "like walking into a womb, which is what a house should be." Sit in har-mony in the carpeted sitting-well, where the longhouse fire pit would traditionally be, and meditate calmly on Vickers's mystical artwork on the surrounding walls.

Not to be outdone, Tofino also has a few wonderful attractions, one of which is **Jamie's Whaling Station** (606 Campbell Street, Box 129, Tofino, V0R 2Z0; 800–667–9913 or 250–725–3919; fax: 250–725–2138; info@jamies.com; www.jamies.com/). The first gray whale tour company on Canada's west coast, Jamie guarantees his customers a whale sighting and even offers a rain check "forever" if they don't see one. Whales can be observed daily in the waters around Tofino for more than ten months a year! Three-hour trips in the 65-foot *Leviathan II,* with two glass-bottom panels (to check out the abundant sea life), range from $48 to $70, and two-hour trips in a Zodiac range from $35 to $50. After whale-watching, enjoy a bite at the ***Alley-Way Garden Café*** (250–725–3105), behind the CIBC bank just up from the Tofino Co-op. It's open from 8:00 A.M. daily for breakfast, lunch, and dinner, serving vegetarian-style Mexican food as well as absolutely delicious meal-size chowders.

Jamie's (which has recently started tours in Ucluelet—phone 877–470–7444 or 250–726–7444) also runs tours on nearby **Meares Island,** the home of the largest Western red cedar in the world. This cedar is more than 2,000 years old, is 72 feet (22 m) round, and is still growing. Meares was also the site of an extremely bitter antilogging lobby by the Tla-o-qui-aht First Nations people and other environmentalists. Another of Jamie's tours passes through the gray whale feeding bays in Clayoquot Sound to Hot Springs Cove, 23 miles (37 km) up the coast from Tofino. Here you can hike along a boardwalk through rain forest to **Macquinna Provincial Marine Park**. At the end of a narrow peninsula, stunningly perched right at the ocean's edge, treat yourself to a decadent soak in steaming natural hot springs. It's advisable to make reservations for these tours with Jamie's.

Should you be looking for somewhere truly "off-the-beaten-path" for accommodation, try the ***Innchanter*** (250–670–1149; innchanter@uniserve.com; www.innchanter.com), a heritage yacht moored near Hot Springs Cove. Luxury staterooms, unbelievable scenery, those glorious hot springs, and memorable gourmet meals prepared by an onboard chef will have you wishing you'd discovered the Innchanter long ago. For those who don't want to simply lie like a lizard on the sundeck, there's plenty to do, such as kayaking, whale watching, and hiking. At $85 per person including meals, you'll probably be returning sooner than you think. *The Tofino Visitor Info Centre* (Box 249, Tofino, V0R 2Z0; 250–725–3414; fax: 250–725–3296; tofino@island.net; www.island.net/~tofino) can also help with your stay in this area.

If it's blowing a gale when you visit the west coast, throw caution to the wind at the celebrated **Wickaninnish Inn** (Osprey Lane at Chesterman Beach, P.O. Box 250, Tofino, V0R 2Z0; 250–725–3100 or 800–333–4604; wick@wickinn.com; www.wickinn.com) with its **Pointe Restaurant, On-the-Rocks Bar,** and **Ancient Cedars Spa**. Luxuriate decadently in soaker tubs in rooms ranging from $160 to $380 and enjoy the truly panoramic, wild Pacific view, often dotted with wet-suited surfboarders. Look for signs on Highway 4 at Chesterman Beach about five minutes south of Tofino.

Denman and Hornby Islands

From the new Inland Island Highway (19) take exit 101, which crosses Oceanside Route 19A (the old Island Highway) to Buckley Bay. A car ferry (250–335–0323) leaves regularly (at least once an hour between 7:00 A.M. and 10:00 P.M.) for Denman Island (affectionately referred to by Hornby Islanders as "The Hornby Speed Bump"). After you cross Denman, a second ferry takes you further east to Hornby Island. These islands are steps back in time, so enjoy them leisurely. Cycling the mostly paved roads is an ideal way to get around, and **JR's Cycledeli** (250–335–1797) can usually oblige with a rental. It's in Denman Village near the junction of Denman and N.W. Roads, up the hill from the ferry dock. Cycle the trails through old-growth Douglas fir in Boyle Point and Fillongley Provincial Parks, both are pleasant with driftwood-littered beaches.

Then take the second ferry to Hornby Island, where Tribune Bay Provincial Park has fine white sandy beaches, and Helliwell Provincial Park has a 3-mile (5-km) circular track with spectacular bluffs. When the herring are running in March, watch for sea lions on nearby Norris Rocks. Bicycle rentals and guides are also available at the **Hornby Island Off Road Bike Shop** (5875 Central Road; 250–335–0444; hornbybikes@yahoo.com), or if you prefer an eye-level view of the sea lions, try some ocean kayaking with **Hornby Ocean Kayaks** (250–335–2726; pennym@mars.ark.com; ark.com/~pennym). For campers, Fillongley on Denman has ten beach sites, and **Tribune Bay Campsite** (250–335–2359) on Hornby has hot showers and cafes nearby.

As on many of these small islands, artisans and bed-and-breakfast

Kids' Stuff on the Islands

establishments flourish, so drop in to the **Denman Island General Store** (250–335–2293) at the top of the hill after you come off the first ferry and ask about accommodations and anything else you need to know about the islands. While there, be sure to pick up some **Denman Island Chocolate** (info@denmanislandchocolate.com; www.denmanislandchocolate.com). You'll have discovered not only the best tasting chocolate in the world but also Canada's only certified organic chocolate. Just around the corner from the general store near the bakery, you'll find a fine collection of local arts and crafts at the **Denman Craft Shop** (3676 Denman Road; 250–335–0881).There's more useful information on Denman at www.denmanis.bc.ca. Or write the **Hornby/Denman Tourist Association**, at Sea Breeze Lodge, Big Tree 3-2, Hornby Island, V0R 1Z0; phone/fax: (250) 335–2321; toll free: 888–516–2321; info@seabreezelodge.com; www.seabreezelodge.com.

Sea Breeze Lodge is delightfully set up with children in mind. Guests stay in waterfront (or close) one- and two-bedroom cottages. In summer the rates (which include all meals) are $122 per person (double) for a waterfront unit, and from September to May, kitchen cottages ($78–$98 double occupancy), some with fireplaces, can make for a very romantic, back to nature getaway, where watching the eagles soar and the herons stand in stately solitude waiting for a fishy meal is part of a normal dreamy day.

For those of you who want to see deeper than the ocean's surface, divers at **Hornby Island Diving** (Ford Cove, Hornby Island, V0R 1Z0; phone/fax: 250–335–2807; info@hornbyislanddiving.com; www.hornbyislanddiving.com) will accompany you in search of the elusive sixgill shark. Hornby Island is one of the few places in the world where the primitive, torpedo-shaped sixgill moves into waters as shallow as 50 feet (15 m). As its name suggests, the sixgill has six gills, instead of the five that most other sharks breathe with. They are both graceful and (according to dive masters on Hornby) surpris-

Beacon Hill Children's Farm, *Beacon Hill Park, Victoria (250–381–2532). Pet baby animals from mid-March to October.*

Watch salmon spawning in **Victoria's Goldstream Provincial Park** *(250–391–2300) between late October and mid-December, or learn about their life cycle at the* **Quatse River Hatchery** *(250–949–9022) near Port Hardy.*

All Fun Recreation, at 2207 Millstream Road, Victoria (250–474–3184) has go-carts, water slides, minigolf, and a batting cage.

See the Chemainus murals (250–246–4701) on a steam-train ride through town.

Swim and slide at **Oak Bay Recreation Centre,** *1975 Bee Street, Victoria (250–595–7946).*

Drag your parents along the whole 12-mile (20-km) length of surf-swept, sandy **Long Beach,** *with a lunch break at the Wickaninnish Centre (250–726–4212), where you'll learn fascinating things about marine life.*

Try your skills in the **kid's sandcastle competition** *in August on Parksville Beach (250–248–3252).*

ingly accommodating to the presence of humans. They grow up to 15 feet (4.5 m) long and frequent the waters off Hornby Island from May through September. The sea off Hornby is also known for giant Pacific octopus, sea lions, and harbor seals, as well as colorful nudibranchs, anemones, sponges, sea cucumbers, sea urchins, and particularly large and strikingly colored sea stars. Hornby Island Diving has group dive packages that include accommodation, two boat dives with a guide, an optional shore dive or night dive, and all air fills for $100 per person. The new dive lodge across from the ocean is equipped with a modern kitchen, sauna, and basic but pleasant bedrooms. And you don't have to be a diver to stay there. From May to September a non-diver pays $35 overnight, and in low season the cost is $30. Children twelve and under stay for free. It's a great place to get together with a group of friends or family to do some beachcombing, craft hunting, hiking, or photography.

One thing you must be sure to visit on Hornby is the **Free Store** at the recycling center on Main Street, where you'll find anything from a glamorous new wig to that old *National Geographic* issue you've been searching for.

The Comox Valley

*C*ourtenay is the city, *Comox* the town, and *Cumberland* the village, three of the communities that comprise the Comox Valley, where some of Canada's tallest fishing tales originate. As well as on the sea, there's plenty to do on land in the Comox Valley. In Comox you'll see Vancouver Island's largest glacier, and in Courtenay, the museum is housed in the largest freestanding log structure in Canada—**Native Sons Hall**—which was built in 1928. Here you'll see a replica of the first *elasmosaur* (an 80-million-year-old prehistoric swimming reptile) found west of the Rockies. Find out about amateur paleontology day trips in the Comox Valley at the Comox Valley Visitor Info Centre, 2040 Cliffe Avenue, Courtenay, V9N 2L3; (888) 357–4471; (250) 334–3234; fax: (250) 334–4908; chamber@mars.ark.com; www.tourism-comox-valley.bc.ca. One attraction 3 miles (5 km) north of Courtenay tweaked my interest. **Outback Emuzing Ranch** (2301 Clark Road, Courtenay, V9J 1T1; 250–338–8227; fax: 250–338–1108; info@emuoilcanada.com; www. emuoilcanada.com) is a small emu farm offering tours to the public. Here, just off the Island Highway, Russ and Karen Davis raise these gentle, flightless Australian birds for their meat and hides and for their valuable healing oil.

High above the emu ranch, 19 miles (31 km) west of Courtenay, looms a mountain rated third in British Columbia (after Whistler/Blackcombe and Big White) for the number of skiers it attracts each year. *Mount Washington Alpine Resort* (Box 3069, Courtenay, V9N 5N3, 250–338–1386; ski@mtwashington.bc.ca; www.mtwashington.bc.ca) is number one to more than 360,000 skiers per year. And with an average seasonal snowfall of more than 30 feet (9 m) it's no wonder. (In February 1999 the resort was closed for a day while the staff dug out the chair-lifts!) If you need help getting started, you could try one of the resort's "Discover" lessons, where you'll be introduced to skiing (cross-country or downhill), snowboarding, telemarking, or snowshoeing. Their reasonable prices include the lift pass, rental equipment, lesson, and sometimes a hot chocolate or coffee in the lodge to warm you up. And the spectacular view across Georgia Strait to the Coast Mountains is free.

In summer the cross-country ski trails of Paradise Meadows become wildflower-thick hiking trails that wind through a corner of *Strathcona Provincial Park,* Vancouver Island's largest park. No matter what the season, if you need condominium-style hotel accommodation at Mount Washington, contact Central Reservations at 888–231–1499 or online at the address above.

Campbell River and Surrounds

You've seen the view from the top. It's time to return to sea level and head north to the other Salmon Capital of the World (and you were told it was Port Alberni!), *Campbell River*. If you arrive in winter, try a backcountry snowshoe trek with *Paradise Found Adventure Tour Company* (800–897–2872; 250–923–0848; paradise @paradisefound.bc.ca; www.paradisefound.bc.ca). Summer visitors (July to October) can enjoy mountain biking, hiking, whale-watching, and caving tours. Ask your guide about *The Spirit of Discovery* video—a visual tour of northern Vancouver Island's outdoor activities and perhaps the perfect souvenir to take home with you. It sells for $15.95 US or $21.95 Canadian.

Not far from downtown Campbell River is the *Discovery Fishing Pier*. For $2.00 a day (from May to mid-October), you can fish off the fully lit, 600-foot (183-m) dock, which sports built-in rod holders, bait stands, fish cleaning areas, and picnic tables. Some huge salmon have been caught off this very pier. The concession stand (250–286–6199) will sell you all the necessary gear, plus bait, licenses, and fantastic ice creams.

For something more substantial than ice cream, head south from the pier to Second Avenue, then right onto Dogwood Street to the **Fusilli Grill** (220 Dogwood Street, V9W 2X9; 250–830–0090; fax: 250–830–0093; info@fusilligrill.bc.ca; www.fusilligrill.bc.ca). The Italian fare here is a huge favorite with locals. Choose from a generous shrimp and scallop fusilli alfredo accompanied by a BC Sumac Ridge Riesling to a healthy grilled chicken focaccia sandwich and much more. Takeout is also available, and prices are more than reasonable. If you're there on the weekend, the prime rib special is a winner.

I've seen some unusual museum settings, but the **Campbell River Optical Maritime Museum** close to the Fusilli Grill, (102–250 Dogwood Street; 250–287–2052) could be unique. Scattered throughout waiting and examining rooms in a suburban optometrist's office is a fine collection of maritime artifacts. Dr. Robert Somerville was for years a keen auxiliary Coast Guard volunteer. He has brought his love of things nautical into his workplace. From antique diving suits to interesting log books, every nook of his small office is filled. The museum is open during regular business hours, admission is free, and if he's not too busy, Dr. Somerville will give you a personal tour between seeing clients.

With a spectacular view of Discovery Passage, the **Campbell River Museum and Archives** (470 Island Highway, V9W 4Z9; 250–287–3103; fax: 250–286–0109; public.programs@crmuseum.ca; www.crmuseum. ca) is on the highway at the corner of Fifth Avenue. Look for First Nations culture and art, film footage of the historic Ripple Rock explosion, a replica pioneer cabin and a coastal floathouse, logging and fishing exhibits, and a 200-year-old Sun Welcome Mask. It is wheelchair accessi-

Ka-BOOM!

*T*he largest ever non-nuclear peacetime explosion occurred in Seymour Narrows near Campbell River on April 5, 1958, when part of **Ripple Rock** was blasted away. Over the years this dreaded hazard to navigation had caused about 114 vessels to sink, with an equal number of lives lost. To complete the task of destroying the rock, a special explosive, Nitramex 2H, was developed. A 500-foot (150-m) shaft was sunk on Maud Island, and a 2,370-foot (722-m)-long tunnel was dug out to the rock. After stuffing the rock with 2,750,000 pounds (1,250,000 kg) of the explosives, the area was cleared for 3 miles (5 km), and the button was pushed. The cost was more than three million dollars, and the top 350,000 tons of the rock disappeared in about three seconds. Film footage of the explosion can be seen at the Campbell River Museum.

ble and is open daily but it's closed Monday in winter. For more information contact **Campbell River Tourism,** Box 482, Campbell River, V9W 5C1; 800–463–4386; 250–286–1616; fax: 250–286–8336; crtour@vquest.com; www.campbellrivertourism.bc.ca.

Quadra and Cortes Islands

or more aboriginal history take a twelve-minute ferry ride to **Quadra Island** and follow the signs to the **Kwagiulth Museum and Cultural Center** (Box 8, Quathiaski Cove, Quadra Island, V0P 1N0; 250–285–3733; fax: 250–285–3753; kmccchin@island.net; www.island.net/~kmccchin), which is shaped like a giant sea snail to reflect the evolution of Kwagiulth culture. It's in the Cape Mudge Indian Village and houses part of a returned potlatch collection confiscated by the government in 1922. An addition to the museum called **Kwikwik Gwillas,** meaning "House of Eagles," has recently been built. Traditional songs and dancing are performed, and courses such as carving, cedar weaving, and native-doll making are taught. Admission is $3.00 for adults, $2.00 for seniors, and $1.00 for children ages six to twelve, plus an extra $1.00 for touring Kwikwik Gwillas.

While on Quadra, plan to hike on some of the often-deserted trails. The **Morte Lake** trail is an easy, pleasant hike, and the **Chinese Mountain** trail provides a panoramic view of the island. Tour the **Cape Mudge Lighthouse** (250–285–3351), where Captain George Vancouver went ashore in his exploration of Discovery Passage, or visit **Drahanchuk Studios** (157 Quadra Loop, Box 74, Quathiaski Cove, Quadra Island, V0P 1N0; phone/fax: 250–285–3160; drahan@oberon.ark.com; www. oberon.ark.com/~drahan). This delightful artists' home and studio is set in picturesque gardens (which are works of art in themselves) with views across Sutil Channel to the Coast Mountains. The studio, where you'll find exceptional paintings and pottery, as well as bronze and soapstone sculptures by Ed and Ethel Drahanchuk, is open most days June through mid-September, but phone ahead for opening hours or stop at the info booth by the ferry for a brochure with directions.

If you plan to stay, there's accommodation to suit everyone on Quadra Island, even a spot for your boat. **Heriot Bay Inn and Marina** (Heriot Bay Road, Box 100, Heriot Bay, V0P 1H0; 250–285–3322; fax: 250–285–2708; marina@heriotbayinn.com; www.heriotbayinn.com) has camping and marina facilities, cycle and kayak rentals, cottages, and a historic bed-and-breakfast inn (rates start at $40) in pretty Heriot Bay near Rebecca Spit. Mariners can check in on VHF channel 73.

Perhaps the best way to learn about some of Quadra's wildlife is from the quiet of a kayak. *Spirit of the West Adventures* (Box 569, Heriot Bay, V0P 1H0; 250–285–2121; fax: 250–285–2104; toll free: 800–307–3982; spirit1@ connected.bc.ca; www.kayak-adventures.com) takes guests in sea kayaks to the Breton Island Archipelago to view seal colonies, porpoises, killer whales, and nesting bald eagles.

From Quadra's Heriot Bay, take a 45-minute ferry ride (runs every two hours) to Cortes Island, "where the earth and the sea touch the sky." There's good camping at *Smelt Bay Provincial Park* (800–689–9025 for reservations but there are also "first-come" sites), 9 miles (15 km) south of the Whaletown Ferry Terminal on Sutil Point Road. The mounds behind the beach are believed to have been built by natives for defense purposes. If you have a valid BC fishing license, at low tide you can help yourself to a few huge oysters, which are delicious cooked on the campsite grill. Take note that this park has only basic facilities—pit toilets, no showers, and RVs to a maximum of twenty-four feet.

For something more upscale than oysters on a campsite grill (can there be?), try *The Tak Restaurant* (250–935–8555; www.cortesisland.com/thetak; open nightly from 5:00 to 10:00 P.M.) on Sutil Point Road. It's opposite the Cortes Market and the island's only bank machine. If you're arriving by yacht, it's about a ten-minute walk up from the Manson's Landing dock. It's fully licensed and offers the use of a computer to pick up your E-mail. The food is superb. Just north of Smelt Bay on Potlatch Road there's excellent waterfront bed-and-breakfast accommodation at *Blue Heron B&B* (Box 23 Mansons Landing, Cortes Island, V0P 1K0; 250–935–6584; www.cortesisland.com/blueheron). Rates range from $40.

Cortes is also home to *Hollyhock* (Box 127 Manson's Landing, V0P 1K0; 250–935–6576; fax: 250–935–6424; 800–933–6339; registration@ hollyhock.com; www.hollyhock.ca), where you can luxuriate in every kind of body, mind, and spirit renewal—an experience that may alter your life forever.

Strathcona Park and the Central West Coast

efore leaving the Campbell River area, head 30 miles (48 km) west on Highway 28 (the Gold River Highway) to **Strathcona Park**. It's British Columbia's first Provincial Park, a hiker's wilderness paradise located almost in the center of Vancouver Island and stretching almost to Nootka Sound on the west coast. At 627,064 acres (253,773 ha), not only is it the largest park on the island, but it also has the island's highest peak, **Mount Golden Hinde,** at 7,218 feet (2,200 m), and Canada's second-highest free-falling waterfall, **Della Falls,** which at 1,443 feet (440 m) is almost ten times higher than Niagara Falls. (See Port Alberni section for hiking details to the falls.) The paved road that hugs the eastern shore of **Buttle Lake** down to **Myra Creek** is spectacular and passes several creeks and water-falls. Two campsites—Buttle Lake, with eighty-five sites, and Ralph River, with seventy-six sites—can be accessed from Highway 28. Both are located on Buttle Lake. Phone (800) 689–9025 for reservations. Information is avail-able at the entrance to the park (seasonal) or from BC Parks, Strathcona District, on Highway 19, 2 miles (3 km) south of Parksville (Box 1479, Parksville, V9P 2H4, 250–954–4600; fax: 250–248–8584).

*In Victoria: Spend a day at the Inner Harbor and visit the **Royal British Columbia Museum** (250–387–3701 or 800–661–5411) and the **Royal London Wax Museum** (250–388–4461); cycle the 43-mile-long (70-km) **Galloping Goose Trail;** visit **Craigdarroch Castle** historic house museum (250–592–5323).*

*In Brentwood Bay: Visit the world-famous **Butchart Gardens** (250–652–4422) and **Butterfly Gardens** (250–652–3822), where the butterflies fly free and the birds are friendly.*

*In Duncan: Ride the steam train at the **British Columbia Forest Museum;** (250–715–1113).*

And all over the islands: Do some whale watching, fishing, hiking, and beachcombing.

As an alternative to camping, you can stay at the **Strathcona Park Lodge and Outdoor Education Centre** (Box 2160, Campbell River, V9W 5C5; 250–286–3122; fax: 250–286–6010; info@ strathcona. bc.ca; www.strathcona.bc.ca), where you can also learn a variety of wilder-ness skills. Everyone is welcome—you're just as likely to see eighty-year-olds perfecting Eskimo rolls as eight-year-olds rappelling down a rocky bluff. Nutritious meals are standard fare, and the package deals are very reasonable.

Gold River, 6 miles (9 km) west of the park border, also has first-class outdoor activities. Fishing in the Gold River and **Nootka Sound**—a 65-pound (30-kg) salmon was taken in 1993—and more than fifty caves within a 30-mile (50-km) radius supplement beautiful views. Enjoy some of these views while hiking the **Peppercorn Trail,** which starts out near the secondary school close to downtown. Steps and a safety rope assist hikers along the trail to Peppercorn Park, where you can cool off in a swimming hole below diving cliffs. For cavers, the **Upana Caves,** located twenty-five minutes northwest of Gold River on the Head Bay Forest Road (toward Tahsis) provide approximately 1,475 feet (450m) of caving bliss. Gold River Visitor Info Centre can be contacted at Box 610, Gold River, V0P 1G0; (250) 283–2418 or 283–2202; fax: (250) 283–7500; goldriv@island.net; www.village.goldriver.bc.ca.

Every year on the first Saturday in June, the Tahsis Lions Club hosts the **Great Walk,** undisputedly North America's toughest charity pledge walkathon. The route runs between Gold River and Tahsis. The top time to complete the approximately 40 miles (63.5 km) is four and a half hours. If you think you can beat that, or just want to have some fun, contact the Tahsis Lions Club (Box 430, Tahsis, V0P 1X0; 250–934–6570; greatwalk@greatwalk.com; www.greatwalk.com) for information. Afterward, soak your toes in the Tahsis River near **Fern's Place Bed & Breakfast Suite** (379 North Maquinna Drive, Tahsis, V0P 1X0; 250–934–7851; fax: 250–934–7871; eastcott@cancom.net; www.cancom.net/~eastcott). Accommodation with continental breakfast is in the $45–$65 range. For more information contact the Tahsis Info Centre/Museum (June–September) at Rugged Mountain Road, Box 278, Tahsis, V0P 1X0; 250–934–6667; fax: 250–934–6679; tahsis@village.tahsis.bc.ca; www.village.tahsis.bc.ca.

Get Ready for a GREAT Walk

*I*f you're set on doing the **Great Walk,** *here are a few very important things to consider:*

• **Socks.** *You'll need a few extra pairs to get you through the forty-odd agony-filled miles (63.5 kilometers to be precise), so bring oodles.*

• **Toilets.** *You'll be sharing the road with about 700 others, so expect long lineups at the potty stops.*

• **Grades.** *At times the terrain is excruciatingly steep, so train in Everest-like territory.*

• **Earplugs.** *Bring these for the screaming sirens, bright lights, and raucous pot-banging at the end, where you'll be greeted by crowds of high-spirited locals.*

• **Fun.** *Finally, despite occasional torture-filled paroxysms, you can expect to have a ton of this.*

From Gold River another logging road leads 39 miles (63 km) north through the Nimpkish Valley to **Woss,** just west of the Highway 19 intersection. It's rough, but if you're in Gold River and heading north to Port McNeil, it will cut off 92 miles (148 km). If you don't mind a few corrugations (maybe a lot!) and have good emergency supplies and the appropriate forestry maps, there's lots more to be explored in this wild, northern part of the island. But perhaps the best-kept secret is **Woss Lake**. The views down the lake to the glacier-topped Rugged Mountain Range are breathtaking. To top it off, you can camp by a lovely white-sand beach complete with boat ramp, which is kept in excellent condition by Canadian Forest Products.

From Woss it's about 12 miles (20 km) north to the turnoff to Zeballos, population 250 and named after a Spanish explorer, Ciriaco Cevallos (close enough!). Drive for fifteen to twenty minutes along the Zeballos Road and look for the well-marked logging road turnoff to Little Huson Caves Regional Park. Another fifteen minutes or so, and you'll be able to explore several caves, rock arches, and a limestone canyon. No, Huson is not a typographical error; you'll see it written as Hustan in maps and government documents (soon to be corrected), but the regional park and the nearby lake are actually named after Mr. West Huson, a North Island pioneer.

When you reach **Zeballos,** 26 miles (42 km) southwest of Highway 19, ask at the Visitor Info Booth on Maquinna Avenue (Box 127, Zeballos, V0P 2A0; 250–761–4070/4158; fax: 250–761–4331, www.zeballos.com) about guided tours of the village. The booth is open July 1 to September 6. The many false-fronted buildings in Zeballos tell a story of a town with an exciting gold mining history. You can read up on this at the library, which offers an Internet service. Or visit the folks at **Mason's Motor Lodge** (203 Pandora Avenue, Box 10, Zeballos, V0P 2A0; 250–761–4044; fax: 250–761–4074; info@masonslodge.zeballos.bc.ca; www.mason slodge.zeballos.bc.ca). They'll fill you in on this exciting history while you lounge on the large deck below the pretty mountains that edge the Zeballos River and the inlet. And don't be surprised if a black bear snuffles by below in search of his salmon supper, especially in late summer during spawning season. Accommodation at Mason's, a charmingly refurbished, historic hospital building with an attached restaurant, is in the $55–$110 range. Zeballos truly fits the description: "Accessible wilderness."

Rat River Enterprises (250–761–4215) has a 26-foot aluminum boat ready to help you explore **Nootka Island** or **Kyuquot Sound,** where perhaps you'll land a thirty-pound king salmon in this scenic wilderness. Kayakers wishing to meet up close and personally the sea otters, bald eagles, and black bears of the stunning **Nuchatlitz** can contact **Zeballos Expeditions and Kayaks** (115 Maquinna Avenue, Box 111, Zeballos, V0P 2A0; 250–761–4137; kayak@netcom.ca; www.zeballoskayaks.com). Three-day wildlife viewing tours in the **Nootka Sound** area aboard comfortable vessels are also offered.

Back on Highway 19 after the Zeballos side trip, the road skirts **Nimpkish Lake** (noted for its world-class windsurfing), with the Karmutzen Range on the opposite side for 40 miles (64 km) to Port McNeill, the ferry terminal for the intriguing island communities of Sointula and Alert Bay.

The North Islands

Six miles (9 km) south of Port McNeill, just before the Nimpkish River Bridge, a 10-mile (16-km) road leads to **Telegraph Cove** and the **Robson Bight (Michael Bigg) Ecological Reserve,** the most predictable location in the world to see killer whales. Walk Telegraph Cove's historic boardwalk, perched on stilts over a rocky shoreline, and wander past the folksy, weatherbeaten houses that front the harbor. **Mothership Adventures Inc.** (Box 130, Victoria, V8W 2M6; 888–833–8887 or 250–384–8422; fax: 250–384–3750; info@mothership adventures.com; www.mothershipadventures.com) will take you right to the whales, as well as to abandoned native villages and the remote rain forests of British Columbia. You'll have a live-aboard, sea-kayaking adventure you won't forget—ever. Captain Bill McKechnie has beautifully refitted the 68-foot (21-m) **Columbia,** a historic mission boat, to take small groups of adventurers to Johnstone Strait, Broughton Archipelago, and the Central Coast (from Port Hardy to Prince Rupert). Costs run about $340 per day, including kayaks, all meals and wine, and comfortable staterooms.

Back on the highway as you head north to Port McNeill on Highway 19, look for an ARTISAN sign after the Nimpkish River bridge that points you to **Henschel Fine Arts Gallery and Studio** (801 Nimpkish Heights Road, Port McNeill, V0N 2R0; 888–663–2787 or 250–956–3539; fax: 250–956–4760; henschel@island.net; www.henschelfinearts.com). Gordon Henschel's delicate North Island scenes grace walls in a handsomely designed gallery.

Just before the gallery **Roseberry Manor Bed & Breakfast** (810 Nimpkish Heights Road, Port McNeill, V0N 2R0; 250–956–4788; www.

bbcanada.com/roseberrymanorbb) has antique, knickknacky decor straight out of a Victorian dining room. Candlelit gourmet breakfasts plus afternoon tea and evening cappuccinos are all included in the $65–$85 (per double in high-season) price range.

If you make the 8:40 A.M. ferry in Port McNeill, it's possible to see both *Sointula* and *Alert Bay* in one day, but give yourself some time or you might miss some of the treasures both Malcolm and Cormorant Islands have hidden away. Check carefully with BC Ferries (888–BCFERRY; www.bcferries.bc.ca/schedules/northern/pmab-current.html); the timetable covering Port McNeil, Sointula, and Alert Bay is complicated, at best!

Sointula, a Finnish word meaning "place of harmony," is aptly named. As soon as you drive off the *Quadra Queen II* thirty-car ferry, you sense the easygoing atmosphere. It wasn't always so, though. The old school building off First Street houses the volunteer-run *Finnish Museum* (250–973–6764), where you can learn about the community's colorful history. It started as a Finnish cooperative community in 1901, but after some dissension and debt, and a fire, which killed eleven people and destroyed the meeting hall, the cooperative disappeared. Many Finns remained, though, and in some of Sointula's back lanes you will still hear a smattering of the old tongue. For more information contact the *Malcolm Island Tourism Association* at Box 23, Sointula, V0N 3E0; sointula@island.net; www.island.net/~sointula.

Window on a Small Town

*T*he walls were as thin as brothel sheets, the pillow slips thick with bleach. Buses idled below, their sickly fumes filtering into the rain-battered hotel. My dreams involved gas masks. I was beginning to have doubts about Port McNeill.

The next morning, I stumbled sleepily to the town's mall. An adorable teapot in *The Window*, a little hole-in-the-wall studio, tweaked my interest. IT'S MY BIRTHDAY, GONE FOR LUNCH was the greeting on an open door. Of course it wasn't **really** painter and potter Heather Brown's birthday. She invited me in to see her superb paintings of island gardens and spawning salmon, and her whimsical pottery.

We chatted about the Ronning Gardens (the subject of many of her paintings) near Cape Scott and of the vicissitudes of living in Port McNeill. I left The Window breathing in deeply the sweet smell of a rain-cleansed earth as speckles of blue broke the gray sky.

When you arrive at the Sointula ferry landing, you'll see *Choyces* (250–973–6433), where you can rent a bike and pedal around the island to see the old Finnish farms and beachfront homes. Choyces, open Monday to Saturday from 10:00 A.M. to 5:00 P.M., also sells a few local arts and crafts. There's attractive waterview accommodation at *Palo Farm Bed & Breakfast* (Box 205, Sointula, V0N 3E0; 250-973-6571; b-b@island.net; www.sointula.com). Choose to stay in the comfortable home or a self-contained honeymoon cottage. Rates range from $60 to $80 for a double.

Recommended Reading - The Islands

FOR ADULTS:
Island Backroads: Hiking, Camping & Paddling on Vancouver Island, by Richard K. Blier. Orca Book Publishers, 1998.

Hiking Trails 1—Victoria & Vicinity, Hiking Trails II—South-Central Vancouver Island and the Gulf Islands; and *Hiking Trails III—Central & Northern Vancouver Island & Quadra Island* by the Vancouver Island Trails Information Society. Orca Book Publishers, Victoria.

More Island Adventures: An Outdoors Guide to Vancouver Island, by Richard K. Blier. Orca Book Publishers, 1993.

Ghost Towns and Mining Camps of Vancouver Island, T. W. Paterson & Garnet Basque. Sunfire Publications Limited, 1989. Langley.

Backroading Vancouver Island, by Rosemary Neering. Whitecap Books. Vancouver, 1996. A nitty gritty approach to exploring Vancouver Island's off-roads, right down to where to buy your ice cream and eggs.

FOR KIDS:
In Like a Lion, by Julie Lawson, illustrated by Yolaine Lefebvre. North Wind Press, Markham Ontario, 1998. A picture book for kids Grades One and Two. Based on a true story about a cougar visiting the Empress Hotel in Victoria.

Jessie's Island, by Sheryl McFarlane, illustrated by Sheena Lott. Orca Books, Victoria, 1992. Ages five to eight. A celebration of West Coast life through a child's eyes.

Ida and the Wool Smugglers, by Sue Ann Alderson, illustrated by Ann Blades. Douglas and McIntyre, Toronto, 1987. The story takes place on Salt Spring Island at the turn of the century. Smugglers row over from the mainland, Ida spots them, and the story continues. For kids at the primary level.

Cougar Cove, by Julie Lawson. Orca books, 1996. Set on the remote west coast of Vancouver Island. The heroine, eleven-year-old Sam, meets a cougar and two cubs. For kids about the grade three and four level.

Trivia

Holberg, named for the Danish historian and dramatist Baron Ludvig Holberg, was once the site of the world's largest floating logging camp.

Alert Bay has an equally fascinating, but quite different history. To the right after you come off the ferry is the **Alert Bay Info Centre** (116 Fir Street, Bag Service 2800, Alert Bay, V0N 1A0; 250–974–5024; fax: 250–974–5026; info@village.alert bay.bc.ca; village.alertbay.bc.ca). Here you'll find a collection of paintings depicting the island's historical waterfront, plus photocopied literature about the island's history and attractions, which will set you off handily on your explorations.

Head back past the ferry terminal along Front Street and past the Anglican **Christ Church** (built in 1892) to the **U'mista Cultural Center** (Box 253, Alert Bay, V0N 1A0; 250–947–5403; umista@island.net; www. umista.org). The name has an interesting origin. In the early days, if captured people were returned to their villages (possibly after a ransom payment or as a result of a retaliatory raid), they were said to have "u'mista." So, too, the return of treasured artifacts from distant museums is a form of u'mista. First learn about these potlatch treasures from the center's informative brochure, watch the twenty-seven-minute award-winning video *Box of Treasures,* then see the famous **Potlatch Collection** of coppers and masks, originally confiscated by the government in 1921. Allow about two hours for a visit. Regular hours are Monday–Friday 9:00 A.M.–5:00 P.M., and the center is open daily May Day to Labor Day. Don't miss the interesting gift store.

High up on a hill behind the U'mista Cultural Center, next to a traditional Big House, the 173-foot (53.7-m) **World's Tallest Totem Pole** reaches for the sky. Carved in the late 1960s (although not raised until 1973) by a team headed by Jimmy Dick, the fourteen figures on this pole represent some of the tribes of the Kwakwaka'wakw. Among these figures look for Sun Man, Whale, Wolf, Thunderbird, and a bear holding a salmon, indicative of the native people's pride in the land. Down on the waterfront in the center of town, the **'Namgis Burial Ground** is an imposing reminder of Cormorant Island's aboriginal ancestry. In **Ecological Park**, stark, dead tree trunks stand amid life-filled reflections, a reminder of the island's commercial past. Check the treetops for eagles, and at the information center, learn the interesting history of how this park was formed.

And don't leave without doing some whale watching. **Seasmoke Whale Watching** (Box 483, Alert Bay, V0N 1A0; 800–668–6722 in BC only, elsewhere phone/fax: 250–974–5225; seaorca@island.net; www.seaorca.

'N̲amgis Burial Ground totems in Alert Bay

com) runs five-hour tours ($40 for children, $70 for adults) from June to mid-October. You'll be served scrumptious hot muffins and Devonshire Tea, while you enjoy the sights and sounds (via hydrophones) of orcas, Dall's porpoises, harbor seals, humpback and gray whales, river otters, and sea lions. There's also an "On the Beach" self-contained unit where you can relax and enjoy the delightful surroundings. Suitable for up to six, it's a great spot to throw fresh fish on the barbecue while enjoying fabulous sunsets from the large deck. Although private, the shops and restaurants are only a minute or two away.

Janet's Guest House Bed and Breakfast (Box 229, Alert Bay, V0N 1A0; 250–974–5947; janets@alertbay.com; www.alertbay.com/janets), on the waterfront at 667 Fir Street, is another cozy spot. Rates at this turn-of-the-century restored home range from $55 single to $70 double—or $160 for the whole house, which is handy for groups. Several other accommodations (including two campgrounds) can also be found on the island.

Back on Vancouver Island, information about Port McNeill and sur-rounds can be found in the new museum building at the ***Port McNeill***

Visitor Info Centre (Box 129, Port McNeill, V0N 2R0; 250–956–3131; fax: 250–956–3132; pmccc@island.net; www.portmcneill.net).

From Port McNeill, Port Hardy lies 27 miles (43 km) northwest. About 3 miles (5 km) from Port McNeill's center, the West Main logging road crosses the highway, and a few hundred feet north along this road sits the *World's Largest Burl.* Weighing more than twenty tons, with a circumference of more than 44 feet (13.5 m), it's worth stopping simply to take in the immensity of this 355-year-old spruce burl. As you approach the Port Alice Road, about 10 miles (16 km) northwest of the burl, you might want to polish up the clubs, as along this very scenic road you'll find two small golf courses. One, the *Seven Hills Golf and Country Club* (250–949–9818) has a restaurant and is about a mile from Highway 19. You'll find here the remains of the only surviving *Hornsby Steam Tractor,* the direct ancestor of all tracked vehicles. Built in England in 1910, it has had a varied past, having been used both for hauling coal in Dawson City in the Yukon and for hauling logs in Holberg Inlet. The other club, the *Port Alice Golf and Country Club* (250–284–3213), is near the town's pulp mill; it's a steep nine-holer, complete with sand traps and water hazards. For information on the area, or accommodation, contact the village of Port Alice at Box 130, Port Alice, V0N 2N0; 250–284–3391; www. village.port-alice.bc.ca.

When you reach Port Hardy, you're at the jumping-off point for *BC Ferries'* fifteen-hour sail through the spectacular *Inland Passage* to Prince Rupert, 305 miles (491 km) north. This journey, at $430 (one-way summer fare, but check www.bcferries. com/fares/inside_passage.html; 250–386–3431 for updates) for a car and two adults, is a splendid means of seeing as much of BC as possible without retracing your steps.

In *Port Hardy* the staff and volunteers of the small museum at 7110 Market Street (Box 2126, Port Hardy, V0N 2P0; 250–949–8143) will share their knowledge on the logging, mining, and fishing history of the area. Hours vary "according to available funds!" Considering the small area avail-

---

Trivia

Names mean a lot in Port Hardy. Ask a local why Carrot Park and Stink Creek Park are so named. Then try to figure out how **Filomi Days,** *the annual mid-July festival, got its name. Finally, visit the Gwa'Sala-'Nakwaxda'xw Tribal Council's big house project—just for the name of it!*

Trivia

During the Second World War, the tiny community of Coal Harbour, twenty minutes west of Port Hardy near the mouth of Holberg Inlet, was a busy Royal Canadian Air Force seaplane base and reconnaissance station. Flying-boat crews flew missions along the Canadian coast. After the war, it was a thriving whaling station, attested to by the huge jawbone from a blue whale on display in the village.

able, the museum shop is well stocked with books and souvenirs.

The locals all have their favorite eating spots, but these three come highly recommended. **Sam's Restaurant** (250–949–9733) is a fifteen-minute walk from the town center. It's near the Petro Canada station in the old mall complex close to the Island Highway. The walk will ready your appetite for some excellent Greek and Italian cooking, or steak if you prefer. It's not on the beaten path, but for the quality and comfortable atmosphere, it's worth looking for. Another choice is the **Airport Inn Restaurant** (250–949–8381), also popular with locals. The fifteen-minute drive (near the airport off Byng Road) is worthwhile for the best Chinese food in town, as well as good quality Canadian cuisine. If it's seafood you're after, the accomplished chef/owner at **Joe's Bar and Grill** (9040 Granville, 250–949–8187) produces consistently delicious meals. It's at the Port Hardy Inn at the corner of Island Highway and Granville Street, a ten-minute walk from town.

If you prefer a pub-style meal, **I. V.'s Quarterdeck Pub** (6555 Hardy Bay Road; 250–949–6922) has just the right mix of local and marine atmosphere. It's a pleasant fifteen-minute walk from town. Head south along Market Street past the Green Apple Restaurant and turn left on Hardy Bay Road at the Robert Scott elementary school. For accommodation and other information, contact the **Port Hardy Visitor Info Centre** (7250 Market Street, Port Hardy, V0N 2P0; 250–949–7622; fax: 250–949–6653). And while you're there, check out the totem poles in and around the building.

If you've come this far north, spare time for **Cape Scott Provincial Park** at the far northwest end of the island. To get there head south from the center of Port Hardy on Highway 19 and turn right (west) onto the Holberg Road. **Holberg** is 28 unpaved miles (45 km) from Port Hardy, and the park entrance is a farther 12 miles (19 km). Watch for the **Shoe Tree,** a visual pun on the north side of the road about 8 miles (12.5 km) from Highway 19. From **Holberg** the tiny fishing hamlet of **Winter Harbor** is 12 miles (20 km) south. Here, in September, the tuna fishing fleet enlivens this sleepy port.

If you're heading to Cape Scott, you'll pass the **Bernt Ronning Garden** (Box 105, Holberg, V0N 1Z0; 250–288–3724), a heritage site presently being restored by Julia and Ron Moe. It's off the San Josef Main logging road, about 8.5 miles (14 km) west of Holberg. It's blooming with a collection of plants from all over the world. Look for the pair of monkey puzzle trees at the entrance to the old house site, as well as brilliant rhododendrons, daffodils, and countless squirrels. Bring peanuts!

Unbelievably dauntless Danish immigrants started a colony near Cape Scott in the 1890s; however, the absence of safe boat landings and lack of an access road led to the failure of the colony. Many independent home-steaders followed the Danes, but most left when the First World War began. At present giant Sitka spruce, some settlement remnants, and the *Cape Scott Lighthouse* are but some of the points of interest. Spectacular *San Josef Bay* is an easy thirty-five-minute walk on the 1.5-mile (2.5-km) trail from the parking lot at the end of the road. Be aware that the trail to the cape (as well as the beaches on the north side of the park) is often muddy and requires most of a day to hike one way. Stand on the *Cape Scott sand neck* from where you can view both sides of Vancouver Island, and think back on those brave Danish settlers. But perhaps think further back to earlier inhabitants who stood on this same sand neck. It was the site of a prehistoric massacre, and it is said that the shifting sands sometimes expose human bones. But the history goes even further back. Native legend has it that Cape Scott is the place where the first people orig-inated. For information (and don't hike here without it), contact BC Parks District Office at Box 1479, Parksville, V9P 2H4; (250) 954–4600, or call the area office at (250) 949–2815; fax: (250) 949–6346; jryan@prkparksvl. elp.gov.bc.ca; www.elp.gov.bc.ca/bcparks. A Web site that has a wealth of information on hiking at Cape Scott is www.village.port-alice.bc.ca/capescott. For information on all areas of the North Island contact Van-couver Island North Visitors Association, Box 1755, Port McNeill, V0N 2R0; phone/fax: 250–949–9094; toll free: 800–903–6660; tourism@ vinva.bc.ca; www.vinva.bc.ca. For more information covering all of "The Islands" visit www.vancouverisland.com.

PLACES TO STAY ON THE ISLANDS

ALERT BAY

On the Beach,
Box 483, Alert Bay,
V0N 1A0; phone/fax: (250) 974–5225; (800) 668–6722 in BC only. Self-contained unit on the water, with ocean and mountain views. Sleeps six.

Janet's Guest House Bed and Breakfast,
667 Fir Street, Box 229, V0N 1A0; (250) 974–5947. Waterfront rooms or a whole house.

BAMFIELD

Woods End Landing,
380 Lombard Street, Box 108, Bamfield, V0R 1B0; phone/fax: (250) 728–3383; (877) 828–3383 toll free. Rustic and beachy cabins and duplex accommodation.

CHEMAINUS
Olde Mill House,
9712 Chemainus Road,
Box 1046, Chemainus, V0R
1K0; (250) 416–0049; (877)
770–6060 toll free; fax:
250–246–4457.
Historic home run as a
bed-and-breakfast inn.

CORTES ISLAND
Blue Heron B&B,
Box 23, Mansons Landing,
Cortes Island, V0P 1K0;
(250) 935–6584.
Waterfront, secluded.

COWICHAN BAY
Old Farm Bed and Break-
fast, 2075 Cowichan Bay
Road, Cowichan Bay, V0R
1N0; phone/fax:
(250) 748–6410;
(888) 240–1482 toll free.
Relaxation plus, with water
and garden views.

GABRIOLA ISLAND
Sunset Bed & Breakfast,
RR 1, Site 1, C–7, Gabriola
Island, V0R 1X0;
(877) 247–2032 toll free;
(250) 247–2032.

Green Gates Bed and
Breakfast, 2345 South
Road, RR 1, Site 23, C–33,
Gabriola Island, V0R 1X0;
(250) 247–9870 or
(604) 680–0673.

HORNBY ISLAND
Sea Breeze Lodge, Big Tree
3–2, Hornby Island, V0R
1Z0; phone/fax: (250)
335–2321; (888) 516–2321
toll free. Waterfront
cottages.

PENDER ISLAND
Brook Point Glade,
(250) 592–5088;
dgreer@coastnet.com. A
cosy all-season cottage in
the woods, a short walk to
a secluded beach.

PORT MCNEILL
Roseberry Manor
Bed & Breakfast,
810 Nimpkish Heights
Drive, V0N 2R0;
(250) 956–4788.

QUADRA ISLAND
Heriot Bay Inn and Marina,
Heriot Bay Road, Box 100,
Heriot Bay, V0P 1H0;
(250) 285–3322;
fax: (250) 285–2708.
Bed-and-breakfast inn
with camping and marina
facilities.

QUALICUM BEACH
Bahari Bed and Breakfast,
5101 West Island Highway,
V9K 1Z1; (250) 752–9278.
Waterfront luxury ocean-
front bed-and-breakfast
accommodation.

SALTSPRING ISLAND
Anne's Oceanfront
Hideaway, 168 Simson
Road, V8K 1E2;
(888) 474–2663 or
(250) 537–0851. First-class
oceanfront bed-and-
breakfast accommodation.

Brooks Point Glade,
(250) 598–3607;
dgreer@coastnet.com.
A secluded, two-day-
minimum, all-season
cottage close to a quiet
beach.

SOINTULA
Palo Farm Bed & Breakfast,
Box 205, Sointula, V0N 3E0;
(250) 973–6571. Home or a
self-contained cottage.

SOOKE
Billings Spit Beach House,
(250) 642–1910 or toll
free (877) 642–1910;
information@billingsspit
beachhouse.com;
www.billingsspitbeach-
house.com. A modern
oceanfront cottage in a garden setting. The welcome
basket is loaded with
gourmet goodies.

TOFINO
Innchanter,
Hot Springs Cove; (250)
670–1149. Luxury yacht
accommodation. First class
menu, too.

VICTORIA
Oak Bay Guest House,
1052 Newport Avenue,
V8S 5E3; (800) 575–3812
or (250) 598–3812. Quality
bed-and-breakfast accom-
modation in quiet suburb
near the water.

ZEBALLOS
Mason's Motor Lodge,
203 Pandora Avenue,
Box 10, Zeballos, V0P 2A0;
(250) 761–4044; fax: (250)
761–4074. Historic hospital
building with an attached
restaurant.

PLACES TO EAT ON THE ISLANDS

CAMPBELL RIVER
Fusilli Grill,
220 Dogwood Street, V9W
2X9; (250) 830–0090;
fax: (250) 830–0093.
Italian fare. Licensed and
very popular.

CORTES ISLAND
The Tak Restaurant,
on Sutil Point Road,
(250) 935–8555. Classy
healthy food.

NANAIMO
Dinghy Dock Pub,
8 Pirate Lane on Protection
Island; (250) 753–2373.

OAK BAY
Blighty's Bistro,
2006 Oak Bay Avenue;
(250) 592–5111. Absolutely
delicious food.

Windsor House Tea Room
and Restaurant,
2450 Windsor Road;
(250) 595–3135. Open
Tuesday–Saturday 11:00
A.M. to 6:00 P.M.

PORT HARDY
Sam's Restaurant,
(250) 949–9733, near the
Petro Canada station. Greek
and Italian cuisine.

Airport Inn Restaurant,
(250) 949–8381, near the
airport. Chinese and
Canadian cuisine.

Joe's Bar and Grill,
9040 Granville;
(250) 949–8187, at the Port
Hardy Inn. Great seafood.

I.V.'s Quarterdeck Pub,
6555 Hardy Bay Road;
(250) 949–6922.

SALTSPRING ISLAND
Bouzouki Greek Café,
2104 Grace Point Square,
115 Fulford-Ganges Road;
(250) 537–4181.

Moby's Marina Pub,
124 Upper Ganges Road;
(250) 537–5559;
(800) 334–MOBY, on the
Ganges Harbour water-
front. Live entertainment
and pub fare.

SIDNEY
The Blue Peter Pub and
Restaurant,
2270 Harbor Road;
(250) 656–4551. On the
waterfront in Shoal
Harbour. Impressive
seafood!

The Stonehouse Pub &
Restaurant, 2215 Canoe
Cove; (250) 656–3498.
Casual; by the marina.

TOFINO
Pointe Restaurant at
Wickaninnish Inn,
Chesterman Beach;
(800) 333–4604 or
(250) 725–3100. Great
views, great food.

Alley-Way Garden Café,
(250) 725–3105,
behind the CIBC bank.
Breakfast, lunch, and
dinner. Vegetarian-style
Mexican food.

VICTORIA
Charters Restaurant at
McMorrans Beach House,
5109 Cordova Bay Road;
(250) 658–5527. On the
beach. The Sandbar Patio
is a popular spot on a
summer day.

John's Place,
723 Pandora Street;
(250) 389–0711. Best free
bread in the city.

Sam's Deli,
805 Government Street;
(250) 382–8424. Casual,
healthy.

Spinnakers Brew Pub and
Guest House,
308 Catherine Street;
(250) 386–2739. Walking
distance along the water-
front from downtown.
Luxury bed-and-breakfast
accommodation also.

The Southwestern Mainland

hether you want to be part of the madding crowd or lose yourself in silent wilderness, this region of British Columbia has it all. Starting out in vibrant Vancouver, rated (out of an international survey of 215 cities) in 2000 for the second year in a row as the best city in the world for quality of life, we'll travel east along the Fraser River to the pretty town of Hope, then north through amazingly engineered tunnels in the Fraser Canyon to the mercifully untouched Stein River Valley. Then it's south through the Coast Mountain peaks and the famous Whistler-Blackcombe ski resort to North Vancouver. From here ferries cross Howe Sound to the warm Sunshine Coast, where from Gibsons Landing, immortalized in the CBC production *The Beachcombers*, we'll pass through laid-back villages and holiday homes to Lund, the last vestige of civilization before the yachting paradise of Desolation Sound.

Vancouver

ancouver is at the center of a very beaten path. With its eclectic mix of residents, there's little challenge in finding elegant eateries, a variety of accommodations, and a huge range of activities, from sailing to skiing to golfing, often possible all on one day, in any season. But where to start?

From almost anywhere in Vancouver, a look up reveals **Grouse Mountain,** at night a sleeping beauty of twinkling lights giving the city a fairy-tale feel. To get there head north through Stanley Park to the Lions Gate Bridge, then east on Marine Drive, north on Capilano Road, and up Nancy Greene Way to the end. For more than 300 stalwarts (5,000 on weekends!), the 2-mile (3.5-km) daily climb, **The Grouse Grind,** to the top of this 3,609-foot (1,100-m) pinnacle keeps them in peak form.

But if you're into taking the easy way up, an aerial tramway, **The Grouse Mountain Skyride** (604–980–9311, ext. 6; info@grousemtn. com; www.grousemountain.com) is an eight-minute alternative. At the top view a thirty-five-minute movie *Born to Fly,* Canada's first

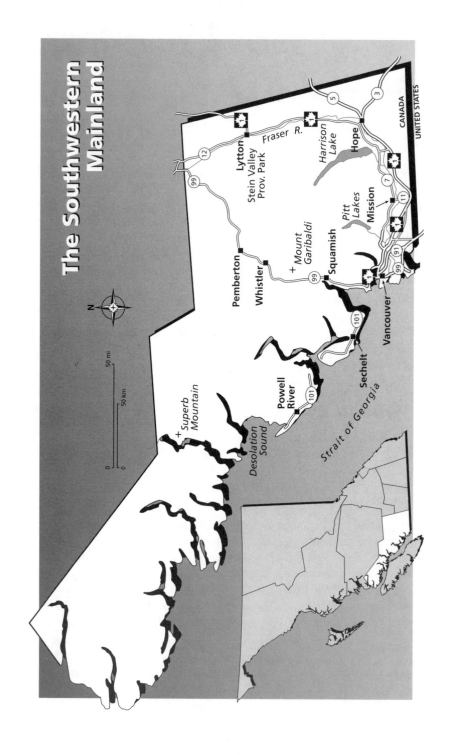

THE SOUTHWESTERN MAINLAND

high-definition video presentation, in the multi-million-dollar *Theatre in the Sky*. Then eat native cuisine in the *hiwus Feasthouse,* impressively decorated with artwork by Coast Salish artist Richard Krentz.

In the cooler months, it's a winter wonderland with skiing, snowboarding, ice-skating, and snowshoeing available. Take advantage of a winter shuttle bus service. *Landsea Tours* makes stops at several downtown hotels. Phone (604) 255-7272 or toll free (877) 669-2277 for information.

Stop off on the way down at the *Capilano Suspension Bridge* (604-985-7474; fax: 985-7479; www.capbridge.com), the world's longest pedestrian suspension bridge, which measures 450 feet (137 m) and sways 230 feet (70 m) above the Capilano River. Here you can enjoy the nature trails or watch native carvers chiseling colorful totem poles at the Big House carving center in *Capilano Park.*

Back at ground level and smack in the center of the city, you'll find a refueling spot at *Harry's Diner* (1078 West Pender Street, near Thurlow; 604-331-0046; www.harrysdiner.com; open weekdays 7:00 A.M.–5:00 P.M.). While sitting beside Billie Holliday and Louis Armstrong photos, enjoy Harry's excellent pizzas, soups, salads, and sandwiches and listen to lively jazz music. You'll also find Harry's Diner at 833 Bute Street (at Robson). Phone (604) 685-3287. For a *loaded* Greek chicken sandwich, try *Uptown Market* (538 West Pender; 604-488-1450). In the Yaletown area, my favorite restaurant is the *Amarcord* (1168 Hamilton Street, 604-681-6500). Try the scrumptious Venetian-style lobster. Entrees are in the $15-$20 range. Or, for something more unusual, *Raku Kushiyaki* (4422 West Tenth Avenue; 604-222-8188) is a small restaurant out near the University of British Columbia. Dishes range from orange-spiced lamb shanks to salmon with Chinese pesto. Raku is open Tuesday through Sunday 5:00-11:00 P.M., and if you're not

Trivia

In 1860, four years before the words "In God We Trust" appeared on an American two-cent coin, these same words appeared on New Westminster's coat of arms. Situated 7.5 miles (12 km) south of present-day downtown Vancouver, "New West" was the first town in British Columbia to be incorporated as a municipality.

into nibbling your way to Sumo wrestler status, prices are reasonable.

While in the university area, visit the **Museum of Anthropology** (6393 N.W. Marine Drive, Vancouver, V6T 1Z2; 604–822–3825; www. moa.ubc.ca), which overlooks the Strait of Georgia and English Bay. The museum houses a fabulous collection of Northwest Coast First Nations artwork, as well as artifacts from around the world. It's open daily in summer from 10:00 A.M. to 5:00 P.M. and in winter Tuesday to Sunday from 11:00 A.M. to 5:00 P.M. Admission is $7.00 for adults, $5.00 for seniors, and $4.00 for students. The family rate is $15.00. Children under six get in free. It's also open Tuesday nights from 5:00 to 9:00 P.M., when admission is free.

Sometimes it rains in Vancouver! Should you need protection from the weather, head over to **The Umbrella Shop** at 1106 West Broadway (604–669–9444), where you'll find an enormous variety of umbrellas —from the fold-away variety, ideal for travelers, to hand-painted originals, an ideal souvenir of your visit.

There's more free entertainment to be found in one of North America's busiest **Chinatown**s. The area, from Carrall Street to Gore Avenue and from Union to Powell Streets, is second only in size to San Francisco's Chinatown. Here you'll find ancient Chinese remedies, delicious dim sum, and all kinds of exotic teas and spices. Don't miss the **Sam Kee Building** at 8 West Pender Street, listed in the *Guinness Book of World Records* as the world's thinnest office building. Built in 1913 out of spite for the city fathers who had expropriated most of the property, it's all of 6 feet (1.8 m) deep.

Sample refreshing teas at **Ten Ren Tea and Ginseng,** 550 Main Street (at the corner of Keefer), then take your camera along to capture some of the details on the traditional gate framing the entrance to the **Chinese Cultural Center**. It's in front of the **Dr. Sun Yat-Sen Garden** (578 Carrall Street, 604–662–3207; fax: 604–682–4008; sun yatsen@telus.net; www.vancouverchinesegarden. com/sun), an authentic Ming Dynasty garden and the first of its kind to be built either inside or out-

Trivia

British Columbia is Canada's most attractive film and television location, generating a record $630 million in direct spending to the provincial economy in 1997. More than 25,000 British Columbians are employed in the industry, which produces approximately twenty TV series. Past successes include The X-Files. *The largest film production ever completed in the province was Michael Crichton's* Eaters of the Dead.

side China since 1492. Admission to the garden is $7.50 adults, $6.00 seniors, $5.00 students. Children under five get in free. The family rate is $18. These prices include tea and a forty-five-minute tour. The gift shop has some delightful souvenirs.

But if it's Canadian ambience you want to be ensconced in, stay at the 1897 *"O Canada" House B&B* (1114 Barclay Street, Vancouver, V6E 1H1; toll free 877–688–1114; 604–688–0555; fax: 604–488–0556; ocanadahouse@home.com; www. ocanadahouse.com). This Victorian-style heritage home is located in a quiet downtown neighborhood, within walking distance of St. Pauls Hospital, Stanley Park, and the beaches. In 1909 Mr. Ewan Buchan, the original owner, wrote Canada's national anthem here; it was first performed in The Canadian Club in Vancouver on February 9, 1910. At "O Canada" House you'll be served sherry in the front parlor in the early evening, and a three-course gourmet breakfast. Off the dining room, there's a "guest's own kitchen," stocked with complimentary snacks, tea, coffee, and juices. Rates in high season range from $175 or if you want to be totally decadent, spend $225 ($175 in winter) for the Penthouse Suite—all 750 square feet of the third floor—from which you can enjoy Vancouver's superb skyline.

For travelers on a budget, there's a comfortable San Francisco–style, elegantly renovated, hundred-year-old hotel within walking distance of just about everything in Vancouver's heart. At the *Victorian Hotel* (514 Homer Street, Vancouver, V6B 2V6; toll free 877–681–6369; 604–681–6369; fax: 604–681–8776; victorianhotel@hotmail.com; www.victorian-hotel.com) you'll be central to the theater district, Gastown, and the waterfront. If you saw the Tommy Lee Jones's movie *Double Jeopardy* you've seen the Victorian! Breakfast is included in the reasonable rates (from $79 for a double), which belie the value offered. I particularly loved the hardwood floors, high ceilings, solid wood furniture, and tiled bathrooms that gave it a modern yet 1800s feel.

Before leaving the Vancouver area, discover for yourself how close the wilderness is to this lively city, by experiencing a day-paddle (including an impressive salmon barbecue lunch on an uninhabited island) in Indian Arm with *Lotus Land Tours Inc.* (2005–1251 Cardero Street, Vancouver, V6G 2H9; 604–684–4922 or 800–528–3531; fax: 604–684–

4921; info@lotuslandtours.com; www.lotusland tours.com). No experience is necessary. You'll be picked up from your hotel and soon be paddling in sea canoes, designed both for safety and to put you close enough to water level to give you that eyeball-to-eagle feel.

For complete information on other city activities, contact the **Vancouver Tourist InfoCentre,** Plaza Level, 200 Burrard Street, Vancouver, V6C 3L6; (604) 683–2000, fax: (604) 682–6839; www. tourismvancouver.com.

East to Abbotsford

From Vancouver the Trans-Canada Highway leads southeast through Surrey to Langley, the Horse Capital of BC. If you're interested in BC history, visit the **Fort Langley National Historic Site** (23433 Mavis Avenue, Box 129, Fort Langley, V1M 2R5; 604–513–4777; fax: 604–513–4798; fort_langley@pch.gc.ca; parkscan.harbour.com/fl). Open to the general public from March 1 to October 31 and to schools and other prebooked groups weekdays from November 1 to the end of February, this fascinating site will let you discover BC's history. Established in 1827 as a Hudson's Bay Company fur trading post, it's also the location where, in 1858, mainland BC was proclaimed a crown colony. You'll find here costumed interpreters ready to guide you through the original storehouse and several reconstructed buildings, as well as exhibits, demonstration vignettes, gold panning, a video/audio tour, a picnic shelter, and a gift shop. You can easily spend a day here lost in BC's engaging history. Take the 232nd Street North

BC-style Recycling

For fifty-eight years two British Columbia sisters, Babe Warren and Dorothea Stafford, have mailed the same birthday card to each other between the Lower Mainland and Victoria. That's 116 trips across the Strait of Georgia via Canada Post, and not once has the card been overdue. Interestingly, the card depicts a penny-pinching Scotsman bragging about a two-for-one card bargain.

THE SOUTHWESTERN MAINLAND

exit to the stop sign on Glover Road. Turn right and follow the BEAVER signs to the village of Fort Langley. Just before the railway tracks, turn right and head to the end of Mavis Avenue Entrance fees are $4.00 for adults and $10.00 for families (parents and dependent children).

From history to the only winery in the Fraser Valley—***Domaine de Chaberton Estates,*** 1064 216th Street, Langley, V2Z 1R3; (604) 530–1736 or (888) DDC–WINE; info@domainedechamberton.com; www.domainedechaberton.com. This winery exists where it does because its owner recognised the area's unique wine-growing characteristics. Vintner Claude Violet, whose family has been in the wine-making business since 1644, came from the south of France in 1981 and established the winery both for its closeness to the Vancouver market and its ideal microclimate (it gets 56 percent less rainfall than downtown Vancouver). It started out as a farm gate winery and, after numerous awards, grew to be an estate winery. It is now working on expanding its export business. Claude's wife, Inge, oversees this as well as the on-site wine shop. Tours are held daily at 2:00 and 4:00 P.M. The shop and a tasting room are open Monday to Saturday from 10:00 A.M. till 6:00 P.M. and from noon till 6:00 P.M. Sunday. To find Domaine de Chaberton from Fort Langley, take Glover Road to 216th Street, turn left, and stay on 216th till Sixteenth Avenue (approximately twenty minutes). At the junction of 216th and Sixteenth, you'll see a WINERY sign. It's about 0.6 mile (1 km) farther on. If you're coming directly from Vancouver, take Highway 1 east to the 200th Street exit. Head south on 200 to 16th Avenue. Turn left (east) to 216th Street, then follow the directions above.

Highway 1A travels east to Abbotsford, Canada's raspberry capital, and the place to be in early August when awe-inspiring aerobatics such as the Wall of Fire and incredible wing-walking are performed at the world-famous three-day-long ***Abbotsford International Airshow*** (604–852–8511; fax: 604–852–6093; info@abbotsfordairshow.com;

TOP ANNUAL EVENTS ON THE SOUTHWESTERN MAINLAND

Brackendale Winter Eagle Festival and Count, Brackendale; January; (604) 898–3333

Lytton Days, Lytton; May 24 long weekend; (250) 455–2523

Hope Seabird Island Indian Festival, May; (604) 796–2177

Alcan International Dragon Boat Festival, Vancouver; June; (604) 688–2382, Ext. 222

Squamish Adventure Festival, Squamish; June/July; (888) 684–8828

Abbotsford Berry Festival, Abbotsford; July; (604) 850–6547

Harrison Festival of the Arts, Harrison; July; (604) 796–3664

International Comedy Festival, Vancouver; July; (604) 683–0883

Festival of the Written Arts, Sechelt; August; (250) 885–9631

Annual Bluegrass Festival, Chilliwack; September; (604) 792–2069

www.abbotsfordairshow.com). Canada's Snowbirds can be seen here performing loops, rolls, and their famous "Candle Burst" formation, as well as many other thrilling events.

The Fraser River Valley

Cross the Fraser River north of Abbotsford to Mission's *Fraser River Heritage Park* (7974 Mary Street, Box 3341, Mission, V2V 4J5; 604–826–0277). Folk festivals, car shows, children's art classes, twilight concerts, and a jam-packed *Canada Day* (July 1) keep the park humming through the warmer months. A concession booth serves light lunches and delicious homemade scones with blackberry jelly (prepared by volunteers in the fall). It's a pretty spot to stop off for a picnic, offering panoramic views of the Fraser River Valley and Mount Baker.

If you want to stay in the area, there's lovely accommodation and delicious home baking at the *Fence Post Lane Bed & Breakfast,* 4 miles (6.6 km) west of Mission at 8575 Gaglardi Street, Mission, V4S 1B2; (877) 833–7009, (604) 820–7009; fax: (604) 820–4974; mperdue@ direct.ca; www.bbcanada.com/906.htm. Room rates range from $50 to $75 double in this peaceful four-star country rancher, close to lakes and walking trails.

Trivia

January 1, 1922. Although no injuries resulted, a traffic accident at a Surrey intersection on this date will go down as one of the most bizarre in history. Two cars collided head-on, one on the left side of the road, the other on the right. The driver on the right, a Mr. Claude Harvie who was a Surrey municipal worker, had been up all night placing signs to warn drivers of a change in the traffic laws: Cars were now required to be driven on the right side of the road.

East of Mission, high up over the Lougheed Highway, you'll see (or hear) the distinctive bells in the tower of the *Westminster Abbey Benedictine Monastery* (34224 Dewdney Trunk Road; 604–826– 8975). The Benedictine monks invite visitors from 2:00 to 4:00 P.M. Sundays and from 1:30 to 4:00 P.M. weekdays to see their beautiful church. Its 22-foot-high stained-glass windows (sixty-four in all), combined with a tall dome of colored glass rising above the altar, make it an architectural beauty. To get there turn left off Highway 7 onto Dewdney Trunk Road. If you come to the DUCKS CROSSING sign, you've passed it. It's also accessible from Stave Lake Street, just west of Mission's Heritage Park.

Leave the serenity of the monastery and head back to Highway 7. East of Dewdney Trunk Road there's another kind of serenity at the *Hatzic*

Rock Site, or, more officially, **XÁ:YTEM Longhouse Interpretive Centre** (35087 Lougheed Highway, Mission, V2V 6T1; 604–820–9725; fax: 604–820–9735; xaytem@dowco.com; www.xaytem.museum.bc.ca/xaytem/). This national historic site is British Columbia's oldest dwelling—it's even older than the Pyramids and Stonehenge. The remains of a semisubterranean house, between 5,000 and 6,000 years old, were discovered in 1990 by Gordon Mohs, an archaeologist for the Stó:lo Nation. Since then, this Coast Salish Indian group and scientists from the University of British Columbia have uncovered tens of thousands of artifacts, some radiocarbon-dated 9,000 years, revealing a long-term Stó:lo presence and evidence of a ceremonially inclined trader people. Kids can enjoy an archaeology tour during which they can sift for artifacts, and adults can try their hand at working with inner cedar bark; everyone can enjoy the storytelling. Two pit houses (underground circular winter dwellings accessed through the top by a notched ladder), examples of homes used by First Nations people over thousands of years, are open to visitors.

The rock, or **XÁ:YTEM**, (pronounced "hay-tum") is associated with an early period in Stó:lo history when Xexá:ls threw three chiefs into a heap and transformed them to stone for not teaching the people the written language he gave them. From late June to early September, the center is open daily 10:00 A.M. to 5:00 P.M.; the rest of year it's open on weekdays from 2:00 to 4:00 P.M. Maximum admission for a family of four is $13.00.

There's more history at the **Mission Museum** (604–826–1011, fax: 604–826–1017), where you'll discover the legends of rivers, rails, and robbers. And one more activity in the area that's sure to get the adrenaline flowing is a nail-biting afternoon at **Mission Raceway Park**

Sasquatch Madness

Sasquatch (from the Coast Salish word sesqac), British Columbia's infamous hairy giant, was not a very popular fellow. His trick was to come down from the mountains, seize young Indian maidens, and seal their eyes with pitch, thus preventing them from knowing their whereabouts. What he did with them is anybody's guess.

Keep your eyes peeled (or pitched) for him as you pass through the Fraser River area. Every May, eyewitnesses, scientists, believers, and nonbelievers gather in Harrison Hot Springs at the Sasquatch Forum to examine the latest evidence. Sasquatch Hikes, Sasquatch Golf, Bigfoot Races, and Sasquatch Parades all add to the craziness.

(604–826–6315; info@missionraceway.com; www.missionraceway.com), just west of town. Drag-car and motor-cross racing is held most weekends between March and October. For more information on other activities and accommodations in the Mission area, contact the *Mission Visitor Info Centre,* 34033 Lougheed Highway, Mission, V2V 5X8; (604) 826–6914; fax: (604) 826–5916; Email@missionchamber.bc.ca; www.missionchamber.bc.ca.

The Lougheed Highway, or the "Scenic 7" as locals like to refer to it, curls east beside the Fraser toward *Harrison Mills,* "the Home of the Bald Eagle," 24 miles (40 km) past Mission. Hundreds of magnificent eagles frequent the area from November through April, and in spring and summer, the Harrison River is a fisherman's paradise, with large runs of coho, steelhead, and sockeye salmon. In late November the area features the *Harrison/Chehalis Bald Eagle Festival.* (Contact the Mission Chamber of Commerce for more information at 604–826–6914, or the organizer at 604–463–2507; driftwood@bc.sympatico.ca).

Nearby, *Kilby Historic Store and Farm* (215 Kilby Road, Box 55, Harrison Mills, V0M 1L0; 604–796–9576; fax: 604–796–9592; info@kilby. bc.ca; www.kilby.ca), 1 mile (1.6 km) off Highway 7, is a must-stop attraction. It's a 1920s living history site, with a general store museum, surrounding heritage buildings, and a working farm. There's also the Waterloo Farm Gift Shop and Harrison River Restaurant to make for complete visitor services. It's open daily April to October from 11:00 A.M. to 5:00 P.M., but for the rest of the year, only on weekends from 11:00 A.M. to 4:00 P.M. Entrance fees range from free to $6.00, with a family pass (two adults plus children) available for $16.00.

Continue enjoying the "days of yore" at the small museum run by the *Agassiz-Harrison Historical Society* (Box 313, 6947 Lougheed Highway, Agassiz, V0M 1A0; 604–796–3545). Housed in the oldest wooden railroad station (1893) still in existence in BC, it's open daily 10:00 A.M. to 4:00 P.M. from the May 24th long weekend until mid-September. There's no charge, but donations are welcome.

The village of *Harrison Hot Springs* lies 4 miles (6.5 km) north. Idyllically set on Harrison Lake, southwestern British Columbia's largest lake, below snow-covered 7,825-foot (2,385-m) Mount Breakenridge, Harrison Hot Springs, with fabulous *Sasquatch Provincial Park* (Lower Mainland District, 1610 Mount Seymour Road, North Vancouver V7G 1L3; 604–924–2200; fax 604–924–2244) just 4 miles (6.5 km) beyond, is a popular spot for a beach holiday.

Every September the words "Ladies and gentlemen, start your buckets" are heard when Harrison Hot Springs hosts the **World Championship Sand Sculpture Competition** (604–796–3425; info@harrisand.org; www.harrisand.org). "Master Sand Sculptors" pit their skills against each other, with solos and international teams competing for $35,000 in prize money and bragging rights to the title of world champion. There's a small fee to view the sculptures. The *Guinness Book of Records* gives Harrison Hot Springs a mention as the site where the world's tallest hand-built sand castle, a 21.5-foot (6.5-m) Christmas tree, was built. With no tides to wash them away, the fantastic sand creations are on display until early October.

Half a block back from the sandy beach, close to shops and restaurants and with a pretty river edging the garden, **Harrison Heritage House and Kottage Bed and Breakfast** (312 Lillooet Avenue, Box 475, Harrison Hot Springs, V0M 1K0; 604–796–9552 or 800–331–8099; rreyerse @bbharrison.com; www.bbharrison.com) has romantic rooms in the $75–$150 range. Deluxe rooms come with private Jacuzzis and/or fireplaces. Separate two-bedroom cottages are also available—and the filling breakfasts are a great start to the day.

Nearby, meals at **The Old Settler Pub** (222 Cedar Avenue; 604–796–1034; oldsettler@uniserve.com; www.oldsetter.com) are also filling. Humorous chain-saw carvings decorate the log building where, on the patio, I found a pleasant spot to enjoy a generous and delicious salmon dinner. For more information on where to eat and stay in Harrison Hot Springs, contact the Visitor Info Centre, 499 Harrison Hot Springs Road, Box 255, Harrison Hot Springs, V0M 1K0; (604) 796–3425; fax: (604) 796–3188; infoserv@harrison.ca; www.harrison.ca.

Hope

Log carvings also decorate **Hope,** dubbed "the Chain-saw Carving Capital," 20 miles (32 km) east of Agassiz on the south side of the Fraser River. It's an incredibly pretty spot, set on a large, flat plain deep in among the mountains.

Hollywood has discovered Hope's beauty, too. *First Blood* (first of the Rambo series), is the best-known of the movies to emerge from Hope. The Visitor Info Centre (919 Water Avenue, Box 370, Hope, V0X 1L0; 604–869–2021; fax: 604–869–2160; hopechmb@uniserve.com; www.hopechamber.bc.ca) has devel-

Trivia
Rumor has it that when filming of First Blood *was announced, chaos struck Hope. Hundreds of people wanted to be featured in the film as extras, but out of 550, only 100 were chosen. A rumor circulated that no one taller than Sylvester Stallone was chosen as an extra.*

oped a walking and driving tour of the film's key locations.

One of these is in the **Coquihalla Canyon Recreation Area,** site of the **Othello-Quintette Tunnels** (called Chapman Gorge in the movie), an amazing engineering feat, which, at a cost of $300,000, is perhaps the most expensive mile of railway track in the world. The chain of now-abandoned tunnels was built between 1911 and 1918 to complete the Kettle Valley Railway. Look for the cliff above the stump at Tunnel No. 2 where Rambo's spectacular canyon jump took place. Other movies shot in this area are *Shoot to Kill, White Fang II, K2, Fire with Fire,* and *Far from Home: Adventures of Yellow Dog.* To get there take Kawkawa Lake Road from the ball park on Sixth Avenue, passing the cemetery and Kawkawa Lake to Othello Road, a distance of about 3 miles (5 km). Turn right onto Tunnels Road and then into a parking lot. Private; campgrounds, such as **Othello Tunnels Campground and RV Park** (67851 Othello Road, Box 2009, Hope V0X 1L0; Phone toll free: 877–869–0543; fax: 604–869–9448; othellocamp@uniserve. com; www.othellotunnels.webprovider.com) operate year-round.

Trivia

On January 9, 1965, an earthquake, with its epicenter in the Nicolum Valley, caused a devastating landslide about 11 miles (18 km) east of Hope, destroying almost 2 miles (3 km) of the Hope-Princeton Highway. More than 1,600 million cubic feet (46 million m³) of snow, rock, and earth crashed in seconds from the 6,500-foot-high (2,000-m) mountain ridge that formed the north side of the Nicolum Creek valley. Four people in three vehicles were killed—two were never found.

Back in Hope forget movie-mania and spend a quiet minute in **Christ Church** at the corner of Park and Fraser Streets. Consecrated in 1861, this Anglican church is the oldest continuously active church on the mainland still on its original foundations. (But then that's a debatable subject in nearby Yale!) Its builder and first vicar was Reverend Alexander St. David Francis Pringle. He arrived in the midst of the Cariboo Gold Rush, when thousands of young men were gathered in hope of striking it rich. Pringle felt that the men needed access to good reading material, so he began raising funds for a building to carry "respectable and readable newspapers of various nations and politics, together with all the standard reviews and periodicals." The result, on December 1, 1859, was the first library on British Columbia's mainland.

With so much history (discover more at the **Hope Museum** next to the Visitor Info Centre 604–869–7322) and such a diversity of outdoor activities—everything from rafting to golf to hiking—in this area, stay a while in one of Hope's many motels (check the glass case outside the Info centre) or book into the **Evergreen Bed** *and Breakfast* (1208 Ryder Street, Box 811, Hope, V0X 1L0; 604–869–9918; fax: 604–869–3763; midway@uniserve.com; www.pixsell-bc.ca/bb/2139.htm), with its lovely mountain views. It operates year-round and is at the corner of the Old Hope-Princeton Way and Ryder Street. Rates are $65 to $75. A block away there's a popular cafe called **The Home Restaurant** (665 Hope-Princeton Highway; 604–869–5558), where you'll find thick clam chowder, barbecue back ribs, pies, and other home-style meals in large portions.

Before leaving Hope stop at the **Hope Station House** (604–869–9495) at the junction of Highway 1 and Old Hope-Princeton Way—also known as Rainbow Junction, a smoke-free restaurant, community arts center, and art gallery located in the restored 1916 Great Northern Railway Station. Specializing in homemade soups and sandwiches and wonderful desserts, it's open between 8:00 A.M. and 8:00 P.M. daily. The **Upstairs Gallery** (located upstairs!) features various artists' work. Check www.hopebc.com for maps and detailed information on the area.

From Hope you can either head north through the Fraser River Canyon via the Trans-Canada Highway 1, northeast via the Coquihalla (toll) Highway 5 to Merritt and Kamloops, or east to **Manning Provincial Park** along the Crowsnest Highway 3, a beautiful but winding extravaganza through the Cascades that leads to Princeton and the Okanagan.

Trivia
Toll revenues collected on the Coquihalla Highway during 1997 were $38.9 million.

"This is Canada!" were my thoughts as I took the latter choice. I was passing snow-powdered alpine larch at the 4,400-foot (1,341-m) Alison Pass and had read there were 175,440 acres (71,000 ha) more of this delightful park. If you're there in June, take a twenty-minute walk through colorful **Rhododendron Flats,** close to the highway about 6 miles (10 km) east of the marmot carving at the west gate. For park information contact BC Parks, Box 3, Manning Park, V0X 1R0; (250) 840–8836; fax: (250) 840–8700; or check the BC Parks Web site listed in the introduction. Accommodation, a store (the only one in the park), and dining (a cafe, pub, and restaurant) are available at **Manning Park Resort** (Box 1480 Hope, V0X 1L0; 800–330–3321 toll free; 250–840–8822; fax: 250–840–8848; info@manningparkresort.com; www.manningparkresort.com). The resort offers a variety of accommodation types, as well as equipment rentals for a host of summer and winter activities. The easterly route to Princeton continues in the Okanagan-Similkameen section. Our journey here, though, follows the route the gold seekers took along the raging Fraser River north to Yale.

The Fraser Canyon

At the WELCOME TO HISTORIC YALE sign, 15 miles (24 km) north of Hope in the Fraser Canyon and just south of the town, a steep hike called the *Spirit Caves Trail* begins. The round-trip is about 3 miles (5 km), and the elevation gain is 1,640 feet (500 m). It's worth the climb for the great views of Yale and the Fraser River. Allow about three hours to enjoy it. But if you prefer to just amble through a lush meadow loaded with history, the *Pioneer Cemetery,* directly across from the trailhead, is one of the prettiest old cemeteries in the province. The ages on many headstones (dating back to 1862) hint at stories of lives prematurely taken.

At the tiny but classy *Yale Museum* (phone/fax: 604–863–2324; www.heritage.gov.bc.ca/yale/yale.htm) you'll learn of the lives of these pioneers who sought their gold fortunes between the 1850s and the 1880s, when Yale was the head of navigation for the Fraser. The costumed museum staff show a thirty-minute film on Yale's history and arrange guided tours that include an Old Yale Town Tour, a Float trip to Hope (via Fraser River Rafting Expeditions), and a Pioneer Cemetery tour. As well, you can learn the fun and skill involved in Gold Panning. The museum is open Thursday to Monday 10:00 A.M. to 5:00 P.M. from mid-May to early September and only on weekends from September 8th to October 7th. Admission prices range from free to $4.50. Tour and gold panning costs are extra.

Included in the town tour is a peek next door at the beautiful *St. John the Divine Anglican Church,* one of the oldest churches on the BC mainland and a designated BC Heritage Site.

To help you enjoy your stay in Yale, there are a couple of bed-and-breakfast establishments in the area ready to pamper you. *Teague House Bed & Breakfast* at 30950 Trans Canada Highway (Box 10, Yale, V0K 2S0; toll free: 800–363–7238; 604–863–2336; fax: 604–863–2355; frre@uniserve.com; www.fraserraft.com) is an 1866 heritage house with lovely views of Fraser Canyon. Get adventurous and sign up for a rafting expedition with *Fraser River Rafting* (same contact information as the Teague House). Rates for the B&B start at $70 double,

Pioneer Cemetery in Yale

while a one-day Boston Bar to Yale rafting trip, including lunch, is $105. Another B&B, *Chrysalis Retreat* (31278 Douglas Street, Box 50, Yale, V0K 2S0; 604–863–0055), features a hot tub, a sauna, and your own registered massage therapist/hydrotherapist to help relax you on the long journey. Ideal for families or a romantic getaway, this year-round retreat has rates starting at $85.

North of Yale is the wonderfully named *Spuzzum* (from the Thompson Native word meaning "little flat"). Less than a mile north of Spuzzum, you'll find *Alexandra Bridge Provincial Park,* a pleasant, 136-acre (55-ha) spot to stop for a break. In the heart of this park is the historic suspension bridge for which the park is named. First built in 1863, it was twice destroyed, only to be rebuilt in its present form in 1926. A ten-minute walk along parts of the now-abandoned highway brings you to this elegant old bridge.

Back on Highway 1 you're into the spectacular *Fraser Canyon* tunnels. Between Yale and Boston Bar, 26 miles (42 km) north, you'll remove your sunglasses seven times as you pass through these fantastic tunnels with names such as Saddle Rock, Sailor Bar, Hell's Gate, and the 2,000-foot (610-m) China Bar Tunnel, one of North America's longest. Here enterprising Chinese found their golden mother lode after reworking an old, supposedly exhausted, area.

There's little gold today other than that in the glint of the turbulent rapids seen from the airtram at *Hell's Gate,* the narrowest—110 feet (33 m)—point of the Fraser River. The canyon reminded early explorer Simon Fraser of "The Gates of Hell." It was hell, indeed, for millions of salmon when, in 1914, with the building of the second railroad, the canyon wall slid into the river, causing British Columbia's worst environmental disaster. It almost destroyed the Fraser River salmon run. Several gigantic fishways now assist approximately two million sockeye salmon yearly to reach their spawning grounds.

You can look down on these fishways from the comfortable safety of a twenty-five-passenger cabin run by *Hell's Gate Airtram Inc.* (Box 129, Hope, V0X 1L0; 604–867–9277; fax: 604–867– 9279; mckinney@hells gateairtram.com; www.hellsgateairtram.com), which runs April through October. At the lower terminal there's the *Salmon House Restaurant* (excellent salmon steaks and chowder), the *Fudge Factory* (ice creams and two hundred flavors of homemade fudge), gift shops, and a fisheries

Worth Seeing/Doing on the Southwestern Mainland

Minter Gardens (604–794–7191 or 888–646–8377; minter@minter.org; www.minter.org). Twenty-seven acres of brilliant show gardens, near Chilliwack; open April through October.

The Lookout! at Harbour Centre Tower (555 West Hastings Street; 604–689–0421; heatherv@lookout.bc.ca; www.harbourcentretower.com). Enjoy the 360° view to orient yourself in Vancouver.

VanDusen Botanical Garden (5251 Oak Street, Vancouver; 604–878–9274). Glorious gardens. Open year-round from 10:00 A.M.

Burnaby Village Museum (6501 Deer Lake Avenue, Burnaby; 604–293–6501; mail@burnabyparksrec.org; www.burnabyparksrec.org). Nine-acre historical village.

Vancouver Museum (1100 Chestnut Street; 604–736–4431; fax: 604–736–5417; www.vanmuseum.bc.ca). First-rate museum with great views of city.

Gulf of Georgia Cannery National Historic Site (12138 Fourth Avenue, Richmond V7E 3J1; 604–664–9009; gogmark@portal.ca; parkscan.harbour. com/ggc/). In the village of Steveston, with many excellent seafood restaurants nearby.

display. Fares range from $6.50 for kids six and older to $26.50 for an immediate family. If you watch all three movies, including the award-winning video *Run, Sockeye, Run,* you can easily spend two hours on the *other side.* And you will have passed where, in Simon Fraser's words, "no man should venture."

The tunnels end at Boston Bar, but from here, there's another 26 miles (42 km) of Fraser River views to Lytton. Just before Lytton, located in Nlaka'pamux tribal territory, the Siska (meaning "uncle") Museum, part of the **Siska Art Gallery** (Box 519, Lytton, V0K 1Z0; 250–455–2219; fax: 250–455–2539; siskaib@goldtrail.com) displays soapstone carvings, wooden masks, beaded crafts, drums, and dreamcatchers. They're open year-round. You can't miss the yellow SISKA MUSEUM sign up on the highway.

We leave the Trans-Canada at Lytton, often named on weather broadcasts as Canada's "hotspot." Here the earthy Fraser meets the pretty, aqua-green Thompson River, and we discover another hotspot, the ecologically important Stein Valley, the spiritual home of the Nlaka'pamux Nation. In past years environmentalists and First Nations people have fought to preserve this wilderness area from the logger's ax. In 1995 the 264,865 acres (107,191 ha) of the Stein Valley were permanently protected as the **Stein Valley Nlaka'pamux Heritage Provincial Park.** For day hikers, there's good hiking in the lower Stein Valley near Lytton. Pick up maps at the **Lytton Info Centre** (400 Fraser Street, Box 460, Lytton, V0K 1Z0; 250–455–2523; fax: 250–455–6669). More in-depth information on the 47-mile (75-km) Stein Valley trail through to the Pemberton area is available from **BC Parks** (1210 McGill Road, Kamloops, V2C 6N6; 250–851–3000; fax: 250–828–4633).

If you prefer the excitement of wild water over walking, **Kumsheen Raft Adventures** (Box 30, Lytton, V0K 1Z0; 250–455–2296 or toll free 800–663–6667; fax: 250–455–2297; rafting@kumsheen.com; www.kumsheen.com), located on the Trans-Canada Highway, 4 miles (6 km) northeast of Lytton, run thrilling rafting trips that range from three hours to six days long. A three-hour Whitewater Quickie costs $89 ($65 for youths ages ten to sixteen), or a one-day Raging River trip from Spences Bridge to Lytton, during which you'll pass through eighteen adrenaline-pumping rapids with such spine-

Trivia

In 1999:

- *The average cost of a hotel room in BC was $114 Canadian.*

- *Total hotel room revenue exceeded $1.3 billion.*

- *American travelers took 6.9 million trips to Canada via BC.*

- *From elsewhere, the number of visitors totaled 1.4 million.*

Trivia

British Columbia's first railway was built between Seton and Anderson Lakes in 1860. This 3-mile-long (almost 5 km), narrow-gauge, wooden railway was powered by mules.

chilling names as Jaws of Death and Washing Machine, costs $119 (youths $89).

Over the years (since 1973), the headquarters have been enhanced to include a swimming pool, disc golf, hot tub, a restaurant, beach volleyball courts, riverview campsites (stay-over packages from $19 for adults, $12 for youth) and uniquely decorated wood-floor tent cabins. These contain two double beds, all linen, and cost $85. In true rafting fun games boards and ironing boards (must look neat in the rapids!) are set up, ready to use. And the Kumsheen coffee! Stop off for a cup of Kumsheen's best Colombian and maybe sign up for a rip-roaring trip down a raging river.

The Sea to Sky Highway

*H*ighway 12 (from the green bridge at the north end of Lytton) follows the dizzying, murky Fraser River, past black trampoline-style tarpaulins shading the world's largest ginseng farms for 40 miles (65 km) north to *Lillooet* (see section on Cariboo Chilcotin Coast). Here we leave the Fraser River and join Highway 99 (previously the rough-and-ready but now paved Duffey Lake Road), where stunning views of emerald lakes and icy glaciers lead to Mount Currie and Pemberton. Still on Highway 99, the *Sea to Sky Highway,* we pass North America's number-one ski resort at Whistler. By the time we reach Horseshoe Bay, north of Vancouver, we will have traversed a highway so aptly dubbed "the gateway to the spectacular."

The Duffey Lake Road is tortuous and remote. The only radio station I could raise was in Mandarin! But, as attested to by movie crews shooting Subaru advertising, its beauty is being broadcast universally. It follows the fast-coursing Cayoosh Creek steeply down to Duffey Lake, Joffre Lakes, and Lillooet Lake.

Organic is the key word at *Sturdy's North Arm Farm* (1888 Sea to Sky Highway 99, Pemberton V0N 2K0; 604–894–5379; fax: 604–894–6650). Drop in to see what's in season at the Sturdy family's fifty-five-acre (22-ha) mixed farm. Bring your bucket along to load up with delicious raspberries and strawberries, fresh greens and herbs, specialty vegetables, nugget potatoes, garlic, sweet corn, even fresh farm eggs with brilliant yellow yolks. Kids will enjoy the *Wagon Rides* to the pumpkin patch in September and October. There's a cut-flower garden, farm animals, and a hay-bale play area for the kids. A commercial kitchen offers cooking classes and produces pies, preserves, and treats—fresh from the farm field to the table! They're open daily May to October from 8:00 A.M. to 6:00 P.M., but call ahead to be sure. Look for the green-and-white sign on the highway.

Nearby at the *Rainbow Valley Inn Bed and Breakfast* (1864 Sea to Sky Highway, Box 257, Pemberton, V0N 2K0; 604–894–3300 fax: 604–894–3323 or toll free 800–555–8042; Jim@rainbowvalleyinn.com; www. RainbowValleyInn. com), you can rest while soaking in the outdoor hot tub surrounded by towering alpine peaks, amid ten acres (4 ha) of beautiful cedar groves and farmland. A duck pond completes the peaceful scene. The rustic home has a huge fireplace with guest rooms ($79–$99 double including gourmet breakfasts), decorated with antique furnishings. There's a two-bedroom family suite as well. Breakfast includes freshly baked cake, smoked salmon, and a special homemade orange juice. The Rainbow Inn is well signed on the south side of the highway, halfway between Pemberton and Mount Currie, and just twenty-five minutes northeast of Whistler. There is a daily shuttle to the *Whistler/Blackcombe Ski School Resort*.

In 1967 Pemberton became the first commercial seed potato area in the

Kids' Stuff on the Southwestern Mainland

Science World and the Alcan OMNIMAX Theatre (1455 Quebec Street, Vancouver; V6A 3Z7; 604–443–7443; www.scienceworld.bc.ca). Amazing *3D Laser Theatre* with magical visual effects and many more hands-on science exhibits. Kids may even get a chance to create their own cyclone under the silver geodesic dome.

Vancouver Aquarium Marine Science Centre, in Stanley Park, featuring the new Gallery of Whales. Phone (604) 659–FISH (3474); information@vanaqua.org; www.vanaqua.org.

CN IMAX at Canada Place (604–682–IMAX or 800–582–4629; kharvey@imax.com; www.imax.com/vancouver). Huge five-story screen. Films are thirty-five to forty-five minutes.

Trans-Canada Waterslides (53790 Popkum Road S., Bridal Falls; 888–883–8852; ; 604–794–7455). Thrilling rapids river ride, giant hot tub, blackhole ride. (East of Chilliwack.)

world to grow virus-free seed potatoes. With that in mind I had to try out the fries in **Willie G's** (10–1359 Aster Street; 604–894–6411). The Caesar salad and pasta on the outside deck were fine fare, too. On Fridays they serve prime rib with Yorkshire pudding.

But I didn't come just for the potatoes. There's so much to see and do in the area. If you'd like a view from above, and this area warrants it, visit the **Pemberton Soaring Center** (Box 725, Pemberton, V0N 2L0; 604–894–5727/800–831–2611; fax: 604–894–5776; pemsoar@direct. ca; www.mountain-inter.net/soaring/). A Valley Flight costs $75 for a fifteen-to-twenty-minute glide over paradise.

To find out about other flights, as well as white-water rafting, horseback riding, jet-boat tours, parasailing, fly-fishing, canoeing, and golfing, stop off at the **Pemberton Info Centre** at the junction of Highway 99 and Pemberton Portage Road in summer, or write to Box 370, Pemberton, V0N 2L0; (604) 894–6175/6984; fax: (604) 894–5571. About 2 miles (3 km) south of Pemberton, there's a pleasant, short hike to the emerald-green waterfalls in **Nairn Falls Provincial Park**. These stunning falls tumble 200 feet (60 m) into a steep, forested valley. Contact BC Parks Garibaldi/Sunshine Coast District, Alice Lake Park, Box 220, Brackendale, V0N 1H0; (604) 898–3678; fax: (604) 898–4171 for information.

Pemberton is just twenty minutes from North America's number-one ski resort, **Whistler-Blackcombe**, 62 miles (100 km) north of Vancouver. (Readers of Japan's prestigious *Blue Guide* ski magazine voted it the best ski resort in the world, four years in a row.) Even in summer you can ski and snowboard at **Blackcombe** on Horstman Glacier. Or if you prefer golf, you have three world-class courses—designed by such prestigious names as Jack Nicklaus, Robert Trent Jones Jr., and Arnold Palmer—each with breathtaking views.

Winter visitors (December to April) might enjoy a little backcountry adventure with **Cougar Mountain Wilderness Adventures** (888–297–2222; 604–932–3474; fax: 604–932–5584; adventures@ whistler.net; www.cougarmountainatwhistler.com). They offer a two-hour ($49) backcountry introductory snowshoeing/nature tour at Cougar Mountain. For $99 there's a combo Sno-Cat/snowshoe guided tour through 1,200-year-old trees in Whistler's Ancient Cedar Grove. The more adventurous might try a three-hour Learn to Ride snowmobile tour ($119 double or $159 single) with a hearty meal at a cozy lakeside cabin. For those who really want some fun, there's a two-and-a-half-hour ($125 per person based on two per sled) dogsled trip through the

Soo Valley Wildlife Reserve. In summer they run fishing trips, ATV tours on Cougar Mountain (one-and-a-half-hour trips start at $79 per person), horseback riding to the Ancient Cedar Grove, and Hummer 4x4 tours into the Soo Valley and Cougar Mountain. Mountain biking and hiking are also offered.

If you need accommodation, contact **Whistler Resort Association,** 4010 Whistler Way, Whistler, V0N 1B4. For reservations, in Canada and the United States call (800) WHISTLER (944–7853), and in Vancouver and outside North America call (604) 664–5625; fax: (604) 938–5758; www.tourismwhistler.com. For other information contact the **Whistler Travel Info Centre,** corner of Lake Placid Road and Highway 99, Box 181, Whistler, V0N 2B0; (604) 932–5528; fax: (604) 932–3755.

The Sea to Sky Highway continues south past the western edge of **Garibaldi Provincial Park** (to contact, use the address listed earlier for BC Parks Garibaldi/Sunshine District). To see what "sea to sky" really means, take a drive in the Diamond Head area in the southwest tail of the park. South of Alice Lake, and 2.5 miles (4 km) north of **Squamish**, turn onto Mamquam Road, marked as DIAMOND HEAD (GARIBALDI PARK). It's paved for 2.5 miles (4 km). Finally, after the last switchback and about 10 miles (16 km), you'll get breathtaking views of the Squamish River Valley, the Stawamus Chief, and Howe Sound. From here if you are equipped (and fit!), there's a two- to three-hour hike to Elfin Lakes, with good views of Diamond Head. At this point you are a mere 40 miles (64 km) north of Vancouver.

Every January at nearby Brackendale, the winter home of the bald eagle, where the Cheakamus and Squamish Rivers meet, hundreds of eagle-eyes gather, cameras and binoculars to the ready, for the annual **Brackendale Winter Eagle Festival.** In 1994 a world-record 3,766 eagles were counted. Enthusiasts leave from the **Brackendale Art Gallery Theatre and Teahouse** (41950 Government Road at Axen Road, Box 100, Brackendale, V0N 1H0; phone/fax: 604–898–3333; gallery@mntn.net; www.mountain-inter.net/~gallery/). Eagles or not, stop off here to sample the first-class soups and croissant sandwiches. Located behind a large white unicorn near the corner of Depot Road, the gallery was established in 1973 as a center for the arts in the Squamish Valley. It features a different west coast artist every month and is open weekends and holidays from noon to 10:00 P.M. One interesting gallery, **The Bell Shop**, houses the famous Brackendale bells, made from recycled steel.

You're soon in Squamish—6 miles (10 km) south—where there are so many recreational activities that it's hard to know where to start.

Rock climbers go nuts here. They love the cracks and chimneys in the 2,139-foot (652-m) *Stawamus Chief*, a huge exposure of granodiorite, which is part of the coast range batholith. You can view it and, if your lens is long enough, capture some colorful climbing photos from the parking lot on Highway 99.

If you missed the eagles in Brackendale, you might catch a view of them during a leisurely horseback ride through the beautiful Paradise Valley, near Squamish. The eagles are so used to seeing horses in their environs that the rider becomes part of their normal scenery. *Sea to Sky Stables* (Box 1083, Squamish, V0N 3G0; 604–898–3934; fax: 604–898–4190; info@seatoskystables.com; www.seatoskystables.com) offers guided trail rides ($35 for one hour, $55 for two hours, and $140 for a group overnighter, all meals included). Group tours (Covered Wagon or Sleigh Rides) are also available.

Horse riding can be a thirsty business, so don't leave Squamish without a visit to the *Howe Sound Inn and Brewing Company* at 37801 Cleveland Avenue, Box 978, Squamish, V0N 3G0; (800) 919–ALES (2537) or (604) 892–2603; fax: (604) 892–2631; hsibrew@howesound.com; www. howesound.com. It opened in 1996 and serves both pub-style meals and moderately priced restaurant meals. The inn's rooms (rates from $95 double) all have panoramic views of Stawamus Chief and the Coast Mountains.

The *Squamish Visitor Info Centre* (37950 Cleveland Avenue, Box 1009, Squamish, V0N 3G0; 604–892–9244; fax: 604–892–2034; information@

Finding an Old Friend

I'm addicted to dock strolling. Barely a week goes by that I don't wander down to the local marina to sniff out the new arrivals. From Vancouver I recently sailed on BC Ferries' Queen of Capilano *to Snug Cove on Bowen Island and headed for the Union Steamship Company's docks. Back in the twenties, when the company's grand ships cruised these waters, this waterfront buzzed with the summer sounds of dancers and drinkers. I wasn't looking for the* ghosts of the booze cruises, though, but for my old mate, the sloop Zeevogel, *our family home for three exciting years in the late eighties. From Victoria she had safely sailed to exotic destinations like Tonga's Niuatoputapu, French Guiana's Devil's Island, and Ecuador's mysterious Galápagos. And now there she lies, snugly protected on Bowen Island, while a new young family pampers and primes her, readying the sweet ship for more exciting discoveries ahead.*

squamishchamber.bc.ca; www.squamishchamber.bc.ca) will help with more information on this exciting area.

BC Museum of Mining (Box 188, Britannia Beach, V0N 1J0; 604–896–2233 or 604–688–8735; fax: 604–896–2260; general@bcmuseumofmining.org; www.bcmuseumofmining.org), 7.5 miles (12 km) south of Squamish, is all underground. An electric train takes you into the mountain on a tour of what was at one time the largest copper producer in the British Empire. Its history has not all been happy, though. Back in 1915 the mine was struck by an avalanche, killing thirty-two miners. It's open May to October (or year-round by arrangement for tours but closed December and January). Adult admission is $9.50, students and seniors $7.50; kids five and under are free, and there are family discounts. You can't miss the museum—just look for the 235-ton Super Mine Truck standing in the industrial yard outside.

You don't need a vehicle to see this fabulous Sea to Sky area. Consider chugging past the spectacular Cheakamus Canyon and Seton and Anderson Lakes by train. The **Cariboo Prospector** leaves North Vancouver at 7:00 A.M. daily, arriving in Lillooet at 12:35 P.M. The return trip leaves Lillooet at 3:45 P.M., returning to Vancouver at 9:15 P.M. The round-trip fare including breakfast, dinner, and taxes is $144—for a trip that is ranked in Paul Taylor's book *The Ten Most Beautiful Rail Journeys in the World* as a "premier scenic route." Sundays, Wednesdays, and Fridays you can travel as far as Prince George for $212 one way—a fourteen-and-a-half-hour trip. Contact BC Rail at (604) 984–5246; fax: (604) 984–5505; toll free in North America: (800) 663–8238; passinfo@bcrail.com; www.bcrail.com/bcrpass.

If you have time restrictions, the **Pacific Starlight** *Dinner Train* leaves from North Vancouver early May to mid-October at 6:15 P.M. It's not just gourmet meals and fabulous scenery though. During the forty-five-minute stop (between dinner and dessert) at *Porteau Cove Provincial Park,* you can dance to (or simply enjoy) the live, big-band sounds of Night Train, or take a walk in the park, which makes this moveable feast an exceptional attraction. Exclusive of drinks and tips, you'll pay $85.95 in Salon Class and $109.95 in Dome Class. Contact BC Rail as above; ask, too, about their family-oriented *Hudson Steam Train* trips and a train/boat combination tour.

The Sunshine Coast

Highway 101, the Sunshine Coast Highway, connects pretty coastal communities with attractive names such as Secret Cove, Smuggler Cove, Sechelt, Halfmoon Bay, Garden Bay, Earl's Cove, and Saltery Bay, sprinkled along the sheltered coastline between Howe Sound and the marine-life-rich waters of Desolation Sound.

The ferry from the terminal at Horseshoe Bay at the western end of the Upper Levels Highway in Vancouver takes forty minutes to cross to Langdale, the southern entrance to the Sunshine Coast. Contact BC Ferries (888–BCFERRY or 250–386–3431) and inquire about the Sunshine Coast Circlepac deal, a four-route travel package that gives up to 15 percent off regular one-way fares.

A few minutes west of Langdale (take the more scenic Marine Drive instead of the bypass), fans of *The Beachcombers* will want to stop off in **Gibsons** to see some of the haunts made famous by the old television series—such as **Molly's Reach** (604–886–9710), but since 1995 a seafood restaurant. You'll find it down near the "Landing." The **Gibsons Visitor Info Centre** (in the Sunnycrest Mall parking lot in Upper Gibsons, 668 Sunnycrest Road, Box 1190, Gibsons, V0N 1V0; 604–886–2325; fax: 604–886–2379; gibsons_chamber@sunshine.net, www.gibsonschamber. com) has other eateries listed and quite a few bed- and- breakfasts. One of these, **Marina House Bed & Breakfast** (546 Marine Drive, Box 1696, Gibsons, V0N 1V0; 888–568–6688 or 604–886–7888; marina house@sunshine.net; www.bbcanada.com/3203.html), was built in 1931 by local medical legend Doc Inglis. It has lovely view rooms (Molly's and Sarah's) with private baths in the $100 double range, including coffee in your room and a full breakfast in the library. The hosts will also pick you up from the ferry.

Before leaving Gibsons take a look at the Charles Bedford shell collection at the **Elphinstone Pioneer Museum** (716 Winn Road, Box 766, Gibsons, V0N 1V0; 604–886–8232; epm@dccnet.com). As well as this world-renowned shell collection, there's a *Beachcomber* series display, which will remind you to take a stroll down **Molly's Lane** and the **Seawalk**. Butterfly fanatics will enjoy the new Don Bland Butterfly Collection. Summer hours are 10:30 A.M. to 4:30 P.M. daily, except Sundays and Mondays. Winter hours are Tuesday, Thursday, and Saturday, 1:00 to 4:30 P.M.

Up the hill from the Landing at **Jack's Lane Bistro** (546 Gibson's Way; 604–886–4898), you'll find specialty coffees, homemade soups and sandwiches, and the best desserts going, as well as fresh Mediterranean

BC Ferry approaching Langdale

food. A tasty, Veggie Combo entree for two costs about $14. The *Wild Blueberry Bakery* (604–886–1616) downstairs has a wide variety of breads and sweets.

Head northwest out of Gibsons past thick forests toward Sechelt. Beside the eighteen-hole *Sunshine Coast Golf and Country Club* (800–667–5022; 604–885–9217; fax: 604–885–6212; $30 per round), you'll find a park akin to a small-scale rainforest. *Cliff Gilker Regional Park* consists of an unusual variety of trees, plants and shrubs, with cedar bridges and waterfalls along pleasant hiking trails.

Turn at the Fire Department building, 6 miles (10 km) from Gibsons and stop at *Roberts Creek.* Take a walk out along the pier at Rock Point, where unsightly propane tanks used to sit. If you haven't seen it lately, you're in for a surprise. It's now a scenic area "furnished" with drift-wood "armchairs." Wander the beach, where you'll sometimes find sea stars, mussels, and oysters, and stay for the glorious sunsets.

Nearby, the *Gumboot Garden Cafe* (1057 Roberts Creek Road; 604–885–4216) serves fresh, tasty foods, in keeping with a back-to-the-sixties Roberts Creek atmosphere. It's open daily from 8.30 A.M. till 3:00 P.M. and for dinner Thursday, Friday, and Saturday until 8:30 P.M. *Casual* is the key word at this funky, friendly feast house! Try the locally caught cedar salmon (baked traditionally on a cedar plank) or something off the extensive (from enchiladas to Thai Noodle Salad) vegetarian or vegan menu.

The Sunshine Coast Highway 101 continues heading west to the best coffee shop on the coast. *Strait Coffee Traders* (4330 Sunshine Coast Highway, Sechelt, V0N 3A0; 800–893–6646 or 604–885–9757; strait_coffee@sunshine.net), in the Wilson Creek Plaza, beckons with its rich aroma of roasting beans. The organic lunches (steaming curried lentil-apple soup in winter and cool gazpacho in summer) and

Recommended Reading - The Southwestern Mainland

FOR ADULTS:
A Guide to Climbing and Hiking in Southwestern British Columbia,
by Bruce Fairley. Vancouver: Gordon Soules Publishing, 1986.

109 Walks in British Columbia's Lower Mainland, by Mary and David Macaree.
Vancouver: Greystone Books/Douglas & McIntyre, 1997.

Whitewater Trips for Kayakers, Canoeists and Rafters in British Columbia, by
Betty Pratt-Johnson. Vancouver/Whistler, Thompson, 1986.

Fort Langley: Birth Place of British Columbia, by B. A. McKelvie. Beach Holme Publishing Ltd., 1991.

Salmonopolis: The Steveston Story, by S. and D. Stacey. Madeira Park: Harbour Publishing, 1994.

Bicycling near Vancouver: Book 1 - Central Fraser Valley, by Margaret Slack.
Vancouver: Gordon Soules, 1994

Daytrips from Vancouver, by Jack Christie. Vancouver: Greystone Books/Douglas & McIntyre, 1997.

Fraser and Thompson Canyons, by Art Downs, ed. Heritage House
Publishing Co. Ltd., 1980.

The Whistler Outdoors Guide, by Jack Christie. Vancouver: Greystone Books/Douglas & McIntyre, 1997.

Sunshine and Salt Air: An Outdoor Guide to the Sunshine Coast, Karen Southern,
Bryan Carson, Peter Robson (eds.). Madeira Park: Harbour Publishing, 1997.

FOR KIDS:
Breakaway, by Paul Yee. Toronto: Groundwood Books, 2000. The hero is a good
student and soccer player whose Chinese family are poor farmers. Set during the
Depression years in Vancouver. For ages nine to twelve.

dreamy desserts make it a triple-the-value coffee stop.

Continue north past the long, sandy beach and engaging galleries at Davis Bay, and you're soon in Sechelt, home of artists, writers, and retirees. Every August the nationally acclaimed *Festival of the Written Arts* is held at the *Rockwood Centre* (at the top of Cowrie Street; 604–885–9631 or 800–565–9631; written_arts@sunshine.net; www. sunshine.net/rockwood), just up from the *Sechelt Visitor Info Centre* in the Trail Bay Centre (45–5755 Cowrie Street, Box 360, Sechelt, V0N 3A0; 604–885–0662; fax: 604–885–0691; visitorinfo@dccnet.com; www.the sunshinecoast.com/secheltchamber). Visit the galleries and shops in town and pick up some local artists' works at *Sunshine Coast Arts Centre* (corner of Medusa Road and Trail Avenue; 604–885–5412).

There's native artwork at the Indian Band Complex, the imposing *House of Hewhiwus* (House of Chiefs), on the highway opposite St. Mary's Hospital as you enter Sechelt. As well as a museum and a 280-seat theater, there's an art gallery in which the raven, an integral feature of the Sechelt Indian band's culture, is a recurring theme. The word *sechelt* means "land between two waters." Indian legend has it that gods carved out the valleys but left a beach along the inlet at nearby Porpoise Bay. Later the transformers—a male raven and a female mink—changed details by carving trees and forming pools of water. Divers love the waters here in Porpoise Bay. In 1992 the 387-foot (118-m) *HMCS Chaudière* was sunk (off Kunechin Point), creating an artificial reef that is now rated as one of the top twenty recreational dives in the world.

If it's the fabulous snow-topped mountain views you're after, stay at the *Casa Del Sol* (6564 Gale Avenue North, RR 2, Shores Site, C20, Sechelt, V0N 3A0; 604–885–0900; toll free: 877–399–2929; casadelsol@sun shine.net; www.thesunshinecoast.com/casadelsol). This first-class bed-and-breakfast accommodation (also offering massage and other pampering delights) is north of Sechelt in a small community (The Shores) edging Snake Bay. To get there from Sechelt, head north along Trail Avenue to the skating arena, turn right on Fairway, and follow this (keeping left) to the end. Turn left onto Gale Avenue North and look for the bed-and-breakfast on the water side. Rates are from $110 per night double.

An unforgettable back-to-nature camping experience can be had with *Tzoonie Outdoor Adventures* (Box 157, Sechelt, V0N 3A0; 604–885–9802; fax: 604–885–9826; tzoonie.adventures@home.com; www.sunshine.net/zoonie). You'll hike, camp, and more in a wilderness camp on traditional native lands.

On Porpoise Bay Road you'll discover what is possibly Sechelt's best restaurant, *The Blue Heron* (604–885–3847 or 800–818–8977; blue-heron@uniserve.com). It's open for dinner Wednesday through Sunday and specializes in seafood, with such delicacies as a bouillabaisse deliciously loaded with fresh fish and shellfish in a lobster bisque broth. The delightful surroundings and high-quality wines, combined with French cuisine, make it very popular with the locals—I suggest you make reservations.

Heading north on Highway 101 from Sechelt, hikers will enjoy *Smuggler Cove Marine Park* (604–898–3678), just past Halfmoon Bay. About 5.5 miles (9 km) northwest of Sechelt (look for the blue-and-white BC Parks sign), go up a long hill and turn left at Brooks Road, following this gravel road for 2 miles (3 km) to the parking lot. The cove, named for the illegal traffic of Chinese workers to the United States, is an easy 1-mile hike. There are a couple of walk-in campsites with pit toilets but no water.

The highway continues north past Halfmoon Bay to *Pender Harbour,* a puzzling jigsaw of inlets and bays, with a few lakes, islands, and reefs thrown in. Here you'll find tiny fishing communities such as Madeira Park, where such signs as BEWARE OF ATTACK SQUIRREL! abound, and you'll find great sandwiches in a hole-in-the-wall cafe called *Madeira Mercantile.* Many of the harbor's community-proud residents are there for the good fishing, both saltwater and fresh. One man who knows this area well is Bryce Christie of *Sunshine Coast Tours* (RR 1, S9, C1, 4289 Orca Road, Garden Bay, V0N 1S0; 604–883–2280; fax: 604–883–2352; Bookings: 800–870–9055; fax: 800–762–9055; info@sunshinecoast tours.bc.ca; www.sunshinecoasttours.bc.ca). Bryce runs the *Harbour Hopper* ferry, where a pass will take you anywhere you want to "hop" to throughout Pender Harbour.

Contact the *Pender Harbour Tourist/Visitor Info Booth* (July–August), 12911 Madeira Park Road, Box 265, Madeira Park, V0N 2H0; phone/fax: (604) 883–2561, for more information on activities and accommodations.

Highway 101 leads north to the ferry at Earl's Cove, but before leaving the peninsula, take a look at the thrilling *Skookumchuck Narrows,* named for a Chinook word meaning "turbulent water" or "rapid torrent." Here, tidal flow associated with Sechelt, Narrows, and Salmon inlets is forced through the narrows to form Sechelt Rapids, perhaps the world's fastest saltwater rapids, with currents surpassing 16 knots per hour. Check current tables (as opposed to tide tables) in the local newspaper (*The Reporter*) for the best viewing times or check with the

Trivia

Statistics show that the number of Canadians traveling to the United States from British Columbia on a single-day automobile trip is strongly affected by the relative value of the Canadian dollar. For every decrease of 1 cent in the Canadian dollar, 30,000 fewer Canadians will make a same-day trip to the United States from British Columbia each month (and the reverse occurs when the currency increases in value).

Chamber of Commerce (they sometimes have a booth on the Langdale ferry) in Sechelt; they display a chart showing the best times and days to view the rapids. (If you go at slack tide, you'll wonder what all the fuss was about!) To get to the rapids, take the turnoff to Egmont (half a mile before you reach the ferry terminal). Drive about 4 miles (6.5 km) to a parking lot marking *Skookumchuk Narrows Provincial Park*. Signs lead you to a 2.5-mile (4-km), easy trail past Brown Lake to North Point (best viewing point on the ebb tide) and Roland Point (best on the flood tide). Allow an hour to walk to the narrows. An alternative to walking is to become one with the whirlpools in a dinner/tour with Sunshine Coast Tours (800–870–9055—more contact information is above in the Pender Harbour section). Before traveling to the Sunshine Coast, you may want to check out the Web site www.bigpacific.com for an extensive exposé of this wonderful holiday area.

Powell River

The BC ferry takes you to Saltery Bay, 19 miles (30 km) from Powell River. In *Saltery Bay Provincial Park,* a 10-foot (3-m) bronze mermaid lies at 66 feet (20 m), holding her arms out to the many scuba divers who believe this area to offer the best diving in the world. *Don's Dive Shop* (4552 Willingdon Avenue, Powell River, V8A 2M3; 604–485–6969; fax: 604–485–7609; info@donsdiveshop.com; www.donsdive shop.com) will take you to the bronze mermaid, as well as to some of the other "best dive sites in the world" aboard *The Shadow,* a customized skiff. It's berthed at Westview Marina, close to the Dive Shop. The Powell River area is renowned for huge ling cod, wolf eels, and giant octopus that thrive in the nutrient-rich waters of this emerald sea. Kayaking, fishing, hiking, diving instruction, or just plain cruising are also part of the scene.

We're almost at the end of the road in *Powell River,* the first pulp and paper town in Western Canada. Despite log booms and spewing chimneys, there's a pleasant *Heritage Townsite,* which in 1995 was awarded historic district status. At the *Powell River Visitor Info Centre* (4690 Marine Avenue, 877–81–SUNNY [78669]; 604–485–4701; fax:

604–485–2822; prvb@prcn.org; www.discoverpowellriver.com) pick up a *Heritage Walk* brochure for a self-guided tour.

For campers, **Willingdon Beach Municipal Campground** (mailing address: 6910 Duncan Street, Powell River, V8A 1V4; 604–485–2242; fax: 604–485–2162) at 4845 Marine Avenue just north of town has campsites with plenty of forest surrounding them, and the sunsets are fabulous. Walk the **Willingdon Beach Trail,** about a 40-minute round-trip, winding its way through forest along a beautiful ocean-front. Afterward, you can sit on a driftwood beach to soak up the final rays, eating fresh-out-of-the-sea fish and chips from **Kathy's Kitchen** next door. Vehicle sites are from $13 to $20 (full hookup).

But if you prefer the comfort of a hot tub and a massage, as well as the company of Jetty the cat, stay at **Beacon Bed and Breakfast** (3750 Marine Avenue, Powell River, V8A 2H8; toll free: 877–485–5563 or 604–485–5563; fax: 604–485–9450; stay@beaconbb.com; www.beaconbb.com), a waterfront home where massage technician Shirley Randall knows how to pamper guests. Look for the red-and-white beacons on the fence, 3 miles (5 km) south of Powell River. High-season rates range from $75 to $135, including a nourishing breakfast. Massage is extra.

Highway 101 continues north to the coastal village of **Lund,** the last frontier before Desolation Sound. **Cedar Lodge Bed & Breakfast** (C8, 9825 Malaspina Road, RR 2, Powell River, V8A 4Z3; phone/fax: 604–483–4414; cedarldg@prcn.org; www.prcn.org/cedar), near Okeover Arm Provincial Park, has nature trails that connect to the Sunshine Coast Trail (see end of chapter). Accommodation with continental breakfast starts at $45. Nearby at 2694 Dawson Road, **Desolation Resort** (C36, Malaspina Road, RR 2, Powell River, V8A 4Z3; 604–483–3592; fax: 604–483–7942; desolres@prcn.org; www.desolationresort.com) is a luxurious, dramatically simple resort hidden in the woods; the chalets and apartments seem to hang over the 900 feet (274 m) of wilderness waterfront overlooking the beautiful Okeover Arm. Rates range from $95 to $190 in low season and $120 to $290 for a triple unit in high season. There are canoes and kayaks to use, and the eagles, whales, seals, and sea lions are free to enjoy from your private deck.

Both accommodations are close to **The Laughing Oyster Restaurant** (604–483–9775; falk@prcn.org; www.laughing-oyster.bc.ca), where you'll find classic cuisine with a West Coast flavor, served in front of breathtaking views over Okeover Inlet. For lunch try the salmon and spinach crepe, and for dinner don't miss the "hilariously delicious" Laughing Oysters. You'll find the Laughing Oyster at the end of Malaspina

Road, just by the Okeover Provincial Park. Further accommodation, the *Oyster Shell Beach House* (self-contained waterfront accommodation —check the Laughing Oyster Web site or write C-4 Vandermaeden Road, RR2, Powell River, V8A 4Z3; 604–414–0234; falk@prch.org), can be found 3 miles (5 km) north of Sliammon Village on the highway to Lund on the west side of Malaspina Peninsula. You can stay for a week for a mere $375 double in high season, or overnight for $65.

A few minutes away is the quiet fishing village of Lund (named after the city of Lund in Sweden), the gateway to Desolation Sound, a sailor's paradise. The historic *Lund Hotel* (General Delivery, Lund, V0N 2G0; 877–569–3999 toll free in North America; 604–414–0474; fax: 604–414–0476; info@lundhotel.com; www.lundhotel.com), built by the Swedish Thulin brothers in 1889 and refurbished by the Sliammon First Nation in May 2000, provides excellent dining and accommodation, and the views are everywhere. As well as the hotel and restaurant, there's a pub, a general store, and a fuel dock. To discover Desolation Sound and take a journey into Coast Salish culture, contact *Coast Salish Journeys* (C–64, RR#2, Sliammon Road, Powell River, V8A 4Z3; 604–483–4505; 800–345–1112 toll free in North America; fax: 604–483–7975; info@ coastsalishjourneys.com; www.coastsalishjourneys.com), located in summer in the Lund Hotel. They'll take you on guided hikes, ocean adventures (in 30-foot dugout-style canoes), sea kayaking to uninhabited islands, or canoeing and sailing into the sound, where you can enjoy traditional Coast Salish salmon barbecues. Craft workshops are also held, to complete a total "back-to-how-it-was" adventure.

Lund is but a water-taxi ride away (*Lund Water Taxi* 604–483–9749, reservations appreciated) from British Columbia's largest arbutus tree and the white sand beaches of one of the prettiest of the Gulf Islands: *Savary Island*.

Stay a while to enjoy Savary's warm waters at *Savary Island Lodge* (604–483–9481; jyuile@armourtech.com), a large log home located directly on one of those endless white beaches. Jim and Jean Yuile serve traditional hot English breakfasts that are included in the tariff, which starts at $75 double. Bring your whites for a game of tennis on the wooden-decked court nearby. You'll find a photo of this historic lodge at www.savary.bc.ca, as well as much more about Savary. For tours of the island, phone Rick Thaddeus at (604) 483–3218 or (604) 979–6863 (free pager from Vancouver), or E-mail him at rick@savary.bc.ca. There are three seasonal restaurants on the island, one of which (Riggers, 604–483–2210) is beside the small general store.

Back on the mainland, experienced hikers can trek the 112-mile (180-km) *Sunshine Coast Trail*, which starts (or ends) at Sarah Point north of Lund, at the tip of the Malaspina Peninsula, the dramatic entrance to Desolation Sound. Lund Water Taxi (604–483–9749) offers transport to Sarah Point. The other extremity of the trail is at the ferry terminal in Saltery Bay. Learn more about this challenging trail at www.sunshinecoast-trail.com. It nudges a couple of bed-and-breakfasts, which can add a touch of cheer to a sometimes difficult hike. One of these, *Fiddlehead Farm* (Box 421, Powell River, V8A 5C2; Radio Telephone 604–483–3018 [let it ring ten times]; fiddlehead@aisl.bc.ca; www.armourtech.com/~fiddlehead), is accessible only from the trail, or by boat up Powell Lake from Powell River. (Fiddlehead Farm staff will pick you up for a $20 return.) It's no ordinary hostel. Visitors are welcome to share the homestead life. (How long since you baked bread, chopped wood, or gathered eggs?) The 80-acre (33-hectare) farm is tranquility itself, surrounded by everything that British Columbia is renowned for—lakes, forests, and magnificent mountains. There's a six-bedroom guesthouse, a bathhouse with a wood-fired sauna, and a dining room/kitchen area. Meals are home-style and, of course, mainly home-grown. Daily rates, including all meals plus the use of canoes, are very reasonable. Non–Hostelling International members pay $40 per person in the guest house or $32 camping, kids ages five to ten pay half price, and the under fives are free. There's also a backpacker's working rate of $26 if you are prepared to do two hours of chores per day.

Malaspina Coach Lines (877–227–8287; 604–485–5030; or 604–485–3894) leaves Vancouver's main terminal at 8:30 A.M. daily and arrives in Powell River (where Fiddlehead staff will pick you up) at 1:50 P.M. The cost is approximately $26. If coming from Vancouver Island, take the mid-morning ferry from Comox to Powell River and meet the Fiddlehead staff in the terminal waiting room. You'll be set for an off-the-beaten-path experience second to none.

PLACES TO STAY ON THE SOUTHWESTERN MAINLAND

HARRISON HOT SPRINGS
Harrison Heritage House and Kottage Bed and Breakfast, 312 Lillooet Avenue, Box 475, V0M 1K0; (604) 796–9552 or (800) 331–8099; www.bbcanada.com/2177.html. Rooms $50–$145.

MISSION
Fence Post Lane Bed & Breakfast, 4 miles (6.6 km) west of Mission at 8575 Gaglardi Street, V4S 1B2; (877) 833–7009 or (604) 820–7009; fax: (604) 820–4974; mperdue@direct.ca; www.bbcanada.com/906.html. Room rates $50–$75 double.

PEMBERTON

Rainbow Valley Inn Bed and Breakfast,
1864 Sea to Sky Highway, Box 483, V0N 2K0;
phone/fax: (604) 894–3300; (800) 555–8042;
sales@rainbowvalleyinn.com; www.RainbowValleyInn.com.
Rooms $79–$99.

SECHELT

Casa Del Sol,
6564 Gale Avenue North, RR2, Shores Site, C20, Sechelt, V0N 3A0; (604) 885–0900; toll free (877) 399–2929; casadelsol@sunshine.net; www.thesunshinecoast.com/casadelsol. Classy bed-and-breakfast plus. From $110.

VANCOUVER

"O Canada" House Bed & Breakfast,
1114 Barclay Street, V6E 1H1; (604) 688–0555; (877) 688–1114 toll free; fax: (604) 488–0556; ocanadahouse@home.com; www.ocanadahouse.com. Downtown. Classy. Rooms from $175.

Victorian Hotel,
514 Homer Street, Vancouver, V6B 2V6; toll free: (877) 681–6369; (604) 681–6369; fax: (604) 681–8776; victorian hotel@hotmail.com; www.victorian-hotel.com. Downtown. Rooms from $79, including breakfast. Newly renovated and great value.

PLACES TO EAT ON THE SOUTHWESTERN MAINLAND

GIBSONS

Jack's Lane Bistro and Bakery, 546 Gibson's Way; (604) 886–4898. Great desserts.

HOPE

Hope Station House,
at the junction of Highway 1 and Old Hope-Princeton Way; (604) 869–9495. A smoke-free restaurant specializing in homemade soups, sandwiches, and desserts. Open 8:00 A.M. to 8:00 P.M. daily.

SECHELT

The Blue Heron,
Porpoise Bay Road; (604) 885–3847 or (800) 818–8977; www.ewest.com/blue heron/. Open for dinner Wednesday through Sunday. Specializes in seafood. Reservations recommended.

SQUAMISH

Howe Sound Inn and Brewing Company,
37801 Cleveland Avenue; (604) 892–2603 or (800) 919–ALES (2537). Moderately priced restaurant and pub meals.

VANCOUVER

Raku Kushiyaki,
4422 West 10th Avenue, near 42nd Street; (604) 222–8188. Japanese-style; classy; reasonable prices. Reservations recommended.

Amarcord,
1168 Hamilton Street, (604) 681–6500. Excellent Italian dining in Yaletown.

Harry's Diner,
1078 W. Pender Street near Thurlow; (604) 331–0046. Pizza, etc. Also at 833 Bute at Robson.

The Okanagan

Apples and wine, water sports, and lots of sunshine are images that prevail on hearing the words *The Okanagan*. Here in Canada's warmest, driest climate, we'll travel through just 3 percent of British Columbia's 366,275 square miles (948,596 sq km), but our diverse journey will lead us from Princeton, in the foothills of the Cascades, along the once gold-rich Similkameen River, past eccentrically shaped mountains and turquoise lakes in Cathedral Provincial Park, and through orchards of cherries, peaches, pears, apples, apricots, and grapes. Down close to the U.S. border, we'll ride the rolling ranges, where painted turtles and rattlesnakes lurk in Canada's only desert. Farther north we'll look for the mystical Ogopogo in the 90-mile-long (145-km) Okanagan Lake, one of more than 250 lakes in the region. And in fall we'll enjoy world-class wine at the Okanagan Wine Festival, for which this land of plenty is fast becoming famous.

Princeton

Starting in the east at the Manning Park border, the mountainous Crowsnest (Highway 3) winds north to *Princeton,* a town mother-loded with a history of gold and copper mining from the 1880s. Originally called Vermilion Forks, after the nearby bluffs of red ocher, a substance prized by the Similkameen Indians for trading and face painting, Princeton, the southern gateway to the populous BC interior, is in the foothills of the Cascade Mountains, where the Tulameen and Similkameen Rivers meet.

Start your visit to Princeton by stopping off near the bridge over the Similkameen River at the **Princeton Visitor Info Centre** (57 Highway 3 East, Box 540, Princeton, V0X 1W0; 250–295–3103; fax: 250–295–3255; chamber@nethop.net; www.town.princeton.bc.ca) to pick up a *Historic Walk* brochure. Numbered plaques on

Trivia
British Columbia's worst road accident occurred July 15, 1975, near Princeton, when a head-on collision caused the deaths of eleven people, including a family of eight.

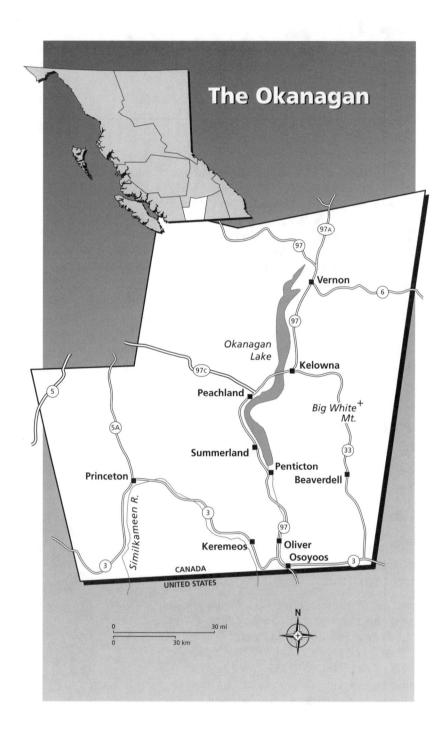

The Okanagan

Vernon

Okanagan Lake

Kelowna

Peachland

Big White Mt.

Summerland

Penticton

Beaverdell

Princeton

Similkameen R.

Keremeos

Oliver

Osoyoos

CANADA

UNITED STATES

0   30 mi
0   30 km

N

AUTHOR'S TOP TEN PICKS IN THE OKANAGAN

Cathedral Provincial Park

The Grist Mill

Princeton Museum and Archives

Haynes Point Provincial Park

Desert Ecological Reserve

Dominion Radio Astrophysical Observatory

Okanagan Pottery Studio

Hainle Vineyards Estate Winery

Myra Canyon

Big White Ski Resort

each historic site correspond with photos and information in the guide.

Historic Site 6, the **Princeton Museum and Archives** (167 Vermilion Avenue; 250–295–7588) is a credit to this population of just three thousand. It features one of Princeton's more infamous characters, the likable train robber and prison escapee Bill Miner. After doing time in the United States for Pony Express robberies, he moved his talents to the Princeton area and started on the trains, where, as "the Gentleman Bandit," he restricted his robberies to the baggage cars, taking only the payrolls and never the ladies' jewelry. One daring robbery near Kamloops ended in his capture and imprisonment. He escaped and fled to the United States, where, after recapture, he died in a Georgia prison. The museum has a vast collection of rocks and petrified wood, as well as one of the largest collections of fossils in British Columbia. This world-class donated collection necessitated the building of a special wing to house it. The museum is open from 10:00 A.M. to 6:00 P.M. Tuesday through Saturday and from 11:00 A.M. to 3:00 P.M. Sunday and Monday in July and August and on weekends 1:00 to 3:00 P.M. in May, June, and September.

A Princeton Treasure

*T*he Princeton Museum was closed, so I inquired at the library.

"Find Margaret Stoneberg," was the answer. "She's usually around somewhere."

I found dear Margaret Stoneberg, a wool hat pulled tightly on, a stuffed bag of books by her feet, and her eyes close to a newspaper she was reading. She parted a ring of keys, selected one, rose slowly from her paper, and shuffled me into the museum.

"At first there was just trees and the mountain," she began.

Two hours later, I was still listening eagerly to stories from the gold and copper heydays, learning how during the war all the beer "from here to Alaska" was Princeton beer, and hearing how things haven't always changed for the better. As we left the museum, she was still pointing out artifacts.

"That organ was $29.50 in the 1903 catalogue," she whispered, a note of nostalgia in her tiny voice.

The Princeton Rodeo Club is busy in the spring, with both team rop-ing and rodeo competitions. If you're visiting on the Canada Day (July 1) weekend, you'll catch Princeton Racing Days, and on the second weekend of September, there's the *Little Britches Rodeo* and the *Annual Agricultural Fall Fair.*

Near the museum enjoy a "Hungry Man Breakfast" at the *Belaire Restaurant* (161 Vermilion Avenue, Princeton, V0X 1W0; 250–295–7711), also popular for its homemade pies, soups, and delicious full meals. For accommodation to suit all budgets, head out of town to *Princeton Castle Resort and R. V. Park* (Princeton-Summerland Road, RR 1, Site 1, Comp 10, Princeton, V0X 1W0; 888–228–8881 or 250–295–7988; info@castleresort.com; www. castleresort.com). Outdoor hot tubs add a little decadence at the new log lodge and cottages, which are set behind the racetrack off Osprey Lake Road on the site of an intended cement plant and powerhouse. For some unknown reason, the massive architectural venture didn't pan out (possibly they ran out of limestone), and what is left looks like the ruins of a medieval castle. You may want to spend some time searching for the notorious Bill Miner's lost treasure, rumored to be hidden in his hideout in the hills near the castle. Locals tell me you'll have more luck panning for gold in the creek, though. Or perhaps flying to the moon!

Winter visitors can experience a scenic and exhilarating dogsled jour-ney along the famous *Trans Canada Trail,* with only the sound of the mushing dogs and the rustle of the pine trees to intrude on the Cana-dian wilderness in all its winter majesty. Contact *Pinewood Expedi-tions* (RR 1, Site 19 C5, Princeton, V0X 1W0; phone/fax: 250–295–7667; toll free for reservations: 877–295–7668; pinewood@uniserve. com; www.pinewoodexp.net) to book tours or to learn to drive your own team. Accommodation in the form of a trapper's wall-tent at $50 per night, including all meals and use of lodge facilities, will add realism to this wonderful old-time adventure. The third weekend in January features the *Sno-X Races,* exciting snowmobile races with contestants from all over Canada and the United States.

Look for the new eighteen-hole *Princeton Golf Club* three minutes from the town center. Camping accommodation is available. The Golf Course Kitchen (250–295–0008; open in summer from 8:00 A.M. to 12:00 P.M.) serves inexpensive deep-fried and grilled meals on its view patio.

The Similkameen Valley

eaving Princeton, the Crowsnest follows the Similkameen River 41 miles (67 km) east to Keremeos, passing through **Hedley**. Stop here to learn of the area's rich gold mining history. Two miles (3 km) before Keremeos, a 16-mile (25-km) southern side trip on the gravel Ashnola River Road brings you into **Cathedral Provincial Park.** California bighorn sheep, mule deer, and porcupines range in this 81,214-acre (33,272-ha) mountain wilderness, the setting for the movie *Clan of the Cave Bear.*

Past the Ashnola River, a privately owned road leads to **Cathedral Lakes Lodge** (888–255–4453 or 250–352–3724; fax: 250–354–0230; journey@ netidea.com; www. cathedral-lakes-lodge.com), Canada's highest full-service hiking and fishing resort, located on Lake Quiniscoe in the very center of the park. From the lodge the most popular hike is the **Cathedral Rim Trail,** which follows a high alpine ridge to unique geological formations such as Devils Woodpile and Smokey the Bear, a jagged gigantic rock looking like a silhouette of old Smokey himself. On a clear day the view is spectacular, as not only can you see Mount Baker and Mount Ranier 200 miles (320 km) to the west, but also the Thompson Plateau and the Kootenays to the north and east. It's definitely a top-of-the-world sensation. Glorious wildflowers and the turquoise Cathedral Lakes make the area a wilderness heaven. But keep in mind it's a "be-prepared" park, with no commercial facilities other than the private lodge. Campers may reserve ahead for the one-hour-long jeep ride (phone: 888–255–4453) to the park center. Costs are $55 per person June–October or $75 July–August. Children twelve and under cost $30, and under four are free. Accommodation rates at the lodge include superb meals and transportation from the base camp.

For camping information (sixteen sites, open April to October, with fees collected June to September), contact BC Parks, Okanagan District,

Funtastic Summer Festival, *Vernon/Enderby; June/July; (250) 260–0973; www.funtastic.org*

Elks Rodeo, *Keremeos; May; (250) 499–5175*

Sunshine Festival, *Oliver; June; (250) 498–6321*

Beach Blanket Film Festival, *Penticton; July; (250) 492–4019*

Annual Peach Festival, *Penticton; August; (800) 663–5052; www.peachfest.com*

Blossum Run, *Summerland; May; (250) 494–2686*

Cowboy Festival, *O'Keefe Historic Ranch, Vernon; early August; (250) 542–7868*

Westside Daze Community Festival, *Westbank; July; (250) 768–3378*

Fat Cats Children's Festival, *Kelowna; July; (250) 763–3212*

Interior Provincial Exhibition and Stampede, *Armstrong; September; (250) 546–9406*

Okanagan Lake Park, Box 399, Summerland, V0H 1Z0, or phone (250) 494–6500; fax: (250) 494–9737. If you're already in the area, **Keremeos & District Chamber of Commerce** (415 Seventh Avenue, Keremeos, V0X 1N0; 250–499–5225) can help with brochure maps and information. A more detailed topographic map (sheet 92H/1) is available for approximately $10 from Nanaimo Maps and Charts (8 Church Street, Nanaimo, V9R 5H4; 250–754–2513; 800–665–2513; fax: 250–754–2313 or 800–553–2313 toll free—include your phone number when ordering) or, in Victoria, at Crown Publications (521 Fort Street, Victoria, V8W 1E7; 250–386–4636; fax: 250–386–0221; crown@pinc.com; www.crown pub.bc.ca). In Vancouver contact World Wide Books and Maps (604–687–3320).

At the route map information sign on Highway 3, 3 miles (5 km) west of Keremeos, the **Login Bed and Breakfast** (C1 Site 27, Highway 3 West, Keremeos, V0X 1N0; 250–499–2781/2664; loginbnb@keremeos.net; www.keremeos.net/loginbnb) caters to people, but if you come for the **Chopaka Rodeo** on the Easter weekend or the **Elks Rodeo** on the May long weekend, your horse is welcome, too. The pleasant log home is on 190 acres (77 ha), a short hike away from the Ashnola wilderness. The rooms have lovely views of the Similkameen scenery, and you might see bighorn sheep right outside your window. Breakfasts are excellent, with enough leftovers to stuff your packs for the hike snack. There's a kitchen for your use and a lovely log fireplace. Rates are moderate, and the hosts, Helen and Eric Falkenberg, will let you use their Internet access. Ask them about rides or hikes outside the park to Crater Lake, Barcelo Canyon, and The Columns.

Keremeos, where in-season fruit stands line the highway, has earned the nickname "Fruit-stand Capital of the World." It is also fast earning a name for its many certified organic orchards and market gardens. Pick up some organic garlic, carrots, and other vegetables, and of course don't miss the organic apples and other delicious fruit the area boasts. In the lovely Similkameen Valley, you'll find lots to see and do, including a visit to the **Orchard Blossom Honey House** (250–499–2821), with its historic beekeeping equipment, and to **Harker's Fruit Ranch** (RR1 Highway 3, Cawston; 250–499–2751), where owners Bruce and Kathy Harker specialize in growing and marketing organic fruits and vegetables. From mouth-watering melons to just-picked peaches to jams, jellies, and juices, the Harkers also offer tours where you can learn the basics of organic farming. They're open daily from July 1 to October 31. Tours should be booked in advance.

**WORTH SEEING/DOING
IN THE OKANAGAN-SIMILKAMEEN**

Windsurf on Osoyoos Lake.

Take a wine tour in the Okanagan Valley.

Ride the rails in Summerland on the Kettle Valley Railway.

Ski at Big White (near Kelowna) or Apex Mountain (near Penticton).

Visit the museums in Kelowna and Oliver.

Climb the Skaha Bluffs, one of the best rock-climbing bluffs in the world.

But the valley's best-known attraction is British Columbia's only water-powered flour mill, the oldest surviving pioneer flour mill west of Ontario, built in 1877. **The Grist Mill** (RR 1 Upper Bench Road, Keremeos, V0X 1N0; 250–499–2888; gmk_chin@keremeos.com; www.heritage.gov.bc.ca/grist) is well signed 1 kilometer off Highway 3A on Keremeos Creek. It features restored, rare, original machinery driven by a 12-foot waterwheel, a **Heritage Gardens** showing the agricultural history of the Similkameen Valley, and hands-on displays about this historic milling process. Pioneer lifestyle activities, enacted by costumed interpreters, give you that 1880s atmosphere. Don't miss the delightful Victorian schoolma'am, Mrs. MacPherson, who is in real life Christine Pilgrim, once a lead comic act in British music halls. She doubles as Julia Bullock-Webster, a British artist and diarist who visited her homesteading sons in the Keremeos area in 1894. She'll charm you in the pretty little Apple House Theatre, built before the days of electricity as an apple storage building.

At the **Tea Room**, you can enjoy light lunches featuring fresh-baked goods made from flour milled as it was in 1877 and organically grown vegetables from the Heritage Gardens. In the **Mill Shop** you'll find seeds and plant-starts from the Heritage Gardens, wheat-straw weavings, corn dolls, dried gourds, and, of course, milled flour. Topical books are a nice addition. The Grist Mill is open formally from May to October and informally the rest of the year. Admission prices are reasonable, with tour discounts available.

The Okanagan Valley

The Similkameen River winds south to the border, and the highway leaves it to take a northeastern route. Just 5.5 miles (8.8 km) west of Osoyoos, the strange **Spotted Lake** (called *Klilok* by the Okanagan Indians) can be seen from the southern side of the highway. Evaporation and crystallization cause the formation of salty, white circular plates on the surface, hence its name. If it weren't on private land, you'd be able to soak away your arthritic pains in this muddy paradise of Epsom salts, calcium, and magnesium, as did the

First Nations people in centuries gone by. Instead, be content to enjoy the unusual view from the highway.

Osoyoos Lake, named from *soi'yus,* an Inkaneep Indian word meaning roughly "gathered together" or "where the water narrows," comes into view. "Seems a zealous Irishman added the 'O'," explained former schoolteacher John Wallace, who, with his wife June, was my host at **Haynes Point Lakeside Guest House** (3619 Jasmine Drive, Osoyoos, V0H 1V0; phone/fax: 250-495-7443; www.bbcanada.com/14.html). The Wallaces know and share a remarkable amount of information about the area, even to preparing handouts on birding or arranging golfing or winery tours (there are five fine golf courses and fourteen wineries within thirty minutes), or you can simply enjoy June's delicious breakfasts (where I learned to put cardamom in my coffee for that special flavor) and unwind in one of the hammocks overlooking the 11.8-mile-long (19-km) lake. Their three guest rooms are distinctively decorated to a theme, and the view over the lake and hills is wonderful. In summer boating and swimming in Canada's warmest freshwater lake is popular. (The average summer temperature is 75° F, or 24° C.) To get there turn south from the Crowsnest onto Highway

Fruity Facts

British Columbia produces 12.1 million pounds (5.5 million kg) of sweet cherries and 2.2 million pounds (1 million kg) of sour cherries a year—about 60 percent of the Canadian cherry crop.

Osoyoos has the earliest fruit season in the Okanagan Valley. The following table will show you when to visit, depending on whether you want to be there for the blossoms (beautiful photography) or the eating (mm!).

Fruit	Blossom	Ripens
Apricots	April 1–30	July 15–August 15
Cherries	April 15–May 1	June 25–July 30
Peaches	April 15–May 10	July 15–August 15
Pears	April 15–May 1	July 15–October 15
Plums	April 15–May 1	August 15–September 20
Apples	April 25–May 20	July 15–September 30
Grapes	April 25–May 20	September 5–October 10

97; after 2 miles (3 km) follow the HAYNES POINT PROVINCIAL PARK sign south down Thirty-second Avenue. Jasmine Street is a left turn just before the park entrance and lake. Rates in high season range from $70 to $95 (double); the pampered feeling you come away with makes these rates quite reasonable.

Two minutes away at the **Haynes Point Provincial Park** (BC Parks Okanagan District, Box 399, Summerland, V0H 1Z0; 250–494–6500; fax: 250–494–9737), a strip of land stretches out into the middle of the lake, narrowing to just a little more than 60 feet (18 m) wide in spots. Forty-one forested campsites line the waterfront, where fishing for trout, kokanee, bass, and lake whitefish is popular. Park personnel offer audiovisual programs and other activities relating to the history of the area. Red-winged blackbirds, ospreys, and eagles are seen regularly. If you're particularly lucky, you may hear the hum of a hovering Calliope hummingbird, Canada's tiniest bird. In summer the park is extremely popular, so reserve a spot up to three months in advance by calling the Discover Camping Campground Reservation Service (800–689–9025), which operates between March 1 and September 15. You'll get to talk to a real person between 7:00 A.M. and 7:00 P.M. weekdays and 9:00 A.M. to 5:00 P.M. on weekends. For more information on Osoyoos's attractions and accommodation, contact the **Osoyoos Visitor Info Centre** at the junction of Highways 3 and 97 (Box 227, Osoyoos, V0H 1V0; 250–495–7142 or 888–676–9667; fax: 250–495–6161; tourism@osoyooschamber.bc.ca; www.osoyooschamber.bc.ca).

Still on the lake, but north and east of Osoyoos (across the bridge) is the famous **Desert Ecological Reserve.** Prickly pear cactus, rock rose, antelope bush, and desert creatures such as the endangered burrowing owl, northwestern Pacific rattlesnakes, western painted turtles, black widow spiders, and scorpions all defy human intrusion in this unique terrain. Creatures found nowhere else in Canada include kangaroo rats, praying

The Wild Rose

*T*he wild rose held spiritual significance for the Okanagan First Nations people. They ritually placed branches of the bush around a recently deceased person's house to prevent him or her from returning to haunt those left behind. The relatives then drank wild rose tea as an extra protection. Before burial, the grave was swept clean with wild rose branches, to keep mourners from being drawn into the earth and to protect the dead person from bad spirits.

mantises, a bird called the sage thrasher, and the Great Basin spadefoot toad. Controversy hovers over whether this is a true desert, and whether this "vest-pocket desert" is the tip of the Sonoran Desert extending up from Mexico into Canada. The truth is that because of the variation in ideas on what a desert is or isn't, there will always be this confusion. Xerophytic vegetation of a type rare in Canada exists here, but this alone does not a desert make. It's located on the Osoyoos Indian Reserve and covers approximately 247 acres (100 ha). Contact the Osoyoos Indian Band, or Nk'mip as it is known in the native Okanagan language (RR 3, Site 25, C1, Oliver, V0H 1T0; 250–498–3444), for permission to visit in the off-season. Between May and September access is via their campground, *Nk'mip Campground and R.V. Park* (250–495–7279; fax: 775–587–8957; campsite@oib.ca; www.campingosoyoos.com), on Osoyoos Lake's eastern shore. Check the map on the Web site for an excellent close-up view of the desert, campground, and lake. A twenty-minute desert walking trail and an all-day trail have been added to aid persons interested in learning about the desert. Turn off Highway 3 East (Main Street) at Forty-fifth Street, just past the windmill and the *Little Duffer Ice Cream Parlor and Mini Golf* (250–495–6354), and drive north approximately a mile. En route you'll pass the *Indian Grove Riding Stable* (250–495–7555 June 28 to Labor Day, 250–498–4478 off-season; fax: 250–498–4463). Aaron Stelkaia and his staff will lead you through this fascinating desert on mild-mannered horses. You'll wind down into a canyon to underground waterfalls, where you'll be treated to a huge steak dinner—barbecued and ready to eat after you've done some fishing or have had a refreshing swim. You'll possibly see rattlesnakes, deer, bear, coyotes, or bighorn sheep on the way. It's an all-day ride (9:30 A.M. to 7:30 P.M.) and costs $125, but small children can double up with a parent for free. Circular (one hour or so) short rides through the desert cost $25. Ask Aaron, too, about pony rides for the kids. He has operated here for about thirty years and has extensive knowledge about the area's history.

You'll see some of this history if you turn off Highway 97 about 7 miles (12 km) north of Osoyoos onto Road 22. Cross a rickety wooden bridge over an irrigation canal ("The Ditch") onto Black Sage Road, a paved but quiet road that passes the old *Haynes Ranch House*. Here you'll find excellent photo opportunities at a historic site.

Haynes Ranch House near Osoyoos, Okanagan

In dramatic contrast as you continue north along Black Sage Road, vineyards replace the arid pastures. The Okanagan has entered the world arena in wine growing, with many high-quality wines winning national and international awards in recent years. One little gem of a winery along this road is *Carriage House Wines* (Black Sage Road, RR 1, Site 46, Comp 19, Oliver, V0H 1T0; phone/fax: 250–498–8818). Keep heading north to just past Orchard Grove Lane. David Wagner, the "only home-grown vintner in the area," works an 8.5-acre (3.4-ha) small winery with his wife, Karen, and produces pinot noir, merlot, cabernet sauvignon, Kerner, and chardonnay wines. Savoring the aroma of a 1996 Kerner, a mandatory prelude before the sip, swirl, and swallow of this delicious wine, even my inexpert nose told me I had found something special. Carriage House Wines, where they "pride themselves on being small," is open daily for tours from 10:00 A.M. to 6:00 P.M. May 1 to October 31 or anytime by appointment. If you're coming from Oliver, take Road 9 left off Highway 97, left again onto Orchard Grove Lane, and left again onto Black Sage Road.

> ### Trivia
>
> *Osoyoos* is the Spanish Capital of Canada (based on its climate and buildings), and *Oliver* is British Columbia's Canteloupe City.

After the First World War, British Columbia's premier, known as "Honest John Oliver," envisioned an irrigation canal, which would bring the dry Sonora Desert region (near the southern Okanagan Lake area) to life. Completed in 1923, the "Ditch" soon transformed this desert region into lush orchards and farms.

From the winery there's a lovely view of the Southern Okanagan Valley to other larger vineyards, notably **Tinhorn Creek** (RR1 S58 C10, Oliver, V0H 1T0; 250–498–3743 or 888–4–TIN-HORN; fax: 250–498–3228; winery@tinhorn. com; www.tinhorn. com) and **Gehringer Brothers Estate Winery** (RR 1, S-23, C-4, Oliver, V0H 1T0; 250–498–3537; fax: 498– 3510), which leads me to understand that there is some truth to the rumor that the Oliver postal code, V0H 1T0, really does stand for "View of heaven in the Okanagan." Oliver & District Chamber of Commerce (36205 Ninety-third Street, Box 460, Oliver, V0H 1T0; 250–498–6321; fax: 250–498–3156; info@oliver chamber.bc.ca; www.oliverchamber.bc.ca) is an extensive source of information on this area, including its beaches and parks, the **Fairview Jail,** the **Oliver and District Museum** (located in the former 1924 police station at 9726–350 Street), and the fascinating **McIntyre Bluff** at the south end of Vaseux Lake. Sometimes called Indian Head, it has pictographs depicting legends about rival Indian bands who drove each other over the edge of these 820-foot (250-m) cliffs.

From Oliver take the Fairview–White Lake Road, which runs northwest from the gold rush town of Fairview to the **Dominion Radio Astrophysical Observatory** (Box 248, Penticton, V2A 6K3; 250–493–2277; fax: 250–493–7767; www.drao.nrc.ca/). If you're coming from Penticton, turn off Highway 97 at Kaleden junction onto White Lake Road; from the west turn off Highway 3A onto the White Lake Road at Twin Lakes. Should you still not find it, simply ask a friendly local where the White Lake observatory is.

A tour of the complex (which is part of the National Research Council of Canada) takes you past a row of seven antennae that work together to simulate a giant 1,969-foot (600-m) telescope. The most prominent "dish" antenna is 85 feet (26 m) across. At the visitors' center displays explain how images from these telescopes are used to probe the invisible gases between the stars. Canadian scientists here are working to understand how stars are born, how they die, and how stars and gas are interrelated in the Milky Way. Beyond the visitors' center is a smaller radio telescope that monitors the radio output from the sun. From these data scientists can research global climate change. Because ignition systems can emit radio waves that interfere with the astronomers' observations, you must leave your car in a parking lot and walk about 600 yards to the observatory grounds. Canada's only radio observatory is open all year during daylight hours. Free lectures and demonstrations are held on Sundays in July and August from 2:00 to 5:00 P.M.

North of Oliver, snugged between Vaseaux and Skaha Lakes, lies Okanagan Falls. Try the cinnamon buns at the *Falls Restaurant* (1032 Main; 250–497–5898)—they're legendary.

As you approach *Penticton,* you'll know exactly where you are by the large sign visible on the east side of the highway on Munson Mountain. Then head for the beach, the most popular area here. Ask at the *Penticton Visitor Info Centre* (888 Westminster Avenue West, Penticton, V2A 8S2; 250–493–4055 or 800–663–5052; fax: 250–492–6119; visitor@ penticton.org; www.penticton.org) about the *SS Sicamous,* a nineteenth-century beached stern-wheeler, now a heritage site, and the *Rose Garden* next door, with hundreds of varieties of roses. You'll never have to worry about losing the kids at the beach; just tell them to meet you at the *Big Peach on the Beach,* a popular concession stand open on those lazy, hazy days.

Just south of Penticton is a world-renowned climbing area known as *Skaha Bluffs*. If coming from the south on Highway 97, turn east at the northern end of Skaha Lake (site of an annual 7.38-mile [11.8-km] Ultra Swim) from South Main Street (where it meets Lakeside Road at Skaha East Park) onto Crescent Hill Road. At the top of the hill turn south onto Valley View Road, which eventually deteriorates into a winding narrow road, to the Braeside parking lot (locked in winter) at the end. From the parking lot, follow the trail east along the fence to the bluffs. There's an honor-system $5-per-day fee here, but climbers attest to the value considering the quality of climbing offered. Don't be put off, though, the Skaha Bluffs cater to all levels of climbing. Look for California bighorn sheep and perhaps a rattlesnake, keeping in mind that this is a fragile wildlife and plant habitat and that any disturbances can have a serious effect.

Okanagan summers are the warmest in British Columbia, so cooling-off spots between Penticton and Summerland (like *Kickinninee* and *Sun-Oka* beaches on Okanagan Lake) are popular spots. With more hours of summer sunshine than Hawaii, though, make sure you're well protected.

Okanagan Salad Days

*S*andra Hainle sent me this wonderful salad recipe that she gleaned from Chef David Forestell of the Amphora Bistro. It makes good use of simple ingredients available from any of the dozens of produce stalls in the area. It's well matched with a dry, full-bodied white wine such as Hainle's certified organic Pinot Blanc. Perfect to accompany your Okanagan beach holiday barbecue.

Green and Yellow Bean Salad Dressed with a Warm Bacon Vinaigrette
(serves 6–8)

For Salad:

1 lb. fresh green beans

3/4 lb. fresh yellow beans

1/2 c. chives (2" lengths)

1/4 c. Italian parsley leaves

1/4 c. celery leaves

2 c. roughly chopped yellow

tomatoes (optional)

For Dressing:

1/2 lb. good quality bacon, diced

1 c. cubed yellow potatoes

1/2 c. thinly sliced shallots

4 cloves garlic, minced

1/4 c. grainy Dijon mustard

1/3 c. apple cider (hard or soft)

1/3 c. apple cider vinegar

1/2 c. good olive oil

salt and freshly ground black pepper

Trim beans and blanch them in boiling water until "al dente." Plunge them into cold water immediately to freshen. Drain and combine in large serving bowl with other salad ingredients (except yellow tomatoes, if using).

To prepare dressing cook bacon in a heavy skillet or Dutch oven over medium heat until crisp. Remove bacon from pan with slotted spoon and set aside. Drain all but 3 tbsp. of fat from pan and return pan to heat. Add potatoes and cook over medium-high heat until they start to brown. Add shallots and continue to cook, stirring frequently, until they are lightly browned. Add garlic and cook for another 1–2 minutes and season lightly with salt and pepper. Add mustard to pan and stir to combine with other ingredients. Cook for a few minutes, and when moisture is almost gone, add apple cider and cook over high heat until volume is reduced by half. Remove from heat and add remaining ingredients, including the reserved bacon. Season to taste with salt and pepper.

While the dressing is still warm, pour it over the salad ingredients, toss to combine, and let sit 15 minutes before serving. If using the yellow tomatoes, add them just before serving.

Summerland is a major fruit-growing and processing center. Pomology (the science of fruit growing) and viticulture (the cultivation of grapes) are carried out at the *Summerland Research Station*. This research is in various fields, including breeding to develop new tree fruit and grape varieties, cultural practices to obtain optimum fruit quality and increase yields, and harvesting and storage research. Visit the *Summerland Research Station Gardens* (250–494–6385; fax: 250–494–0755), a project of the Friends of Summerland Research Station, and wander through ten acres of spectacular ornamental gardens. There's also an interpretive center in a country-style cottage. The station is operated by Agriculture Canada and is open to the public in summer. Contact PARC Summerland, 4200 Highway 97 South, Box 1363, Summerland, V0H 1Z0; PARC@em.agr.ca for more information.

The fruit-growing industry was helped in its early days by steam trains. A ride on the *Kettle Valley Steam Railway* (Box 1288, Summerland, V0H 1Z0; 877–494–8424; 250–494–8422; toll free: 877–494–8424; kvr@telus.net; www.kettlevalleyrail.org) will help transport you back to this time. It departs from Prairie Valley Station (May to October). Phone ahead for operating days and hours. Adult fares are $14.00, seniors and youths $13.00, children four to twelve $10.00, under four free; the family rate is $49.00.

There's more railway memorabilia at the *Summerland Museum Historical Society* (9521 Wharton Street, Box 1491, Summerland, V0H 1Z0; 250–494–9395; smhschin@vip.net; www2.vip.net/~smhschin) as well as a collection of historical photographs and pioneer tools used in fruit growing. The museum is open year-round: Monday–Saturday in June, July, and August from 10:00 A.M. to 4:00 P.M.; Tuesday–Saturday September–May from 1:00 to 4:00 P.M. For more information ask at the *Summerland Visitor Info Centre* (15600 Highway 97, Box 1075, Summerland, V0H 1Z0; 250–494–2686; fax: 250–494–4039; schamber@vip.net; www.summerlandchamber.bc.ca).

If you need accommodation, *Beachside B&B* is located, as its name implies, right on the beach at 15811 North Lakeshore Road, Summerland, V0H 1Z0; phone/fax: (250) 494–8977; carroyl@vip.net. Head toward the lake from Highway 97 along Peach Orchard Road, just south of Summerland, and turn north on North Lakeshore Road.

From the comfort of the beachfront patio, you might be lucky enough to see Ogopogo, as members of the BC Cryptozoology Club (BCCC) did during the summer of 1989. The following is a quote from their report:

The focus of the investigation turned to Summerland, and a particularly good vantage point was located at Peach Orchard Beach, Lower Summerland, on July 30. All four members of the investigating team were stationed at various points on the beachfront when, at 3:55 P.M., a most extraordinary occurrence took place. A large patch of white water materialised close to a headland at the southern end of the beach, drawing the attention of the BCCC observers. It was about 1,000 feet distant at this point, and it was clear that a large animal was swimming in a northerly direction against the prevailing wind and slight swell . . . this was the classic Ogopogo, with its humps well above the water level . . . The animal displayed, variously, five and sometimes six humps . . . the animal's skin was whale-like, and there appeared to be random, calcium-like deposits under the skin which appeared to be similar to barnacles in shape. All the team members agree that the animal was between 30 and 35 feet (9-10 m) in length, and was almost 3 feet (1 m) above the surface at its highest point—that being the middle hump.

Cynics and skeptics may laugh, but you just never know . . .

Back on Highway 97 the winding highway climbs past vineyards and rocky cliffs bordering Okanagan Lake to Peachland, 13 miles (21 km) north. Here Peter and Daffnaee Flanagan operate a small, bright, family business, **Okanagan Pottery Studio** (6030 Highway 97S, Peachland, V0H 1X0; fax: 250–767–2010; fax: 250–767–2540). Here you'll see many of the artists' works decorated in strong purples and greens and with grape-leaf designs inspired by the beauty of the Okanagan. The studio was built by Daffnaee's father, Des Loan, in 1968, and the original kiln is still in operation. Peter's work has been honored with the Special Judges' Award at Mino, Japan. Look for French butter dishes in varying sizes. The butter sits in the "lid." Water in the bottom forms a seal, preserving the butter without refrigeration. The dishes are small, practical, and inexpensive if you're looking for an Okanagan souvenir. The Flanagans have joined forces with Roy and Jean Lysholt to create wrought-iron patio furniture and lamps beautifully combined with pieces of their unique Okanagan pottery.

Another interesting stop heading north along Highway 97 (just past the huge Golf Ball on the roadside) *is Hainle Vineyards Estate Winery* (5355 Trepanier Bench Road, Peachland, V0H 1X0; 250–767–2525; fax: 250–767–2543; 800–767–3109 for wine orders; tilman@hainle.com; www.hainle.com), a small, family-run winery producing naturally dry, fully fermented wines. In addition to a tasting room, wine shop, and bistro (*Amphora Bistro*), where tasty lunch specials both complement and compliment their wines, the winery offers a spectacular view of the valley. Their Icewine is a rare wine made by allowing the fruit to freeze on the vine to at least 17° F (-8° C). This requires an early morning workforce frantically picking, crushing, and pressing before the warm sun thaws the grapes. The frozen water from the fruit remains in the press, and from the concentrated juice, wines result that range from sherrylike to fruity and from almost dry to rich and sweet. Hainle Winery boasts several firsts: It's located on what used to be the first peach orchard in the area, giving Peachland its name; it has the first winery-based cooking school (classes started in September 1998); Tilman's father, Walter Hainle, was the first person in Canada to make Icewine (1973), a product that is now making Canadian wines renowned around the world; it's the first winery to label its bottles "certified organic"; and as well, it's the first British Columbia winery to have its own Web site (through which wines can be ordered). Summer hours are Tuesday to Sunday, 10:00 A.M. to 5:00 P.M. (closed Monday). At the Amphora Bistro lunch is served noon to 3:00 P.M., but reservations are required. In winter the winery is open Thursday to Sunday, noon to 5:00 P.M., but call ahead for Bistro hours.

All over the Okanagan, *wine* is the word. The Okanagan Wine Festivals have been recognized as being among the *Top 100 Events in North America* for the past seven years. For four days during the first weekend of every May, the *Okanagan Spring Wine Festival* takes place when valley vintners release their new wines. If you time your visit for early

Recommended Reading - The Okanagan-Similkameen

Ogopogo: The True Story of the Okanagan Lake Million Dollar Monster, by Arlene Gaal. Hancock House. Surrey, 2000.

Exploring the Kettle Valley Railway, by Beth Hill. Polestar Book Publishers, 1989.

McCulloch's Wonder: The Story of the Kettle Valley Railway, by Barrie Sanford. Graphic Arts Center Publishing Co., 1998

Similkameen and South Okanagan, by Murphy Shewchuk. Surrey: Hancock House, 1987.

Okanagan Trips and Trails: A Guide to Backroads and Hiking Trails, by Judy Steeves and Murphy Shewchuk. Sonotek Publishing, 1999

Trivia

October, you'll be inundated with bacchanal choices at the *Annual Fall Okanagan Wine Festival,* a hopping event with more than one hundred diverse choices, from grape stomps, wine biking tours, and pig roasts to a chocolate and port buffet. Winter visitors (late January) can discover the magic and delicacy of icewine at the *Annual Icewine Festival.* Contact the Okanagan Wine Festivals Office (1527 Ellis Street, Kelowna, V1Y 2A7; 250–861–6654; fax: 250–861–3942; info@owfs.com; www.owfs.com) for information and bookings.

From the west your introduction to *Kelowna* (population 100,000 and growing fast) is via a 2,000-foot (640-m) floating bridge, North America's first and largest. You're still in Ogopogo territory, so keep a look out as you cross Okanagan Lake. Long before the first mission settlement by Father Pandosy in 1860, Interior Salish folklore told of a mysterious monster called N'ha-a-itk, the Devil of the Lake. According to the tale, if you see a long, snake-like, humpy, greenish oddity with a horselike head, you'll be the next believer. Could this be the reason Kelowna is labeled "City of Smiles"?

Just past the community of Westbank (home of *Mission Hill Winery,* which was awarded the International Wine and Spirits Avery Trophy in 1994 for the best chardonnay in the world), both avid golfers and beginners have a chance to play on Canada's first All-Putting golf course at *19 Greens* (2050 Campbell Road, Kelowna, V1Z 3X7; 250–769–0213), a par 72, eighteen-hole course, creatively configured with putting in mind and with a spectacular view of Okanagan Lake. Turn right onto Campbell Road just before the floating bridge. Designed by Les Furber, the course is fully lit for starlight putting.

For a panoramic view of this smiling city, named Canada's most beautiful small city in 1998, hike or bike a route created by the *Kettle Valley Railway* through the horseshoe-shaped *Myra Canyon.* A one-hour bike trip over eighteen trestle bridges and through two tunnels will reveal breathtaking views of the canyon and Kelowna below. Local enthusiasts (Myra Canyon Trestle Restoration Society, PBC Box 611, Kelowna, V1Y 7P7; www.members.cnx.net/myra) are restoring these old trestles in what is soon to be a provincial park. The railway was first used in 1915, but it was abandoned in the seventies, and the trestles left to rot. The best time to hike or bike is on the weekend, as the very rough logging roads leading up to the canyon are active logging roads. For a guided tour contact *Monashee Adventure Tours* (250–762–9253 or 888–76CYCLE; fax: 250–868–9214; monasheeadventure tours@home.com; www.vtours.com/monashee/). They specialize in tours of the Kettle Valley Railroad no matter what level of rider you are; recently the local "tourist watchdog" honored them with a Best of Kelowna rating. Bike tours run mid-May to October, and everything is provided, right down to the water bottle. Depending on numbers in the group, rates range from $60 to $100 including lunch and trail snacks, for an afternoon in the glorious Myra Canyon.

If you prefer a one-way ride, *Air-Hart Aviation* (1326 Water Street, Kelowna, V1Y 9P3; 250–762–9830; toll free: 877–766–6699; fax: 250–762–9840; airhart@home.com; www.air-hart.com) will fly you and your bike to McCulloch Lake for a full day's cycle along the Kettle Valley Railway to the Okanagan's oldest orchard, where you'll savor freshly pressed juice and seasonal fruit. The $159 cost includes the floatplane ride, guide, gear rental, snack, and return transport to Kelowna.

After a strenuous hike you'll need a restful night. *A View to Remember Bed and Breakfast* (1090 Trevor Drive, Kelowna, V1Z 2J8; 888–311–9555; phone/fax: 250–769–4028; bnbview@cnx.net; www. kelownabandb.com), will provide all the rest you may need. This elegant home is decorated with antiques inside and lovely gardens outside. Enjoy the fruit from these gardens on a patio with a superb view of the lake and mountains. From Highway 97 take the Hudson exit south, turn right on Guidi Road and left onto Trevor Drive. Rates are in the $80–$95 (double) range.

Kelowna is fast gaining a reputation as a cultural destination, attested to by the soon to be completed 35,000-square-foot (3,252-sq-m) *Kelowna Visual and Performing Arts Centre* and the impressive *Kelowna Art Gallery* (1315 Water Street, Kelowna, V1Y 9R3; 250–762–2226; fax: (250) 762–9875; kelowna.artgallery@home.com; www.galleries. bc.ca/ kelowna). Nearby, next to the BC Orchard Museum, *The Wine Museum* (1304 Ellis Street; 250–868–0441; fax: 250–868–9272) not only offers tastings of world-class Okanagan wines, but also displays early wine-making and barrel-making equipment. A feature is a 3,000-

Trivia

Drive over to Magnetic Hill in northeast Vernon and experience the strange forces involved when you and your car mysteriously seem to be pulled "uphill." The "magnetic" spot is on Dixon Dam Road, between Hughes and Hartnell Roads. Go to Hughes Road and then travel south on Dixon Dam Road past seven alder trees; stop at the second tree, put the car in neutral, and then listen to the kids say: "Oh wow!"

year-old clay drinking horn excavated in Iran. The museum is open Monday to Saturday 10:00 A.M.–5:00 P.M. and Sunday noon–5:00 P.M.

South of the city, off the KLO Road near Pandosy Street, is the **Tutt Street Square** (3045 Tutt Street). Here a charming teahouse called **The Gathering Room** (250–861–4188) serves wonderful homemade soups and herb breads, English and herbal teas, chocolates, Caesar salads, lattes, cappuccinos, award-winning cheesecakes, and lemon curd tarts—such a deliciously eclectic array of food. A stained-glass division separates the tearoom from its small gift shop. The Gathering Room is open Monday–Saturday 9:30 A.M. to 4:30 P.M. and Sunday in summer from 11:00 A.M. to 3:00 P.M. Across from the Gathering Room at the **Tutt Street Gallery** (#9, 3045 Tutt Street, Kelowna, V1Y 2H4; phone/fax: 250–861–4992; www.tuttstreetgallery.com), watercolors, oils, raku, bronzes—all top-quality works by Canadian artists—are displayed for sale. The gallery is open Tuesday to Friday 10:00 A.M. to 5:00 P.M. and to 4:00 P.M. Saturdays.

Whatever your needs in the Kelowna area, the **Kelowna Visitor Info Centre,** just east of the Floating Bridge at 544 Harvey Avenue (Highway 97), Kelowna, V1Y 6C9; (250) 861–1515 or (800) 663–4345; fax: (250) 861–3624; info@tourismkelowna.org; www.tourismkelowna.org, will help you enjoy all aspects of this lovely city.

> **Trivia**
>
> *Vernon has Western Canada's only floral clock. It's located in Polson Park, south of town on the corner of Highway 97 and Twenty-fifth Avenue.*

The staff will probably convince you that wine rules in the Okanagan! Not to be outdone by California's Napa Valley Wine Train, the **Okanagan Valley Wine Train** (888–674–8725; 250–712–9888; fax: 780–482–7666; funtrain@telusplanet.net; www.okanaganwinetrain.com) is one of Kelowna's newest and most popular attractions. It runs between Kelowna and Vernon from June 28 to October 1, Fridays, Saturdays, and Sundays, and combines the love of wine (preferred seating in the Club Galley Car offers wine tasting), the beauty of the Okanagan, and the romance of the rails. It leaves from Kelowna, taking ninety minutes to reach Vernon, and passes three beautiful lakes: Okanagan, Wood, and Kalamalka. In Vernon passengers have about two and a half hours to perhaps enjoy a cooked-to-perfection meal at **Andy's Added Touch** (3006 Thirtieth Avenue; 250–549–4706)—on Main Street at the Kamalka Hotel—before heading back to Kelowna.

The North Okanagan

I f you didn't get the chance to discover the northern Okanagan on the Wine Train, take Highway 97 along the east coast of Okanagan Lake for 29 miles (46 km) north to **Vernon**. **Agri-tourism** is a word often heard in this area; it refers to the many specialty livestock and fruit and vegetable operations open to the public. Just a few miles north of Vernon at Armstrong, Tony and Connie Seale welcome visitors to their llama-breeding establishment at **The Llama Farm** (250–546–3038; llmafarm@junction.net). Take Highway 97A northeast from Armstrong to McLeod Road, then to the corner of Heighton Road. Farther on at the end of McLeod Road you'll find **Chickadee Ridge Miniatures** (Box 71, Armstrong, V0E 1B0; 250–546–9323; fax: 250–546–8905; info@ chickadeeridge.com; www.chickadeeridge.com), where they invite you to bring the kids to "Come talk to the animals." There are several varities of miniature animals, a gift store, and a concession stand. It's open season-ally from 10:00 A.M. to 4:00 P.M. at 1403 McLeod Road. At **Little Mountain Peruvians** (5231 Stepney Road, Armstrong; 250–546–3970; little mountain@ telus.net), visitors are always welcome to watch Peruvian *pasos* being trained. Take Highway 97A 3 miles (5 km) north to Stepney Road and follow it for 3 miles (5 km) to the end.

And if you've never seen alpacas, Canada's largest herd can be found at **Okanagan Alpaca Company** (3285 Mabel Lake Road, Site 14A, Comp 9, RR 2, Enderby, V0E 1V0; phone/fax: 250–838–9559; okalpaca@ cnx.net; www.okalpaca.com). In 1989 Harold Berkholtz brought the first alpacas into Canada from Peru. Now he and his wife, Linda, wel-come visitors to tour their one-hundred-acre farm on the Shuswap River, 20 miles (32.85 km—hence the address) east of the Enderby bridge in the scenic Monashee Mountains. And it's all free! Children love having their photos taken with these gentle animals, and if visit-ing between mid-May to mid-September, they may have an opportu-nity to pet *las crías* (the baby alpacas). You'll see both huacuya and the rare, silky-fleeced suri alpaca—about 500 animals in all—as well as a herd of about sixty llamas. A gift shop specializes entirely in alpaca and llama products.

Plan to stay a few days in the area. As well as a few B&B establishments, next door to the llamas there's a twenty-site campground, **Kingfisher Campground and Store** (3303 Mabel Lake Road, Enderby, V0E 1V0; 250–838–7730; fax: 250–838–6697), where delicious homemade pizzas and other meals are served. About 7 miles (12 km) west of the alpaca farm is the **Kingfisher Environmental Interpretive Centre** (250–838–0004). Call for more information or a tour of the hatchery, which has one of the most successful salmon enhancement programs in Canada. You'll also see here a half-sized replica of a kekuli, the traditional underground home of the Shuswap Indians.

"U-pick" farming is becoming popular in the North Okanagan. At **MacDonald's Pure Beeswax** (250–546–3237), between Vernon and Armstrong at 4663 North Grandview Flats Road, you'll find not only prize-winning honey and beeswax candles, but apricots and cherries ripe for the picking. Take Highway 97 north to St. Anne's Road. Continue north to South Grandview Flats Road, then west onto North Grandview Flats Road and look for the HONEY FOR SALE sign. If you'd prefer to pick apples, pears, or plums, call **Cayford's Orchard** (250–546–3411) at 4377 Hallam Road, about 2 miles northwest of Armstrong off the Salmon River Road. Of course, you have to be there in season. Contact the **Vernon Visitor Info Centre** (701 Highway 97 South, Box 520, Vernon, V1T 6M4; 250–542–1415; fax: 250–542–3256; 800–665–0795 for reservations only; info@vernontourism.com; www.vernontourism.com) for information on fruit-growing seasons and to find out about other farms involved in this fast-growing agritourism industry.

Kettle River Valley

Four miles (6.5 km) east of the Kelowna floating bridge, the lonely Highway 33 winds south from Highway 97 for 80 miles (129 kms), following the course of the Kettle River through pretty, pastoral landscapes. A side road (watch out for cattle and deer) brings you to the **Big White Ski Resort** (800–663–2772 or 250–765–8888; fax: 250–765–8200; bigwhite@bigwhite.com; www.bigwhite.com), 34 miles (55 km) from Kelowna and on the edge of the Monashees. With more than 24 feet (7.5 m) of champagne powder annually, expect some superb skiing here. You'll also find Canada's fastest and longest quad chairlift, the Gem Lake Express. It runs at 20 feet (6 m) per second. In summer, the slopes are more peaceful. With beautiful views of the Monashees, good fishing, and lovely walks, consider a stay at the award-winning **White Crystal Inn,** located in the heart of the village. The rooms are large; it's open year-round and offers excellent dining. Double accommodation starts at $59 in summer.

Halfway along Highway 33, at Beaverdell, is the historic **Beaverdell Hotel** (Box 40, Beaverdell, V0H 1A0; 250–484–5513), where a wall inscription in The Ladies Parlour reads: "Oh what stories she could tell," and promenades us back to an exciting era invoking memories of the heady days of old. The hotel, built in 1901, claims significance as the oldest operating hotel in British Columbia. Check out the old car in the yard beside the hotel (there isn't much more) and then get ready to explore the Kootenays when you reach tiny Rock Creek (population fifty-one) 31 miles (51 km) south, just north of the Canada–U.S. border on Highway 3. We're back on the Crowsnest.

PLACES TO STAY IN THE OKANAGAN-SIMILKAMEEN

KELOWNA
A View to Remember Bed and Breakfast,
1090 Trevor Drive,
V1Z 2J8; (888) 311–9555;
phone/fax: (250) 769–4028; bnbview@cnx.net;
www.kelownabandb.com.
Rates: $80–$95.

KEREMEOS
Cathedral Lakes Lodge,
(888) 255–4453 or
(250) 352–3724;
fax: (250) 354–0230;
www.cathedral-lakes-lodge.com.

Login Bed and Breakfast,
C1 Site 27, Highway 3 West,
V0X 1N0;
(250) 499–2781/2664;
loginbnb@keremeos.
com; www. keremeos.
net/loginbnb.

OSOYOOS/OLIVER
Haynes Point Lakeside
Guest House,
3619 Jasmine Drive,
V0H 1V0; phone/fax:
(250) 495–7443;
www.bbcanada.
com/14.html. $70–$95
double.

Nk' mip Campground and
R.V. Park,
45th Street, Osoyoos,
(250) 495–7279.
Open June–September.
Serviced sites, store, wash-
rooms with showers, play-
ground.

PRINCETON
Princeton Castle Resort
and R.V. Park,
Princeton-Summerland
Road,
RR 1, Site 1, Comp 10,
V0X 1W0;
(888) 228–8881 or
(250) 295–7988;
info@castleresort.com;
www.castleresort.com.
Cottages, lodge, and RV
park.

SUMMERLAND
Beachside B & B,
15811 North Lakeshore
Road,
V0H 1Z0;
phone/fax: (250) 494–
8977; carroyl@vip.net.
Rates: $75–$95.

PLACES TO EAT IN THE OKANAGAN-SIMILKAMEEN

KELOWNA
The Gathering Room Tea
House,
3045 Tutt Street,
V1Y 2H4; (250) 861–4188.
Inexpensive and creative.

Water Street Grill,
1346 Water Street,
V1Y 9P4; (250) 860–0707.
Casual, interesting menu.
Open daily from 11:30 A.M.

KEREMEOS
The Grist Mill Tea Room,
RR 1, Upper Bench Road,
V0X 1N0; (250) 499–2888.
Inexpensive.

PEACHLAND
The Amphora Bistro,
at Hainle Vineyards,
5355 Trepanier Bench
Road,
V0H 1X0; (250) 767–2525.
Delicious stuff. Reservations required.

PRINCETON
The Belaire Restaurant,
161 Vermilion Avenue,
V0X 1W0; (250) 295–7711.
Popular for its homemade
pies and soups.

VERNON
Andy's Added Touch,
3006 30TH Avenue;
(250) 549–4706.
On Main Street at the Kalamalka Hotel. Full meals.

The Kootenays

The Monashee, Selkirk, and Purcell ranges straddle glacier-fed rivers and lakes to form this scenic area of British Columbia's interior, where the Ktunaxa people trace their unbroken presence back to before the last ice age. In the late 1800s a frenzied rush for precious metals brought newcomers. Many of the towns they built are now but ghostly remnants, but some grew, and today, with an excellent system of highways and free ferries, serve travelers wanting to explore this mountainous wilderness.

Our trek through the Kootenays starts in **Boundary County** close to the U.S. border in historic Greenwood and follows the Crowsnest Highway to Rossland, where a tour of a hard-rock gold mine gives us a taste of the fever that shook those early immigrants. We'll experience the Russian influence in the south as we enjoy borscht near a Doukhobor museum, then relive the mining past in a ghost town. We'll meet the interesting people of east Kootenay Lake, where ashrams, weavers, broom makers, blacksmiths, and an embalming-bottle house will arouse our curiosity.

Greenwood

After leaving the Okanagan we rejoin the Crowsnest (Highway 3) and travel east to **Greenwood,** Canada's smallest incorporated city. Located near the Washington State border, Greenwood features many historic buildings and sites. As you enter the city from the west, you'll see an old chimney on the north side of the highway. This marks the ruins of the **BC Copper Company Smelter** that operated between 1901 and 1918. It stands as a reminder of the mining history of the city. A sign indicates a track to the 120-foot (40-m) chimney near **Lotzkar Memorial Park,** where an abandoned underground shaft and slag heaps evoke images of dusty miners.

You're still surrounded by history at the restored **Greenwood Inn Saloon/Restaurant** (321 Copper South; 250–445–6623), where his-

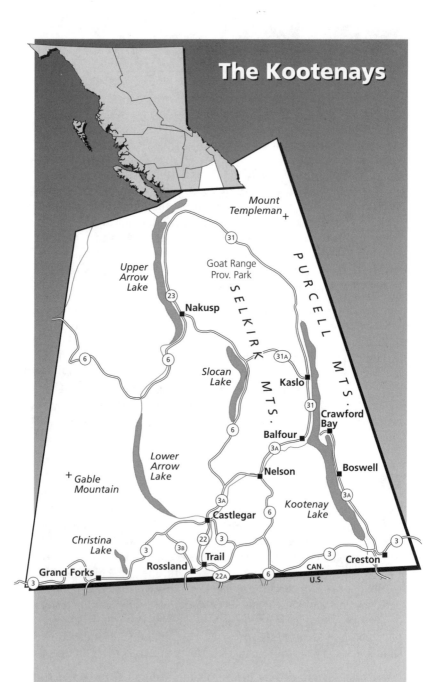

The Kootenays

Mount Templeman +

Upper Arrow Lake

Goat Range Prov. Park

PURCELL MTS.

S E L K I R K M T S.

31

23

Nakusp

Slocan Lake

31A

Kaslo

31

Crawford Bay

6

6

Balfour

3A

Boswell

Lower Arrow Lake

Nelson

+ Gable Mountain

3A

Kootenay Lake

3A

Castlegar

6

Christina Lake

22

3

3

Grand Forks

3

3B

Trail

Rossland

22A

6

CAN.
U.S.

3

Creston

AUTHOR'S TOP TEN PICKS IN THE KOOTENAYS

Phoenix Forest and History Tour, Greenwood

Red Mountain, Rossland

Doukhobor Village Museum, Castlegar

Ainsworth Hot Springs Resort

S.S. Moyie, in Kaslo

Sandon Ghost Town

Yasodhara Ashram, Riondel

North Woven Broom Company, Crawford Bay

The Glass House, in Boswell

Creston Valley Wildlife Management Area

toric photos depict Greenwood at the turn of the century. In those days the city supported one hundred businesses, including fourteen hotels, two newspapers, two banks, and a thousand-seat opera house. At present its population is just 900, and there's certainly no sign of an opera house. But the Greenwood Inn has survived and operated continuously for more than one hundred years. Check out (or perhaps do a little leaning on) the 30-foot-long (9-m) antique bar. Next door, at the **Greenwood Art and Expresso Cafe** (250–445–2234; jovan@sunshine cable.com), you'll enjoy home-style breakfasts and lunches surrounded by some exciting artwork. There's more history in the form of a player piano and several other antiques at the **Copper Eagle Cappuccino and Bakery** (325 Copper South, 250–445–6121), where the cinnamon buns and lattes are legendary.

On a city walking tour, take a look at Hammersly House (perhaps the friendly owners may give you a tour), the City Hall (excellent stained glass upstairs in the court room), the Sacred Heart Catholic church (high up on the hill), and the red-brick, towered Greenwood Post Office, with its antique, hourly chiming clock. Ask at the **Greenwood Museum** (214 Copper Street, Greenwood, V0H 1J0; 250–445–6355), in front of City Hall, or at the seasonal Visitor Info Booth for directions. Check www.city.greenwood.bc.ca for extensive information. The museum is open daily in summer from 10:00 A.M. to 5:00 P.M. and is worth a visit for its interesting collection of mining relics and photos of nearby Phoenix, now defunct, but at one time the highest city in Canada and home of the first Canadian professional hockey team.

The **Phoenix Forest and History Tour** is a two-hour, self-guided driving tour that takes you past the old **Phoenix Cemetery,** where towering Douglas fir trees now grow beside graves of young miners and victims of the 1918–1919 influenza epidemic. A detailed brochure that makes the tour much more interesting is available from the Ministry of Forests, Boundary Forest District, 136 Sagamore Avenue, Grand Forks, V0H 1H0 (250–442–5411), or at either the Greenwood or Grand Forks museums or the Chamber of Commerce in Grand Forks. The drive starts (or ends) in Greenwood at the junction of Highway 3 and

Phoenix Road, covering 13.6 miles (22 km) of well-maintained road. You'll pass an area around Marshall Lake that is now a cross-country skier's dream, with more than 10 miles (17 km) of trails. Alpine skiing is nearby at the **Phoenix Ski Hill** (250–442–2813), where runs are named after the old copper mines. Ask, too, (at the museum) for brochures to do a hiking/biking/horseback-riding tour.

The folks (Faith and Ron) at the **Lind Valley Guest Ranch** (Box 362 Greenwood, V0H 1J0; phone/fax: 250–445–6585; lindra@felus.net; www. boundary.bc. ca/LindValley/) will also take you to this Phoenix area—on easygoing horses. Take Greenwood Street past the Post Office to Lind Creek Road and drive 3 miles (5 km) to the ranch, where you'll discover more of an adventure than a place to sleep. It's set high up in the mountain valley. Guests see firsthand how an active cattle ranch works and can enjoy trail rides to deserted mining towns. Or if you really want to get into the backcountry, you can try an overnight wagon trip complete with campfire singing and storytelling—a trek into the past. Rates are very reasonable at $52 (double) including breakfast, or $95 (double) with three meals.

Grand Forks

Six miles (9.5 km) west of **Grand Forks** along Highway 3, keep an eye out for the abandoned two-story, red-brick **Doukhobor houses** and barns on the south side of the highway. The Doukhobors (or "spirit wrestlers") were a group of Russian pacifists who fled from persecution in Russia to Saskatchewan and Manitoba, only to be evicted again when they rejected the oath of allegiance. In 1908 they arrived in the Grand Forks area, where they farmed simply and were self-sufficient in almost every way. Although the communes are now deserted, the religion lives on.

As does the cuisine! Try a typical Russian meal at the **Chef's Garden Restaurant** (4415 Highway 3; 250–442–0257), 3 miles (5 km) west of Grand Forks at Rilkoff's General Store. "Russian Food from Russian Folks" is the claim, and delicious it is, too. Try the Galooptsi (cabbage rolls) or Nalesniki (Russian crepes filled with cottage cheese) or the Voreniki (potato-based dumplings). They also sell Russian souvenirs. Nearby, off Reservoir Road, enjoy country hospitality and homemade preserves at the **Orchard Bed and Breakfast** (5615 Spencer Road, RR 1, S850C, C3, Grand Forks, V0H 1H0; 250–442–8583).

Continue north along Reservoir Road to the **Fructova Doukhobor**

THE KOOTENAYS

Heritage Centre, open for tours from 1:00 to 4:00 P.M., Monday and Thursday, at 6110 Reservoir Road (250–442–3523), and on to Hardy Mountain Road, where you'll learn more about Doukhobor culture at the **Mountain View Doukhobor Museum**. Displayed here are handmade household articles, tools, costumes, and photographs. It's open June 1–September 30, 9:00 A.M. to 7:00 P.M. Phone the curator (250–442–8855) for information.

Continue down Hardy Mountain Road into **Grand Forks,** once a lively (perhaps raunchy) hub, with a colorful red-light district and a Chinatown. Rum running, logging, mining, and railroading ruled "The Forks," where the Granby and Kettle Rivers meet. Now the railways are gone, as are the smelters, but you can relive its history at the **Grand Forks Boundary Museum** (7370 Fifth Street, V0H 1H0; 250–442–3737; fax: 250–442–5688; jomiller@direct.ca) on the main street at the corner of Central Avenue. It's open Monday–Friday 8:00 A.M. to 4.30 P.M. and daily in summer.

Beside the museum at the **Visitor Info Centre** (7362 Fifth Street, Box 1086, Grand Forks, V0H 1H0; 250–442–2833; fax: 250–442–5688; gfchambe@sunshinecable.com), pick up a pamphlet to guide you on an 18-mile (30-km) drive or bike ride past the **Granby Mining and Smelter Company,** at one time the largest nonferrous copper smelter in the British Empire. Today a couple of slag heaps (now processed as Kleen Blast and used in sandblasting and roofing) are all that remain of the Granby smelter. Take the steel bridge over the Granby River (Granby Road) north to the **Hummingbird Bridge** (a fishing and swimming spot). Cross the bridge and take North Fork Franklin Road, which brings you back south to town past an old Columbia and Western Station, now the **Grand Forks Station Pub** (7654 Donaldson Drive; 250–442–5855), where you can enjoy pub-style meals.

Up on Rattlesnake Hill, overlooking Grand Forks (as you head east out of town) sits a huge Victorian mansion. The **Golden Heights Inn and Restaurant** (7342 Bluff Street; 250–442–0626; 888–933–5339; www.goldenheights.com) was shipped in pieces from California at the

Summer Theatre Production: Gold Fever Follies, *Rossland; July/August; (250) 362–5666 or (250) 362–9912*

Golden City Days Celebration, Fall Fair, and Rubberhead Classic Mountain Bike Festival, *Rossland; September; (250) 362–5666*

Silver City Days, *Trail; May; (250) 368–3144*

Nelson Artwalk, *Nelson; July/September; (250) 352–2402*

Kaslo Jazz Festival, *Kaslo; July/August; (250) 353–7538*

SS Moyie, Model Boat Regatta, *Kaslo; August; (250) 353–2525*

Castlegar Sunfest, *Castlegar; June; (250) 365–6313*

Castlegar Kayak Rodeo (on Slocan River), *Castlegar; September; (250) 365–6313*

Creston Blossom Festival, *Creston; May; (250) 428–4342*

turn of the century by a wealthy dentist-cum-mining-speculator, Dr. A. W. Averill, whose specialty was diamond fillings! His Golden Heights home featured a ballroom, a guest cottage, six fireplaces, and a stable. Even if you don't stay overnight or come for a gourmet meal, take a walk in the parklike gardens, complete with an orchard, a pond, and a gazebo.

Thirteen miles (20 km) beyond Grand Forks, the Crowsnest heads north, hugging the long and lovely *Christina Lake,* one of the warmest and clearest lakes in British Columbia. There are two provincial parks with lakefront sites (Gladstone and Christina Lake—contact BC Parks Okanagan District, Box 399, Summerland, V0H 1Z0; 250–494–6500; fax: 250–494–9737) and one Forest Service recreation site, which is accessible only by boat. As well, several commercial campgrounds (some with cabins) and a number of motels are located along the lake. Reservations for all accommodations at this very popular lake are recommended. Golfers will enjoy the eighteen-hole *Christina Lake Golf Course* (Box 1106, Grand Forks, V0H 1H0; 250–447–6104; fax: 250–447–6628; www.christinalakegolfclub.com), set among majestic pines next to the Kettle River, with the rugged Christina Range as a scenic backdrop. The course is professionally designed by Les Furber, and with a good sprinkling of bunkers and water hazards, it's a fair challenge. It's open April 1 to October 31.

My Personal Tour Guide

Years ago I lived in the Eastern Arctic, where I knew Richard and Trish Exner. Today they live in a pretty, blue-roofed house on a hilltop in Rossland. Twenty-one Christmas cards later, we strolled Rossland's San Francisco–like hills, remembering our Baffin days. Trish introduced me to some of the town's colorful characters. I met Lee Flanders, the barber, who joked he'd rather be a barber than one of those "schlubs down in the mine." We said hello to Jack McDonald, Rossland's historian, and Harry Lefebvre, who used to be the mayor. Maurice Samuelson ambled by; he used to be the postman. Trish was the consummate tour guide, taking me from hot pools to osprey nests to beautiful lookouts in the Silvery Slocan, and finally back to the Exner cottage on Kootenay Lake, which was mine to stay in "for as long as you like." That northern hospitality I remembered so well is alive and kicking in Rossland.

Kootenay South

ifteen miles (24 km) east of Christina Lake on Highway 3, the highway passes through mountains of scenic forests. Cedar, birch, fir, and hemlock stands lead to the Paulson Bridge, where the views down into McRae Creek are spectacular. *Bonanza Pass,* 6 miles (10 km) farther, cuts through the Monashees at 5,036 feet (1,535 m) shortly before the highway meets the 3B south to Rossland. At the junction winter travelers can enjoy the *Paulson Cross Country Ski Trail,* with its 28 miles (45 km) of track-set trails. Adjacent to it, *Nancy Greene Provincial Park* features a subalpine lake and pleasant hiking trails. For more information (and for all other provincial parks in this chapter, unless otherwise specified), contact BC Parks Kootenay District, Box 118, Wasa, V0B 2K0; (250) 422–4200; fax: (250) 422–3326.

Rossland

he Crowsnest follows Blueberry Creek to Castlegar, but first visit *Rossland,* 17 miles (28 km) south on Highway 3B. It sits at 3,398 feet (1,036 m) above sea level in the crater of an ancient volcano. In all seasons it erupts with life. In winter just ask any Red Mountain ski bum, and in spring, summer, or fall, dare to stop a mountain-biker blazing down one of the trails. Of the 3,800 folks who live in Rossland, more than 50 percent are under thirty-four, which might explain its lively, small-town feel.

Rossland is Nancy Greene country. A nationally recognized name for Olympic Gold success in alpine skiing, Nancy Greene has had named for her a lake, a mountain, a provincial park, and a recreation area. She started her climb to fame back in the sixties at the fabulous *Red Mountain* (Box 670, Rossland, V0G 1Y0; 250–362–7384; fax: 250–362–5833; 877–969–7669 for reservations; redmtn@ski-red.com; www.ski-red.com) home of Western Canada's first chairlift. The mountain itself is legendary among hard-core skiers and snowboarders for its steep, challenging terrain. But beginners need not fear, as Granite Mountain (part of the complex) features a few easier runs including the seemingly never-ending Long Squaw. Located just a mile north of town, its full-tilt diamond

Leroi Mine

runs tower over Rossland. Some might find the nearby *Black Jack Cross-Country Trails,* with more than 30 miles (50 km) of groomed classic tracks and skating lanes, just as exhilarating. Check the Web site for detailed information: www.rossland.com/blackjack.

The Swiss Alps Inn (250–362–7364; fax: 250–362–7315; 800–663–0203 for reservations only; info@swissalps.net; www.swissalps.net), at the junction of Highways 22 and 3B, offers package deals with Red Mountain (accommodation, lift pass, and taxes) from $130 double. Regular double rates are from $49. There's the added convenience of a restaurant (good hearty Swiss fare), plus the decadence of a twelve-person outdoor hot tub. In summer, the Swiss Alps offers golf packages and rents out mountain bikes.

At this same highway junction (in summer the Visitor Info Centre site), the **Rossland Historical Museum** (Box 26, Rossland, V0G 1Y0; 888–448–7444; 250–362–7722; fax: 250–362–5379) features mining history and, as well, houses the **Western Canada Ski Hall of Fame** (where local champions Nancy Greene and Kerrin Lee-Gartner are honored). Open from mid-May to mid-September, it's the site of the **Leroi Mine,** the only hard-rock gold mine in Canada that offers public tours. Try your luck at gold panning during the forty-five-minute guided walking tour. then enjoy a light lunch in **The Tea Room Restaurant,** next to the museum lobby. After being sold for a $12.50 recording fee, the Leroi eventually grossed more than $30 million. In the late 1890s it produced 50 percent of Canada's gold at a time when Rossland's population was around 7,000. It ran dry in 1929, a black year for Rossland, as it was also the year of a disastrous fire.

Francis Mawson Ratten-bury designed the impres-sive British Columbia Legislature building and the Empress Hotel in Victo-ria. His private life was also impressive. A married man, he openly courted his mistress, Alma Packen-ham. After the death of his wife, he married Alma and left Victoria to settle in Bournemouth, England. Alma soon had designs on the family chauffeur, though, and the pair were charged with murdering Rattenbury. She was acquitted, but her lover, George Stoner, was sen-tenced to death. Unable to go on, Alma committed suicide. Stoner had his sen-tence commuted to life imprisonment and was eventually released.

Despite fires, in Rossland you'll get that turn-of-the-century feel when you see its heritage buildings. The city has pro-duced a brochure *(Historical Heritage Walking Tour)* to guide you through its architectural history. Contact the Rossland Red Mountain Resort Association (Box 1385, Rossland, V0G 1Y0; 877–969–7669; 250–362–5666; fax: 250–362–5399; chamber@rossland.com; www. ross land.com) or check at the Info Centre to find out more about these thirty designated heritage buildings.

One of the grandest, the **Bank of Montreal,** on the corner of Washington Street and Columbia Avenue, was designed by Francis Mawson Ratten-bury. The restored, wooden counters and ornate plaster ceilings sit above the **Golden City Barber Shop** (formerly a telegraph office), where many tales of fortunes won or lost must have been heard. You can still have your hair cut (and talk about lost fortunes) in an original 1926 porcelain revolving chair that was reupholstered with Naugahyde from the old Rossland theater seats.

Next door to the barbershop on Washington Street was once the town bathhouse. It's now *The Cellar* (2002 Washington Street; Box 1575, Rossland, V0G 1Y0; 250–362–7600) and features kids' clothes, weaving, and pottery, mostly work of Kootenay locals. Drop in and hear tales of miners who hid their gold under the floorboards.

On the other side of Washington Street is a funky bookstore, coffee bar, and micro bakery with yummy, homemade delectables. *Gold Rush Books and Espresso* (open seven days per week at 2063 Washington Avenue; 250–362–5333; 800–668–0140; fax: 250–362–5566; goldrush@ rossland.com) serves delicious coffees, homemade muffins, rustic sourdough breads, cookies, soups, and gourmet teas. An eclectic book selection covers everything from philosophy to cooking.

Other buildings of historic note are the *Post Office,* built in 1910 on the corner of Queen Street and Columbia Avenue, and the *Courthouse,* on the corner of Monte Cristo Street and Columbia Avenue. Completed in 1901 at a cost of $53,000, the stained glass and woodwork in the court-room are exquisite. The building holds National Heritage status. Then take a look at Saint Andrew's United Church and the *BC Firefighter's Museum* (Box 789, Rossland, V0G 1Y0; 250–364–1194/1126; fax: 250–364–1164), on opposite corners at Queen Street and First Avenue. The museum features a hose tower, horse-drawn hose-and-reel wagons, uniforms, and old fire trucks. It's open May to September and admission is $3.00.

Trivia

Trail is called the Home of Champions. Two of these champions include Olympic Gold medalists Kerrin-Lee Gartner (skiing) and Kathleen Heddle (rowing).

There's no need to pay a mother lode for accommodation in Rossland. West of the Rossland Red Mountain Resort Association at 2125 Columbia Avenue, *Mountain Shadow Hostel* (Box 100, Rossland, V0G 1Y0; 250–362–7160; 888–393–7160; fax: 250– 362–7150; mshostel@look.ca) is but $17 per night for a basic bed, shower, kitchen facilities, TV room, reading room, and storage area. There are three family rooms, as well as seven other rooms that sleep four, six, or eight. Another cozy place in town is *Angela's Bed and Breakfast* (1520 Spokane Street, Rossland, V0G 1Y0; phone/fax: 250–362–7790). It's renowned for its good food, relaxing fireplace, outdoor redwood hot tub, delicious breakfasts, and warm atmosphere. A standard double room starts at $50.

Trail

hen you've had your fill of Rossland, and that isn't easy, head down Highway 3B east to *Trail*. Here the road drops 2,000 feet (610 m) in 7 miles (11 km) into one of British Columbia's major industrial cities. This is the home of *Cominco,* the world's largest integrated *lead-zinc smelter*. Retired Cominco employees give two-hour tours of the Cominco complex weekdays during summer at 10:00 A.M. and by reservation only the rest of the year. Children under twelve are not admitted, and visitors must wear long-sleeve shirts, slacks, and covered shoes. No cameras, videos, or pacemakers are allowed. Tours are free. Cominco also has an *Interpretive Centre* (a miniscience center) at 200–1199 Bay Avenue (above the TD Bank). Here you'll find exhibits concerning Cominco's history and products, and as well you can watch videos on a big screen TV or play an interactive computer game called Groundwork—Exploring for Minerals in Canada. Contact the *Trail Visitor Information Centre* (200–1199 Bay Avenue, Trail, V1R 4A4; 250–368–3144; fax: 250–368–6427; info@trailchamber.bc.ca; www. trailchamber. bc.ca) for information.

After the smelter tour enjoy a swim at the *Trail Aquatic and Leisure Centre* (1875 Columbia Avenue; 250–368–6484) beside the baseball park, followed by a spaghetti dinner at the *Colander Restaurant* (1475 Cedar Avenue, Trail, V1R 4C5; 250–364–1816), where all the pasta you can eat, and meatballs, salad, a bun, and coffee, costs less than $12.00. Italian food is not uncommon fare in Trail, a city with a long Italian heritage. It proudly maintains the only Italian archives in North America at *Cristoforo Colombo Lodge* (584 Rossland Avenue, Trail, V1R 3M8; 250–368– 8921). The public is welcome here (for free) to learn about Trail's dynamic Italian history. Learn, too, how Trail received its "Home of Champions" designation at the Alan Tognotti Sports Hall of Fame in the Trail Memorial Centre, which is beside the bridge at 1051 Victoria Street. There's a special section featuring the story of the 1939 and 1961 World Champion Trail Smoke Eaters Hockey Team.

And if you need a spot to put up the tent or park the RV, where else in this Home of Champions but *Champion Lakes Provincial Park*. Located about 12 miles (20 km) northeast of Trail on Highway 3B (and in fact named for James W. Champion, one of the area's earliest orchardists), it features three adjacent lakes, ninety-five campsites, an adventure playground, hiking, boating, and fishing. Phone (800) 689–9025 for reservations. First-come, first-served sites are also available. There's also a spot to park at the City of Trail RV Park beside the Waneta Mall. The park includes a playground, showers, and electrical hook-ups.

Castlegar

ighway 22 travels north from Trail beside the Columbia River for 16 miles (26 km) to *Castlegar*, where the Columbia meets the Kootenay River and, as in Grand Forks, where the Doukhobors have left their mark.

For a taste of this Russian influence, at the junction with Highway 3 cross the Columbia River Bridge, turn left onto Highway 3A, and left again onto Frank Biender Way, opposite the Castlegar airport. The *Doukhobor Village Museum* (RR1 S2 CB4, Castlegar, V1N 3H7; 250–365–6622 or 250–365–5327; cds@kootcom.kootenay.net) is on Heritage Way. This museum portrays the history of what was the largest communal enterprise in western Canada until 1938. It's easy to appreciate the turn-of-the-century hardships when you see this reconstructed Doukhobor community. Check out its bread oven, blacksmith shop, and wood-fired banya (sauna). The museum is open daily May to September from 10:00 A.M. to 6:00 P.M. Admission is $4.00 for adults, $2.00 for students and fifty cents for children under twelve; preschoolers get in free.

Next to the museum the *Kootenay Gallery of Art, History and Science* (120 Heritage Way, Castlegar, V1N 4M5; 250–365–3337; fax: 250–365–3822; kgal@netidea.com) features local exhibits and offers a variety of creative workshops throughout the year. It also features performance art, readings, concerts, lectures, and audiovisual presentations. The gallery is open daily in July and August and every day but Monday the rest of the year. Call for opening hours. Admission is by donation.

Castlegar offers more than history and culture, though. Golfers will enjoy the scenically set challenges of the *Castlegar Golf Course* (Box 3430, Castlegar, V1N 3N8; 800–666–0324 or 250–365–5006; fax: 250–365–7788), which *Golf Digest* has given a 3.5 rating, recognizing it as one of the top one hundred courses in North America. You'll find it behind the airport. From Highway 3A, which heads north to Nelson, take Ootischenia Road; turn left onto Columbia Road and left again onto Aaron Road. Contact the Castlegar Chamber of Commerce/Visitor Info Centre (1995 Sixth Avenue, Castlegar, V1N 4B7; 250–365–6313; fax: 250–365–5778; cdcoc@kootenay.net; www.castlegar.com) for information on other recreational activities. These activities include camping at *Syringa Provincial Park,* with its variegated habitat of sandy beaches, grasslands, steep canyons, and cliffs, an important habitat for Rocky Mountain bighorn sheep, elk, and deer; hiking the *Waldie Island Trail,* which winds along the Columbia River's northern shoreline from the CPR train bridge to Brilliant; exploring the *Zuckerberg Island Heritage Park,* where you'll see an unusual sculpture of a seated woman carved from a tree stump, one of revered Russian sculptor Alexander Zuckerberg's best-known works; and visiting the *Castlegar Museum,* located in the old railway station at 400 Thirteenth Avenue in downtown Castlegar, where you'll find aboriginal history and tales of the beginnings of Castlegar as well as modern history.

Nelson

Twenty-three miles (38 km) northeast of Castlegar along Highway 3A, *Nelson* graces the West Arm of Kootenay Lake in the heart of the Selkirk Mountains. As you approach from the south, keep an eye out for *osprey nests* on the bridge pylons at Taghum, about 3 miles (5 km) before *Grohman Narrows Provincial Park.* The park is a pleasant picnic spot overlooking Kootenay Lake (just before you enter Nelson), with a pond and walking trails.

Nelson is in a picture-perfect setting. It's long been appreciated for movie backdrops, among them the Steve Martin/Darryl Hannah film *Roxanne.* Martin's Pinocchio-nosed character would have appreciated the clean mountain air of this lovely city of heritage buildings, artisans, and steep streets overlooking Kootenay Lake's West Arm.

Trivia
• *With so many designated heritage buildings, **Nelson** is known as the "Heritage Capital of British Columbia."*
• *Nelson was the first city in British Columbia to be electrified! Electricity was turned on in early February 1896.*

Take in the lake views at the *Nelson Guest House* (2109 Fort Sheppard Drive, Nelson, V1L 6A2; phone/fax: 250–354–0198; toll free: 888–215– 2500; nelsonguest@yahoo.com; www.nelsonguesthouse.com), a newly constructed cedar home that is close to town, yet you can ski, hike, or bike from the door, or simply sit on the deck and enjoy the mountain air. Accommodation is either a two- or three-bedroom self-contained suite, with kitchen, deck, and laundry facilities. There's also the choice of two main-house rooms with en-suite baths. Rates range from $59 to $119 and include a hearty breakfast.

Nelson has several fine restaurants to choose from, including *Max & Irma's Restaurant* (515A Kootenay Street; 250–352–2332), where they bake their daily specials in a brick oven and *The Rice Bowl* (301 Baker Street, 250–354–4129), an organic restaurant with a Thai influence that serves sushi as well. For $1.75 you can have a bowl of miso soup, or for $12 try a Red Thai Curry stir-fry with caribou and a choice of jasmine rice or noodles. If you want to head a little more upscale, take a detour down a back alley one block from Baker Street between Josephine and Hall Streets to the *All Seasons Cafe* (620 Herridge Lane, 250–352–0101; fax: 250–352– 7499; www.allseasonscafe.com). Main dinner items include rosemary smoked chicken fettuccine and grilled Slocan Valley wild boar sausage, with prices ranging from $12 to $27. The Sunday brunch (in the $4.00 to $13.00 range) has been applauded loudly and widely. Its restored heritage home setting comes complete with pretty mountain views.

Still on the theme of heritage buildings, the *Nelson Visitor Info Centre* (225 Hall Street, Nelson, V1L 5X4; 250–352–3433; fax: 250–352–6355; information@nelsonchamber.bc.ca; www.city.nelson.bc.ca) has self-guided tour brochures for an architectural heritage walking (or driving) tour as aids in viewing some of the 350 heritage buildings the city boasts.

During your walk you're sure to pass several arts, crafts, and antiques stores, such as *The Craft Connection Co-op* (441 Baker Street, Nelson, V1L 4H7; 250–352–3006; fax: 250–352–9398; lhall@netidea. com), where you'll find a selection of some of the best work of west Kootenay artisans—everything from raku to wreaths—in the "best little art town" in BC. It's open 9:30 A.M. to 5:30 P.M. year-round (noon to 4:00 P.M. Sundays).

During the snow-free months there's a delightful way to view the Nelson waterfront and the lovely *Lakeside Park,* and that's aboard the historic *Streetcar 23,* built in 1906 for service in Cleveland, Ohio, and then used in Nelson from 1924 to 1949. In those days it ran through the winter, but with a snow buildup it sometimes derailed. After enough shopkeepers complained about the tram crashing through their storefronts, it was discontinued in winter. Costs are $2.00 for adults and $1.00 for children.

Kootenay Lake West

A 21-mile (34-km) drive northeast from Nelson along Highway 3A beside the Kootenay Lake West Arm brings you to Balfour and the world's longest free ferry ride, but first we'll take Highway 31 north along the west shore of *Kootenay Lake,* renowned for its good fishing. Drop the hook for Dolly Varden, kokanee, and rainbow trout.

Nine miles (15 km) north of Balfour at Ainsworth Hot Springs is the *Silver Ledge Hotel* (250–229–4640), a one-hundred-year-old hotel restored to its late nineteenth-century glory, but now operating only as a museum. It houses a collection of old photos of the Ainsworth Mining District. Once home to 3,000 silver seekers, Ainsworth now has fewer than one hundred permanent residents. The museum is open 1:00 to 5:00 P.M. from the May long weekend till September (daily in July and August, but only weekends in May, June, and September).

For a hot soak go to the caves at the **Ainsworth Hot Springs Resort** (Box 1268, Ainsworth Hot Springs, V0G 1A0; 250–229–4212; fax: 250–229–5600; 800–668–1171 for reservations; reserve@hotnaturally. com; www.hotnaturally.com). You'll soak in 114° F (42° C) water in a 66-foot (20-m) dripping, U-shaped cave. This hot springs water has reputedly the highest mineral content in Canada. The springs originate in the Cody Caves area, which is directly above and to the west of Ainsworth Hot Springs. The water works its way down deeply through porous rock, increasing in temperature at a rate of 104°F (40°C) per kilometer, until it strikes what is known as the Lakeshore Fault. Hydraulic pressure forces the water up along the fault to emerge at Ainsworth Hot Springs. In the dark patches you may bump into a quietly meditating mortal as you drift through the steamy caves. Cost is $6.50 single entry for adults (day pass $10.00) and $4.50 for kids ages three to twelve (day pass $6.50). Towels and disposable swimsuits are available for a small fee. For the hardy there's a 39° F (4° C) glacier-fed pool to alternate with the sizzling dips. The resort provides fine dining at moderate prices, and the lovely lake views are free.

Two miles (3 km) north of Ainsworth, a 9-mile (14-km) rugged and steep forest road leads to **Cody Caves Provincial Park.** Here an underground stream flows for 800 yards through an ancient limestone system of tunnels and galleries containing stalactites, stalagmites, soda straws, and other cave features. Wear sturdy shoes and warm clothing, because although it may be hot outside, the interior temperature is about 42° F (6° C). Also, it's a long walk to the caves from the parking lot, so bring drinks and snacks. Guided tours (and this is the only way to see the caves) are led daily in the summer by Highadventure Corporation (250–353–7425), which provides helmets, headlamps, and gloves.

Kaslo

Thirteen miles (21 km) north of the hot springs, the plain street names (numbers and letters) of **Kaslo,** located between the

Selkirk and Purcell Mountains, belie her prettiness. In 1893, when silver, galena, and gold enriched the mountainsides, Kaslo's population grew to 3,000; at present it's fewer than 1,000. Steamers helped develop the area, and to this memory the Kootenay Lake Historical Society has restored the oldest intact passenger stern-wheeler in the world, the **SS Moyie**. She sits majestically on the waterfront in downtown Kaslo, after having steamed an estimated two million miles between 1898 and 1957. Prefabricated in Toronto, all 830 tons were shipped in sections in 1898. The **SS Moyie National Historic Site** (324 Front Street, Box 537, Kaslo, V0G 1M0; phone/fax: 250–353–2525; ssmoyie@klhs.bc.ca; www.klhs.bc.ca), complete with historic trapper's cabin, is the main museum in town and is open daily mid-May to mid-October from 9:30 A.M. to 5:00 P.M., with admission fees ranging from $2.00 (ages six to twelve) to $5.00 for adults.

There's more history at the **Woodbury Mining Museum** (402 Front Street). Open June–September from 10:00 A.M. to 5:00 P.M., here you'll get a good introduction to those booming, mining days. Admission is $2.00 for adults and $1.00 for children.

Across from the Post Office at the corner of Fourth and B, the **Langham Cultural Center** (Box 1000, Kaslo, V0G 1M0; 250–353–2661, fax: 250–353–2820; langham@pop.kin.bc.ca; www.kin.bc.ca/Langham/Langhom.htm), one of sixty officially designated heritage buildings in Kaslo, was a hotel for miners in the 1890s. Now it comprises two galleries, a ninety-seat theater, and an ecomuseum. Poignant photographs on the walls tell the story of Kaslo's 1,200 resilient Japanese-Canadian internees, seventy-eight of whom were housed in the Langham during World War II. It's open daily all year, except January, from 9:00 A.M. to 5:00 P.M. Admission is by donation.

Kaslo was the setting for the Mark Harmon movie *Magic on the Water*. If you stare at the lake long enough, you may see Orky, the movie's odd but genial lake monster. A walking tour of this Switzerland of the Americas village and its environs is well worthwhile. It's hard to imagine that it has seen devastation in the form of fire, flood, and even hurricane.

To view Kaslo panoramically take a walk up A Avenue and turn right on Wardner Street. After a block you'll see a trailhead on the left side. Turn right and 300 yards (275 m) up you'll come to a sharp left turn followed by some steep switchbacks. At the top you'll get a breathtaking view of Kaslo and Kootenay Lake. In fall mountain ash trees add flaming color to the scene.

After the hike stop at **The Rosewood Cafe** (213 Fifth Street, Box 1435,

Kaslo, V0G 1M0; 250–353–ROSE or 7673; rosewood@netidea.com). This attractive restaurant serves calamari, Camembert fondue, blackened Cajun shrimp, and tortellini in a curry sauce, at moderate prices. In summer outdoor barbecue specials are popular.

To appreciate the intimacy and quality of life this little town offers, stay a while. **Beach Gables B&B** (Box 962, Kaslo, V0G 1M0; 250–353-2111; fax: 250–353-2240), opposite the beach, is open year-round. This restored heritage home, beautifully furnished with exquisite antiques, offers private decks, views of the lake and mountains, and a continental breakfast served to your private suite. Rates are in the $80 to $90 double range (cash or check only).

The **Kaslo Visitor Info Centre** (324 Front Street, Box 537, Kaslo, V0G 1M0; phone/fax: 250–353-2525) can lead you to other lodgings and fill you in on the history of this charming little town. If you visit in early August, you're in time for the Kaslo Jazz Etc. Festival (250–353-7538; kaslojaz@netidea.com; www.netidea.com/~kaslojazz). Check out www.kin.bc.ca on the Web for up-to-date Kaslo information before you leave home.

From Kaslo you can head north along Kootenay Lake on Highway 31 over mostly unpaved road for 88 miles (142 km) to **Galena Bay.** The road edges **Goat Range Provincial Park** and **Trout Lake.** Ask in Kaslo about road conditions; then set out to explore the ghost town of Gerrard (at the south end of Trout Lake), where in early to mid-May you can watch the Gerrard rainbow trout spawn. This is the world's largest breed of rainbow trout, with some reported up to 50 pounds (23 kg). "No-trace" camping is available in the park, with five drive-in spots and

A Not-So-Friendly Monster

*T*he movie Magic in the Water, *filmed in Kaslo, may not have been all fiction. Several reported sightings of a "monster" in Kootenay Lake have occurred over the past hundred or so years. A couple of years ago a highway crew reported sighting "humps and a huge wake, much larger than those made by houseboats and fishing boats." Another sighting by a reputable local who "got a good look at it for at least a* couple of minutes before it dove" was *described as "a head on the end of a long neck lifted up . . . just like the images of the Loch Ness monster that we have all seen." Unlike the lovable Orkie in the movie, this creature does not seem to be friendly and has been blamed for various accidents on the lake, which many locals avoid unless they are in a very large boat. Strangely, the monster has yet to be named.*

some wilderness walk-in sites. No potable water is available, and anglers must have a valid non-tidal angling fishing license. Stop at the one-hundred-year-old (plus) **Windsor Hotel** (RR2, Site 3, Box 49, Nakusp, V0G 1R0; 250–269–2244; fax: 250–369–2246; windsor@ columbiacable.net; www.windsor-troutlake.com) in **Trout Lake** (at the northwest end of the lake) for a piece of great pie. The Windsor offers three-night accommodation and all-meals-included package deals that might feature a cruise on Trout Lake; a four-wheel-drive guided tour to see abandoned mines, ghost towns, and alpine scenery; and a gold-panning excursion to Lardeau Creek. Package rates range from $215 to $295. Room rates start at $30.

From Galena a free ferry crosses Upper Arrow Lake to Shelter Bay, 31 miles (50 km) south of Revelstoke. Highway 23 (now paved) continues for 30 miles (49 km) south to Nakusp.

An easier route to Nakusp is via a paved road, Highway 31A, which leads 29 miles (47 km) west from Kaslo to New Denver on Slocan Lake. Here, between Kaslo and Sandon, you'll pass through the Valley of the Ghosts, with its many abandoned mines and ghost towns. Ask in Kaslo or New Denver to help locate these sites. Twenty-four miles (38 km) from Kaslo—or 5 miles (8.3 km) from New Denver—look for a sign indicating the turnoff to **Sandon**. This junction is known as Three Forks. Here a 3.4-mile (5.5-km) unpaved road leads to this formerly rowdy town that once supported twenty-four hotels, three newspapers, and an opera. It had electricity even before Vancouver. At one time the silver-mining capital of Canada, Sandon's population of 5,000 gradually decreased, only to grow briefly again when the Japanese-Canadians were interned there in 1942. A collection of historic photographs and artifacts is located in the visitors center in the restored **Slocan Mercantile Building**. When space ran out in its early days, Sandon was enlarged by building a flume to contain the river, then planking over it to add a boardwalk "street." A washout in 1955 devastated the city center, but the City Hall and western Canada's oldest operating hydroelectric station still remain. The visitors center is open June to October, with tours of the **Silversmith Hydroelectric Station** (with its amazing collection of operating, turn-of-the-century machinery) held daily in July and August from 10:00 A.M. to 4:30 P.M. Hikers will enjoy the easy 3.8-mile (6.1-km) walk to Payne Bluffs along the **K & S Historic Railway Trail**. You can even drive the first 1.4 miles (2.3 km). Poke around the old mine sites, admire the views, and then hike back to Sandon, where you can enjoy a homemade meal at the **Tin Cup Cafe**. The Sandon Historical Society has put together a comprehensive Web site. Ghost-town aficionados can learn more about Sandon's fascinating history at www.slocanlake.com/sandon.

Six miles west of the Sandon turnoff is *New Denver,* where you can visit the *Nikkei Internment Memorial Centre,* a memorial to the thousands of Japanese-Canadians displaced to the area during World War II. A feature of the center is a splendid Japanese garden.

Here, too, Highway 31A meets Highway 6 at Slocan Lake on the edge of the aptly named *Valhalla Provincial Park* (250–422–4200). Access to this isolated, undeveloped wilderness is mostly by boat across the lake or via Little Slocan Lake Road, after crossing the river in Slocan. It's beautiful, with lucid lakes, wild creeks and waterfalls, and majestic stands of timber—a paradise for hikers and climbers. The park has only wilderness/walk-in camping sites (pit toilets and no potable water) and a day-use picnicking area.

Quiet accommodation in the village of Slocan, close to the Slocan River and Lake, can be found at *Three Maples Bed & Breakfast* (710 Arthur Street, Box 270, Slocan, V0G 2C0; 250–355–2586; fax: 250–355–2220. Rates, from $50 double, include a full breakfast served on crystal in the delightful solarium.

If you're a hot-springs zealot, a 29-mile (47-km) side trip from New Denver along Highway 6 leads northwest to Nakusp on Upper Arrow Lake. Here the clear air of the Selkirks is rivaled only by the pure waters of *Nakusp Hot Springs* (250–265–4528; fax: 250–265–3788 or 800–909–8819; info@nakusphotsprings.com; www.nakusphotsprings.com), 8 miles (13 km) farther east along a paved road. With two pools, one hot at 100.4° F (38° C) and the other hotter at 105.8° F (41° C) to soak in, hot-springs' connoisseurs insist it's number one in the Kootenays. Camping is available May to November beside the Kuskanax River, a short walk from the hot springs (no reservations necessary). There are also cedar chalets (ranging from $60 to $90 double) on-site that are open year-round. Phone 250– 265–4505; fax 250–265–3596 for chalet reservations. Contact Nakusp & District Chamber of Commerce/Visitor Info Centre at 92 West Sixth Avenue (Box 387, Nakusp, V0G 1R0; 250–265–4234; fax: 250–265–3808; 800–909–8819; nakcom@columbiacable.net; www.nakusp-chambercommerce.com for more information on Nakusp.)

Twenty miles (32 km) north of Nakusp is BC's newest (and perhaps oldest) hot springs resort. Fascinating history, as well as fabulous scenery, surrounds *Halcyon Hot Springs Resort* (Box 37, Nakusp, V0G 1R0;

888–689–4699; 250–265–3554; fax: 250–265–3887; info@halcyon-hot springs.com; www.halcyon-hotsprings.com), located on Highway 23 along the shores of Upper Arrow Lake. At the turn of the century, it was renowned for its fancy dress balls and as a riotous "in" place to holiday, but after 1924, the drinking and gambling stopped when a sedate and charitable general and doctor, Frederick Burnham, bought the resort. The emphasis turned to making use of the health-restoring waters of the springs. Before long Halcyon's healing powers were touted internationally with mind-boggling claims—one man even claimed his hair grew back. Burnham allowed no bathing trunks in the segregated pools, as he believed clothing interfered in the healing process; stories circulated that the surrounding trails were closed in the mornings, as he used to run naked there "to harden" himself. He was killed in 1955 when the hotel burned to the ground, but the shingle-roofed chapel that he built after his beloved wife passed away in 1945 has been restored and now functions as a museum and chapel. What a romantic spot to tie the knot! Now, as of March 1999, a new resort with four pools with water temperatures ranging from 107° F (41.6° C) to 85° F (29.4° C), combined with a Kids Waterpark, 40 RV sites, camping facilities, cabins, chalets, a store, and a bistro-style restaurant set by the lake with a view of Mount Burnham, make for a spectacular holiday spot. Bring along your arthritis, osteoporosis, and gout, and return home rejuvenated—and perhaps married!

A third way to reach Nakusp is from the west (from Vernon) along Highway 6, via the 3,900-foot (1,189-m) Monashee Pass and a free ferry across Lower Arrow Lake from Needles to Fauquier.

Just 3 miles (5 km) south of New Denver on Highway 6, as you wind through the beautiful *Slocan Valley,* is historic *Silverton.* You'll find a really pretty campground on the lakeshore right in town, down the road from the *Silverton Outdoor Mining Museum,* 408 Fourth Street, which displays forty-eight pieces of vintage mining machinery and is well worth a visit, as is the *Silverton Resort* (Box 107, Silverton, V0G 2B0; phone/fax: 250–358–7157; www.silvertonresort.com), with its lovely log lodge and loft-cabins on the shores of Slocan Lake. From November to March a sauna is available, and throughout the year you can rent canoes, motorboats and kayaks. The 1,500-square-foot lodge will sleep eight and has rates as low as $120 in the off-season; late June to early September rates are $230; its deck overlooks Slocan Lake and the Valhalla Mountain Range.

Less than a mile (1.5 km) south of Silverton is a *viewpoint* on a high cliff overlooking Slocan Lake. Don't miss it, or you'll miss one of the best views in British Columbia.

Slocan is 17 miles (27 km) south of Silverton, and 5 miles (7 km) south of Slocan is the turnoff to a rustic, year-round guest lodge. The front field of the *Lemon Creek Lodge* (Box 68, Slocan, V0G 2C0; phone/fax: 250–355–2403 or 877–970–8090; lemoncrk@telus.net; www.lemoncreeklodge.com), at 7680 Kennedy Road, was home to hundreds of Japanese-Canadian wartime internees. A photo of the internment camp in the warmly furnished living room in the lodge shows how it looked in those difficult years. Located between Valhalla and Kokanee Glacier Provincial Parks, accommodation at Lemon Creek Lodge offers ten neat and clean bedrooms with five shared bathrooms, two cabins, a fabulous Finnish sauna, a hot tub, a Japanese Garden, a twenty-eight-site campground, and a restaurant serving fresh-from-the-garden vegetables, home-baked bread, and creative desserts. Double accommodation with breakfast costs $65 in the lodge and $75 in the cabins (breakfast not included).

Our side trip through the Slocan Valley returns via Nelson to Balfour and then back to the world's longest free ferry ride (*Kootenay Lake Ferry;* 250–229–4215). Eighteen forty-five-minute runs daily (twelve in winter), starting at 6:00 A.M., sail between the Purcell and Selkirk Mountains to Kootenay Bay on the eastern shore. Watch for *Canada geese* on the beach at Balfour. At Lang's Restaurant near the ferry lineup, you can buy grain (or "cwackers") to feed them. There's also a large osprey colony nearby, so keep the binoculars handy.

Aboard the MV *Anscomb* or the MV *Balfour,* the ferry cafe serves inexpensive but tasty food. In winter change your watch back one hour after

Recommended Reading - The Kootenays

Ghost Towns and Mining Camps of the Boundary Country, by Garnet Basque. Heritage House Publishing Company Surrey, 1999.

West Kootenay: The Pioneer Years, by Garnet Basque. Heritage House Publishing Company Surrey, 1996.

Ghost Towns and Drowned Towns of West Kootenay, by Elsie Turnbull. Heritage House Publishing Co., 1988.

Whitewater Trips and Hot Springs in the Kootenays of British Columbia: For Kayakers, Canoeists and Rafters, by Betty Pratt-Johnson. Vancouver: Adventure Publishing, 1989.

you disembark at Kootenay Bay. You're now on Mountain Standard Time. Just to confuse you, though, in April, when Daylight Savings Time comes into effect, the time doesn't change, because Kootenay Bay maintains Mountain Standard Time year-round. You'll soon learn that time really does stand still on Kootenay Lake's eastern shore!

Kootenay Lake East

Some strange, inexplicable force urged me to take the Riondel Road turnoff after the ferry. Two miles (3 km) from this turnoff, along a gravel road (Walker's Landing), I found *Yasodhara Ashram* (Box 9, Kootenay Bay, V0B 1X0; 250–227–9224 or 800–661–8711; fax: 250–227–9494; yashram@netidea.com; www. yasodhara.org), a vibrant spiritual community and educational institution founded in 1963 by the late Swami Sivananda Radha. You'll experience here yoga courses and retreats in an atmosphere of peace and harmony. The ashram also offers programs (by application only) for working guests, and families are always welcome. An attractive study center, a well-stocked bookstore, a beautiful white-domed Temple of Divine Light on the lakefront, and residents working quietly in vegetable gardens make up the tranquil scene. The cedar log guest lodge overlooks the lake and mountains.

Back on Highway 3A, a few miles south of the ferry landing at the *North Woven Broom Company* (Box 126, Crawford Bay, V0B 1E0; 250–227–9245; broom@northwovenbroom.com; www.northwovenbroom.com), a pungently sweet odor permeates everything inside an old barn. You can almost feel the time warp as you watch Janet and Rob Schwieger fashion brooms from Mexican unprocessed broomcorn. Their machinery consists of a turn-of-the-century treadle-stitcher to sew the brooms flat and an antique vise for gripping the hand-stitched whisks and crooked-handled brooms. They spend their days listening to CBC radio, peacefully wetting and weaving, tying and treadling, as they turn out these nifty brooms. They're open daily from 9:00 A.M. to 5:00 P.M. from April to October. Winter hours vary, so call ahead.

Close by is the *Kokanee Springs Golf Resort* (Box 96, Crawford Bay, V0B 1E0; 800–979–7999 or 250–227–9226; fax: 250–227–9220; info@kokaneesprings.com; www.kokaneesprings.com), one of Canada's finest eighteen-hole golf courses magnificently set beneath the Purcell Mountains.

A few hundred yards south of the broom "factory," the *Kootenay Forge* artist-blacksmiths (Box 119, Crawford Bay, V0B 1E0; 250–227–9466;

toll free: 877–461–9466; fax: 250–227–9535; info@kootenayforge.com; www.kootenayforge.com) produce practical household accessories such as door knockers, umbrella stands, magazine racks, fireplace accessories, candlesticks, and lamps. John Smith (his real name!) and his staff of traditional smiths have been forging and riveting these timeless articles in their "smithy" for more than twenty years. A sign in the gift shop reads: ON THIS DAY IN 1895, NOTHING HAPPENED. Perhaps this is *black*-smith humor? Next door, Tim Elias transforms sand into glowing molten glass at **Breathless Glass** (Box 85, Gray Creek, V0B 1S0; 250–227–9598; blewglass@lightwave.bc.ca). Visitors watch mesmerized as he brings the artistry of glassblowing to life in the form of delicate goblets, vases, and flasks. Also in the same building, at **Fireworks Enamelled Copper and Glass** (250–227–9467), beautiful jewelry, bowls, scenic pieces, and more are created by firing colored glass powders onto a copper sheet.

Yet another cottage industry in this close-knit Crawford Bay community is **Weavers' Corner** (Box 160, Crawford Bay, V0B 1E0; phone/fax: 250–227–9655; weaverscorner@telus.net; www.weaverscorner.com). Owner Janet Wallace and friends weave colorful natural fibers on traditional looms. One-of-a-kind items, from sweaters vests, hats, and blankets, to placemats, prayer shawls, and teddy bears, are sewn and sold on site. They are open from May to October daily and weekdays in winter. And keeping it in the family, Ted Wallace, a teacher at the Crawford Bay School (the smallest kindergarten-to-grade-twelve school in British Columbia), creates visionary paintings created in pencil, colored inks, and acrylics on a variety of media. His latest "Shield" series is made of acrylic on shaped masonite. Many of his pieces are reproduced on cards for sale at Weavers' Corner.

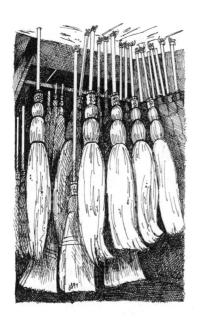

North Woven Broom Company

There's a lovely residence (a heritage mansion) just over the Crawford Creek Bridge, 4 miles (7 km) south of the ferry terminal at 16002 Crawford Creek Road.

Wedgwood Manor Country Inn (Box 135, Crawford Bay, V0B 1E0; phone/fax: 250–227–9233 or, for reservations, 800–862–0022; wedgwood@netidea.com; www.bctravel.net/wedgwood) is lavishly Victorian. Originally built in 1910 by a daughter of the English Wedgwood china family, the inn is entirely set apart for guests, but the accommodation rates ($79–$125) include a hot breakfast and evening tea. You'll feel you're on a country estate as you stroll through its fifty acres (20 ha) of lovely woods and gardens or perhaps as you relax by the parlor fireside, curled up with a mystery from the library shelf. The manor is open from April to mid-October. Even if you don't stay, stop by to take a complimentary tour of this historic house.

At Gray Creek, 7 miles (11 km) south of the ferry dock, a warning of what is to come is right there on the highway. The winding lakeshore highway passes a sign proclaiming: POPULATION 354—METRIC FREE. So, of course, gas still sells by the gallon, and the store is like a page out of a *Waltons* television script. But the variety of products in this overstuffed emporium is second to none. At the **Gray Creek Store** (1979 Chainsaw Avenue, Gray Creek, V0B 1S0; 250–227–9315; fax: 250–227– 9449; graycrk@lightwave.bc.ca), you're likely to trip over wheelbarrows, woodstoves, kitchen sinks, chain saws, of course, and the best darned collection of books on British Columbia this side of Vancouver. Oh, and you can resupply your food stocks here, too.

Store owner Tom Lymbery knows the area well. Ask Tom about the 55-mile (86-km) seasonal (July–October) alpine route from Gray Creek to Kimberley. About 10 steep miles (16 km) from Gray Creek, just before the 6,800-foot summit, you'll pass near an alpine lake (Oliver Lake) that features a path made of split colored stone. This route to Kimberley, deserted for the most part, is a "be-prepared" no-services road.

Three miles (5 km) south of the Gray Creek Store, the **Windwalker Ranch** (Box 146, 14434 Highway 3A, Gray Creek, V0B 1S0; toll free: 800–694–2277; 250–227–9372; fax: 250–227–9610; coach@windwalkerranch.com; www.windwalkerranch.com) provides comfortable, total relaxation. But Dan and Kathryn Cook offer much more than just a place to stay. Trail rides and riding clinics using an ancient breed of Russian horses called Bashkir Curlies, beautiful gardens, a farm (chickens, ducks, and goats), and delicious baking make a stay here memorable. The cabin ($129.50 per night for a family of five) is secluded and has spectacular views of the mountains and lake. Weekly rates are available.

Twenty minutes south of the Windwalker Ranch and 4 miles (7 km) past Boswell on Highway 3A, which is 25 miles (40 km) south of the ferry terminal, is an extraordinary house made from embalming bottles. Funeral director David Brown's son Eldon had me fascinated with stories of growing up in *The Glass House* (RR1, #1, Boswell, V0B 1A0; 250–223–8372; fax: 250–223–8332). After thirty-five years in the funeral business, the late David Brown retired and began building this unique house. He collected the square bottles from other funeral directors across western Canada (500,000, weighing 250 tons) and built this 1,200-square-foot cloverleaf-shaped house. Inquisitive passersby started showing up, and soon the Browns started charging them to take a look inside after a minister friend had advised them: "If you want to break up a congregation, either pass the plate or ask them to sing!" Since 1952, when building began, other parts have been added—terraces, patios, a glass bridge, a moss-covered wishing well, and a lighthouse on the lakefront. It's open daily May, June, September, and until the Thanksgiving weekend in October from 9:00 A.M. to 5:00 P.M. and in July and August from 8:00 A.M. to 8:00 P.M.

Creston

At the bottom end of Kootenay Lake, only 8 miles (13 km) north of the U.S. border, lies *Creston,* population approximately 5,000. Grain elevators and scenic fields of alfalfa give it a prairie look. This "Valley of the Swans" comprises some of the province's most fertile fruit-growing land. Raspberries, cherries, and apricots are ripe in July, peaches and plums in August. In May, Highway 3 is a sea of color as the town springs to life with its *Blossom Festival.*

> **Trivia**
>
> *The Crowsnest (Highway 3) contains Canada's highest paved road, at 5,820 feet (1,774 m). It's between Salmo and Creston at the summit of Kootenay Pass.*

There are a number of quality bed-and-breakfast and other accommodations in the area. One, the *Sweet Apple Bed & Breakfast* (3939 Highway 3 East, Box 93, Erickson, V0B 1K0; phone/fax: 250–428–7205; doull@kootenay.com; www.sweetapple.bc.ca), is a modern country home with a panoramic view (from a 60-foot balcony) of the Selkirk Mountains to the west and the Skimmerhorns to the east. The Scottish hosts serve a full breakfast, and if you get there early enough, they may invite you to join them in a round of golf. Or if you prefer to fish, drop a fly onto the Goat River, which runs through the property, and perhaps land a trout or kokanee salmon. Accommodation, which is on a separate floor from the hosts, is $60 double; or if you prefer a golf package, double accommodation plus two green-fees at the challenging *Creston Golf Course* is $120. The eighteen-hole, par 72 course is just 3 miles (5 km) south of Creston off Highway 21 on Mallory Road. Phone (250) 428–5515 for a tee-off time.

Another accommodation in the area is *Goat River Lodge Bed & Breakfast* (1108 Lamont Road, S40, Box 8, RR 1, Creston, V0B 1G1; 250–428–7134; fax: 250–428–4713; allmi@kootenay.com; www.bbcanada.com/1379.html), with a heated swimming pool and lovely mountain views. Rates are from $50 to $70 double.

Attractions around Creston include the *Columbia Brewing Company* (1220 Erickson Street; 250–428–9344), which offers tours Monday to Friday mid-May to mid-September, the *Kootenay Candle Factory* (1511 Northwest Boulevard; 250–428–9785), and the *Creston Historical Museum* (219 Devon Street; 250–428–9262). Open daily from 10:00 A.M. to 3:30 P.M. mid-May to October, this stone house museum is small but of excellent quality. The building itself, with its thick walls, fireplaces, crypt, and animal figures and windshields embedded in the walls, is interesting. Contact *Creston Visitor Info Centre* (1711 Canyon Street, Box 268, Creston, V0B 1G0; 250–428–4342; fax: 250–428–9411; crescofc@kootenay. com; www.crestonbc.com) for more information on these attractions. Ask about the Creston mural walk, an interesting way of viewing the town and its environs. Another information source is Web site www.crestonvalley.com.

Without doubt the main attraction in the vicinity is the *Creston Valley Wildlife Management Area* (Box 640, Creston, V0B 1G0; 250–428–3260; fax: 250–428–3276; info@cwildlife.bc.ca; www. cwildlife.bc.ca). From Creston travel west along Highway 3 for 7 miles (11 km) to this lush, 17,000-acre (7,000-ha) wetland ecosystem drained by the Kootenay River. It's a staging and nesting area to more than 265 bird species and is a breeding ground for a number of rare species. During March and April ducks, swans, and geese in the thousands transform the area into a chattering, marshy amphitheater. Bald eagles, tundra swans, bank swallows, western grebe, osprey, and the rare Coeur d'Alène salamander are some of the species. Viewing is facilitated by boardwalks, a three-story birding tower, and a trail system. You'll possibly see white-tailed deer and coyotes as you hike, bird-watch, or fish in this ever-changing area, no matter what time of year. An *Interpretive Center,* which includes a gift shop, a library, a theater, and a variety of wildlife programs, opens the last weekend in April with an annual *Osprey Festival* celebration and closes on the Thanksgiving (mid-October) long weekend. Hours in summer (from

May long weekend to Labor Day) are from 8:00 A.M. to 6:00 P.M. daily. Shoulder-season hours are from 9:00 A.M. to 4:00 P.M. Wednesday to Sunday. Also available from the center are interpretive walks and guided canoe rides ($5.00) through the marsh.

PLACES TO STAY IN THE KOOTENAYS

CRAWFORD BAY
Wedgwood Manor Country Inn,
Box 135,
V0B 1E0; (250) 227–9233
or, for reservations,
(800) 862–0022;
wedgwood@netidea.com.

CRESTON
Sweet Apple Bed & Breakfast,
3939 Highway 3 East,
Box 93, Erickson
V0B 1K0; phone/fax:
250-428-7205;
doull@kootenay.net;
www.sweetapple.bc.ca.

GREENWOOD
Lind Valley Guest Ranch,
Box 362,
V0H 1J0; phone/fax:
(250) 445–6585;
www.boundary.bc.ca/
LindValley/.

NAKUSP
Halcyon Hot Springs Resort,
Box 37,
V0G 1R0; (888) 689–4699
or (250) 265–3554;
fax: (250) 265–3887;
info@halcyon-hot
springs.com;

www.halcyon-
hotsprings.com.

NELSON
Nelson Guest House,
2109 Fort Sheppard Drive;
(888) 215–2500;
phone/fax:
(250) 354–0198;
www.nelsonguesthouse.
com;
nelsonguest@yahoo.com.

ROSSLAND
Angela's Place Bed and Breakfast,
1520 Spokane,
Box 944,
V0G 1Y0; (250) 362–7790.

SLOCAN
Lemon Creek Lodge,
7680 Kennedy Road,
Box 68,
V0G 2C0; phone/fax:
(250) 355–2403;
lemoncrk@telus.net;
www.lemoncreeklodge.
com.

PLACES TO EAT IN THE KOOTENAYS

GRAND FORKS
Chef's Garden Restaurant,
4415 Highway 3,
V0H 1H0; (250) 442–0257.

Grand Forks Station Pub,
7654 Donaldson Drive,
V0H 1H0; (250) 442–5855.

GREENWOOD
Copper Eagle Cappuccino and Bakery,
325 Copper South;
(250) 445–6121.

KASLO
The Rosewood Cafe,
213 Fifth Street,
Box 1435,
V0G 1M0; (250) 353–ROSE.

ROSSLAND
Gold Rush Books and Espresso,
2063 Washington Avenue,
V0G 1Y0; (250) 362–5333;
(800) 668–0140;
goldrush@rossland.com.

TRAIL
Colander Restaurant,
1475 Cedar Avenue,
V1R 4C5; (250) 364–1816.

The Rockies

No matter where you stand in this rugged southeastern corner of British Columbia, there's a good chance that if you close your eyes and spin around, when you open them, you'll be facing a mountain. From rolling hills to crenelated, snow-covered peaks, the Rockies contains twenty-six provincial parks bearing names like Top of the World Park and Height of the Rockies Park. Two national parks, Yoho and Kootenay, occupy most of the northeastern section. The heart of the region is the Rocky Mountain Trench, the longest valley in North America, where the Columbia River begins its 1,245-mile (2,005-km) meandering journey to the Pacific.

On the Rockies adventure list, we'll start with a mix of railway history and marshlands wildlife viewing in the "Key City of the Rockies," Cranbrook, followed by a side trip to the southeastern corner of the province, the Elk Valley, where *wilderness* is the key word. In Kimberley, where yodelers in the Platzl sing out a Bavarian theme, we'll eat German fare and ski in powder-perfect snow, followed by a trip back to 1897 frontier life at Fort Steele Heritage Park. Following the Columbia River, our journey passes through the Windermere Valley, famous for hot springs and golf courses, to Radium Hot Springs, where Rocky Mountain bighorn sheep walk the streets. We'll finish our adventure with a trip through the fabulous Kootenay National Park. Finally, we'll kick our way out of the Rockies with some white-knuckle, white-water rafting on the Kicking Horse River.

The Crowsnest to Cranbrook

As with the Okanagan and the Kootenays, we begin close to the U.S. border on the Crowsnest Highway 3, which at Yahk joins Highway 95. With the Rockies to the east and the Purcells to the northwest, the highway cuts and weaves northward beside the Moyie River on its path toward Cranbrook, passing en route four provincial parks (Yahk, Ryan, Moyie Lake, and Jimsmith Lake).

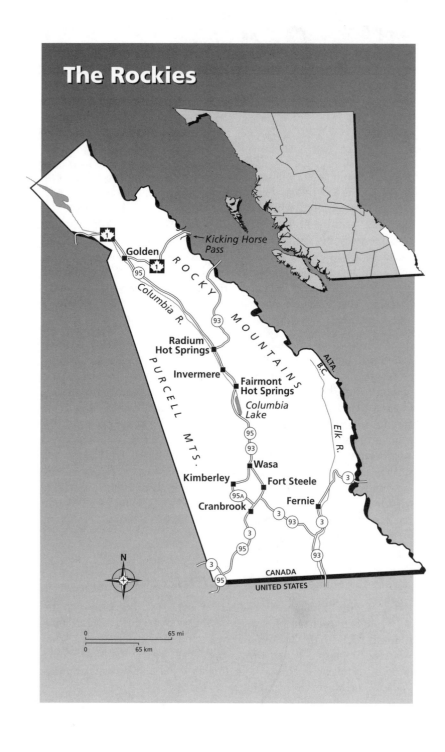

THE ROCKIES

Moyie Lake Provincial Park is a 222-acre (90-ha), forested playground 13 miles (21 km) south of Cranbrook, with a good swimming lake and a sandy beach. It has more than one hundred well-shaded campsites, pleasant picnic shelters and showers, and lots of room on the lake for boaters, windsurfers, and fishing enthusiasts (the Dolly Varden and rainbows bite well). Reservations can be made ahead by calling the Discover Camping number (800–689–9025 or, in Vancouver, 604–689–9025). For information on this (and all other provincial parks in this section), contact BC Parks Kootenay District, Box 118, Wasa, V0B 2K0; 250–422–4200; fax: 250–422–3326. Closer to Cranbrook, *Jimsmith Lake Provincial Park* (250–422–3212) is extremely popular with canoeists, campers, and picnickers and has wheelchair access to a table and toilet facilities. Powerboats are prohibited here.

On the southwestern outskirts of Cranbrook near the *Splash Zone Water Slides* (250–426–3389), the 249-acre (100-ha) *Elizabeth Lake Wildlife Sanctuary* is a must-stop for bird-lovers. Walking trails lead to blinds at different spots around the lake, allowing excellent bird-watching. You're likely to see Canada geese, mallard, teal, bufflehead, and ruddy ducks. In summer the *Cranbrook Visitor Info Centre* is located at the entrance.

There's another kind of bird-watching at the *Raptor Rescue Society* (250–489–2841; fax: 250–489–2831; raptors@telus.net), where interpretive programs using live falcons, owls, hawks, and eagles operate from June 1 to the end of September. Phone first; then take Highway 95A toward Kimberley, turn left onto Wycliffe Park Road, and follow it for 2.5 miles (4 km).

Cranbrook has a long railway history. Displays at the *Canadian Museum of Rail Travel* (Box 400, Cranbrook, V1C 4H9; 250–489–3918; fax: 250–489–5744; office@trainsdeluxe.com; www.trainsdeluxe.com) feature, among others, seven original cars from the luxurious CPR *TransCanada Limited* of 1929. This set of cars (dining, parlor, sleeping, and business cars), possibly the only surviving set of this vintage in the world designed as a traveling hotel, once provided service from Montreal to Vancouver. The invalid walnut-paneled dining car, the *Argyle,* is an elegant summer spot to have afternoon tea. Other earlier trains, such as the 1907 *Soo-Spokane Train Deluxe,* feature stained glass and art nouveau–style inlays. The museum is located in the town center at 1 Van Horne Street (Highway 3/95) across from Baker Street, an apt position considering that Cornelius Van Horne was the famous railroad building pioneer and Colonel James Baker was the town's founder. At the museum ask for a map to do a self-guided tour that includes many historic buildings, notably the 1888 home of Colonel Baker. These maps are also available at the **Cranbrook Visitor Info Centre** (2279 Cranbrook Street North, Box 84, Cranbrook, V1C 4H6; 800–222–6174 or 250–426–5914; fax: 250–426–3873; cbkchamber@cyberlink.bc.ca; www.cranbrookchamber. com). As well, you'll find here information on eateries and accommodations.

One of the best places to eat in this city of more than 18,000 people is **The Art Café** (20 C Seventh Avenue South; 250–426–4565), where not only is the food excellent, but so, too, is the entertainment and local artwork on the walls.

Of a number of pleasant accommodations in Cranbrook, the **Cedar Heights Bed & Breakfast** (1200 Thirteenth Street South, Cranbrook, V1C 5V8; 250–426–0505 or 800–497–6014; fax: 250–426–0045; cedarheightsbc@home.com; www.bbcanada.com/cedarheights) is hard to beat. A beautifully built executive home with mountain views and an outdoor spa, it has all the class and comforts you'd expect with a Canada Select 4½ Stars–rated B&B. To add to these comforts, artistically presented delicious breakfasts turn a memorable stay into an unforgettable one. Rates are $85–$105 double. From the highway take Third Street South, turn south on Eleventh Avenue South, then east on Thirteenth Street South.

Four miles (6 km) north of Cranbrook on Mission Road heading toward the Cranbrook-Kimberley airport, a scenic detour leads to the **St. Eugene Mission and Church.** The 1897 church was restored in 1983 by the St. Mary's Band and the East Kootenay Historical Association. It is viewed as the finest Gothic-style mission church in British Columbia and has beautiful, hand-painted stained glass.

The Ktunaxa/Kinbasket Tribal Council is redeveloping the buildings associated with the former Residential School that occupied this area. One of these buildings is now the clubhouse of the **St. Eugene Mission Golf Course** (7725 Mission Road, Cranbrook, V1C 1E5; info@golf steugene.com; www.golfsteugene.com), a championship course designed by Les Furber that opened in May 2000. Phone toll free: (877) 417–3133 or (250) 417–3417 to book a tee-off time, or visit the comfortable 19th Hole for a meal and a drink. Tee times can also be booked on the Web site.

The Southeastern Corner

Tucked into the extreme southeastern alcove of British Columbia are the towns of Fernie, Sparwood, and Elkford, lined up south to north in the *Elk Valley* near the Albertan border. To do a side trip to this often forgotten hunting-fishing-skiing utopia, follow the Crowsnest Highway 3 east from Cranbrook 62 miles (100 km).

The largest of the three towns, *Fernie* (population almost 5,000), is proof that from adversity hope occasionally springs eternal. Two fires in 1904 and 1908 destroyed the city, leaving thousands homeless. The reconstruction in brick and stone has resulted in a city full of beautiful, turn-of-the-century buildings, some of which can now be toured. Contact the Fernie Chamber of Commerce, (Highway 3 and Dicken Road, Fernie, V0B 1M0; 250–423–6868; 888–754–7325; fax: 250–423–3811; fernie@ elkvalley.net; www.chamber.fernie.bc.ca) to obtain a self-guided walking-tour map to see these architectural beauties.

TOP ANNUAL EVENTS IN THE ROCKIES

Wings over the Rockies Bird Festival, Invermere/ Radium Hot Springs; Late April/early May; (888) 933–3311 or (250) 342–3210

Golden Wildlife Festival of Birds and Bears, Golden; second week of May; (800) 622–GOLD or (250) 344–7125

Sam Steele Days, Cranbook; June; (250) 426–4161

Pro Rodeo, Cranbrook; August; (250) 426–5792

Elk Valley Art Walk, Fernie; July/August; (250) 423–6868

Coal Miner Days, Sparwood; late June; (250) 425–2423 or (250) 425–0552

Wildcat Charlie Days, Elkford; July; (250) 865–2241

Marysville Daze, Kimberley; June; (250) 427–3666

Kimberley July Fest, Kimberley; (250) 427–3666

Golden Rodeo, Golden; July; (800) 622–GOLD

British Columbia Fact

British Columbia's most easterly point is Akamina Pass in the Rocky Mountains.

The fires were just part of a series of disasters to hit the city. Floods and a horrifying coal-mining explosion in 1902, in which 128 men died, added to its woes. According to Indian legend a curse was placed on Fernie to revenge the coal-mine developer, William Fernie, who spurned a young Indian woman of the Tobacco Plains band. Perhaps the proof of this curse can be seen some evenings at dusk when you look up at *Hosmer Mountain,* just north of Fernie. Some people have even heard the ghostly hoofbeats filling the mountain air as a horse and rider gallop down the sheer, rocky walls. Fortunately for the town, Chief Red Eagle of the Tobacco Plains band lifted the curse shortly before he died in 1964, but the specter is still up there. I asked my waitress at **Rip'n Richard's Eatery** (301 Highway 3, beside the West Fernie Bridge; 250–423–3002) about this famous "ghost." She immediately stopped what she was doing and led me outside to point out where (and when) to look. The Wile E. Coyote Burger at Rip'n Richard's was ready when we came back in, and was it ever good! I was camped a mile west of the restaurant at the **Mount Fernie Provincial Park**, a delightful spot to photograph and hike.

What a fantastic part of British Columbia this Elk Valley is. It's difficult to decide which is the best time of year to visit. The **Fernie Alpine Resort,** 3 miles (5 km) south of Fernie on Highway 3, sports everything from dogsled rides and snowmobiling to snowboarding, cross-country skiing, and downhill skiing. In summer there's mountain biking, horseback riding, and hiking—or you can be lazy and ride the quad lift up to enjoy the beautiful wildflowers and the view. Phone (250) 423–4655 or, for reservations, (800) 258–SNOW; fax: (250) 423–6644; info@skifernie.com; www.skifernie.com. Fernie Destinations (888–754–7325; book@ferniemtnproperties.com; www.fernie.net) will also arrange package holidays and provide information.

<table>
<tr><td>

Trivia

What's in a name? Fernie is the Outdoor Capital of British Columbia, **Sparwood** *is the* Clean Coal Capital of the World, *and* **Elkford** *is the* Wilderness Capital of British Columbia.

</td><td>

There's also golf at **Fernie Golf and Country Club** (250–423–7773; www.golffernie.com), where the clubhouse sits right in the center of the course, and the restaurant's wraparound deck allows you to watch someone else dig up the fairways! Perhaps you'd rather practice a little fly-fishing with **Lost Creek Angling** (250–423–7561; fax: 250–423–7598) or if you've ever wanted to try white-water kayaking or rafting, **Mountain High River Adventures Inc.** (1042 Fifth Avenue, Fernie, V0B 1M0; phone/fax: 250–423–5008 or toll free

</td></tr>
</table>

877–423–4555; fun@mountainhigh.bc.ca; www.mountainhigh.bc.ca) will have your adrenaline flowing as fast as the water. They use inflated kayaks for trips on the Bull and Elk Rivers—or more difficult rivers if you prefer. There are three levels of adventure: Wet Your Appetite Scenic Float Trips, Wet Your Friends White-Water Rafting, and Wet Your Pants Inflatable Kayaking.

Stop over a while to take it all in at **Willow Creek Bed and Breakfast** (5375 Boomerang Way, Box 6049, Fernie, V0B 1M6; 250–423–7731; fax: 250–423–7723; go2far@yahoo.com; www.go2far.com). Rates are moderate in this cozy home located a stone's throw from the base of the ski lifts. Built of tamarack logs, the home has a beautiful river rock fireplace with a sitting-room loft above and a private hot tub just outside the door. There's also a suite available (breakfast not included) on a nightly, weekly, or monthly basis; it sleeps up to six. From Highway 3, take Ski Hill Road to Highline Drive (first right), then turn right onto Boomerang Way. In town, accommodation is available at **Barbara Lynn's Country Inn B&B** (Box 1077, 691 Seventh Avenue, Fernie, V0B 1M0; 250–423–6027; toll free: 888–288–2148; fax: 250–423–6024; Barbs CountryInn@discoverfernie.com; www.bbcanada.com/barbscountryinn). It's just off the highway at the corner of Seventh Avenue and Seventh Street. Rates are in the $50 to $85 double range, with some excellent discounts for cyclists.

Heli-hike with guides or take a sight-seeing tour, leaving from Fairmont Hot Springs Airport.

Float down the Columbia River with experienced rafting guides.

Visit the pets or take a ride in a Spin-n-bump car at the Fairmont Fun Park.

Dine at the Eagle's Eye in Golden, Canada's loftiest restaurant.

Hike to the impressive Josephine Falls near Elkford.

Sparwood (population 4,000 plus), 17 miles (28 km) northeast of Fernie, is a little smaller than its sister and a lot newer. The residents moved there in 1968 from nearby Michel and Natal, now bulldozed into oblivion because they were an environmental headache. The National Film Board's movie *That's the Price,* which documents the town move, can be borrowed from the local library.

Artist Don Sawatzky (of Chemainus murals fame) and several local artists have spruced up Sparwood with some excellent *murals* depicting its mining history. *The Sparwood Visitor Info Centre* (Highway 3 and Aspen Drive, Box 1448, Sparwood, V0B 2G0; 250–425–2423; fax: 250–425–7130; spwdchamber@titanlink.com) can direct you to the footprints on the sidewalk to do the twenty-minute tour. Next door to the Chamber of Commerce office is the *Terex Titan,* the world's largest dump truck. It weighs in at 350 tons, and its box can stuff in two huge buses and two pickup trucks. It stands by Canada's largest open-pit coal mine, where tours (ask at the Chamber) are held Monday to Friday in July and August.

From Sparwood Highway 43 travels north for 22 miles (35 km) along the Elk River to *Elkford,* the "Wilderness Capital of British Columbia" and the jumping-off point for the *Elk Lakes Provincial Park* (250–422–3212), a walk-in-only camping park. Elkford is truly a wilderness town, with elk, bear, bighorn sheep, and deer some times seen in the environs. Inquire at the *Elkford Info Centre* (4A Front Street, Box 220, Elkford, V0B 1H0; 877–355–9453 or 250–865–4614; fax: 250–865–2442;

ecofc@titanlink.com; www.chamber.elkford.bc.ca) for details about accommodation, restaurants, and the many hiking trails (notably one to the breathtaking Josephine Falls) in this spectacularly scenic area.

North to Kimberley

Kimberley, at 3,652 feet (1,113 m), is BC's highest incorporated city. It lies 20 miles (32 km) north of Cranbrook along Highway 95A. Four miles (7 km) before Kimberley, in *Marysville,* look for a sign indicating a boardwalk track to *Marysville Falls,* a thundering 100-foot (30-m) cascade quite near the highway. It's just before the turnoff to the scenic *Kimberley Golf Course* (250–427–4161), which is set among Ponderosa pines with the Purcell Mountains as a backdrop.

If you're feeling particularly energetic, a 3.7-mile (6 km) nature and fitness trail developed by the Kimberley Rotary and Lions Clubs starts at the bridge at the north end of Main Street in Marysville and leads north to Kimberley along Mark Creek. Walk quietly and you may see mule deer, Rocky Mountain elk, northern flickers, sometimes great blue heron, and lots of wildflowers. Occasionally in summer a moose and calf can be seen in the marshes.

In Kimberley the *Platzl* monopolizes center stage with a brilliant red and green theme. You may enjoy (or not!) Happy Hans's yodeling as the world's largest *cuckoo clock*'s doors pop open at the drop of a quarter.

The clock sits in front of the amazing *Chef Bernard's Platzl Inn and Restaurant* (170 Spokane Street, Kimberley, V1A 2E4; 250–427–4820 or 800–905–8338; fax: 250–427–4829; chefbernards@cyberlink.bc.ca; www.cyberlink.bc.ca/~chefbernards). Why amazing? First, the food is delicious. Second, the confusion of knickknacks inside will keep you gawking for the length of your dinner and then some. Model trains "toot-toot" around the ceiling, sometimes carrying birthday greetings for an unsuspecting diner. Originally the restaurant was fondue-only, until Bernard could afford a stove. His cuisine has won several awards. After many years on *Love Boat* Sunprincesses and serving the rich and famous (from Alfred Hitchcock to the King of Tonga), this Hamburg-born immigrant displays his cosmopolitan past through an eclectic menu—from Cajun Two-Step Jamabalaya to Szechwan ginger crab pot and Drunken Black Tiger Shrimps, all delicious. My lobster-and-steak special at $18.95 went down very well as I sat below accordions and beer steins, while trophy goatheads watched clown fish swim by in colorful aquariums. No kidding!

Upstairs, reasonably priced accommodations, with a hot tub on the outside deck, make Chef Bernard's Inn and Restaurant a one-stop shop. The chef also provides mountain chalets, with self-contained kitchens and spectacular views of the Rocky Mountains, and hotel suites at the base of the *Kimberley Alpine Resort,* a few minutes from town.

The ever-expanding Kimberley Alpine Resort (800–258–7669 or 250–427–4881; fax: 250–427–3927; info@skikimberley.com; www. skikimberley.com), only a few minutes' drive from the city, has sixty-seven runs, ten lifts, one of the longest lit runs in North America, and, consistently, nine feet of pure white powder each year. Other winter activities at the resort are dogsledding, snowshoeing, cross-country skiing, skating, and snowmobiling. In the summer, mountain biking, hiking, river rafting, horseback riding, fly-fishing, and waterskiing are offered. Another feature kids will love is the *Family Fun Park* with its 3,500-foot (1,067-m) alpine slide, go karts, bumper boats, and mini golf course. It's open daily late June to early September, 10:30 A.M. to 5:20 P.M.

Next door to Chef Bernard's is the *Yodeling Woodcarver Arts and Crafts Shop* (140 Spokane Street, Kimberley, V1A 2Y5; 250–427–7211). If you aren't quite yodeled to death, Adi Unteberger will complement your purchase with one of his famous yodels. If it sounds familiar, it's because his is the voice of Happy Hans of cuckoo-clock fame.

Still on the Platzl, *The Snowdrift Café* (110 Spokane Street, Kimberley, V1A 2Y5; 250–427–2001; snowdrift@cyberlink.bc.ca) is a friendly, lively place to go for a beer or wine, play cards, or read a newspaper, while you enjoy the best Manhattan clam chowder this side of the Rockies. Roy Cimolai serves "natural" foods at supernaturally low prices. His lentil soup, served with homemade whole wheat bread ($3.35), and his freshly baked pies ($3.25), make a great lunch between exploring Kimberley's nooks and crannies. Oversized muffins are $1.00, and his huckleberry bars—they're so good, price doesn't matter! Roy buys huckleberries from local pickers and occasionally picks them himself with his authentic Norwegian plastic berry rake. The Snowdrift Café, almost entirely vegetarian, is a favorite among the locals, who come not just for the great cheesecakes and the best coffee in Kimberley, but also for the daylong, small-town chatty ambience. It's open Monday to Saturday, 10:00 A.M. to 10:00 P.M. and Sundays' from noon to 6:00 P.M.

The warm Kimberley summers may entice you to head for the river. Just a block from the Snowdrift, drop in to the Technosport shop to book a rafting trip with *Canadian Rockies River Expeditions* (250 Spokane Street, V1A 2Y3; toll free: 877–777–RAFT; 250–427–3266; fax:

250–427–4666; www.riverraftkimberley.com). They'll take you to the **St. Mary's River** to teach you some river basics, while ensuring three hours of fun at the same time. The more adventurous may want to try some cliff jumping and body-surfing during a riotous one-day white-water rafting trip, followed by a full riverside gourmet buffet that will have you hooked and back for more in no time. Kayaking lessons are also offered—choose from three-hour, one-day, or two-day formats.

A short, steep walk from the Platzl via Howard Street (about fifteen minutes) brings you to the **Cominco Gardens** (306 Third Avenue; 250–427–2293). In season 48,000 blooms overwhelm your optical and olfactory senses. First planted in 1927 to advertise Cominco's Elephant Brand Fertilizer, the 2.5-acre (1-ha) site was later given to the community. It's open dawn to dusk, May through September. You can drive there also from Highway 95A. From the Platzl head north on Wallinger Avenue, following the signs to the hospital; go one block farther, and it's on the left. Entrance is free, but a donation for upkeep is welcome. **The Garden Treasures Restaurant and Gift Shop** serves coffee, tea, and light snacks in the original Cominco greenhouse.

It's an adventure into the past on the **Bavarian City Mining Railway,** built as a labor of love by volunteers who salvaged the equipment from old mines. The 7.5-mile (12-km) round-trip starts at the Happy Hans Campground and passes through a bear-infested tunnel and by a

History and Hot Tubs

It was one of those crisp, Rocky Mountain November days when I serendipitously arrived in Wasa Lake. I meandered around the lake and happened upon the Wasa Lakeside Bed and Breakfast Resort. I was a stranger at the door, but that didn't concern James Swansburg, who invited me in and introduced his family, insisting I return for a longer visit. I then drove down to nearby Fort Steele. As it was winter, it was almost deserted, but an enthusiastic groundsman unlocked doors first opened in the 1890s: The Prospector newspaper office, its antique presses still reverberating with sounds that once pumped out the dramatic and the mundane; Bleasdell's Pioneer Drug Store advertising NOTHING CHEAP HERE, BUT YOUR MONEY'S WORTH EVERY TIME. Shadows from the past. With history permeating every pore, I headed back to Wasa. My evening ended with a game of badminton with locals in the school gym, followed by a decadent soak in the Swansburg's hot tub amid the silence of the dark mountains and the occasional call of a distant wolf. And only the day before, I had never heard of Wasa Lake!

haunted schoolhouse. It then goes through a steep-walled, tight valley, past a miner's cave, and ends up near downtown Kimberley. Alternatively pick up the train from the downtown station. It's not a luxury trip, but it's fun, and the views of the Kimberley Ski Hill and the Thousand Peaks mountain range are spectacular. The train runs on the hour on weekends in June and daily through July to Labor Day.

For campers **Happy Hans Campground** on Gerry Sorensen Way, (Box 465 Kimberley, V1A 3B9; 250–427–2929 or 250–427–4877 off-season; fax: 250–427–2917) has vehicle sites ranging from $16.50 to $20.00—the swimming pool is a bonus.

According to Ktunaxa (pronounced Tun-ah-hah) legend, hoodoos at the north end of Columbia Lake are the remains of a giant fish that was wounded by a coyote. It tried to travel through the Rocky Mountain Trench, but finally died. Its flesh decomposed and its ribs broke up. Half of its ribs became these hoodoos, and the other half became hoodoos located farther south near St. Mary's, just north of Cranbrook.

Find out more from the **Kimberley Visitor Info Centre** (350 Ross Street, Kimberley, V1A 2Z9; 250–427–3666; fax: 427-5378; kimbchamber@cyberlink.bc.ca) or contact Kimberley Vacations (800–667–0871; kimbvac@rockies.net; www.kimberleyvacations.bc.ca). Another useful site is www.kimberleybc.net.

Kimberley to Canal Flats

Fifteen miles (24 km) north of Kimberley, Highway 95A rolls through mysteriously named Ta Ta Creek and then joins Highway 93 heading north to Radium Hot Springs and the Kootenay National Park. A mile south of the Highway 93/95 junction, **Wasa Lake Provincial Park** (250–422–4200; 800–689–9025 for reservations) hugs a gem of a lake of the same name. It's a water-sports utopia. A few years ago, a couple of Albertan hang gliders soared off from a road cut in nearby Mount Estella. While ecstatically suspended over **Wasa Lake**, they decided to throw in their tidy nine-to-five Calgary life and head west for some real adventure. Now James and Mary Swansburg operate **Wasa Lakeside Bed and Breakfast Resort** (Box 122, Wasa, V0B 2K0; 250–422–3688 or 888–422–3636; fax: 250–422–3551; info@wasalakeresort.com; www.wasalakeresort.com) on the northwest side of Wasa Lake, the warmest lake in the Canadian Rockies. The resort offers Hobie Cat sailing, waterskiing, pedal boating, windsurfing, hot tubbing, hang gliding, paragliding, elegant rooms, and the best "honeymoon" steam shower I've ever experienced. It's decorated beautifully with stained glass and a skylight. Delicious breakfasts are served beside the private 100-foot (30-m) beach. Guests are welcome to use the beachside kitchen, barbecue, or fire pit to prepare lunches and dinners.

Ten minutes south of Wasa, almost to Fort Steele, history buffs can visit the site of the first gold rush—and the first town—in the East Kootenay: *Fisherville*. When a rich gold vein was discovered under Fisherville (a town of 5,000 by 1885), the town site was moved farther up the hill and renamed *Wild Horse*. Stroll through the Wild Horse graveyard, following a trail past a Chinese burial ground, along Victoria Ditch to Walker's grave, and back through the site of Fisherville. The East Kootenay Historical Association has prepared a brochure detailing the history of the area and what to look out for on your hike (allow at least an hour). You'll find the brochures at the Fort Steele ticket booth or in the Kimberley and Cranbrook Chambers of Commerce. To get to Wild Horse/Fisherville, turn east off Highway 93/95 at the Fort Steele RV Resort onto Bull River Road, then left onto a logging road for about 4 miles (6 km).

There's much more to discover in the Bull River Road area including a spectacular gorge on the Bull River (look for the BC Hydro Dam sign) and the *Kootenay Trout Hatchery* (250–429–3214; fax: 250–429–3202) on the Wardner-Fort Steele Road, where six million rainbow, brook, and cutthroat trout are produced annually. Take a free, self-guided tour of the special viewing areas and displays. Located 5 miles (8 km) north of Wardner on the east side of the Kootenay River, the hatchery is the second largest in British Columbia. It's open daily from 8:00 A.M. to 4:00 P.M.

Just 12 miles (20 km) south from Wasa on Highway 93/95—or 10 miles (16 km) northeast of Cranbrook—is the *Fort Steele Heritage Town* (9851 Highway 93/95, Fort Steele, V0B 1N0; 250–417–6000; fax: 250–489–2624; info@fortsteele.bc.ca; www.fortsteele.bc.ca), named after Samuel Steele, a North-West Mounted Police superintendent blessed with conflict-resolution skills and a certain amount of charisma. He dealt successfully with the tension that had been rising at nearby Galbraith's Ferry between the white settlers and the Chief of the Upper Kootenay Indians. The resulting settlement was the first North-West Mounted post west of the Rockies. The restored town, set at the confluence of the St. Mary and Kootenay Rivers, with the magnificent Rockies as a backdrop, is a must-see attraction. It's open year-round from dawn to dusk or from 9:30 A.M. to 5:30 P.M. May 1 to October 11 (when admission is charged). In summer it operates as it would have in its heyday, with fresh bread coming from a baker's wood-fired oven, chickens pecking

Trivia

Fairmont Hot Springs is Canada's largest odorless natural-mineral hot springs.

in the dust, lambs gamboling in the fields, and transport provided by steam train or Clydesdale-drawn wagon. Twice daily (except Monday) from late June to early September check out the Wild Horse Theatre for "A Steele of a Show" staged by Rosebud Theatre (800–267–7553 or 250–426–5682; info@rosebudtheatre.com; www.rosebudtheatre.com). Shows can be seen at 2:00 and 8:00 P.M. Make sure to eat lunch or dinner at the *International Hotel,* where in summer an 1890s theater/dining package is a feature. You'll be seated in period furniture with nineteenth-century prints gracing the walls. Many of the stores—*H. Kershaw and Son General Store*, the *Prospector Print Shop,* the *Pioneer Tinshop,* the *blacksmith,* and *Mrs. Sprague's Confectionery* (hard-candy sticks and yummy Canadian maple sugar)—are working establishments, and the array of old-fashioned goodies for sale will assure you that you really have walked back into another century. Special events, such as an unbelievably spooky *Hallowe'en Extravaganza*, and the *Great Fort Steele Easter Egg Hunt* are held throughout the year.

Admission is valid for two days and ranges from $5.50 down to free for children under six. A family two-day pass is $10.75. Season passes ($12.00 per family!) and group rates are available.

The Windermere Valley

Eight miles (13 km) north of the Highway 93/95 junction lies *Skookumchuck,* where the Lussier and Skookumchuck Rivers meet the Kootenay. Stop for a fill-up at the area's cheapest gas station, Skookumchuck Centre (250–422–3737). Seventeen miles (28 km) north, you're in for some pretty scenery around *Canal Flats,* population 680. This legendary area, according to Ktunaxa Indian elders, is where the giant Natmuqcin molded with his knees the mile-wide portage separating Columbia Lake (headwaters of the north-flowing Columbia River) from the south-flowing Kootenay River. If you have a canoe and a couple of days to spare, a trip down the Kootenay River to Fort Steele will take you through some of the best scenery in British Columbia, with lots of wildlife viewing on the way.

About 3 miles (5 km) south of Canal Flats, a turnoff to the east (Whiteswan Lake Road) leads for 14 miles (23 km) along a gravel road to *Whiteswan Lake Provincial Park* (250–422–4200), with ninety vehicle camping sites plus three wilderness sites. Just inside the park boundary is the *Lussier River Hotsprings*. This fabulous, undeveloped springs (except for a covered stairway and change room) is maintained

Trivia

Because of the canal between the Kootenay River and Columbia Lake, the government, in anticipation of an influx of settlers, built a road from Fort Steele to Golden, thus opening up the valley—so the canal was not all for naught.

by volunteers, so please respect this by taking out what you bring in.

Two miles (3 km) north of Canal Flats, near **Canal Flats Provincial Park** (250–422–4200—no camp-sites), the remains of the bizarrely conceived Baillie-Grohmann Canal, an 1880s endeavor to link Columbia Lake to the Kootenay River in an effort to reduce flood-ing, can be seen. On a windy day, windsurfers flock to the lake.

The highway caresses Columbia Lake's west bank up to the fast-growing golfing community of **Fairmont Hot Springs Resort** (Box 10, Fairmont Hot Springs, V0B 1L0; 250–345–6311 or 800–663–4979; fax: 250–345–6616; info@FairmontResort.com; www.fairmontresort.com). Two classy courses are located here: **Mountainside Golf Course** (800–663–4979), which sits in the shadow of the Rockies and has been awarded the title of Canada's Most Unique Golf Resort, and **Riverside Golf Course** (800–665–2112), Canada's Golf Course of the Year in 1998, which incor-porates in its design the Columbia River as a natural hazard. **Fairmont Hot Springs Resort** offers package deals of two nights lodging, two rounds of golf at either course, two breakfasts, and unlimited use of the odorless, sulfur-free pools for $219 per person in low season and $266 in high season. In all, eight eighteen-hole championship courses and several executive-length and mini-putt courses can be enjoyed in the area known as the **Windermere Valley.**

Another accommodation that is located centrally to all the action in the valley and with a spectacular view is **McMillan Chalet Bed & Break-fast** (5021 Fairmont Close, Box 989, Fairmont Hot Springs, V0B 1L0; 250–345–9553; 800–856–9551; fax: 250–345–9518; Kenmcm@ rockies. net or call the toll-free Supernatural BC Reservation Line at 800–HELLOBC; www.bbexpo.com/mcmchalet). Turn east off Highway 93 at the large FAIRMONT HOT SPRINGS RESORT sign; then turn left on Hot Springs Road, right on Falcon Drive, and right onto Fairmont Close. The McMil-lans serve excellent breakfasts and sometimes refreshments in the evening. Double rates are in the $75 to $95 range.

Ten miles north of Fairmont, on the eastern side of Lake Windermere, tiny **Windermere** (population 800) packs quite a punch. Glassblow-ers, wood-carvers, artists, and potters line an artisan's village near the 1887 Whitehouse Hotel. There's even a **Stolen Church** (on the corner of Kootenay Street and Victoria Avenue). The story goes that the church was built in Donald in 1887. When the CPR decided to move their railway divisional point from Donald, 115 miles (185 km) north of Windermere, to Revelstoke, it was agreed that several important buildings, including the church, would be moved, too. Rufus and Celina Kimpton of Donald loved this church. But they were moving to Windermere. So they purloined the church, piece by piece, on wagons and barges, and had it reassembled on a lovely hill, where it now stands as Windermere's only church.

Garden lovers visiting Windermere shouldn't miss **Creekside Flower Gardens** (Box 113, 4795 Dell Road, Windermere, V0B 2L0; phone/fax: 250–342–6354; gardens@AdventureValley.com; www.adventurevalley. com/gardens). Comprised of twenty-two separate theme gardens, too many to list here, the site has fragrant herb gardens, a sunflower forest walk, lily and wildflower hills, rose gardens, a tea house, a gardeners' library, a gift shop, and a suite for overnight guests. The gardens are located on Dell Road, off Sinclair Road and Quartz Street just a few minutes from town.

On the highway just north of the post office, there's fun for all at **Wild Mountain Adventure Park** (250–342–7227; mail@wildmountain.com; www.wild-mountain.com). It has eighteen, fun putting greens and a go-cart track in a pleasant setting of ponds, waterfalls, and shrubs. It's open daily in summer from 10:00 A.M. to 11:00 P.M. In its clubhouse **Cowpuccino on the Green Pie Company** serves homemade pies, ice creams, coffee, and pizza.

Stay over and get to know the golf courses and beaches in the valley at **Windermere Creek Bed & Breakfast Cabins** (1658 Windermere Loop Road, Box 409, Windermere, V0B 2L0; phone/fax: 250–342–0356; 800–946–3942; www.bbexpo.com/bc/windcreek.htm). It's a bit of the old and a lot of the new. Five private, secluded log cabins—one (the Heritage Cabin) built in 1887, the other four just recently—all featuring double Jacuzzi tubs and showers, plus a main house set in 107 acres, make up this unique bed-and-breakfast. The new cabins have a loft bedroom and a kitchenette (perfect for longer stays). To top it off there's a small orchard and miles of trails to wander, hike, or ski. Hammocks by the creek running through the property make for complete relaxation. Rates are from $85 to $105 (double) high season. The Windermere Loop Road is on the eastern side of Highway 93/95, and the Windermere Creek B&B is about 2 miles in (halfway along the loop) across from the fifth tee of the **Windermere Valley Golf Course** (250–342–3004).

Invermere (population 2,200) is on the northwestern side of Lake Windermere and was known by the Ktunaxa as *Kyaknuqti?it,* meaning "prairie on top of a hill." It has quite a holiday atmosphere. In 1807 David Thompson, the first European in the area, settled here, calling it Kootenae House. One of its more famous establishments is **Strands Old House Restaurant** (818 Twelfth Street, Invermere, V0A 1K0; 250–342–6344). Lovely surroundings and to-die-for food make Strands one of the best places to dine in the Rockies. There are at least four innovative chef's features daily, loads of fresh seafood, and a lobster tank. If you can't decide what to choose from the extensive menu, try the Rack of Lamb Anthony (named for the chef and owner, Tony Wood) or the pork fusilli bok choy. If you eat between 5:00 and 6:15 P.M., they offer a three-course, four-choice, early-bird special for $12.95. You'll find Strands 1 block west of the Invermere post office between Eighth and Tenth Avenues.

To experience Canadian adventure in this neck of the woods at its most exciting, call **Purcell River Odysseys Ltd.** (Box 15, Panorama, V0A 1T0; 250–342–6941; fax: 250–342–3936; info@panoramarafting. com; www. panoramarafting.com). You'll be hooked after a four-hour lesson/ excursion in one of their inflatable kayaks, where for $64 you'll be introduced to the basics of kayaking-à-la-ducky, followed by a run down a Class III river. Purcell's supplies all the necessary kayaking gear. There's also white-water rafting: Try a Toby Creek Odyssey, a two-hour adrenaline-pumping thriller at $39 (less for oldies, youngies, and groupies) or a three-hour Toby Ultimate ($44 and down), sure to be a wild and wet one. They also run four-hour Evening Wildlife Safaris ($39) with a naturalist, beginning at Mineral King, the site of an abandoned silver mine, passing through avalanche meadows and subalpine forests to Earl Grey's Cabin, a Canadian historical site. Wine and cheese completes the adults-only Toby Valley wilderness experience. Purcell's base is at Panorama Resort, just 10.9 miles (17.5 km) west of Invermere.

Panorama Mountain Village (800–663–2929 or 250–342–6941; fax: 250–342–3395; paninfo@intrawest.com; www. panoramaresort.com) is legendary, a recreation utopia both winter and summer. Breathtaking scenery and an intimate mountain-retreat village accompany skiing terrains ranging from double black-diamond glades to wide-open groomed cruising. The mountain features a vertical drop of 4,000 feet (1,200 m), runs more than 2.2 miles (3.5 km) long, and nine lifts. There's ski-to-your-door lodging, night skiing, cross-country skiing, heli-skiing, skating, snowmobiling, tubing, sleigh rides and hot tubs. And that's just in winter. In summer you can golf at the Greywolf Golf course, play tennis, swim, and participate in many more activities.

When you reach **Radium Hot Springs,** where Highways 93 and 95 diverge, you need to decide whether to head east (Highway 93) to wonderful parks and eventually Alberta or northwest (Highway 95) along the Columbia River to Golden. My suggestion, if you have time, is to do both. To miss either **Kootenay** or **Yoho National Parks** (in one of the world's largest protected areas) would be a shame. But first, let's look at Radium Hot Springs.

Here I discovered the Victorian-style **Village Country Inn & Tea Room** (7557 Canyon Avenue, Box 15, Radium Hot Springs, V0A 1M0; 250–347–9392; fax: 250-347-9375; mail@VillageCountryInn.bc.ca; www. VillageCountryInn.bc. ca). My first clue that I was in a wilderness setting was when a herd of Rocky Mountain bighorn sheep, refusing to let development interfere with their traditional beaten path, thundered by as I ate breakfast. Later I looked up to see an osprey and an eagle fly by. The main living room/dining room area is set around a large stone fireplace, and, upstairs, hosts Sasha and Gorm have decorated elegantly twelve bedrooms plus a honeymoon suite. Gourmet breakfasts cost $5.50–$7.00, and there's afternoon tea (don't miss Sasha's decadent desserts) from 2:00 to 5:00 P.M. for the general public. Room rates range from $94 to $115 in high season.

Ask at the Village Country Inn about the scenic (gravel but well-maintained) West Side Road, which runs south from Radium Hot Springs on the opposite (west) side of the Columbia River, parallel to Highway 93/95. It passes through beautiful valleys and crosses creeks and rivers before coming to bluffs that overlook the valley, eventually arriving at the small hamlet of Wilmer. It then joins the road to Panorama just north of Invermere. Another road leads from the West Side Road to a trailhead, the start of a three-hour hike leading to the glacier at the Lake of the Hanging Glacier, one of the most spectacular areas in the Canadian Rockies. Detailed maps are recommended.

> ## Trivia
>
> *The Banff-Windermere Road (now called Highway 93, the Banff-Windermere Parkway) was completed in 1922. It was the first motor road to be built through the central Canadian Rockies and is one of the most scenic roads in British Columbia, passing through Kootenay National Park to Banff National Park in Alberta.*

You'll find an excellent meal in Radium at the new **Helna's Stube**

Restaurant (250–347–0047; fax: 250–347–0049; mail@helnas.com; www.helnas.com). The Austrian-style menu has a variety of schnitzels and steaks, as well as delicious homemade desserts; locals swear it's the best meal you'll find in the valley. It's open year-round (except November) from 5:00 to 10:00 P.M. on the corner of Main Street West and St. Mary's Street. It's closed Tuesdays and Wednesdays in winter.

Just 2 blocks from town along Forsters Landing Road—turn west at the highway junction and follow the signs—is the highly acclaimed *Springs Golf Course* (Box 310, Radium Hot Springs, V0A 1M0; 800– 667–6444 or 250–347–9311; www.radiumresort.com), and but a mile away, you might take a dip in the Radium Hot Springs (see next section), where you can soak up the minerals and the stunning view from Sinclair Canyon. Should you be visiting in mid-September, you'll catch the *Show and Shine Columbia Valley Classic Car Show.* To help you find these attractions and more, the Chamber of Commerce in Radium has produced a comprehensive map of the area. Inquire at the *Radium Hot Springs Visitor Info Centre* (7556 Main Street East, Box 225, Radium Hot Springs, V0A 1M0; 800–347–9704 or 250–347–9331; fax: 250– 347–9127; chamber@rhs.bc.ca; www.rhs.bc.ca).

Kootenay National Park to Golden

From Radium Hot Springs you enter the UNESCO Rocky Mountain Parks World Heritage Site at *Kootenay National Park* (Box 220, Radium Hot Springs, V0A 1M0; 250–347–9615 or 800–748–7275; fax: 250–347–9980; www.worldweb.com/parkscanada-kootenay). Drop in to the Visitor Information Centre at the south end of Radium Village first, then keep your eyes peeled for bighorn sheep as you pass through the dramatic Sinclair Canyon. Then take a dip at the famous Radium Hot Springs (800–767–1611 in North America or 250–347–9485; hot_springs@pch.gc.ca) in either the hot pool, which, at an average temperature of 100° F (38° C), is great for a soak, or the cooler 84° F (29° C) pool, ideal for a swim. There's also a small Jacuzzi-style plunge pool. Don't miss a luxurious massage after your soak. (Phone 250–347–9714 or 6420 for reservations.) A restaurant and gift shop complete the complex. Hours mid-May to mid-October daily are 9:00 A.M. to 11:00 P.M. and from October to May Sunday to Thursday, noon to 9:00 P.M. (till 10:00 P.M. Friday and Saturday).

Head east along Highway 93 following Sinclair Creek, then north through the Kootenay River Valley, where from the safety of your vehicle, you may see elk or deer. Drive with care, as there is a significant

Radium Hot Springs

problem with highway mortality of wildlife. Stop off at the **Kootenay Valley Viewpoint,** 10 miles (17 km) from Radium, and feast on the panorama of the Mitchell and Vermilion ranges. Fifty-three miles (86 km) from Radium a mile-long (1.5-km) trail leads to the **Paint Pots,** natural pools where a vivid orange color is formed by iron-rich springs bubbling up through the pools and overflowing to the ocher beds, thus staining the clay red.

At colorful **Marble Canyon,** 55 miles (89 km) from Radium Hot Springs, there's a half-mile trail through a narrow gorge to a thundering waterfall. It's a great leg stretcher and shouldn't be missed. Four miles (7 km) farther, **Vermilion Pass,** at 5,416 feet (1,651 m), marks the Continental Divide (the rivers now flow toward the Atlantic) and the entrance to **Banff National Park** in Alberta. The Trans-Canada Highway then takes you north to the lovely Lake Louise and through Kicking Horse Pass to Golden, where you again meet up with Highway 95. Contact Canadian Heritage Parks Canada at (800) 748–PARK (7275) from anywhere in Canada; natlparks-ab@pch.gc.ca; www.worldweb.com/parks canada-banff/ springs.html for information on fees for all the National

Parks. A Western Canada Annual Pass is $35 per adult, with lower rates for children, seniors, and groups.

If instead you continue north from Radium Hot Springs, 7 miles (11 km) along Highway 95 is Edgewater, where every Saturday (from 10:00 A.M. to 2:00 P.M.) for the past thirty years the **Edgewater Open Market** has been the spot for farmers and artisans in the valley to show their wares.

Another 11 miles (18 km) north you'll pass through Brisco, population 140, where you may wonder, *why stop?* The **Brisco General Store** (250–346–3343), built in 1906, is why! It seems to sell everything, including liquor, videos, mousetraps, coffee, groceries, newspapers, and rubber boots. It's also the post office and the one original general store left in the Columbia River Valley that hasn't burned down yet. Like the other small towns in this wonderful valley, Brisco has a beautiful view. And if you should be coming on horseback, the hitching post is right out front.

A 30-mile (48-km) gravel logging road just south of Brisco leads to the **Bugaboo Glacier Provincial Park** (250–422–4200), famous for its huge glaciers, church-spire mountains, and heli-skiing. Should you ever see pictures of climbers hanging off impossible, jagged, rocky cliffs, chances are they were taken in the Bugaboos in the rugged Purcell Mountains. Hiking here can be steep and demanding, so check with park officials before venturing out.

From Brisco to Golden there's not much other than rambling ranches and beautiful scenery. Some people might ask, "What else do you

Recommended Reading - The Rockies

Yoho: A History and Celebration of Yoho National Park, by R. W. Sanford. Altitude Publishing, 1993.

Fort Steele: Here History Lives, by Derryl White. Heritage House Publishing Co. Ltd., Surrey, 1988.

Classic Hikes in the Canadian Rockies, by Graeme Pole. Canmore: Altitude Publishing, 1994.

Central Rockies Mammals, by John Marriott. Luminous Compositions Ltd., 1997.

The Canadian Rockies SuperGuide, by Graeme Pole. Altitude Publishing, 1998.

BC Parks Explorer, by Maggie Paquet. University of Toronto Press, 1986.

Central Rockies Wildflowers, by Mike Potter. Luminous Compositions Ltd., 1996.

want?" The Columbia continues its northern pursuit, and at *Golden* it's joined by the wild Kicking Horse River. Seated between the imposing Rockies and the Columbia Mountains, with five National Parks close by, Golden is indeed a crossroads. Here Highway 95 meets the Trans-Canada, from which you can travel east to *Yoho National Park,* (Box 99, Field, V0A 1G0; 250–343–6783; fax; 250–343–6012; www.world-web.com/ParksCanada-Yoho) with its fabulous canyons and glaciers, spectacular scenery, and more than 250 miles (400 km) of hiking trails. Yoho is also one of the four Rocky Mountain parks that form the UNESCO World Heritage Site. Features include the superb *Takakkaw Falls,* one of the highest waterfalls in Canada (and highest in BC); the *Natural Bridge,* carved out of solid rock; and the *Burgess Shale,* with fossil deposits of internationally recognized significance.

Golden is popular with sports enthusiasts of every ilk, in any season. One activity gaining popularity is white-water rafting. Several companies offer all levels of rafting trips on the Blaeberry and Kicking Horse Rivers, including *Glacier Raft Company* (250–344–6521; fax: 250–344–6591; glacierraft@redshift.bc.ca; www.glacierraft.com); *Alpine Rafting* (888–599–5299; alpinerafting@redshift.bc.ca; www. kickinghorseriver.com/alpinerafting); *Wet 'n Wild Adventures* (800–668–9119; 250–344–6546; fax: 250–344–7650; wetnwild@red shift.bc.ca; www.canadianrockies.net/wetnwild); and *Rocky Mountain Rafting Company* (888–518–7238; 250–344–6979; fax: 250–344–6985; info@rockymountainadventure.com; www.rockymountain adventure.com). If you want to experience the true thrill of white-water rafting, try a one-day Kicking Horse River rollick, which is probably one of the wildest one-day raft trips in Canada. It begins fast, and the river never really slows as you accelerate through such exhilarating rapids as Man Eater, Shot Gun, and Twin Towers. Most companies offer transportation, rafting gear, and a riverside lunch at the halfway point, then it's on to the lower canyon, which has more than 2 miles (3.5 kms) of continuous rapids through steep, narrow canyons. Wild, wet, and what a wallop! Full-day rates are in the $85 to $99 range.

You'll need a few days here—or at least one in which to relax after that rafting thrill. *H.G. Parson House Bed & Breakfast* (815 Twelfth Street South, Box 1196, Golden, V0A 1H0; 250–344–5001; fax: 250–344–2782; hgparsonhousebb@redshift.bc.ca; www.bbcanada.com/2612.html) is a restored 1893-built heritage house decorated with antiques and conveniently located 1 block west of Highway 95 on Twelfth Street South. Rates are $85.50 to $89.50 double in high season.

Rafting is not the only outdoor activity in Golden. There's paragliding in tandem on *Mount Seven*, hang gliding, fishing, cycling, mountain biking, bird-watching, golfing, and more. *Golden Mountain Adventures* (Box 296, 1417 Highway 1, Golden, V0A 1H0; 250–344–4650; fax: 250–344–4651; toll free reservations: 800–433–9533; info@Adventure Rockies.com; www.adventurerockies.com) will book your activities.

The *Golden Golf and Country Club* (250–344–2700; fax: 250–344–2922; golfgolden@redshift.bc.ca; www.golfcanada.com) is in BC's Top Ten list and Canada's Top Thirty. It's located right by the Columbia River, with each hole built to take in the incredible scenery. Look for the pair of eagles who make the fourteenth hole their home.

Kinbasket Adventures (Box 4137 Golden, V0A 1H0; 250–344–6012; 866–344–6012 toll free; fax: 250–344–6140; kbasket@rockies.net; www.bcrockiesadventures.com) runs two-and-a-half hour Wetland Tours, a float through the Columbia River wetlands (the largest area of wetlands west of Manitoba, covering 64,246 acres—26,000 ha), to view osprey, bald eagles, great blue herons, and many other species in their natural habitat. Rates are $40 for adults and $20 for kids twelve and under. They also offer canoeing and fishing, and in winter, snowmobiling.

Purcell Heli-Skiing (877–435–4754 or 250–344–5410; fax: 250–344–6076; info@purcellhelicopterskiing.com; www.purcellhelicopterskiing.com) offers helicopter skiing (of course!).

In early May the *Golden Festival of Birds and Bears* is a hit with bird lovers from all over the world; and throughout the year the old Brisco schoolhouse is a feature at the *Golden Historical Society Museum,* 1320 Eleventh Avenue; (250) 344–5169. To learn more about these attractions contact the *Golden Visitor Info Centre* at 500 Tenth Avenue North, Box 1320, Golden, V0A 1H0; (800) 622–GOLD (4653); (250) 344–7125; fax: (250) 344–6688; goldcham@rockies.net; www.go2rockies.com.

The activities Golden offers are mostly energy-eaters, so it has a few good spots for refueling. You'll probably run into fellow rafters or hang gliders at the *Mad Trapper Neighborhood Pub* (1203 Ninth Street South; 250–344–6661; food line: 250–344–6262; madtrap@rockies.net). Prices are moderate and the daily specials (halibut and chips on Fridays) always a bargain. Coming from the south on Highway 95, take a right on Ninth Street at the first set of lights just before the Kicking Horse River. Or walk down the street and try the international cuisine at *The Kicking*

Horse Grill (1105 Ninth Street South; 250–344–2330; khgrill@ rockies.net). This popular restaurant was once an old log cabin. Or you could sit in the peaceful garden at *Sisters and Beans* (1122 Tenth Avenue South; 250–344–2443), a renovated heritage building with views of the Purcell Mountains.

New to Golden is the *Kicking Horse Mountain Resort* (1500 Kicking Horse Trail, Box 839, Golden, V0A 1H0; 866–754–5425; 250–439–5400; fax: 439–5401; www.kickinghorseresort.com), a $200 million all-season resort. Enjoy rides on the eight-person gondola to the top of the mountain, where you can dine at Canada's loftiest restaurant, *The Eagle's Eye,* standing at 7,705 feet (2,350 m) elevation. Your meal price includes a complimentary gondola ticket to experience five-star dining. For viewers only, two-way gondola tickets are $15.00 adults, $11.50 youths thirteen to eighteen, $13.00 seniors, and $6.00 ages seven to twelve.

If you are heading toward Rogers Pass on the Trans-Canada, you will find quiet country accommodation on fifty-nine acres (24 ha) at *Hillside Lodge Chalets & B&B* (1740 Seward Frontage Road, Box 2603, Golden, V0A 1H0; phone/fax: 250–344–7281; hillside@rockies.net; www.mistaya.com/hillside). It's 8 miles (13 km) northwest of Golden (halfway to Donald) and just 500 yards off the highway on the Blaeberry River. The cabins are new, and the views of the river and the Rockies are spectacular. Guest rooms including delicious breakfasts and chalets with kitchenettes range from $98 to $125 double in high season.

The Trans-Canada follows the Columbia River north through Donald and west to Rogers Pass in *Glacier National Park.* Here at 4,534 feet (1,382 m), Canadian Pacific Railway workers performed the formidable task of pushing a railway line through, while avalanches and rock slides took their toll. At Rogers Pass we head into High Country.

PLACES TO STAY
IN THE ROCKIES

CRANBROOK
Cedar Heights
Bed & Breakfast,
1200 13th Street South,
V1C 5V8; (250) 426–0505
or (800) 497–6014;
fax: (250) 426–0045.

FERNIE
Willow Creek B&B,
5375 Boomerang Way,
Box 6049, V0B 1M6;
(250) 423–7731.
Moderate. Near ski hill.

Barbara Lynn's Country
Inn B&B,
Box 1077, 691 7th Avenue,
V0B 1M0;
(250) 423–6027; (888)
288–2148. In town.

Moderate. Discounts for
cyclists.

GOLDEN
Hillside Lodge Chalets
Bed and Breakfast,
1240 Seward Frontage
Road, Box 2603,
V0A 1H0; phone/fax: (250)
344–7281. Rooms
$98–$125 high-season
double.

RADIUM HOT SPRINGS
Village Country Inn
and Tea Room,
7557 Canyon Avenue,
V0A 1M0; (250) 347–9392.
$94–$115 high-season
double.

WASA
Wasa Lakeside Bed and
Breakfast and More,
Box 122,
V0B 2K0; (250) 422–3688
or (888) 422–3636. Action-
packed holiday or a roman-
tic getaway.

**PLACES TO EAT
IN THE ROCKIES**

CRANBROOK
The Art Café,
20 Seventh Avenue;
(250) 426–4565.
Moderately priced,
tasty food.

FERNIE
Rip 'n Richards Eatery,
301 Highway 3,
(250) 423–3002. Casual
and colorful.

GOLDEN
The Mad Trapper,
1203 9th Street South,
V0A 1H0; (250) 344–6661.
Pub style.

The Eagle's Eye,
(250) 439–5400;
Canada's loftiest restaurant.
Five-star dining.

INVERMERE
Strands Old House
Restaurant,
818 12th Street,
V0A 1K0; (250) 342–6344.
Moderately priced classy
food. Reservations.

KIMBERLEY
Chef Bernard's Inn and
Restaurant,
170 Spokane Street,
V1A 2E4; (800) 905–8338.
International menu.

The Snowdrift Café,
110 Spokane Street,
V1A 2E4; (250) 427–2001.
Inexpensive,
healthful foods.

RADIUM
Helna's Stube Restaurant,
corner of Main Street West
and St. Mary's Street;
(250) 347–0047. Austrian-
style menu.

High Country

From the east, entry into High Country through Rogers Pass in Glacier National Park is dramatic. The Trans-Canada Highway leads west through Revelstoke, the site of one of the largest hydroelectric developments in the world, to Craigellachie, where in 1885 a plain iron spike completed the railway line linking Canada from east to west. From Canada's houseboat capital on Shuswap Lake, we follow the North Thompson River from Kamloops, British Columbia's largest city in area, through Wells Grey Provincial Park to Mount Robson, at 12,972 feet (3,954 m), the highest peak in the Canadian Rockies. A region of superlatives and diversity, High Country has something for all wanderers eager to find a road less traveled.

Southeastern High Country

My first trip into High Country through Rogers Pass was memorable. It was November, and the snow was falling thick and heavy. Trucks lined the roadside as they stopped to fit wheel chains; an occasional car lay abandoned in a ditch like highway litter. This was Rogers Pass in all its winter fury. But in warmer weather **Mount Revelstoke** and **Glacier National Parks** are a hiking and camping wonderland of more than 400 glaciers, unique cave systems (although restricted) and alpine tundra. Information is available from the Park Superintendent (Box 350, 301 Third Street West, Revelstoke, V0E 2S0; 250–837–7500; fax: 250–837–7536; revglacier_reception@pch.gc.ca; park scan.harbour.com/glacier) or at the **Rogers Pass Information Centre** (250–837–6274), just west of the pass. Ask staff guides about joining one of their informative hikes or, if necessary, about borrowing an all-terrain wheelchair to enjoy the trail to the Summit Monument. Park passes can also be purchased here. Everyone stopping in national parks must have a park pass, even if just visiting

Trivia

Between 1885 and 1916, 250 railway employees were killed by the "White Death." The tragedy at Rogers Pass in 1910 was Canada's worst avalanche disaster.

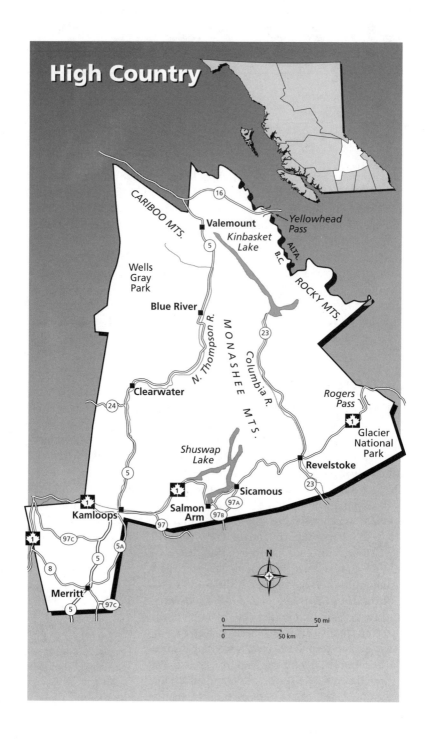

High Country

Yellowhead
Pass

Valemount
*Kinbasket
Lake*

Wells
Gray
Park

CARIBOO MTS.

16

5

Blue River

N. Thompson R.

MONASHEE MTS.

ROCKY MTS.

ALTA
B.C.

23

Columbia R.

Clearwater

24

5

*Shuswap
Lake*

1

Kamloops

97C

97

*Rogers
Pass*

1

**Glacier
National
Park**

Revelstoke

23

**Salmon
Arm**
97A
97B

Sicamous

1

5A

5

8

Merritt

5

97C

N

| 0 | | 50 mi |
| 0 | | 50 km |

the Rogers Pass Centre. Day passes are $4.00 adults, $3.00 seniors, $2.00 children six to sixteen, and $10.00 for groups of two to seven; or inquire about annual passes valid at all western Canadian national parks.

From the pass the highway threads through snowsheds, erected for protection from all-too-frequent avalanches. One, in 1910, buried fifty-eight railway workers. To learn more about avalanches, visit the *Canadian Avalanche Centre* in Revelstoke (250–837–2435). Backcountry hikers and skiers can check snow conditions by calling (800) 667–1105.

Tucked between Mount Glacier and Mount Revelstoke national parks in these spectacular Selkirk Mountains is Albert Canyon Hot Springs. *Canyon Hot Springs Resort Ltd.* (Box 2400, Revelstoke, V0E 2S0; 250–837–2420; fax: 250–837–6160 in winter or 250–837–3171 in summer; info@canyon hotsprings.com; www.canyonhotsprings.com) is set amid 200 acres (81 ha), with superb hiking trails, good fishing, mountain climbing, horseback riding, and river rafting. Open May to September, it's a convenient and relaxing stopover. Watch for the red umbrellas halfway—22 miles (35 km)—between Rogers Pass and Revelstoke. Railway workers enjoyed these soothing waters at the turn of the century. Choose from two pools, a 104° F (40° C) hot pool and an 80° F (26° C) swimming pool. As well as the pools, there are cabins and campsites, a B&B, a laundry, a cafe, and stores.

AUTHOR'S TOP TEN PICKS IN HIGH COUNTRY

Renting a house boat to explore the 621 miles (1,000 km) of Shuswap Lake's shoreline

Touring or horseback riding at Douglas Lake Ranch, Canada's largest working cattle ranch

Hiking to Margaret Falls in Herald Provincial Park, near Salmon Arm

Learning about the bats in Squilax at the Squilax General Store

Learning First Nations traditions at Quaaout Lodge on Little Shuswap Lake

Viewing the Adams River October sockeye salmon run

Exploring Kamloops Wildlife Park

Photographing the alpine meadows at Trophy Mountain, near Clearwater

Heli-skiing or heli-hiking at Blue River

Taking in the awesome views around Mount Robson, the highest peak in the Canadian Rockies

---

Revelstoke

The Trans-Canada passes through *Mount Revelstoke National Park* and follows the Illecillewaet River for 40 miles (65 km) down into Revelstoke, which lies in the heart of the Monashees, looking like a giant model-railroad town. Here the Illecillewaet joins the Columbia in its southerly sweep to Upper Arrow Lake.

Momma, Poppa, and Baby grizzly-bear stone sculptures guard the entrance to **Grizzly Plaza** in downtown Revelstoke, causing local jokers to call it Sesame Street! From 7:00 to 10:00 P.M. in July and August, the plaza perks up with comedy acts, jazz combos, and Bluegrass bands. It's great entertainment and all free!

From the plaza on Mackenzie Avenue, the streets are numbered in order east or west of here, making it easy to find your way around. The city was settled in the 1800s by gold prospectors, but it was the building of the Canadian Pacific Railway that contributed to its becoming the dynamic city of 8,500 that it is today. Learn of the city's history and more at the **Revelstoke Visitor Info Centre,** 204 Campbell Avenue, Box 490, Revelstoke, V0E 2S0; (250) 837–5345 or (800) 487–1493; fax: (250) 837–4223; manager@revelstoke.cc.bc.ca; www. revelstokecc. bc.ca/. It's open all year, and as well there's a summer office at the junction of Highways 1 and 23 North. Perhaps request a Virtual Visit CD-ROM containing video footage and photos that will give you a taste of the area in all seasons.

With railway history in mind, follow the tracks (which will inevitably have a train on them, so be patient) to the **Revelstoke Railway Museum** (719 West Track Street, P.O. Box 3018, Revelstoke, V0E 2S0; 877–837–6060 or 250–837–6060; fax: 250–837–3732; railway@revelstoke.net; www.railway museum.com). Here you'll be able to experience the thrill of operating a diesel locomotive via a coin-operated simulated ride and also learn the history of the construction of the most treacher-

ous section of the transcontinental railway. Volunteers (ex-railway engineers) donate their time to tell you of their experiences on the rails. The museum is open year-round: daily July/August 9:00 A.M. to 8:00 P.M., shoulder season 9:00 A.M. to 5:00 P.M., and December to March weekdays from 1:00 to 5:00 P.M. Admission prices for adults are $6.00, seniors $5.00, youths (ages seven to sixteen) $3.00; children six and under are free. Railway memorabilia is available in the gift shop. On the third weekend in August, the Railway Museum hosts Revelstoke Railway Days, with tours, hikes, slide shows, and equipment demonstrations.

There's more railway history at the **Revelstoke Museum** (315 First Street West; 250–837–3067; fax: 250–837–3094; rm_chin@revelstoke.

net). Housed in the 1926-built original post office, the museum has interesting pieces, such as a 1911 fur press and many artifacts and photographs (over 3,000) relating to logging, mining, transportation, and farming. It is open 10:00 A.M. to 5:00 P.M. Monday to Saturday June 15 to August 31, and 1:00 to 4:00 P.M. weekdays the rest of the year. Ask about cemetery tours and children's programs held throughout the year.

Outdoor enthusiasts will appreciate that Revelstoke places high in the Top 10 Adventure Towns in North America and is number one in Canada, with the area just outside Revelstoke described as "the heart of heli-skiing in BC's interior," having both the Monashees to the west or the Selkirks to the east to choose from. Another sport gaining popularity, sometimes referred to as "poor man's heli-skiing," is Cat skiing. *Cat Powder Skiing* (877–4CATSKI or 250–837–5151; fax: 250–837–5111; catski@revelstoke.net; www.catpowder.com) boasts " almost too much snow" as they load about a dozen skiers into a modern Sno-Cat (five Bombardier Sno-Cats make up the litter!) for a memorable journey to the summit of Mount Mackenzie. Stronger skiers can descend as much as 18,000 feet (5,500 m) in virgin powder snow. *Powder Springs Resort* (recently purchased by Cat Powder Skiing 250–837–3199) is the local favorite for regular downhill enthusiasts. This 1,000-foot (305-m) vertical-drop hill has one double chair and a handle tow serving twenty-seven runs. There's a day lodge, ski shop, cafeteria, lounge, rental shop, and ski school. In summer golfers will find the *Revelstoke Golf Course* (250–837–4276) challenging, with its fairways scenically located along the Columbia River. Contact the *Powder Springs Inn* (200 Third Street West, Box 1479, Revelstoke, V0E 2S0; 250–837–5151 or toll free 800–991–4455; fax: 250–837–5111), about two minutes away from the golf course, to arrange golf packages (from $69). For more information on any of these activities and accommodation packages, call (877) 4–CATSKI or check out www.catpowder.com.

Loggers Day Sports, *Revelstoke; July;* *(250) 837–5345*

Railway Days, *Revelstoke; August; (250) 837–5345*

Squilax PowWow, *Squilax; July; (250) 679–3203*

Grebe Festival, *The Nature Bay, Salmon Arm; May; (250) 833–4886*

Shuswap Rodeo, *Shuswap; June; (250) 838–2367*

Sicamous Moose Mouse Days, *Sicamous; August; (250) 836–3313*

Valemount Days, *Valemont; June; (250) 566–4846*

Annual Shuswap Lake Festival of Arts, *Sorrento; July; (250) 955–2390*

Kamloops Cattle Drive, *Kamloops; July; (250) 372–7075; (800) 288–5850 toll free*

Kamloops International Air Show, *Kamloops; August; (250) 828–1404*

Kamloops Pow Wow Days, *Kamloops; August; (250) 828–9708*

Mountain Music Festival, *Merritt; July; (604) 525–3330*

Revelstoke has a number of historical buildings. A *Heritage Walking and Driving Tour* booklet (available at the museum and Info Centre) adds interest to a walk through the town. The most conspicuous on the list is the **Revelstoke Courthouse** at 1100 Second Street. It stands prominently about 10 blocks from the plaza, with its 30-foot (9-m) copper-covered dome. Other buildings include the **Holton House** (1897), at 1221 First Street West, and Revelstoke's first brick home, the Fromey home, built in 1897 at 912 Second Street West.

Another one of these older homes is a seventeen-room beauty built in 1905. It has since been restored to provide elegant accommodation. *Four Seasons Manor Bed and Breakfast,* at 815 MacKenzie Avenue (Box 2628, Revelstoke, V0E 2S0; toll free: 877–837–2616; phone/fax:250–837–2616; four seasonsmanor@rctvonline.net; www.revelstokecc.bc.ca/vacation/4seasonsbb.htm) features impeccable Edwardian queen-size beds and hearty full breakfasts. An elegant tea room serves home-baked traditional English afternoon tea. High-season rates range from $90 to $140 double; off-season $75 to $85.

There's good coffee (and great desserts) downtown at *Conversations Coffee House* (203 Mackenzie Avenue; 250–837–4772). But for something more substantial, the ranch-style *Frontier Family Restaurant* (Box 1239, Revelstoke, V0E 2S0; 250–837–5119 or 800–382–7763; fax: 250–837–6604; welcome@revelstoke.net; www.revelstokecc.bc.ca/frontier), at the corner of Highways 1 and 23 North, is a good bet. The Frontier also shouts "Y'all welcome!" if you also need accommodation or gas.

BC Hydro's *Revelstoke Dam and Generating Station* is five minutes north of the city on Highway 23. Visitors use audio wands to learn about hydroelectricity and the dam's construction. Take the elevator to the Dam Crest Lookout to see over Lake Revelstoke reservoir and the Columbia River. The two-hour, free tour runs daily from mid-March to late October. Phone (250) 837–6211 for information or check the Web site at www.bchydro.bc.ca/recreation/revelstoke.html.

Twelve miles (19 km) west of Revelstoke is the resort of *Three Valley Lake Chateau Ltd.* and *Three Valley Gap Heritage Ghost Town* (Box

The Four Seasons Manor Bed and Breakfast in Revelstoke

860, Revelstoke, V0E 2S0; 250–837–2109; fax: 250–837–5220; 888–667–2109 for reservations; 3valley@revelstoke.net; www.3valley. com for reservations; open mid-April to mid-October). This popular modern holiday spot, situated on a lake in the spectacular Eagle Pass, comes complete with a restored historic town (guided tours daily) and a theater. At 8:00 P.M. from mid-May to the end of September, listen to the songs of the Old West and watch a trick roping act at the *Walter Moberly Theatre's* **Trails and Rails West Musical Revue** (reservations required). Moberly was the surveyor who chose Eagle Pass for the Trans-Canadian railroad's final stretch through the Monashees. Double accommodation rates at Three Valley Gap are from $100 to $135 in mid-summer.

Ten miles (16 km) west of Three Valley Gap is the *Enchanted Forest* (Box 2938, Revelstoke, V0E 2S0; phone/fax: 250–837–9477 or 837–9655 off-season; enchant@rctvonline.net). Open mid-May to mid-September, it features 350 handmade fairy-tale figures, a nature trail, and an 800-year-old hollow cedar tree. Six miles (10 km) farther is *Beardale Castle Miniatureland* (250–836–2268; RR1 Malakwa,

V0E 2J0; www.shuswap.bc.ca/sunny/beardale.htm), a unique attraction featuring multicultural displays and international villages. Here you can experience a 1950s Canadian prairie town, a Swiss mountain village, a German town, and an English Tudor village, all with large-scale model railway layouts. Six of the fifteen trains on display are running at all times. Also featured is a *Last Spike* heritage display, western Canada's largest animated toy-land exhibit, and Mother Goose nursery rhymes in motion. It's open daily May 1 to September 30, 9:00 A.M. to 7:00 P.M.

West of Beardale Castle is Craigellachie, 28 miles (46 km) west of Revelstoke, the site where on November 7, 1885, Sir Donald Smith, a Canadian Pacific Railway financier, drove in the famous **Last Spike.** A souvenir shop is open from May to October. Attendants will enlighten you with some of the stories surrounding this symbol of Canadian unity. For more information contact Revelstoke Railway Museum (250–837–6060).

The Shuswap

The Trans-Canada moves away from the Monashees and follows the Eagle River past the hiking trails and ancient cedars of the *Eagle River Nature Park* to Shuswap Lake, where more than 600 miles (1,000 km) of shoreline make for a very popular vacation spot. Several arms and channels of the H-shaped lake system appear as tentacles spreading among the intersecting valleys in the Shuswap Highlands. Salmon Arm, Seymour Arm, Anstey Arm, Mara Lake, Shuswap Lake, Little Shuswap Lake, White Lake, and Adams Lake, plus all the hiking trails, sandy beaches, beautiful waterfalls, and friendly people make up this holiday area known as *The Shuswap.*

Trivia

Copper Island in Shuswap Lake reminded Sorrento's founder (J. R. Kinghorn) of Sorrento in Italy, where he and his wife honeymooned; hence the name.

Sicamous, 43 miles (70 km) east of Revelstoke, is *Canada's Houseboat Capital.* Everything, including the kitchen sink, the hot tub, and a waterslide to keep the kids occupied for days, is provided on a houseboat rented from several companies including *Bluewater Houseboat Rentals* (Box 248, Sicamous, V0E 2V0; 800–663–4024 or 250–836–2255; fax: 250–836–4955; bluwater@sicamous.com; www. shuswap. bc.ca/bluewater). Contact Sicamous and District Chamber (Box 346, Sicamous, V0E 2V0; 250-836-3313; fax: 250–836–4368;

WORTH SEEING/DOING IN HIGH COUNTRY

Hike in Glacier National Park.

Stop at Rogers Pass Centre to see railroad models and learn of the struggles endured by CPR workers in the building of the railroad.

Cruise Shuswap Lake from Sicamous to Seymour Arm aboard the MV Phoebe.

Ski at Sun Peaks Resort.

Explore the provincial marine parks in the Shuswap from the comfort of a houseboat.

chamber@sicamous.com; www. sicamouschamber. bc.ca) for more information on houseboating and accommodation, plus hiking and fishing opportunities.

From Sicamous Highway 97A leads southwest to Vernon, where it joins Highway 97 to Kelowna. Twelve miles (19 km) south of Sicamous, there's an excellent family private campground at the end of Mara Lake. **Whispering Pines Tent and RV Park** (RR 1, Site 3, Comp 2, Mara, V0E 2K0; 250–838–6775; fax: 250–838–2332) has a heated pool, minigolf, and a free daily tractor ride—just a few of the family-oriented friendly features at this 160-site campground. RV rentals that sleep four to six are also available.

Trivia

Need a new hubcap? Tiny Grinrod, southwest of Sicamous, and just past Mara Lake on Highway 97A, is home to an eclectic collection of hubcaps and old licence plates, as well as books and other paraphernalia. At last count Gordon Packham, owner of Gord's New and Used, had almost 24,000 hubcaps.

Salmon Arm, 19 miles (31 km) west of Sicamous on Highway 1, along the southwestern arm (Salmon Arm) of Shuswap Lake, is the main business center in the area. Dubbed the "Gem of the Shuswap," it has a population of about 16,000 and boasts the largest freshwater pier in North America. **Shuswap Lakes Vacation Inc.** (Box 1480, Salmon Arm, V1E 4P6; 250–832–2745; fax: 250–836–4824; 800–663–4026; houseboat@twinanchors.com; www.twinan chors.com) is on the pier and rents boats that sleep up to fifteen persons. Sea-doos and ski boats are also available for a day of water fun. If you'd rather have land-based accommodation, call (800) 661–4800 or check www. shuswap. bc. ca for listings.

Also by the pier is the **Salmon Arm Bay Nature Enhancement Center,** a waterfowl sanctuary, where a boardwalk, a viewing platform, and bird blinds are aids in experiencing this very special wildlife area. If you're there between April and June, you might catch sight of Clark's and western grebes (the "water dancer" often seen doing his mating ritual on the water's surface) or any of the other 150 species familiar to the area. Fishing (Eastern brook and rainbow trout) and hiking are very popular here, too.

Over on the northwest shore of Shuswap Lake's Salmon Arm, *Herald Provincial Park* (119 vehicle campsites; phone 800–689–9025 for reservations) is a cooling spot on a hot summer's day (quite common in the Shuswap). Located 9 paved miles (13 km) northeast of Tappen off Highway 1, Reinecker Creek meanders through the park. *Margaret Falls* is at the end of a wheelchair-accessible trail through Reinecker Gorge. Nobody seems too sure who Margaret was, but I've been told that if you look closely into the falls, you may see her apparition. Here the cedars are enormous, and the cool moistness of the twenty-minute round-trek is refreshing. For more information on the area, contact the *Salmon Arm Visitor Info Centre* (#1 751 Marine Park Drive Northeast, Salmon Arm, V1E 2W7; 250–832–6247 or 877–SALMON–7 [725–6667]; fax: 250–832–8382; sacofc@shuswap.net; www.sachamber.bc.ca). Staff have prepared information on golf courses (two championship, two executive, and three nine-holers in the vicinity), dozens of campgrounds, hotels, motels, and cabins, and such attractions as a gouda cheese factory, double go-carts, a free petting zoo, "J" Lanes bowling, and the *R.J. Haney Heritage Park and Museum* (250–832–5243; fax: 250–832–5291; hpark@jetstream.net), on the corner of the Trans-Canada and Highway 97B—the road to Vernon. In summer you can take a step back into Salmon Arm's past at a pioneer village. The museum is open Wednesday to Sunday 10:00 A.M.

Life in the Bat House

*H*ere's a tale of love that needs to be told. When the historic Squilax church burned to the ground, 2,000 female yuma bats (Myotis yumanensis) lost their home. Concerned for the welfare of the bats, students from Haldane elementary and NorKam secondary schools, with the aid of a wildlife biologist, erected bat houses in the vicinity. Interestingly, with a total of thirty-eight houses to choose from, at first most of the bats squeezed into the few houses at the original church site. Lately, they have been moving from house to house, favoring nine houses, three of which are on the old church site. Today these bat houses are an aid in counting the bat population and are part of a North American Bat House Research Assistance Program. Local volunteers count the bats once a week. Visitors are invited to come out—divesting themselves of whatever bat phobias they may have—and help count the bats. The Squilax site is recognized by Bat Conservation International in Austin, Texas, and is listed in their Vacationer's Guide to Viewing Bats in North America.

Trivia

Rockhounding is a popular occupation on Squilax Mountain near Chase, the Enderby Cliffs, and Mount Ida near Salmon Arm. Blue-gray and banded agate, cyrstalline geodes, and amethyst are some of the sought-after stones.

to 4:00 P.M. May through September. There's also a 1.2-mile (2-km) nature trail to hike, where you'll learn about the Shuswap's natural history.

The Trans-Canada heads north from Salmon Arm for 20 miles (32 km) to **Sorrento** (population 6,400), where the air is thick with community spirit.

About 2.5 miles (4 km) before Sorrento, up on a hill with a great view of Copper Island and Shuswap Lake, you can roost for the night at **Pheasant Heaven** (2833 Hilltop Road, Box 202, Sorrento, V0E 2W0; 250–675–4966; fax: 250–675–3420; pheasant@shuswap.net; www. shuswap.bc.ca/sunny/ pheasant.htm). Here Mandi and Laurier Fleury run a pleasant bed and breakfast and aviaries, where they breed and raise more than forty different kinds of pheasants. Their aviaries contain many varieties including a Monal Impeyan, the national bird of Nepal. They enjoy giving personalized tours, and with plenty of parking space and the free use of their picnic tables, you can make a day of it. There's a small gift shop with displays of exotic bird eggs.

While in Sorrento, stop at **Toby's** (250–675–4464), which is on the highway beside the hardware store, for one of Dave and Cherie's homemade pizzas and Caesar salads. Learn about Sorrento's history through a series of murals decorating some of the buildings.

Down behind the Sorrento elementary school on the northern side of the highway, **The Evergreens Bed and Breakfast** (2853 Vimy Road, Box 117, Sorrento, V0E 2W0; 250–675–2568; fax: 250–675–3100; ever greens@jetstream.net; www.bbexpo.com/bc/evergreens.htm) is just a short walk to Shuswap Lake's southwestern shore. Berry-filled gardens provide food for delicious breakfasts as well as afternoon teas, served in a gazebo on Wednesday, and Thursday, or by reservation for parties. The gazebo has made the Evergreens a popular wedding spot, so hosts Linda and Verna have added a tiny chapel and an antique buggy for ambience! The accommodations are pleasant, featuring a sauna and a guest kitchen. With an aviary full of chirping canaries and finches and a few wild turkeys gobbling about outside, it has a laid-back, holiday atmosphere. Take Passchendaele Road to Vimy Road; the Evergreens is on the left. Rates are $60 to $75 double.

Tiny Sorrento (population 662) is full of pleasant surprises. The **Sorrento Centre** (Box 99, Sorrento, V0E 2W0, 250–675–2421; fax: 250–

675–3032; sorrento@jetstream.net; www.sorrento-centre.bc.ca) is an ecumenical conference, retreat, and holiday center on Shuswap Lake just off the highway on Passchendaele Road. Here children, teens, and adults can sign up for courses including such wide-ranging topics as wilderness recreation, meditation, social and environmental justice, and therapeutic touch. It can accommodate up to seventy persons in two modern lodges year-round, and as well, there are private rooms, cabanas, and camping facilities. The meals are cafeteria-style with a set menu. Check the Web site for a full description of courses available.

The highway follows Shuswap Lake, and about 6 miles (10 km) farther west, the historic **Squilax General Store and Caboose Hostel** (Trans-Canada Highway, Squilax, RR 2, Site 2, Comp 11, Chase, V0E 1M0; phone/fax: 250–675–2977; squilax@jetstream.net; www.hihostels.bc.ca) sells "funky foods and groovy groceries." Stay in renovated cabooses overlooking Shuswap Lake for $19, or if you're a Hostelling International member, a mere $15.

From the store take the bridge over the river and turn left onto Little Shuswap Lake Road to the Shuswap Band Reserve. Every summer drummers, singers, and dancers from all over North America arrive for the **Squilax International Powwow** (Box 1100, Chase, V0E 1M0; 250–679–3203). Traditional native food is served, arts and crafts are displayed, and generally a good time is had by all. There used to be a colony (or was it a congregation?) of about 2,000 female **Yuma bats** living in the attic of the old church nearby. In 1993 the church burned down, so some local enthusiasts built bat houses on 14-foot poles near the old church site. The bats are returning, so the mission was successful! Ask at the Squilax Store for up-to-date information.

Exceptional accommodation is available at **Quaaout Lodge Resort** (Box 1215, Chase, V0E 1M0; 800–663–4303 or 250–679–3090; quaaout@quaaout.com; www. quaaout. com). This native-run hotel emphasizes its aboriginal heritage. Traditional native cultural activities, canoeing, a recently built sweat house, and a kekuli, as well as First Nations cuisine in the restaurant, add to the modern lake-view rooms, half-mile of sandy beach, pool, Jacuzzi, fully equipped gym, and steam room at this architectural marvel, inspired by a native pit house. Renowned native dancer and storyteller Ernie Philip is the cultural advisor. He freely gives of his time

Trivia

Peter Wing, elected mayor of Kamloops in 1966, was the first mayor of Chinese descent in North America.

to explain the traditions behind the features at Quaaout Lodge. Double accommodation in high season ranges from $119 to $170.

From Squilax Bridge the Squilax-Anglemont road leads north about 3 miles (5 km) to **Roderick Haig-Brown Provincial Park** (no camping) and the **Adams River**, famous for its October sockeye salmon run, possibly the largest on the continent. The river was called Chu Chua on early maps but was renamed after a Shuswap Indian Chief, Selhowtken, who had been baptized Adam. Every four years (1998–2002, etc.), the river sees a boom run. A slide at Hell's Gate during railway construction in 1913 all but wiped out the run, but through the building of fishways and hatcheries, and upgrading habitats, the runs are gradually coming back to their historic numbers. To see this tide of salmon after their 305-mile (490-km) Fraser and Thompson River run, their battered crimson backs thrusting compulsively to return home to spawn and die in the gravel reaches of the Adams River, is a stirring experience. Writer, poet, avid angler (and conservationist) Roderick Haig-Brown saw it thus: "River-borne fugitives, red muscled under sheathing silver. . . ." Trained staff are in attendance during the run to explain this incredible phenomenon. For more information on this park and all other provincial parks in the Shuswap or Kamloops area, contact BC Parks, Thompson River District Office, 1210 McGill Road, Kamloops, V2C 6N6; (250) 851–3000; fax: (250) 828–4633.

Before leaving the area explore the northern shore of Shuswap Lake, where the tiny communities of Lee Creek, Scotch Creek, Celista, Magna Bay, Anglemont, and St. Ives serve visitors who come to enjoy a wide variety of outdoor activities. The North Shuswap Chamber (Box 101, Celista, V0E 1L0; phone/fax: 250–955–2113; 888–955–1488; requests@northshuswapbc.com; www.northshuswapbc.com) has the pertinent information.

As you pass **Chase** (population 2,575), just past the western end of Little Shuswap Lake, watch for Rocky Mountain bighorn sheep on the hills east of town. A small herd was transplanted to Squilax in 1927. A number of hiking trails are found in the area. One that is a bit of a climb, but with excellent views of Shuswap and Little Shuswap lakes and the South Thompson River, begins near the cemetery. Turn south at the **Chase Country Inn** (250–679–3333). Contact **Chase Visitor Info Centre** (400 Shuswap Avenue, Box 592, Chase, V0E 1M0; 250–679–8432; fax: 250–679–3120) for directions. Ask, too, about Chase Falls, not far off the

Trans-Canada Highway, and **Neskonlith Meadows,** where you'll find glorious wildflowers in late April. For the meadows, though, you must check first with the Adams Lake Band office (Box 588, Chase, VOE 1MO; 250–679–8841) and purchase a permit.

Kamloops to Merritt and the Nicola Valley

Where the North and South Thompson Rivers meet sits Kamloops, 130 miles (210 km) west of Revelstoke. In the Shuswap (Secwepemc) Indian tongue, it means "meeting place." It's also where three highways and two railroads meet, making it a very reachable city for the many forestry workers, miners, and ranchers who call this area home. It's big—at 144 square miles (373 sq km), BC's largest city in area—it's growing fast, and it has all the facilities you would expect to find in a city of 80,000.

One such facility is just 10 miles (16 km) east of Kamloops. The **Kamloops Wildlife Park** (Box 698, Kamloops, V2C 5L7; 250–573–3242; fax: 250–573–2406; info@kamloopswildlife.org; www.kamloopswildlife.org) is home to two Siberian tigers (Zef and Czarina) and Sheba and Shardic, two orphaned grizzly bears. The park is the largest captive breeding center in North America for the endangered burrowing owl. As well, there are seventy species of local and endangered wildlife, a miniature train ride, a gift shop, farmyard animals, and a walking trail leading to waterfalls. Prices of admission are adults $6.75, youths and seniors $4.75, and children $3.75. The park is open from 8:00 A.M. to 4:30 P.M. daily year-round (except Christmas Day) and until 6:00 P.M. in July and August. Throughout December, hours are extended to 9:00 P.M. for the largest festive light show (200,000 lights) in BC's interior. Free marshmallow roasting, haywagon rides, and entertainment, including a giant outdoor movie, add to the winter fun.

Right next door, in this area of Mojavelike, weirdly shaped hoodoos and rocky hills, is the **Kamloops Waterslide and R.V. Park** (250–573–3789; fax: 250–573–3933). On a blazing hot, western summer day, these 2,000 feet of coolwater dips and curves may be the best place to hang out. It's open from May to Labor Day. For more information on the area, contact **Kamloops Visitor Info Centre** (1290 West Trans-Canada Highway, Kamloops, V2C 6R3; 250–374–3377 or 800–662–1994; fax: 250–828–9500; tourism@ kamloopschamber.bc.ca; www.venturekamloops. com). The staff there can guide you to the **Farmers Market,** held downtown every Saturday morning from May to October; or you could spend a day at the **Secwepemc Museum and Heritage Park** (202-355 Yellowhead Highway, Kamloops, V2H 1H1; 250–828–9801; fax: 250–372–1127; museum@secwepemc.org; www. sec wepemc.org). Trails here pass archaeological remains of 2,000-year-old Shuswap winter and summer villages, as well as reconstructed winter pit houses. The Museum Store sells arts and crafts, many of which are traditional to the Shuswap area, such as pine needle and birch bark baskets, moccasins, dream catchers, and beaded and silver jewelry. Other attractions include a tour of the **Sunmore Ginseng Factory** (925 McGill Place, Kamloops, V2C 6N9; 250–374–3017; fax: 250–374–3011; sunmore@ sunmore.com; www.sunmore.com) and a cruise on the **Wanda-Sue Sternwheeler** (250–374–SHIP; wandasue@sageserve. com) to enjoy a cool sunset dinner cruise. Departures are from the old Kamloops Yacht Club on River Street.

Another cooling-off idea is to head south toward the thriving city of **Merritt,** where the slogan "A lake a day, as long as you stay" would still hold true if you stayed almost half a year. Centrally situated where four major highways meet, Merritt is less than three hours from Vancouver via the Coquihalla (sounds almost like "Coca Cola") Highway 5. But coming from Kamloops, you can take a more leisurely drive down Highway 5A, past forested peaks and rolling, grassy ranch lands, and (nearer to Merritt), the deep, azure, and lovely Nicola Lake.

All the lakes in the **Nicola Valley** are popular fishing spots. Kamloops trout, a wild strain of rainbow trout, makes a splendid catch. Ice fishing for burbot during the winter months is popular, too. Other nearby fishing spots are **Marquart** and **Lundbom** Lakes, a few miles east of Merritt off Highway 5A. They both have forestry service campsites with boat launches. Local enthusiasts tell me that the best time to land rainbow, Kokanee, and brook trout is during spring and fall.

Stop off at the historic and charming **Quilchena Hotel** (Highway 5A North, Quilchena, V0E 2R0; 250–378–2611; fax: 250–378–6091; hotel@quilchena.com; www.quilchena. com), sitting regally on the edge of Nicola Lake and at the center of one of BC's largest working cattle ranches. It's open early spring through late fall and serves excellent meals in its elegant dining room. In 1908 the hotel's builder, Joseph Guichon, believed the railway from Spences Bridge to Princeton would pass through Quilchena, and although this didn't happen, the hotel was still a success. It was closed between 1921 and 1958, but today, Guichon's grandson, Guy Rose, continues to maintain the splendor and antique originality of this lovely hotel. The sixteen rooms are furnished with antiques. There's fine dining and a 1900s saloon—look for the bullet holes in the bar! Rates are $71 to $125 double. Nearby, the **Nicola Valley Golf Course and R.V. Park** (General Delivery, Quilchena, V0E 2R0; 250–378–2923; fax: 250–378–6091; nvalgolf@uniserve.com) has a pleasant nine-hole course offering inexpensive golf and comfortable camping services. Quilchena Creek winds through the property crossing five fairways, thus creating some of the course's hazards in the process.

Just before Quilchena on Highway 5A is the turnoff to the famous **Douglas Lake Ranch** (800–663–4838; resort@douglaslake.com; www. douglaslake.com), Canada's largest working cattle ranch. The ranch runs close to 20,000 head of cattle over almost 500,000 acres (200,000 ha). It also boasts eleven private lakes with world-class fly-fishing, conducts ranch tours (by reservation), and offers horseback riding. You'll find more information on Nicola Valley activities—ranging from hiking, cross-country skiing, sailing, and windsurfing to, of course, fishing—at the red-roofed, log-construction **Merritt Travel Info Centre** (Box 189, Merritt, V1K 1B8; 250–378–2281; fax: 250–378–6485), situated at the junction of Highways 5 and 97C. If you're needing a leg stretch, there's a nice hike along a nature trail at the back of the Info Centre.

Another major highway that meets in Kamloops is Highway 5, the Yellowhead South, named for the fair-haired Iroquois trapper Pierre Bostonais (known as *Tête Jaune,* which means "yellow head" in French) who, as a Hudson's Bay Company guide, frequently crossed through the spectacular Rocky Mountain pass that also bears his name. The Yellowhead begins in Winnipeg, Manitoba, and completes its route in Masset in the Queen Charlotte Islands. It covers 1,973 miles (3,185 km), including the 211 miles (340 km) of the Yellowhead South between Kamloops and Tête Jaune Cache, which we shall now begin.

The North Thomson River

The first part of our Yellowhead journey hugs the eastern bank of the North Thompson River for 39 miles (63 km) to **Barriere.** On the way about 11 miles (19 km) north at Heffley Creek, is the turnoff to the famous **Sun Peaks Resort** (800–807–3257; info@sunpeaksresort. com; www.sunpeaksresort.com). **Father's Country Inn B&B** (on Mc-Gilliviray Creek Road, Box 152, Heffley Creek, V0E 1Z0; 800–578–7322 or 250–578–7308; fax: 250–578–7334; mmfathers@telus.net; www. dconover. com/bedandbreakfast) is located near the resort and has all the luxuries of a resort. Imagine an indoor pool with a fireplace at one end, a wood stove and a hot tub at the other, all in a tropical setting. The decadence, which includes breathtaking mountain views, in-room fireplaces, candlelit Jacuzzi tubs, and four-poster beds, doesn't match the $75–$135 (double) rates. "Father's" refers to David Conover Sr., father of the owner, who "discovered" Marilyn Monroe. His original photos of the lovely lady are displayed here.

Barriere, 27 miles (44 km) north of the Sun Peaks junction, is a farming and forestry town, where every Labor Day weekend the **North Thompson Fall Fair and Rodeo** (Box 873, Barriere, V0E 1E0) is held.

There's excellent riverside camping 34 miles (55 km) north of Barriere at the **North Thompson River Provincial Park** (250–587–6150 or 250–851–3000), 3 miles (5 km) before **Clearwater.** The park is situated where the muddy brown North Thompson River meets the green Clearwater River. There's a playground for the kids (Poggy Park) and excellent fishing. At times the rivers can be swift and powerful, so children should always be supervised; swimming alone is not advised. Near the river's edge in the picnic area, look for **kekuli sites,** winter pit-house depressions used by the Chu Chua or Simpcw (pronounced "sim-kwhoo") people.

Don't even think of going into **Wells Gray Provincial Park** without first dropping into the **Wells Gray Info Centre** (Box 1988, Clearwater, V0E 1N0; 250–674–2646; fax: 250–674–3693; clwcofc@mail. wellsgray.net; www.profiles.net/chamber). You'll find here displays of the geology and volcanic activity in the park, a wildlife display, artifacts, and a gift and book section. It's open daily April to mid-October and closed for the rest of the year. The knowledgeable staff will tell you what not to miss in British Columbia's fourth-largest park and will alert you to the dangers, too. The park entrance is 22.2 miles (35.8 km) north of the Info Centre along Clearwater Valley Road.

Right outside the Info Centre, which is on the corner of Clearwater Valley Road and the Yellowhead South, *Jerry the moose* stands guard. He's possibly the most photographed moose in Canada. He started life as a shiny steel creature, refusing to rust for many years. Finally, the sculptor from Victoria urged him along using saltwater-soaked cloths, and today he's a fine-looking brown beast.

If you're looking for a place to stay, 2 miles (3km) up the road towards Wells Gray from the Info Centre, there's year-round self-catering and bed-breakfast accomodation at *Tanglewood Lodge* (1048 Clearwater VAlley Road, Box 1785, Clearwater, VOE 1N0; 250–674–3537; www. tanglewoodlodge.net). This family-friendly home was built with sunsets and spectacular views of Trophy Mountain in mind, and isa good base for hiking the alpine meadows.

In those *alpine meadows* at *Trophy Mountain,* you'll see subalpine daisies, cow parsnips, Indian paintbrush, Lewis's monkey flowers, and arnica. To get there take the Bear Creek Correctional Centre turnoff 6 miles (10 km) up the Clearwater Valley Road, on the right just past *Spahats Creek Provincial Park.* Ask the staff at the Info Centre for the best time to see the flowers.

If quilting is your passion, check out *Country Cabin Quilts & Fabric Shop* (Box 1770, RR 1, Clearwater, V0E 1N0; 250–674–2321; fax: 250–674–3780). Letta Mae Colborne (and other locals) create a variety of quilted products; she also sells other crafts and antiques. The store is open year-round Monday to Saturday from 10:00 A.M. to 5:00 P.M. It's on Clearwater Valley Road but ask at the Info Centre for directions.

A Centennial Trek

*C*learwater's inhabitants include some pretty gutsy folk. Back in 1967, a young woman named Ida Dekelver, aged forty-four and a mother of six, set out with her two donkeys, Bill and Jack, to walk the Yellowhead Highway to Wadena, Saskatchewan. That's more than 890 miles (1,434 km)! She wanted to visit her aunt. Newspapers from all over the country covered her trek, giving publicity to Clearwater and Wells Gray Park. Ironically, she and her donkeys got a ride back home in a truck driven by two Saskatchewan men, also named Bill and Jack. Until recently, Mrs. Dekelver ran the Yellowhead Museum, which consisted of two rustic cabins on the Clearwater Valley Road, full of artifacts and natural history displays, as well as memorabilia collected during her centennial-year trek.

In this wilderness area where good craft stores are a pleasant surprise, it's also a bonus to find good food. Near the park entrance 22 miles (35 km) from the turnoff, *Helmcken Falls Lodge* (Box 239, Clearwater, V0E 1N0; 250–674–3657; fax: 250–674–2971; helmfall@mail. wellsgray.net; www.helmckenfalls.com) serves hearty meals with a reputation for high standards of excellence. They also offer wilderness camp trips, white-water rafting, guiding and outfitting services for horseback riding, hiking, berry-picking rides, sight-seeing tours, and canoeing. The recently upscaled lodge accommodations in this reach-out-and-touch-nature setting range from $120 to $150 double. Campsites are also available.

We're finally at *Wells Gray Provincial Park,* with its breathtaking scenery in all seasons. You'll see snow-covered peaks, glaciers, extinct volcanoes, old-growth cedar forests, and dozens of waterfalls, the most famous being the 450-foot (137-m) *Helmcken Falls* (more than two and a half times higher than Niagara), 6 miles (10 km) inside the park.

A few miles past Helmcken Falls is a naturally carbonated cold-water mineral spring, where you can add juice crystals to the water and presto! You have pop. At *Bailey's Chute,* a few miles farther up in the park, forty-

Recommended Reading - High Country

FOR ADULTS:
A Taste for the Shuswap, by Fran Kay—self published. RR2 Chase, BC, V0E 1M0. Very detailed coverage of the area.

Shuswap Pathways - A Trail Guide, by Estelle Noakes. Sunshine Studios, Chase, BC. 1993.

Magnificent Yellowhead Highway, Volume Two: Edmonton To Kamloops, by Frontier Books. Surrey, BC. ISBN 919214-46-0. 1980

Exploring Wells Gray Park, by Roland Neave. Sandhill Books.

FOR KIDS:
Goldstone, by Julie Lawson. Econo-Clad Books, 1999, Hardcover. Based on a true incident in the Rogers Pass area when an avalanche in 1910 killed sixty-six railway workers. The heroine is Karen, whose Swedish father works for the railway. For grades five and up.

Bats, by Gail Gibbons. Holiday House, 2000; Ages nine to twelve (see the section on Squilax). Learn about their protection and the myths surrounding them. Beautifully illustrated.

four-pound (20-kg) salmon (in season) leap up the rapids. Park your car just past the mineral springs, and it's about a fifteen-minute walk.

Back at the Yellowhead Highway in Clearwater, the road now runs slightly south and east to **Birch Island,** formed by an eddy in the North Thompson River. Either take the back road east to **Vavenby,** which runs from Birch Island via an old, one-lane wooden bridge (lots of character) and Lost Creek Road, or turn right off the highway at Vavenby, 16 miles (26 km) east of Clearwater. Here you can experience a working ranch at **Vavenby Trail Rides** (Box 250, Vavenby, V0E 3A0; 250–676–9598; fax: 250–676–9550; shooked@telus.net; www.profiles.net/shook.htm). The Shook family takes small groups on guided rides through open pasture, woodlands, and hay fields along the scenic North Thompson River. Help herd the cows or just hold the reins and enjoy the scenery. Rides are $20 per hour, $35 for two hours, and $50 for three hours. In May and June they have several cattle drives, to which they invite up to six guests ($125 per person) to join. Ask about their **Saturday Sleepovers,** which include two campfire meals, lots of riding, and all your sleeping gear (tents and sleeping bags). Six is the maximum and two the minimum, and children must be accompanied by an adult. The cost is $125 per person. Or there's the **Ride and Stay** package (also $125 per person per day) for "like-minded guests," which includes a full day's riding, home-cooked meals, and comfortable beds. The following day could involve any number of activities for a real ranch experience. Vavenby Trail Rides operates from April to late October.

Rustic accommodation is just a five-minute drive away at **Aveley Ranch** (250–676–9598; fax: 250–676–9550), one of the largest sheep ranches in Western Canada. A specially built bed-and-breakfast log cabin in the woods sleeps six. Double rates range from $90.

Back on the Yellowhead, heading north, there's another entrance to the **Wells Gray Provincial Park** 62 miles (100 km) north of Clearwater. Turn onto a 17-mile (27-km) narrow, winding, gravel forestry road (not suitable for large RVs) just past Blue River. A 1.5-mile (2.5-km) portage from the parking lot will bring you to **Murtle Lake,** North America's largest "no-motors-allowed" freshwater lake. With more than 62 miles (100 km) of shoreline to explore and only the call of the loon to listen to, if you have a canoe, you can really get away from it all. A dawn paddle may bring you face-to-face with black or grizzly bears, eagles, moose, beavers, deer, or wolves. And if you have a BC fishing license (and don't leave it in the car!), the trout are huge. You must pick up a permit in Blue River for camping at Murtle Lake. You'll find permits on the western side of the highway in Blue River at the **Blue**

River Campground and R.V. Park (Box 38, Murtle Lake Road and Highway 5, Blue River, V0E 1J0; 250–673–8203). They also provide canoe rentals, fishing licences, showers, heli-fishing, full hookups, and if you'd like to spend the night on a bed of cedar chips in a Blackfoot or Cree tipi, that's available, too. An on-site store sells the necessary topographical map for Murtle Lake and a guidebook on Wells Gray Park (also available at the Info Centre in Clearwater). The campground operates May 1 through October 15.

But if teepee camping, portaging canoes, and roughing it on Murtle Lake is not your thing, check into the luxurious year-round resort at *Mike Wiegele Helicopter Skiing* (Harrwood Drive, Box 159, Blue River, V0E 1J0; 250–673–8381; fax: 250–673–8464; 800–661–9170 for reservations only; reservations@wiegele.com; www.wiegele.com) for some backcountry hiking through alpine wildflowers, fly-fishing, biking, skiing, helicopter sight-seeing, or picnicking (gourmet picnics at 7,000 feet!). The luxuries include a health club, a private beach, fireplaces— and the list goes on. There's a choice of accommodation ranging from $145 to $360 double.

Northern High Country

ifty-five miles (88 km) north of Blue River is Valemount, the midpoint between Edmonton and Vancouver. It sits in a valley where the Cariboo, Monashee, and Rocky Mountains meet, where the views become spectacular, and where the birds flock in the millions.

Just 2 miles (3 km) south of town, the *Robert W. Starratt Wildlife Sanctuary* (Cranberry Marsh) is the site of a Ducks Unlimited project to improve waterfowl habitat. The Canada geese love it here, as do northern harriers and red-tailed hawks. You can hike the whole 600-acre (243-ha) marsh in an hour and a half. Contact the Valemount Visitor Info Centre, open May 15–September 15 (99 Gorse Street, Highway 5, Box 168, Valemount, V0E 2Z0; 250–566–4846; fax: 250–566–4249; tour@valemount_bc.org; www.valemount-bc.org) for year-round information. They'll also direct you to the *Valemount Museum* (Box 850, Valemount, V0E 2Z0; 250–566–4177/4324; museum@valemount.com) to discover some valley and railroad history or, if you're visiting in late summer, to Swift Creek in the George Hicks Regional Park, where the world's longest chinook salmon migration occurs.

If you have some extra time, *Mount Robson Adventure Holidays* (Box 687, Valemount, V0E 2Z0; 250–566–4386; fax: 250–566–4351;

nature@mountrobson.com; www.mountrobson. com/) offers back-packing, canoeing, rafting, and fly-in/hike-out activities. Do a three-day hike on the *Berg Lake Trail,* considered by many people to be the most spectacular hike in North America. Imagine standing at cool, blue Berg Lake, mesmerized by a spectacular view of Mount Robson and Berg Glacier and listening to chunks of ice calving from the glacier into the lake. Activities requiring no more than two to three hours are also available. The office is located in the Mount Robson Adventure Centre, 50 miles (82 km) west of Jasper on the Yellowhead Highway 16.

If you'd prefer to just spend a night in Valemount and pass on, from June to October the *Dream Catcher Inn* (Box 1012, Valemount, V0E 2Z0; 250–566–4226 or 800–566–9128; fax 250–566–9128; dream@valemount.com; www.valemount.com/dream) has log chalets as well as bed-and-breakfast accommodation. There's an outdoor hot tub and delicious breakfasts. My hot apple cereal, blueberry muffins, and poached eggs on toast kept me going well into the afternoon. In the bed-and-breakfast, you have a choice of five Indian-named rooms, each with a dream catcher (to catch your dreams before they float away) hanging above a comfortable bed. The inn is located in a ten-acre (four-ha) wooded setting just north of Valemount, within walking distance of the Swift Creek Chinook salmon spawning grounds in George Hicks Park and the nine-hole *Valemount Pines Golf Course* (250–566–4550) on the west side of the highway.

Five miles (8 km) north of Valemount is the *Mount Terry Fox View-point.* In Canada the name Terry Fox is a household name. Having lost a leg to a rare form of bone cancer, twenty-two-year-old Fox attempted to run across Canada to raise funds for cancer research. After running at a pace of almost a marathon a day, covering 3,339 miles (5,373 km), he had to retire after the cancer returned. He died ten months later, and today yearly runs are held throughout Canada to continue the fund-raising effort and honor his memory. Look to the east at the viewpoint and you'll see the 8,694-foot (2,650-m) Mount Terry Fox.

To access the Terry Fox Trail, cross the highway from the viewpoint and follow the trail sign at Stone Road. Take this road for a little over a mile to the trailhead. It's 4.5 miles (7 km) to Mount Terry Fox—easily a full-day hike by the time you get back to the parking lot. It's quite steep, but the alpine views are worth the effort.

It's now time to leave the Yellowhead South (Highway 5) and join the Yellowhead Highway 16 at Tête Jaune Cache, once a thriving town of 3,000, complete with pool halls and flophouses in the early 1900s when the

Grand Trunk Railway was under construction. Now it's all but deserted. At this point we are 63 miles (101 km) from Jasper in Alberta and 150 miles (240 km) from Prince George. The easterly drive is spectacular, especially when Mount Robson comes into view just near the Mount Terry Fox Provincial Park. The road to the northwest is a long and lonely drive into BC's north, which we'll explore in the section on the Northeast.

PLACES TO STAY IN HIGH COUNTRY

CHASE
Quaaout Lodge Resort, Box 1215, Chase V0E 1M0; (800) 663-4303; (250) 679-3090. Deluxe rooms on the shores of Little Shuswap. Restaurant also.

REVELSTOKE
Canyon Hot Springs Resort Ltd., Box 2400, V0E 2S0; (250) 837-2420. Camping, cabins, hot springs.

Four Seasons Manor Bed and Breakfast, 815 MacKenzie Avenue; (877) 837-2616 toll free; (250) 837-2616. Bed and breakfast in a heritage home.

SALMON ARM
The Log Bog Friendship Farm B&B, 540 Highway 97B N.E., Salmon Arm, V1E 1X5; phone/fax: (250) 832-5581; logbog_bb@hotmail.com. Beautifully crafted log home on nineteen acres.

SORRENTO
The Evergreens Bed and Breakfast, 2853 Vimy Road, Box 117, V0E 2W0; (250) 675-2568. Near lake.

Sorrento Center, Box 99, V0E 2W0; (250) 675-2421. Camping, cabanas, and lodge accommodation. On Shuswap Lake.

VALEMOUNT
Dream Catcher Inn, Box 1012, V0E 2Z0; (250) 566-4226 or (800) 566-9128; dream@valemount.com; www.valemount. com/dream. Bed-and-breakfast accommodation.

PLACES TO EAT IN HIGH COUNTRY

CLEARWATER
Helmcken Falls Lodge, Box 239, V0E 1N0; (250) 674-3657. Buffet. Wilderness location.

KAMLOOPS
Storms Restaurant, 1502 River Street, V2C 1Y9; (250) 372-1522. Riverside deck; excellent dining.

REVELSTOKE
Conversations Coffee House, 203 Mackenzie Avenue; (250) 837-4772. Good coffee and great desserts.

Frontier Family Restaurant, corner of Highways 1 and 23 North; (250) 837-5119 or (800) 382-7763. Fast foods.

SORRENTO
Toby's Restaurant, Trans-Canada Highway, V0E 2W0; (250) 675-4464. Good pizzas. Open from 7:00 A.M. to 9:00 P.M.

Cariboo Chilcotin Coast

The Cariboo Chilcotin Coast area is located in central British Columbia, with the Pacific coast to the west and the Cariboo Mountain Range to the east. Hudson's Bay fur traders could never have anticipated the gold-hungry throngs that would stampede into the area after the first bright nuggets reached San Francisco in the late 1850s. Thousands marched north to the beckoning land in hopes of filling their pokes with the brilliant booty. And so it all began.

But in less than thirty years, towns like Barkerville, once the gold capital of the world, were empty of both the gold and its seekers. Roadhouses that had catered to exhausted travelers spread their wings to become centers for rambling ranches, and another way of life began.

South Cariboo

Mile Zero of the old *Cariboo Waggon Road* is at Lillooet at the junction of Highways 99 and 12, majestically perched above the muddy Fraser River. It started out as a landing point for motherlode seekers who had come north through Harrison and Anderson Lakes. Other roadhouses like 100 Mile House and 70 Mile House emerged, their names rising from their distances from Lillooet. A cairn on Main Street marks the Mile Zero spot. A busy town of 16,000 in the gold rush days of the 1860s, Lillooet was at one time the second-largest settlement north of San Francisco and west of Chicago. It also holds the unenviable claim to the hottest recorded spot in BC, when it reached 111.9° F (44.4° C) in 1941, and the more enviable claim as the best location outside of Myanmar (Burma) to find jade. The biggest cash crop in the area is ginseng—that's what all those huge black tarpaulins are hiding! Try some ginseng candy, available at the health-food store.

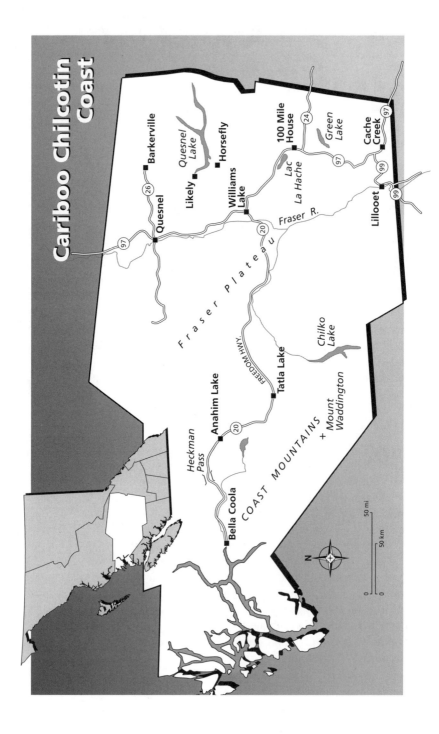

CARIBOO CHILCOTIN COAST

AUTHOR'S TOP TEN PICKS IN THE CARIBOO-CHILCOTIN

Sheep Pasture Golf Course

Green Lake

Historic Hat Creek Ranch

Cornwall Mountain

Painted Chasm

Barkerville Historic Town

Xats'ull Heritage Village

Bowron Lake

Lac la Hache

The Freedom Highway

Opposite the cairn, at 790 Main Street, *St. Mary's Anglican Church* houses the seasonal (open June to September at varying hours) *Lillooet Museum and Information Centre.* The District of Lillooet (Box 610, 847 Main Street, Lillooet, V0K 1V0; 250–256–4289; www.lillooetbc.com) is your best bet for obtaininhg information from afar. The Murray Collection in the church basement is a display of newspaper and printing equipment owned by straight-talking publisher Margaret "Ma" Murray and her politician husband, George. Founded in 1934, the *Bridge River-Lillooet News,* laced with her crusty commentaries, made Ma (who was honored with an Order of Canada medal) a household name. Outside the museum there's a rusty little jail jumbled among antiquated machinery. Ask at the Info Centre about Lillooet's Golden Mile of History from the Bridge of 23 Camels to the Old Bridge, made more interesting if you walk or bike along it using a self-guided tour brochure.

Next door, *Elaine's Coffee Garden & Books Etc.* at 824 Main Street, (250–256–4633) is a lunch bar serving tasty soups, salads, bagels, sandwiches, chili, ice creams, and more. It also sells a few books and souvenirs.

Across at 719 Main at the *Lillooet Bakery* (250–256–4889), *bäckermeister* Axel Sterrmann and his wife, Elke, serve European-style breakfasts, delectables such as eclairs and rum balls, wonderful bread, and excellent coffee, attested to by the busloads of tourists who stop by.

If you need a place to stay, in addition to the three or four hotels, there's a comfortable spot down on the river. *River-Side Bed and Breakfast* (562 Summer Street, Box 1000, Lillooet, V0K 1V0; phone/fax: 250–256–4477) has two rooms (one a family suite for $90) starting from $60 double. Turn right at the Esso station opposite the bakery (Seventh Avenue), cross the railway line, and turn left.

Other B&Bs include *Conway Park Bed & Breakfast* (250–256–4519), *Elephant Cottage Bed & Breakfast* (phone/fax 250–256–7139), *Henri's Bed & Breakfast* (250–256–0005), and *Queens Grove Bed & Breakfast* (phone/fax 250–256–0337). There's a comfortable campground ten-minutes walking distance from town at *Cayoosh Creek Campground* (Box 1548, Lillooet, V0K 1V0; 250–256–4180; fax: 250–256–4174; rjansen@lillonet.org). It's located at the junction of the Fraser and Cayoosh Rivers. While there, plan on doing some gold panning on the Fraser River or perhaps fish for trout in the Seton River. Several times a day *Fraser River Jet Boat Adventures* (1–877–RIVBOAT; www.rivboat.com) runs trips from the campground along the Fraser River through some impressive scenery.

Leaving town as you head north on Highway 99 toward Cache Creek, you cross the Fraser at the *Bridge of 23 Camels,* named for the poor Bactrian beasts of burden (purchased in San Francisco in 1862 for $300) used and abused during gold rush days. It's worth a stop just past the bridge to view the town and the railway line that snakes along the river.

But before heading north, check out Canada's most unusual golf course. *Sheep Pasture Golf Course* (Box 217, Lillooet, V0K 1V0; 250–256–4484), 5 miles (8 km) south of Lillooet on the Texas Creek Road (turn south before the bridge) is a par-35 nine-holer with quite a few moving, bleating hazards, as well as panoramic views of the mountains and river. Owner David Jones built the course after years of losing his sheep to predators; he figured if he had two-legged animals walking around, the predators would disappear! As well as the living hazards, there's water on the course—but no bunkers "because the sheep dig in"—and a few apple trees. Feel free to pick an apple as you play.

Once north of town on Highway 99, you'll twist and climb along the Fraser benchlands toward the 4,987-foot (1,520-m) Pavilion Mountain.

Ma Murray

*M*argaret "Ma" Murray was a mighty woman. Born in Windy Ridge, Kansas, in 1887, she arrived in Lillooet in 1933 with her politician husband, George. To fulfill a campaign promise to his constituents, George established the Bridge River-Lillooet News. Before long, his wife's candid (and often damning) views on the Canadian political situation (and society in general) were widely quoted; she was soon a household name. She also took every opportunity to inform the world of Lillooet's virtues, thus putting it on the map.

In fact, her name became synonymous with that of Lillooet. The flag on page two of the Bridge River-Lillooet News always stated: "Printed in the sage brush country of Lillooet every Thursday, God willing. Guarantees a chuckle every week and a belly laugh once a month or your money back. Subscriptions $5.00 in Canada. Furriners $6.00. This week's circulation 1,726 and every bloody one of them paid for." Ma Murray died in Lillooet on September 25, 1982, at the age of ninety-five, and is buried beside her husband in Fort St. John.

Until recently, you could stop at the *Pavilion General Store,* at one time a one-day trip away from Lillooet by horse and buggy. Unfortunately, it has now been destroyed by fire. Here the horses were watered before continuing up over the mountain. The slope was so steep that they would have to use log "anchors" to help them down the hill, some of which can still be seen. Passengers would have to get out and push the wagons on the uphill sections.

Farther on, after passing a few shimmering lakes, you'll approach Marble Canyon, about 30 miles (48 km) east of Lillooet. Watch for *Chimney Rock* on the north side of the highway and other Utah-like towering cliffs of colored limestone. Camping at *Marble Canyon Provincial Park* is available (twenty-six sites), and there's first-class swimming in Pavilion and Crown Lakes. For information on Marble Canyon, contact BC Parks, Thompson River District, 1210 McGill Road, Kamloops, V2C 6N6; (250) 851–3000; fax: (250) 828–4633.

As you leave the dramatic scenery of Highway 99, you'll come to *Historic Hat Creek Ranch* (Box 878, Cache Creek, V0K 1H0; 800–782–0922 or 250–457–9722; fax: 250–457–9311; explore@ hatcreekranch.com; www.hatcreekranch. com) at the junction of Highway 97, which leads south 7 miles (11 km) to Cache Creek or north 18 miles (29 km) to Clinton. Hat Creek Ranch, originally the property of the murderous Donald McLean and his three horse-stealing sons, was an overnight stop for early travelers on the Cariboo Waggon Road. Today it's a holiday attraction, complete with stagecoach and wagon rides. A blacksmith demonstrates his trade, pigs snuffle in the troughs, and chickens scratch in their coop. A reasonably priced full buffet lunch is available. The ranch is open daily from mid-May to mid-September from 9:00 A.M. to 6:00 P.M.. Admission cost, which includes a guided tour of the Roadhouse, the Blacksmith Shop, and

Top Annual Events Cariboo Chilcotin Coast

Williams Lake Stampede, Williams Lake; July; (250) 398–8388 or (800) 71RODEO

Billy Barker Days, Quesnel; July; (250) 992–1234

Barlow Creek Music Festival, Barlow Creek; July; (250) 992–9322 or 992–8716

Bella Coola Rodeo, Bella Coola; July; (250) 392–5330

Gold Rush Trail Dog Sled Races, Quesnel; January; (250) 992–9143

Quesnel Rodeo, Quesnel; July; (250) 249–5170

Bridge Lake Cattle Drive, 70 Mile House to Bridge Lake; July; (250) 593–4853

Fall Harvest Fair, Williams Lake; August; (250) 398–7678

Gymkanas, Watch Lake and Green Lake; July; (250) 456–7741

Square Dance Jamboree, 100 Mile House; June; (250) 397–2076

Trivia

Cache Creek is the home of the last stop sign that existed on the Trans-Canada Highway. The sign was taken down and replaced with a traffic light on February 4, 1984, and is now on display in the Village Office.

the Native Interpretation Center, is $11 for a family of four.

Before heading north to follow the old Cariboo Waggon Trail, take a look around Cache Creek and Ashcroft, a few miles to the south on Highway 97. Tune into 105.9 FM to find out what's happening first; then just before Cache Creek visit *Horsting's Farm Market* (open 8:00 A.M. to 7:00 P.M.; phone/fax: 250–457–6546), colorful with fresh berries, vegetables, and hanging flower baskets. Try a piece of Donna Horsting's berry pies or buy a bottle of her delicious Saskatoon berry jam and a loaf of homemade bread. The kids can play on the trampoline, go for a wagon ride, or visit the goats and rabbits after a picnic in Horsting's park. *The Country Cafe,* next to the market, serves sandwiches (circle your favorite ingredients) and homemade soups.

From jam to jade: British Columbia is the Jade Capital of the World. You can watch jade being cut, polished, and mounted, as well as buy jade souvenirs at the *Cariboo Jade and Gift Shoppe* (1093 Todd Road, Box 280, Cache Creek, V0K 1H0; 250–457–9566) in Cache Creek. It's opposite the bus depot and is open late daily in summer.

The streets of Cache Creek are lined with neon signs and flowers. Some businesses and residents display antique cars in keeping with a "Nifty Fifties" theme. Here in Cache Creek, where the Trans-Canada crosses Highway 97 and the rolling grasslands of the Bonaparte River Valley combine with a semi-desert climate, you'll get that Old West cowboy feel.

From Cache Creek head south along Highway 97 past the tumbleweed and cactus to historic Ashcroft on the Thompson River. Cross the bridge into town, and stop at the bright red *Ashcroft Fire Hall.* This building is a replica of the first fire hall, which was built in 1889. Go down the hill toward the riverbank to a small campground at *Legacy Park* (Box 183, Ashcroft, V0K 1A0; 250–453–2642). The sites are right on the bank. Next door is the *Ashcroft River Inn* (Box 1359, Ashcroft, V0K 1A0; Phone: 250–453–9124; fax: 250–453–2565 or 800–465–4800), where you can enjoy a meal or spend a night overlooking the river. Rates start at $48 double. The restaurant opens at 7:00 A.M., and there's often live entertainment in the pub.

If you're interested in Cariboo history, the *Ashcroft Museum and Archives* (Box 129, Ashcroft, V0K 1A0; 250–453–9232/9161; fax: 250–453–9664), built in 1916 on the corner of Brink and Fourth Streets, is, as I was told by several residents "definitely worth a visit." Along with a collection of tools, lamps, and Indian and Chinese items, there's a gift shop. It's open daily from 10:00 A.M. to 6:00 P.M. in the summer. Admission is by donation. Next door you'll find the *Ashcroft Journal,* started up in 1895. Originally called the *BC Mining Journal,* it was one of British Columbia's first papers and still churns out the news today.

If you head back across the bridge and turn south on Cornwall Road, you'll reach the **Ashcroft Manor** site (Box 127, Cache Creek, V0K 1H0; 250–453–9983; fax: 250–453–9600). If you're coming from Cache Creek, it's 7 miles (11 km) south on the Trans-Canada Highway. Developed

Ashcroft has a Superman connection. The parents of Margot Kidder, who played Lois Lane in the movie, live there. The actress herself has purchased 245 acres in the Ashcroft area.

by the Cornwall brothers in the early 1860s, these historic buildings, about seven in all, are a must-stop attraction. There's the **Teahouse,** with possibly the best restaurant food in the area, and the **Manor,** which houses a gift shop (excellent selection of jade), a museum (free), and an art gallery. Hours are from 9:00 A.M. to 5:00 P.M. daily from May 1 till October 31. This building was one of BC's oldest roadhouses, which has served also as a post office and a courthouse—the "hanging judge" Matthew Begbie once presided here. An RV campground is on site.

Follow the sweet smell of ponderosa pine and sagebrush for about 9 miles (14 km) south and take a drive up the Hat Creek–Oregon Jack Road to **Cornwall Mountain.** The alpine meadows are thick with wildflowers, but this beautiful drive is really only recommended for 4x4s. There are no services, no campgrounds, a few bears, and if you're as lucky as I was to be guided by an immensely hospitable local, you'll find pictographs and a hidden ice cave containing ice stalagmites, seeming to grow like delicate ferns from the cave floor. But that's my secret!

Five miles (8 km) south of Ashcroft off Highway 97C South, the Rowe family at **Sundance Guest Ranch** (Box 489, Ashcroft, V0K 1A0; 800–553–3533; 250–453–2422; fax: 250–453–9356; sundance@ wkpowerlink.com; www.sundance-ranch. com) offer a genuine bit of the old West. With a herd of more than eighty buckskins, bays, chestnuts, pintos, and Appaloosas—horses to suit all levels—and miles of scenic trails, combined with a heated pool, a tennis court, a kid's wing, games' room, dances, and barbecues, and with a nine-hole golf course and excellent fishing nearby, you're assured of an unforgettable holiday. Rates (including all meals in the licensed dining room, riding, and use of all ranch facilities) range from $195 per person double occupancy in high season. Children's rates are lower, with kids under three free.

Clement Cornwall, who with his brother built Ashcroft Manor, was one of British Columbia's first senators. He became lieutenant governor of British Columbia in 1881.

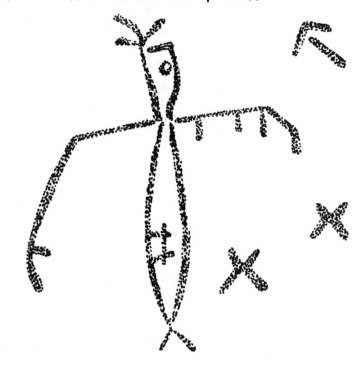

Pictograph near Ashcroft

Circle back to Cache Creek on the Trans-Canada and rejoin Highway 97 heading north to the copper-colored mountains and rolling hills surrounding laid-back Clinton, 25 miles (40 km) north of Cache Creek. A popular spot halfway between Clinton and Cache Creek is Loon Lake. From Cache Creek drive 13 miles (21 km) north and turn east. Six miles (10 km) along the paved Loon Lake Road see kokanee-salmon and rainbow-trout fry at the *Loon Creek Hatchery* (974 Loon Lake Road, RR1 Cache Creek, V0K 1H0 250–459–2454). A farther 10 miles (16 km) on is the *Loon Lake Provincial Park* (BC Parks Cariboo District, 281 First Avenue North, Williams Lake, V2G 1Y7; 250–398–4414; fax: 250–398–4686). (Use this address for all provincial parks in this section, unless otherwise stated.) The 7.4-acre (3-ha) park, set in a forest of Douglas fir and ponderosa pine, is midway along the 7-mile-long (12-km) lake. The rainbow trout usually bite well here, especially during June and September. There are fourteen campsites (pit toilets, no showers) and a small boat launch.

From the Loon Lake Road, Clinton is another 12 miles (19 km) north. *Cariboo Lodge Resort* (Box 459, Clinton, V0K 1K0; 250–459–7992; fax: 250–459–0060; cariboo-lodge@goldtrail.com; www.cariboolodge bc.com) is on the highway in town. It's conspicuous as it is one of the largest log structures in British Columbia. Wonderful old photos on the walls will give you a feel for the past, and with its pretty hanging baskets, swimming pool, pub, and a restaurant with tasty lodge-burgers, it's an inviting rest stop. Room rates (double) start at $80. Ask about riding, sledding, rafting, skiing, and other tours the resort offers.

Across the road at the tiny *South Cariboo Historical Museum,* (Box 25, Clinton, V0K 1K0; 250–459–2442/2533; fax: 250–459–0058), built in 1892 from locally made bricks, check out the backyard with displays that include a bull-press (which was used to keep the beast from doing the blacksmith in as he bravely shod it), a model of the now-burnt-down Clinton Hotel, and a BC Express Company sleigh. In winter, the museum closes, but you can still see the displays in the back. In summer it's open daily 9:00 A.M. to 5:00 P.M.

Walk along to *Robertson Square* and have a giggle at the Bucking Ham Palace Hotel, where you can "Eat and sleep like a king for $2.00 a day." Perhaps you'd prefer to try "Fitzwillies purifying black paste" for your "painful piles, pustules, pimples of acne, pox, bunions, tonsils, and teething grief." If you're still a mess, at *Hickory Daiquiri Doc's,* you can get "mouthwash, whitewash, hogwash, distilled water, toilet water, tonic water, holy water, bones set, blood let, holes patched, and babies hatched." It's right beside the *Grill and Chop Suey Restaurant* (now

From Canned Cream to Claim Staking

*W*hen I arrived in Ashcroft, one of those special little towns where everybody knows everybody and conversations come easy, I headed down to the River Inn for a piece of blueberry pie and a coffee. A chat with a stranger about canned whipped cream ended with a visit to a remote cabin on a hillside. Sweet-smelling wildflowers, wandering bears, and serenity are what brings Trevor Parker, a ship's captain from Vancouver, back regularly to where he grew up. Trevor introduced me to how to stake a claim, to esoteric pictographs and hidden ice caves, and to the friendliness of Ashcroft's people. We dropped in to the Irlybird, where he bought two wooden garden chairs. When they wouldn't fit in his small Toyota, it was "no problem" for the lovely woman who served him to drop them off on the way home. That's the kind of friendly little town it is.

called Lees Family Restaurant, 250–459–2343). Enjoy a Chinese meal on the rustic tables in "the square."

There's decidedly more refinement next door at **Crafts with Class** (1521 Cariboo Highway, Clinton, V0K 1K0; 250–459–2573). Here you can buy Vallance pottery, gourmet coffee, and classy sweatshirts. For more than ten years Jill Robinson has featured Bruce Vallance's exceptional pottery, bringing in customers from as far afield as Vancouver.

Just north of Clinton near Chasm is a northwestern turnoff to wide-open spaces and big ranches, with such cowboylike names as Big Bar, High Bar, Gang Ranch, Dog Creek, and Alkali Lake, stretched out along a road that edges the Fraser River and ends in Williams Lake via the back door. Stay on one of the guest ranches in the area to appreciate the varied terrain and wildlife along this unpopulated pathway, in former times a busy gold rush wagon route.

Any traveler to this part of British Columbia should not miss the spectacular **Painted Chasm,** Canada's Grand Canyon, located in **Chasm Provincial Park.** The turnoff is 9 miles (15 km) north of Clinton; then drive 2 paved miles (3 km) east off Highway 97. There's no fanfare of garish signs announcing its coming, just a small blue PROVINCIAL PARK sign on the roadside. But don't be fooled. This geological wonder, a mile wide and almost 400 feet (120 m) deep, will dazzle you with its display of bright orange and pink rock. Take note of the individual lava flows in the horizontal layering. One modern legend going the rounds is that a Scottish gold digger lost a penny and, in his effort to retrieve it, dug the mighty chasm. If you saw the movie *Grey Fox,* then you've seen scenes shot at the Chasm.

Colorful scenes of a different variety are found at the **59 Mile Bed and Breakfast/Arctic Artists' Gallery** (Box 518, Clinton, V0K 1K0; phone/fax: 250–459–7076). Fred (also known as Iyak) and Laurie Trimble offer bed and breakfast. But there's more. Stop off to see (or buy) the soapstone carvings, for which Fred (from Inuvik) is renowned. His dad, Lyle Trimble, exhibits his oil paintings of northern scenes here, too. An unusual arctic find in a Cariboo setting.

Just as it happened at Arctic Artists Gallery, an unplanned turnoff at 70 Mile House, 19 miles (31 km) north of Clinton, also led to some unexpected finds. Turn east onto Old Bonaparte Road, and less than 5 pleasant miles (8 km) later, you're at **Green Lake.** Many locals have their own reasons for the color of the lake (a reflection of the trees), but the one that makes a lot of sense is that it has no outlet; hence, it has accumulated large deposits of soda, salt, and sulfur, which combine to create its glorious shade of green. It's more than just a pretty green lake, though. There are three campgrounds—on both sides of the lake and all with beach sites—plus a plethora of guest ranches surrounding both Green and Watch Lakes, which means you'll probably find somewhere pleasant to stay. For campers *Green Lake Provincial Park* (281 First Avenue North, Williams Lake, V2G 1Y7; 250–398–4414; fax: 250–398–4686) has 121 camping sites. The park entrance is 10 miles (16 km) northeast of 70 Mile House. Of the three campgrounds at the provincial park (Emerald Bay, Sunset View, and Little Arrowhead), only Emerald Bay on Green Lake's northeast shore can be reserved ahead (800–689–9025).

Little Horse Lodge (6143 Green Lake Road North, RR 1, Comp 1, Site E, 70 Mile House, V0K 2K0; 250–456–7524; fax: 250–456–7512; little horse@100 mile.net; www.cariboovacations.com/littlehorse), a year-round resort, has everything from restaurant to store to laundry, as well as a host of activities from fishing to canoeing to snowmobiling to ice fishing (the best fishing is in winter—you can do it in your T-shirt from the comfort of a warm cabin, playing cribbage while the fishing lines bob!). Gymkhanas and fishing derbies are held regularly. Accommodations are varied: five log cabins, fourteen camping sites, and three bed-and-breakfast guest rooms in the lodge. Rates start at $50 double, plus $7.50 for additional guests.

Discover some of the history of the area at the *Flying U* (Box 69, 70 Mile House, V0K 2K0; 250–456–7717; flyingu@bcinternet.net; www.flyingu.com), a cattle ranch since 1849. It's an international destination with its own BC Rail whistle stop and is Canada's oldest and largest guest ranch with a history and spirit of the early West. Here meals are eaten ranch-style and are announced by the clanging of a bell. There's a two-day minimum stay April to July (adults $130 per day, children from $100 to $70 per day) and a three-day minimum from July to September (adults $140 per day, children from $110 to $80 per day). These rates cover everything from three square meals to unsupervised trail riding to square dancing. Take the northern fork at Green Lake; the ranch is 4 miles (6 km) farther on.

Tall Timbers Resort (Site 3, C8, Watch Lake, 70 Mile House, V0K 2K0; 888–228–8255 or 250–456–7668; timbers@bcinternet.net; www2.bcin ternet.net/~100mile/talltimbers/ttr.html), **Ace High Resort** (Site 2C, C28, RR#1, 70 Mil House, V0K 2K0; 250–456–7518; acehigh@bcinternet. net; www.acehighresort.com), and **Watch Lake Lodge** (RR 1, Watch Lake Road, 70 Mile House, V0K 2K0; 250–456–7741; fax: 250–456– 7492) are three more accommodation choices a little farther along on Watch Lake. At Watch Lake Lodge, 3 miles (5 km) on from Little Horse Lodge, you can ride trail, roll your own, and wear a straw hat with Shorty, Enid, and Dimps Horn, who've been doing it for more than fifty years. Just pick a pair of boots that fit from the thirty or so lined up on the veranda, and it's Happy Trails time.

Head north from Green and Watch Lakes to **Lone Butte,** named for the prominent flat-topped rock that is all that remains of the plug of an ancient volcano that once erupted in the Cariboo. Climb the butte for an excellent view of the surrounding area. Park at the corner of Watch Lake Road and Highway 24 and take the trail up the east face.

An easterly turn on Highway 24 will take you through the Interlakes District to Little Fort, 57 miles (92 km) north of Kamloops on Yellowhead Highway 5. Highway 24 is also known as the **Fishing Highway,** such is the profusion of well-stocked lakes in the area. Fly-fishers and photographers shouldn't miss Lac Des Roches, a few miles east of Bridge Lake. One beautiful view is from the eastern end of the lake at the Pioneer MacDonald Ranch rest area. And for the anglers, try for rainbow trout, kokanee, or brook trout. If you're after a trophy rainbow, stop off at Sheridan Lake and perhaps land one in the ten-pound (4.5 kg) range. Licenses, tackle, and hand-tied flies are available at **Loon Bay Resort** (C1 Airmail Road, Lone Butte, V0K 1X0; 250–593–4431; fax: 250–593–4188; loonbay@bcinternet.net; www.loonbayresort. com) on Sheridan Lake. Cabin accommodation is also available at Loon Bay, as well as campsites near sandy beaches. Rent a canoe for a quiet paddle on the lake and wonder at the stunning scenery. From May to September, the Saturday Market at Loon Bay Resort features local crafts, woodworking, and baking for sale.

You'll find more works by some of the area's artisans, of which there are many, at *Country Pedlar Too* (250–593–4133) in the Sheridan Lake Store Complex. Pottery, folk art, and toys are a few of the items here.

Head east and north via the Old Cariboo Gold Rush Trail (Highway 97) into "town," which is *100 Mile House,* and you can't miss the *South Cariboo Info Centre* (422 Cariboo Highway 97 South, Box 340, 100 Mile House, V0K 2E0; 250–395–5353; 877–511–5353 toll free; fax: 250–395–4085; visitors@bcinternet.net; www.tourism.100mile.com) with the 36-foot-long (11-m) *World's Largest Cross Country Skis* standing outside. This is a reminder that every February, 100 Mile House hosts Canada's second-oldest cross-country ski race, the *Cariboo Ski Marathon,* a 30-mile (50-km) race that brings up to a thousand Nordic enthusiasts from all over the world.

Less obvious than those gigantic skis, but ever so lovely, are the *Bridge Creek Falls* near Centennial Park. They're so close to downtown, but even some locals, unfortunately, have never appreciated their beauty. Turn east on Fourth Avenue (opposite the Visitor Information Centre), take a right on Cedar, and turn immediately left by the school to the parking lot. A chip-trail leads to the falls, where a 30-foot (9-m) pipe, once used by a sawmill to harness the power of the water, still stands erect. Look out for mule deer near the falls. From the pipe, trails continue upstream to the *100 Mile Village Campground* (385 South Birch Avenue, Box 340, 100 Mile House, V0K 2E0; 250–395–2434) on Horse Lake Road. This municipal R.V. park is a pleasant close-to-town campsite with several shaded spots.

There's more natural beauty in 100 Mile House at the *Marsh Wildlife Sanctuary,* beside the Visitor Information Centre. This 20-acre (8-ha) wetland marsh, surrounded by grassy meadows and bluffs of aspen and white spruce, is a nesting ground for Canada geese and several species of ducks. Informative signs help with identification.

Another way of seeing the area is with BC Rail (604–984–5246; toll free 800–663–8238; passinfo@bcrail.com; www.whistlernorthwind.com). The new *Whistler Northwind* luxury train journey leaves Vancouver for Prince George Sundays, early May until late September, with overnight stops in Whistler and 100 Mile House. Northbound fares start at $900, including accommodation in Whistler and 100 Mile House and all meals with the exception of dinner in Whistler. Fares for the two-day southbound trip from Prince George start at $600, including all meals and overnight accommodation in 100 Mile House.

Head up the highway toward (where else?) *108 Mile House,* famous for its internationally acclaimed resorts. **The Hills Health Ranch** (Box 26, 108 Mile Ranch, V0K 2Z0; 250–791–5225; fax: 250–791–6384; thehills @bcinternet.net;www.thehillshealthranch.com) is the best known. Check out the photo-board inside the main lodge to see some of the celebrities who have enjoyed cross-country skiing, horseback riding, aerobics, and other activities "The Hills" offers. High-season rates in the deluxe bed-and-breakfast accommodation (wonderful wilderness views) are $65.95 per person (double occupancy) including hot ranch-style breakfast and a guided hike. Three-bedroom, fully equipped (just like home) family chalets that sleep up to six are $169 per night in high season. Or you can sign up for a weeklong "lifestyle adjustment" vacation package of Smoking Cessation, Stress Reduction, Weight Loss, and several other wellness programs held in a large, well-equipped fitness center. There's also an indoor pool a sixteen-room spa, four lounges, two dining rooms, two skating rinks, a lit downhill ski run, and tube runs with a lift. Two golf courses are located nearby: a challenging nine-holer at **Marmot Ridge** (250–395–4169) north of 100 Mile House and **108 Resort Golf Club** (250–791–5465), a Canadian Professional Golfer's Association approved eighteen-hole course just across the highway from The Hills.

Highway 97, the Gold Rush Trail, continues north to Williams Lake, passing through **Lac La Hache,** 16 miles (25 km) north of 100 Mile House. It's the longest town in the Cariboo and, with its lakeshore setting, possibly the prettiest. Several camping, cottage, and resort facilities can be found along the lake. **Lac La Hache Provincial Park** (250–398–4414), near the north end of the lake, has a beach playground and a boat launch to complement the eighty-three shaded sites. A resort 8 miles (13 km) north of Lac La Hache and very close to the highway, **Crystal Springs (Historical) Resort** (RR 1, Lac La Hache, V0K 1T0; 250–396–4497 or 888–396–4497; doug@crystalsprings resort.net; www.crystalspringsresort.net), has three fully equipped log chalets ($120 double), as well as fifty-seven camping spots on the water. There's also a store and boat rentals.

The Northern Cariboo

Nine miles (15 km) east of Williams Lake is 150 Mile House, the gateway to towns with such unlikely names as *Horsefly* and, yes, *Likely*. But your first stop must be at the *153 Mile Store.* It operated as a store until 1964 but is now a museum containing many mint-condition artifacts. Horsefly, the site of the first gold discovered in the Cariboo, is another 32 miles (51 km) east. You'll still see prospectors washing gravel in the creeks. Horsefly Lake is one of the largest in BC, and the Horsefly River, famous for excellent fly-fishing, is home to the second-largest sockeye run in BC. September is the best month to see the run, and the best place is from the bridge area in the village. Phone (250) 697–2314 for more information. While in Horsefly, visit the *Jack Lynn Memorial Museum* (250–620–3304), also filled with many interesting artifacts of those good old days. On a gravel road 15.5 miles (25 km) east of Horsefly, you'll find *Likely,* named after John Likely, a gold miner (quite likely, you had thought up all kinds of other reasons!). This drive is very pretty, along the western shore of *Quesnel Lake* (the deepest lake in BC and second-deepest in North America), but not suitable for RVs. Check road conditions (especially in the wet season) before leaving Horsefly. An easier way to Likely is by a 50-mile (80-km) paved road north from 150 Mile House. Some of the richest gold fields were found around Likely, and prospecting is still the main activity. The area has many abandoned mines and ghost towns, including *Quesnel Forks,* which had at one time the largest Chinese population in North America. Photographers will love capturing images here of the old log buildings surrounded by fields of wildflowers.

Williams Lake

At Williams Lake you're suddenly back in the big city, and the signs of forestry (four major sawmills and a plywood mill), responsible for the city's incredible growth, are everywhere. Williams Lake became the area's commercial center after 1920, when the Pacific Great Eastern Railway arrived. Forestry, mining, agriculture, and the province's most active stockyard now all contribute to its economy.

Trivia
Canadians will remember Rick Hanson, "Man in Motion," who wheeled his wheelchair around the world to raise money for spinal cord research and rehabilitation. Rick hails from Williams Lake.

Despite all the bustle it is possible to find a quiet, classy place to stay. *Rowat's Waterside Bed and Breakfast* (1397 Borland Road, Williams

Lake, V2G 1M3; 250–392–7395 or 866–392–7395; reservations @wlakebb.com; wlakebb.com/rw2.htm) is right by the **Scout Island Nature Center** (Box 4575, Williams Lake, V2G 3R2; 250–398–8532), a bird-watcher's paradise. From the south as you approach the city, turn left at the Husky station onto Mackenzie Avenue, then left onto Borland Road. Visa and Mastercard are accepted, but it's advisable to book ahead for this quality accommodation, which starts at $68 double in high season. Watch the waterfowl from the deck as you enjoy a down-home cooked breakfast!

The Scout Island Nature Centre (off Borland Road) is operated by Williams Lake Field Naturalists Volunteers, who have interactive exhibits set up in **The Nature House.** It's full of interesting displays, showing small wildlife, waterfowl, birds, fish, and shells, all indigenous to the Williams Lake area. There's also a bee colony on display. An observation deck and walking trails aid in viewing the beaver lodge, native pit house, otters, muskrats, birds, and ducks that inhabit this conservation area. Reached via a causeway at the west end of Williams Lake, the center is open from 8:00 A.M. to 5:00 P.M. Monday to Friday, May to August, and on Sunday afternoons April through October, but the trails are open daily from 8:00 A.M. to dusk. Bring a picnic lunch and a swimsuit to make use of the tables and sandy beach.

Near the City Hall at the **Museum of the Cariboo Chilcotin** (113 North Fourth Avenue, Williams Lake, V2G 2C8; phone/fax: 250–392–7404; mccwl@uniserve.com), rodeo and ranching history is the theme. Displays include a working model of the Pacific Great Eastern Railway, which brought the first stockyards to Williams Lake in 1919. It is also the home of the **BC Cowboy Hall of Fame,** honoring working cowboys who made contributions to the ranching community. Learn here of the history of western Canada's first cattlemen. Admission is $2.00, and children are admitted free. It's open Monday to Saturday from 10:00 A.M. to 4:00 P.M., May to August, and in winter Tuesday to Saturday from 11:00 A.M. to 4:00 P.M.

The museum also features the **William Lake Stampede,** which is held over the July 1 weekend, offering barrel racing, calf roping, steer wrestling, wild-horse racing, bull riding, and other events included on the Canadian Professional Rodeo Association circuit. This four-day event was originally started in the 1920s and is now a major professional rodeo. For more information contact the Williams Lake Stampede Association at (800) 71RODEO (717–6336) or (250) 392–6585; office@williamslakestampede.com; www.williamslakestampede.com.

Hikers can take advantage of the easily accessible **Williams Lake River Valley Trail,** a 9-mile (14-km) hiking trail that takes you from downtown to the Fraser River. It's a scenic, easy family hike passing through varying ecosystems. It starts by the highway near the cemetery, and as it nears the Fraser River, the valley narrows with spectacular cliffs rising over 500 feet (150 m) with deep gullies on each side. To get directions, drop in to the **Williams Lake Visitor Info Centre** (1148 Broadway South, Williams Lake, V2G 1A2; 250–392–5025; fax: 250–392–4214; wldcc@stardate.bc.ca; www.bcadventure.com/wlcc) at the crossroads of Highways 97 and 20 and pick up even more information on the area.

If it's delicious specialty coffees, salads, soups, wraps, desserts, or frittatas (and more) that you're after, you won't go wrong at the **Beanstalk Coffee Company** (phone/fax: 250–392–5656; monster@telus.com). An armchair-friendly atmosphere plus local entertainment at 8:00 P.M. every Saturday night (jazz, blues, acoustic folk music, etc.) is what's offered. Pick up a book in the adjoining new library near the corner of Third Avenue and Borland and settle back for a truly relaxing (and delicious) respite.

Golfers can play till they drop at the **Williams Lake Golf & Tennis Club,** (104 Fairview Drive, Box 4006, Williams Lake, V2G 2V2, 250–392–6026/6548), where a special daily eighteen-hole rate is offered. The fairways overlook the town and the attractive lake with the Chilcotin hills in the background. Non-golfers can take in the view and enjoy a meal in the dining room.

As you drive farther north in the Cariboo, you have a chance to experience hands-on both the native history and the more modern gold rush history. First, at **Xats'ull Heritage Village** (Site 15, Comp. 2, RR 4, Williams Lake, V2G 4M8; 250–297–6323; fax: 250–297–6300), 23 miles (37 km) north of Williams Lake near Soda Creek Reserve, you'll be able to experience the spiritual and cultural magic of a Shuswap heritage village. There are one-day programs (Tuesday, Thursday, and Saturday 10:00 A.M. to 4:00 P.M. from June to fall) at Xats'ull (pronounced "hat-shul"), where you can learn toolmaking, basketmaking, and traditional food preparation. Stay in teepees and reconstructed pit houses (*kekulis*) near the banks of the Fraser River and become spiritually cleansed and rejuvenated in sweat lodges. Ancient petroglyphs can be found near the teepee circle, where you can listen to traditional storytelling and discuss the old ways with Shuswap elders for an experience different from any other you're likely to have in the Cariboo.

From Xats'ull Heritage Village Highway 97 continues north, parallel to the Fraser River for another 51 miles (82 km) to Quesnel. This is where the hands-on gold rush experience starts—where the Fraser and Quesnel Rivers meet. From here, back in the 1860s, thousands of gold seekers left the Fraser and trekked east to historic Barkerville. *Quesnel* is dubbed "Gold Pan City," loudly proclaimed by the *World's Largest Gold Pan,* located north of the city at the junction of Highways 97N and 26E. The *Quesnel Visitor Info Centre* is downtown in LeBourdais Park at 705 Carson Avenue, Quesnel, V2J 2B6 (250–992–8716 or 800–992–4922; fax: 250–992–2181; visitorinfo@city.quesnel.bc.ca; www.city.quesnel.bc.ca). Ask there about gold panning in the Quesnel River, or phone the Gold Commissioner (250–992–4301) for details first, or you could unwittingly become a claim-jumper. At low water during fall, you're most likely to strike it rich!

Next door to the Info centre is the *Quesnel & District Museum and Archives* (705 Carson Avenue, Quesnel, V2J 2B6; 250–992–9580; fax: 250–992–9680; stubbsr@sd28.bc.ca; www. sd28.bc. ca/museum/), one of the best small museums in BC. The museum houses a rare collection of nineteenth-century Chinese items. The major fun event in Quesnel is held the third week of July with four days of revelery called *Billy*

Mysterious Mandy

Since 1991, staff at the **Quesnel Museum** at 705 Carson Avenue have been feeling a little creepy. Several antique dolls reside there, but none so unusual as the eighty-year-old Mandy, who came to live at the museum after many years in a local resident's basement. The resident had often heard a baby's cry coming from the basement but on investigation could find nothing. Mysteriously, after the doll's departure, the resident was no longer disturbed by the crying. Today Mandy sits in the museum, smiling awkwardly, several deep cracks disfiguring her head, and one eye wandering disconcertingly. Before she arrived the aura in the museum was tranquil, even fun. But after she arrived that aura was disturbed and "things" started to happen until the curator, both to contain the doll's ghostly spirit and to prevent more havoc than she had already caused, placed her in another room inside her own special glass case. On two separate occasions attempts were made to develop photos of Mandy in two different labs. In one case contact sheets mysteriously disintegrated, and in the other the lab was found in disarray! Things are tranquil now. Could Mandy have calmed down when she realized that the museum was safe? Who knows, but many visitors to the museum are still spooked.

Trivia

Barker Days. If you're visiting in late January, don't miss the **Gold Rush Trail Sled Dog Mail Run,** which ends with festivities in Wells at the **Wells Winter Carnival.** For more information visit www.wellsbc. com.

*During the 1860s when the gold rush was in full swing, tiny **Barkerville** had the largest North American population north of San Francisco and west of Chicago.*

With two rivers passing through Quesnel, how could it help but be attractive? But it wasn't always so. The town has been spruced up now with the very attractive **River-Front Trail** system, which consists of the 3-mile (5-km) North Quesnel Trail and the 2.6-mile (4.3-km) West Side Trail (along the shores of the Fraser River and Baker Creek). Here you can see the city at your leisure and meet a few locals at the same time. Ask at the Info Centre for a guide.

From Quesnel a turnoff 3 miles (5 km) north at the junction of Highways 97 and 26 leads 55 miles (88 km) to **Barkerville Historic Town** (Box 19, Barkerville, V0K 1B0; 250–994–3332), now fully restored and surely one of British Columbia's most remote, yet biggest, tourist attractions. It's a walk back into those fascinating gold rush days of yore. In summer (when admission is charged) all activities, from live theater to guided tours, are in full swing. Barkerville is open 8:00 A.M. to 8:00 P.M. year-round.

Between Wells and Barkerville on Highway 26, a 14-mile (23-km) road leads northeast to **Bowron Lake Provincial Park** (250–398–4414 for information), one of North America's premier canoeing circuits. Six major lakes connected by several smaller lakes provide solitude and scenery unsurpassed, with plenty of wildlife as well. To paddle in the park, you need a park permit, which costs from $50 per one-person canoe/kayak or from $100 per two- or three-person canoe/kayak. Voyageur canoe permits costs $50 per person. In summer phone (800) HELLOBC (435–5622); outside North America phone (250) 387–1642. Payment must be made at the time of reservation (there is an $18 non-refundable fee applied) by Visa or Mastercard only.

You could take the easy way out by staying at **Becker's Lodge** (Highway 26, Bowron Lake, Box 129, Wells, V0K 2R0; 250–992–8864 or 800–808–4761; fax: 250–992–8893; Radio phone: N698552 Wells Channel; beckers@beckers.bc.ca; www.beckers.bc.ca). Relax in one of the cabins or go completely "wild" and sign up for a weeklong canoe trip. You'll camp in such idyllic spots as Indian Point Lake, Wolverine Bay, Rum Lake, and Spectacle Lake. The all-inclusive tour costs $1,100 plus GST, or stay overnight at rates starting at $70. Perhaps rent a canoe for the day. Park permits are not needed for day rentals. Keep in mind that there are no regular phone lines to Bowron Lake. To get there go through Wells, and 0.3 miles (500 m) before Barkerville, turn left to Bowron Lake. After 13 miles (24 kms) along a good gravel road, you'll see the BECKERS sign and their Trading Post Store. A transfer service is available from Quesnel.

The Freedom Highway

It was the summer of 1953, and the folks in the Chilcotin were tired of hearing that a road couldn't be put through to the coast. George Dalshaug started from the west, and Alf Bracewell pushed downward from the east. They would show them. And show them they did. On September 26, 1953, Dalshaug and Bracewell touched bulldozer blades and shook hands; thus, BC's last frontier, the vast Chilcotin, was laid open. Today the *Freedom Highway* (Highway 20) is a tribute to those stubborn souls who said it *could* be done. To describe the whole of the enormous, dramatic Chilcotin Coast area, which is served by the Freedom Highway, is a book in itself. This small section will hopefully give you enough of an adventurous nudge that you'll be tempted to explore it. As services on the highway are limited, careful planning is in order: Before you set out make sure that your vehicle is in top-notch order and that you have adequate safety equipment and a good map. Staff at the Williams Lake Visitor Info Centre (250–392–5052) have prepared a two-page pamphlet on Highway 20 (*The Chilcotin—Highway 20 Guide*) outlining services and interesting spots along the road. Seasonally, phone (888) 863–1181 for more Freedom Highway Information.

From Williams Lake to the west coast at Bella Coola, you'll cover 288 miles (463 km), of which 212 miles (341 km) are paved or sealcoated. Without question the section most talked about is *The Hill,* a 5.5-mile (9-km) series of gravel switchbacks (with grades to a nail-biting 18 percent) that descend through the 5,000-foot (1,524-m) Heckman Pass in *Tweedsmuir Provincial Park* (BC's largest) into the *Bella Coola Valley.* You might ask yourself, why risk this baptism of fire? There are three answers.

The first is that the views in the Chilcotin of wide-open spaces, crystal-clear lakes, thick-forested mountains, marshes, and meadows, palettes of wildflowers, and the majestic Bella Coola Valley, home of the mythical thunderbird, are second to none. You're also likely to encounter wandering bears and head-knocking California bighorn sheep.

The second reason is the people you will meet: people who are not "chicken" to try a new venture and who love their Chilcotin. People like the Christensens of Anahim Lake, who for more than one hundred years—three generations of the family—have provided service as *A. C. Christensen General Merchants* (Box 3449, Christensen Road, Anahim Lake, V0L 1C0; 250–742–3266). Outside, the store is decorated with a mural of rearing stallions; inside, the ceiling is studded with baseball caps from the four corners of the earth. The Christensen motto is "If we don't have it, you don't need it." Present owners, the McLeans, give a double-or-nothing guarantee with purchases. Flip a coin, and if you win, it costs nothing; if you lose—well, you did agree to double or nothing!

A detour south of Tatla Lake will bring you to folks like the Bracewells at Circle X Ranch. The family runs *Bracewell's Alpine Wilderness Adventures* (Box 8, Tatlayoko Lake, V0L 1W0; phone/fax: 250–476–1169; alex@bracewell.com; www.bcadventure.com/brace well). During the day they'll take you riding the ranges and in the evening may show home movies of Alf Bracewell's impressive road-building feat. Ask Alex and Connie about their new houseboat venture on Tatlayoko and Chilko Lakes. These piloted boats are suitable for two couples or a family of four. A two-night stay aboard, followed by an exciting ATV guided tour, could make for the most incredible wilderness holiday of your lifetime.

Chilko Lake is in Ts'yl-os Provincial Park (250–398–4414). It is the largest natural high-elevation freshwater lake in North America. Fishing enters a new realm here, with rainbow and Dolly Varden trout reaching 22 pounds (10 kg). You'll find exciting rafting on the Chilko River (featured in the Alan Alda movie *The White Mile*), with thrilling rapid drops that thunder through spectacular scenery, including one section through Lava Canyon that provides an adrenalin rush for 12 miles (19 km).

Trivia

In 1935 in an area just above Taseko Lake, seven men were left working in a gold mining camp, well-stocked with supplies for the winter. At breakup runners who were sent in to make a routine check were astonished to find the camp empty. Everyone had disappeared—but there were some human bones lying about. Then a body, presumably that of the cook who may have been collecting supplies, was found in a root cellar. Apparently, an avalanche had occurred while he was in the cellar, sealing it off from the air and preserving the only body of the seven.

Contact *Chilko River Expeditions* (Box 4723, Williams Lake, V2G 2V7; 250–392–0300; www.pennywiser.com/chilko) and get set for a true wilderness rafting trip that will leave you exhilarated. Ts'yl-os (sounds like "sigh-loss") Provincial Park is situated about 100 miles (160 km) west of Williams Lake and is one of BC's newest (1994) parks. Keep a sharp eye out for bald eagles and peregrine falcons. Accommodation is available at *Chilko Lake Resort* (Box 17, Tatla Lake, V0L 1V0; 250–481–3333; fax: 250–481–3334; holiday@chilko lake.com; www.chilkolake.com), located a four-hour drive west of Williams Lake. Rates at this luxury wilderness resort start at $145 and include the use of the swimming pool, sauna, hot tub, tennis court, games room, canoes, pedal boats, and fishing rods. There are also packages available that include air transportation to and from Vancouver, just over an hour away.

Nearer the coast, halfway between Hagensborg and Bella Coola, you'll meet people like Barb of *Barb's Pottery* (Box 363, Bella Coola, V0T 1C0; 250–799–5380). Barb's studio, where she creates lovely stoneware, raku, and porcelain pottery, is in an early 1900s log heritage building of a type constructed by Norwegian settlers who arrived in Bella Coola in 1894.

Recommended Reading - Cariboo- Chilcotin Coast

FOR ADULTS:
Backroads Explorer Volume 1, Thompson Cariboo, by Murphy Shewchuk. Maclean Hunter, Vancouver, 1985. This book is a wonderful in-depth source with detailed maps and historical snippets.

Stein Valley Wilderness Guidebook, by Gordon R. White. Stein Wilderness Alliance, 1991.

Gold Panning in the Cariboo - A Prospector's Treasure Trail to Creeks of Gold, by Jim Lewis and Charles Hart. Heritage House Publishing Ltd. 1997.

Cariboo Chilcotin, Pioneer People and Places, by Irene Stangoe. Heritage House Publishing Company, Surrey. 1994.

They Call it the Cariboo, by Robin Skelton. Sono Nis Press, Victoria, 1980.

Stagecoach and Sternwheel Days in the Cariboo and Central British Columbia, by Willis J. West. Heritage House Publishing Company Ltd. Surrey, 1985.

FOR KIDS:
Three against time, by Margaret Taylor. 1997, Orca Books. Three boys are taken back in time to the great Barkerville fire—a gold rush story. For grades four to seven.

Note the hand-hewn cedar logs and dove-tailed corners. Look for the ARTISAN sign on the highway.

The third tongue-in-cheek reason for driving the Freedom Highway is that you can then honestly flaunt a bumper sticker (if they don't exist, they soon will): I SURVIVED THE HILL!

You finally emerge from the lushly forested Bella Coola Valley, home of the Coast Salish Nuxalk nation, to the fresh ocean smells and dockside activity of Bella Coola at the head of North Bentinck Arm, in total contrast with the dramatic pinnacles, blessed with names like Stupendous Mountain and Matterhorn Peak, so recently passed. Valleys, fjords, countless islands, and thousands of miles of wilderness coastline are waiting to be explored. Breathe in the clean ocean air while hiking the *Gray Jay Lake Trail* to the *Big Cedar Recreation Site*; then drop into *Chloe's Café at the Hitching Post* (250–799–5533; www.bcadventure.com/chloes/) on Cliff Street for a scrumptious feed of fish and chips or maybe a burger. Here you can sit on a patio and enjoy the sensational Bella Coola scenery. There are even more glorious views if you join *Seafair Adventures* (Box 274, Bella Coola, V0T 1C0; phone/fax: 250–982–2547; seafair@bcadventure.com). Cruising in wonderful wilderness, hot-springs bathing, fresh halibut, crab, or prawns cooked to perfection, and classy staterooms aboard the 75-foot (23-m) *Nitinat Chief* are what you'll be treated to. Ask the skipper about stopping in at Ocean Falls, where resorts like the *Ocean Falls Fishing Lodge* (General Delivery, Ocean Falls, V0T 1P0; 250–289–3220 or 800–661–7550; fishing@planet.eon.net) bring keen fishers from all over the world in search of freshwater trout, salmon, and halibut. The lodge is open August and September.

And finally, if you're reluctant to retrace your Freedom Highway steps, consider booking a passage aboard BC Ferries (888–BCFERRY). Ships leave from Bella Coola every two days from June to September (early morning) on a fourteen- to twenty-four hour sail (depending on stops). You'll land in Port Hardy, from which you can drive the length of Vancouver Island to Victoria.

PLACES TO STAY IN THE CARIBOO-CHILCOTIN

70 MILE HOUSE
Little Horse Lodge,
Green Lake Road North,
Comp 1, Site E,
RR 1, 70 Mile House,
V0K 2K0; (250) 456-7524.
fax: (250) 456-7512;
littlehorse@100mile.net.
Lodge, cabins, or
campsites.

108 MILE RANCH
The Hills Health Ranch,
Box 26, 108 Mile Ranch,
V0K 2Z0; (250) 791-5225;
fax: (250) 791-6384;
thehills@bcinternet.net.

BOWRON LAKE
Becker's Lodge,
Highway 26, Bowron Lake,
Box 129, Wells, V0K 2R0;
(250) 992-8864;
(800) 808-4761;
fax: (250) 992-8893;
radio phone: N698552
Wells Channel;
beckers@beckers.bc.ca;
www.beckers.bc.ca.
Wilderness
accommodation.

CHILKO LAKE
Chilko Lake Resort,
Box 17, Tatla Lake,
V0L 1V0; (250) 481-3333;
fax: (250) 481-3334;
holiday@chilkolake.com;
www.chilkolake.com.
Wilderness accommoda-
tion four hours west of
Williams Lake.

CLINTON
Cariboo Lodge Resort,
Box 459, Clinton
V0K 1K0; (250) 459-7992;
fax: (250) 459-0060;
cariboo-lodge@
goldtrail.com.

LONE BUTTE
Loon Bay Resort,
C1 Airmail Road,
Lone Butte,
V0K 1X0; (250) 593-4431;
fax: (250) 593-4188;
loonbay@bcinternet.net.
Cabins and campsites on
Sheridan Lake.

WILLIAMS LAKE
Rowat's Waterside Bed and
Breakfast,
1397 Borland Road,
Williams Lake,
V2G 1M3; (250) 392-7395.

PLACES TO EAT IN THE CARIBOO-CHILCOTIN

BELLA COOLA
Chloe's Café at the Hitching
Post, (250) 799-5533,
on Cliff Street.
Fresh fish and chips.

CACHE CREEK
Ashcroft Manor Teahouse,
Box 127, Cache Creek,
V0K 1H0; (250) 453-9983.
Excellent meals in a
historic roadhouse.

HAGENSBORG
The Bentinck Arms Pub at
The Bay Motor Hotel,
Highway 20,

Box 216,
Bella Coola,
V0T 1C0; (888) 982-2212
or (250) 982-2212;
fax: (250) 982-2330;
bayhotel@
bcadventure.com.
Nine miles (14 km) east of
Bella Coola. Patio cafe and
coffee shop. Free shuttle to
ferry terminal or airport.
Accommodations,
too, from $69 double.

LILLOOET
Elaine's Coffee Garden,
824 Main Street,
V0K 1V0; (250) 256-4633.
A lunch bar serving soups,
salads, bagels,
ice creams, desserts.

WILLIAMS LAKE
Beanstalk Coffee Company,
phone/fax: (250)
392-5656;
monster@telus.com. Near
the library at Third and
Borland, offering soups,
salads, wraps, desserts, and
specialty coffees.

The Northeast

O nly since the completion of the Alaska Highway in 1942 has even a scant section of this huge, beautiful region been accessible to tourists. From the Yellowhead/Trans-Canada Highway junction at Tête Jaune Cache, we'll follow the Fraser River northwest to Prince George, British Columbia's fourth-largest city. From here we'll head to the big skies of the Peace River district and Dawson Creek, where we'll tackle the legendary Alaska Highway to the Yukon border. In total the journey will be more than 930 miles (1,500 km) through some of the most spectacular scenery the province has to offer.

Following the Fraser to Prince George

A bout twenty minutes northwest of Tête Jaune Cache on Highway 16, there's an easily missed sign to **Dunster.** Go down the hill and just after a one-lane Bailey bridge, take the first right to the end of the road. Another right and you're at **Bonnie and Curtis Culp's farm**; perhaps just follow the smell of the wool. Peacocks, llamas, and crossbred Rocky Mountain sheep roam near antique sheep wagons built for herders one hundred years ago. The Culps have redecorated the wagons to operate a unique bed-and-breakfast business. The double beds are covered with Bonnie's quilts, filled with wool from their sheep. Some wagons have woodstoves, and all are decorated and repainted in their original brilliant colors by the Culp's daughter Kitty. Double accommodation (by prebooking only, no drop-ins)is $50, including breakfast. Take a tour of Bonnie's quilt-making studio above the farmhouse, where quilts can be ordered and knitting wool is for sale. If prearranged, meals can be served. Contact **Robson Valley Wools** (Station Road, Dunster, V0J 1J0; 250–968–4309) for information and bookings.

Another choice for *get-away-from-it-all* accommodation is **The Mother Land Inn** (River Road, Dunster, V0J 1J0; 250–968–4356; arlene@ bcnorthweb.com; www.bcnorthweb.com/motherland). Turn right before

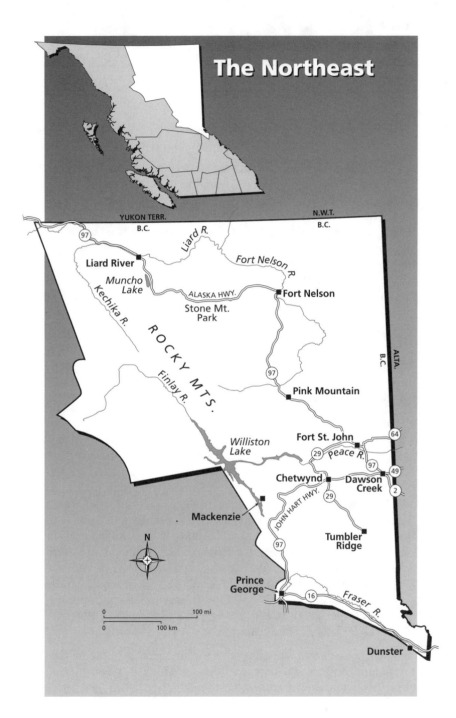

The Northeast

YUKON TERR.
B.C.

N.W.T.
B.C.

ALTA.
B.C.

Liard River

Liard R.

Fort Nelson R.

Muncho Lake

Kechika R.

ALASKA HWY.

Fort Nelson

Stone Mt. Park

R O C K Y   M T S.

Finlay R.

97

Pink Mountain

Williston Lake

Fort St. John

64

29

Peace R.

97

49

Chetwynd

Dawson Creek

2

Mackenzie

JOHN HART HWY.

29

Tumbler Ridge

N

97

Prince George

16

Fraser R.

0   100 mi
0   100 km

Dunster

the bridge and drive to the end of River Road. A variety of accommodation choices are available, from double bed and breakfast ($75), to renting the whole property for a week ($1,200), to budget tent/tipi accommodation ($10), which includes use of an outside kitchen, a tree-house lounge, and a wood-fired sauna next to the Fraser River. With 168 acres (68 ha) and more than 2.5 miles (4 km) of river frontage, there are plenty of activities offered—canoeing, birding, hiking the ridges and riverbank trails, or just simply relaxing in pristine, "no-electricity," awe-inspiring surroundings.

Back on the road into Dunster, drive for a mile or so to *Hill's General Store* (250–968–4488). Since 1973, Claude and Lilly Hill have sold everything and anything in this eclectic grocery-cum-post-office-cum-hardware store. It's the epicenter for a community of about 150 families who ranch, farm, log, and create in this quiet rural area. Ask Claude about the *Dunster Farmers' Market,* held in the parking lot of the Community Hall most Saturday mornings in August and September. Locals bring fresh produce and home-baked goods, and as well there's a friendly old-fashioned flea market. Across the street from the store is the

Fur Out Friendliness

*A*n old black car sat abandoned in a field, a television intriguingly propped on its hood, encouraging me to explore more of this laid-back area in BC's northeast. I stopped at the nearby Dunster store and met Claude Hill. He has loved this Robson Valley since he came here hunting in the sixties and has worked at everything from logging to highway construction. But he has "never looked back" since he "picked up the store" in 1973.

"It's a fantastic community," he enthused, between selling eggs and stamping mail.

He told me of a board game called Fur Out, for "Ages 10–110" invented by local trappers Rod and Deb Reimer.

"A whole bunch of us invested thinking we had the new Trivia," he joked. When I left Hill's Store, Claude was explaining how he was happily anchored to this neighborly community.

"Someone will always need a rat trap, so you just can't go away," he said, insistently tucking a game of Fur Out under my arm.

old **Dunster Train Station,** one of the last of the original CNR train stations built in the early 1900s.

Continue south on gravel road, watching on the right for **Terri's Attempts** (Box 20, Dunster, V0J 1J0; 250–968–4468). Terri creates hand-stitched teddy bears, reverse appliqué wall hangings, dream catchers, and other craft items.

Seven and a half miles (12 km) southeast of Dunster is an area called South Croydon. When the railways were being built, the village of South Croydon was a lively spot. Now only a few stalwarts remain. At the foot of the Old South Croydon Ferry Road is **Mountain Pottery** (250–968–4310), where Stefi McLean's studio overflows with aesthetic, medium-fired porcelain. It's an unlikely discovery on a sheep farm set in the fertile Robson Valley.

If you don't mind a little dust or mud on your vehicle, you might want to drive farther south and try your luck at hooking a few rainbow trout in **Shere Lake.** This recreation area makes for an excellent picnic spot. It's about 14 miles (23 km) from Dunster. A mile or so on, hikers can enjoy a ninety-minute steep hike from Kiwa Lake to the forestry lookout tower on Shere Point. The superb views extend to Valemount and McBride. And yet another valley viewpoint is found 6 miles (10 km) farther southeast at Watertank Hill. Watch for wildlife in the slough by the road as you continue on toward Tête Jaune Cache. If you're visiting between mid-August and mid-September, don't miss the McLennan River salmon spawning area, just past the original village site of Tête Jaune Cache.

You're back on the tar now. Nine miles (14 km) northwest of the junction is **Terracana Resort and Chalets** (12155 Yellowhead Highway 16 West, Box 909, Valemount, V0E 2Z0; 250–968–4304; fax: 250–968–4445; booking@terracana.com; www.terracana.com). Located on the Fraser River, and with views of the mountains second to none, this resort is much more than just a place to sleep. Jet-boat tours, guided canoeing and hiking, and llama trekking are but the beginning of a host of activities offered. Rates for double accommodation in modern chalets start at $123. The chalets are available from June 1 to September 30.

McBride, a town that owes its beginnings to the Grand Trunk Railway, is 40 miles (75 km) northwest of Tête Jaune Cache. Logging and farming are the main industries in this scenic Robson Valley location. A display of local art, craft, and photography can be seen at the **McBride Arts Centre** (Main Street and First Avenue, McBride, V0J 2E0; 250–569–2229) in the newly renovated historic railway station. Artists work here, and there's also a railway history display. Hours are from 9:00 A.M. to 5:00 P.M. or by

Top Annual Events in the Northeast

appointment in winter. Bird lovers will enjoy the **Horseshoe Lake Bird Viewing Station,** where swans, Canada geese, blue herons, and goldeneye ducks can be observed. It's but a short distance from downtown. A wheelchair-accessible viewing platform leads out over the lake. To get there, turn left off Main Street onto Second Avenue, then left onto Horseshoe Lake Road. There are few services on the lonely Yellowhead Highway after McBride, and as Prince George is another 125 miles (202 km), make sure to top up the gas tank. The **McBride Visitor Info Centre** (100 Robson Center, Box 2, McBride, V0J 2E0; 250–569–3366 or 250–569–2229; fax: 250–569–3276) has information on restaurants and accommodation in the area.

Prince George

Prince George (P.G. to northerners) has all the amenities of a modern city. With a population of more than 78,000, the city enjoys first-class live theater, its own symphony orchestra, a university, and modern museums and art galleries. But with 1,500 lakes in the area (it's dubbed the "Lakes and Rivers District") and 140 parks in the city alone, P.G. has managed to maintain a laid-back, northern atmosphere.

You'll see what I mean if you have a day or two to spend and set off with **Strider Adventures** (17075 Perry Road East, Prince George, V2K 5E3; 800–665–7752 or 250–963–9542; fax: 250–963–8446; strider@pgweb.com; www.pgweb.com/strider). They'll take you packing out onto alpine trails with calm, inquisitive llamas on either day hikes or two-, three-, five-, and seven-day camping adventures. The llamas do all the work; you just have to walk and enjoy the scent of the wildflowers and the superb scenery. The turnoff to Strider Adventures is at the Willow River and Upper Fraser sign on the Yellowhead Highway, 10

Robson Valley Fall Fair, McBride; August; *(250) 569-0321*

Prince George and District Music Festival, Prince George; February/March; phone/fax: (250) 614-1004; www.pgmusicfestival.com

Prince George Rodeo, Prince George; mid-June; *(250) 964-0389 or (800) 668-7646*

Saulteaux Pemmican Days, Moberly Lake; June; *(250) 788-9754*

Alexander Mackenzie Day, Mackenzie; June; *(250) 997-5775*

West Moberly First Nations Days, Moberly Lake; November; *(250) 788-3663*

Chetfest Music Festival, Chetwynd; July; *(250) 788-1830*

Tumbler Ridge Grizzly Valley Days, Tumbler Ridge; August; *(250) 242-4246*

Dawson Creek and District Fall Fair and Stampede, Dawson Creek; August; *(250) 782-9595 or (250) 782-8911*

World's Invitational Gold Panning Championship, Taylor; August; *(250) 789-3004*

North Peace Fall Fair, Fort St. John; August; *(250) 785-2020*

Fort Nelson Rodeo, Fort Nelson; August; *(250) 774-1035*

miles (16 km) east of the Yellowhead Bridge in Prince George. Take the first turn right for 2 miles (3 km) to the A-frame at 17075 East Perry Road. Rates are in the $150 to $180-per-day range. Phone or check Dan and Dorothy's Web page for full information.

P.G. is conveniently located where two major highways, two prominent rivers, and two railway lines intersect, making it a convenient transportation hub. Restaurants are plentiful, as are accommodations—in fact, you might call it Bed-and-Breakfast City. Two phone numbers (888–266–5555 and 877–562–2626) will link you to most of the B&Bs in P.G.

One of the sights to take in is the new $5 million *Two Rivers Art Gallery* (725 Civic Plaza, Prince George, V2L 5T1; 888–221–1155 or 250–563–6447; fax: 250–563–3211; annette@tworiversartgallery.com; www.tworiversartgallery.com), which has displays of local and regional artists exhibited in a state-of-the-art gallery next to the *Civic Center Plaza,* which is opposite *Connaught Hill Park* (a good spot for a view of the city and a picnic). If you're interested in native arts and crafts, try the *Prince George Native Art Gallery* in the nonprofit Native Friendship Center. Here, while learning some First Nations' history, you can also purchase a souvenir of the true north directly from the artists—items range from mukluks and moccasins to beaded jewelry and original paintings. The gallery is at 1600 Third Avenue, V2L 3G6; (250) 614–7726. Or for more information visit the Web site at www.pgnfc.com/gallery.

If you're still seeking history, visit *Fort George Park* on the banks of the Fraser River and *The Exploration Place,* operated by the *Fraser-Fort George Regional Museum* (333 Becott Place, Box 1779, Prince George, V2L 4V7; 250–562–1612; fax: 250–562–6395; info@theexplorationplace.com; www.museum.princegeorge.com). This is the site of the original Hudson's Bay Trading Post. Displays give a good overview of the area's history, and as well there's a hands-on *Northwood Explorations Gallery.* The Discovery Boxes are educational and fun for the kids. In summer a small-gauge steam train chugs around, picking up kids at the historic station in the park. For the true trainaholic the *Prince George Railway and Forest Industry Museum* (Box 2408, 850 River Road, V2N 2S6; 250–563–7334; fax: 250–563–7337; site phone: 250–563–7351; trains@pgrfm.bc.ca; www.pgrfm.bc.ca) is a hands-on railway experience. It's next to Cottonwood Island Park, where the Nechako and Fraser rivers meet.

There's lots more to do in P.G., so much so that the *Prince George Visitor*

Info Centre has set up two offices: one on the corner of Victoria Street and Fifteenth Avenue (250–562–3700) and a summer site (250–563–5493) at the junction of Highways 16 and 97. They also regularly update an events Web site: www.afterhours.org. Contact them from outside the area by phoning (800) 668–7646; fax: (250) 563–3584; or by writing to them at 1198 Victoria Street, Prince George, V2L 2L2. The E-mail address is information@tourismpg.bc.ca, and the Web site is www.tourismpg.bc.ca.

North to Peace River Country

From Prince George we leave the Fraser River and cross the Nechako River past thinning suburbs and rolling farmlands along the John Hart Highway (97 North). Twenty-five miles (40 km) north is the **Huble Homestead**, now part of a regional park. In 1900 a trapper named Albert Huble operated a trading post from here. The business became a regular stop for steamboats running the Fraser River to Tête Jaune Cache. Today the steamboats are gone, but Huble Homestead remains as a historic site and a popular hiking area. To get there follow the signs from the highway for 4 miles (6 km) along Mitchell Road. The site includes the Giscome Portage Interpretive Centre, an original 1912 log house, the 1914 general store, farm animals, a blacksmith shop, and other heritage buildings. Costumed staff work at the site, gardening and demonstrating tasks from the May long weekend to the Labor Day weekend in September. Contact the Huble Homestead/Giscome Portage Heritage Society (Suite 1, 245 Quebec Street, Prince George, V2L 1W4; 250–564–7033; fax: 250–962–4628; cbelfry@mag-net. com) for more information. From the homestead, a pleasant hike, the **Giscome Portage Trail,** runs for 5 miles (8.5 km) northwest to a pull-out on Highway 97.

Ninety-eight miles (158 km) north of Prince George on Highway 97,

WORTH SEEING/DOING IN THE NORTHEAST

Watch beavers swimming in the pond at Forests for the World Park in Prince George.

Visit the Little Prairie Heritage Museum in Chetwynd (beautiful antique quilts).

Paddle the Fort Nelson River from Fort Nelson.

Float down the Liard River in a raft.

Take a train trip on VIA Rail's The Skeena for a memorable two-day trip from Prince Rupert to Jasper, Alberta.

Enjoy colorful skies as the northern lights (aurora borealis) dance over Fort Nelson.

Hike the 7-mile (11-km) Heritage River Trails in Prince George.

Join a forestry or mill tour in Fort St. John.

Tour Walter Wright Pioneer Village in Dawson Creek. See the log schoolhouse, the smithy, general store, two churches, and a trapper's cabin.

See the best fossil collection in the Peace River area at Hudson's Hope Museum.

there's a turnoff to Mackenzie, which is located on the shores of **Williston Lake,** North America's largest man-made reservoir. A 2-mile (3-km) drive north of town takes you up **Morfee Mountain** for a spectacular view of the lake through the unpolluted crystalline air of the Rockies. Mackenzie was named for fur trader and explorer Alexander Mackenzie, who camped nearby in 1793, during his historic journey to Bella Coola on the coast. The town is a pulp, paper, and lumber manufacturing center, surrounded by countless logging roads to access the multitude of rivers and lakes. It's also home to the world's largest **tree crusher,** weighing 177 tons (160 metric tons), which was used to clear timber to form the 746-mile (1,200-km) shoreline of Williston Lake. It sits in state on Mackenzie Boulevard. For information on the area, contact the Chamber of Commerce (Box 880, Mackenzie, V0J 2C0; 250–997–5459; fax: 250–997–6117; mchamber@macbc.com; www.mackenzie chamber.bc.ca) year-round.

The next town traveling northeast along Highway 97 is Chetwynd, The Gateway to the Peace Country, 190 miles (306 km) north of Prince George. It's here that you decide whether to go north to Fort St. John via the **Bennett Dam** or east via Dawson Creek. The former is very scenic, following the Peace River to join the Alaska Highway 8 miles (13 km) past Fort St. John; the latter is slightly longer but will take you to Mile Zero of the Alaska Highway.

Those traveling to Alberta might consider doing a circle tour through Chetwynd along Highway 29 north to Hudson's Hope and Fort St. John, then south through **Taylor** to Dawson Creek, west 11 miles (17 km) on Highway 97 to **Arras,** and south along the **Heritage Highway** 60 miles (98 km) to Tumbler Ridge. Then head north on Highway 29 back to Highway 97 (near Cetwynd), then east for 60 miles (98 km) back to Dawson Creek and on to Alberta. You'll have covered it all, and in 330 miles (532 km) of paved roads, you'll have retraced your steps only 11 miles (17 km).

While in Chetwynd try out the **Leisure Pool,** which includes a wave pool, a hot tub, and a dry sauna. Another activity is to take a walk round to seek out the **Chetwynd Chainsaw Sculptures**. After being greeted by three huge bears at the entrance, you're sure to want to see more of the two dozen or so carvings that decorate the town. Ask at the **Visitor Info Cen-**

tre on Highway 97 next to the three bears (Box 594, Chetwynd, V0C 1J0; 250–788–1943; fax: 250–788–1846; chetwyndtourist@nlc.bc.ca; www. gochetwynd.com) for a brochure showing sculpture locations. Learn some of the area's history at the tiny **Little Prairie Heritage Museum,** Chetwynd's oldest building, once having served as the first post office. Quilters will enjoy seeing the antique quilts. (Admission is free.)

Moberly Lake Provincial Park, 16 miles (25 km) north of Chetwynd on Highway 29, is set on the south side of Moberly Lake. It's a beautiful park, with a boat launch, nature trails and a playground. The **ChetFest Music Festival** (250–788–1830) is a big draw to the area every July. Check out the structure on the north shore of Moberly Lake, reputed to be the world's largest log building. For information on Moberly Park and all other provincial parks listed in this section, contact BC Parks, Peace-Liard District, 150–10003 110th Avenue, Fort St. John, V1J 6M7; 250–787–3407; fax: 250–787–3490.

Highway 29 from Moberly Lake heads west and north to the **Peace Canyon Dam.** Drop in at the Visitor Centre (see below for contact information), open daily Victoria Day (the Monday before May 24) to Labor Day from 8:00 A.M. to 4:00 P.M. to learn here, via self-guided tours, of dinosaur evidence discovered when the Peace River was dammed. You'll see two life-size dinosaurs plus photographic displays of the building of the Peace Canyon Project.

Fourteen miles (23 km) upstream from the Peace Canyon Dam is the **W.A.C. Bennett Dam,** an enormous structure—1.2 miles (2 km) wide—constructed from glacial moraine left over from the last ice age. This damming formed the 225-mile-long (362-km) Williston Lake, which took a whole five years to fill. Take the Dam Access Road (Canyon Drive) just west of Hudson's Hope and drive along good road for 15 miles (24 km). In the Visitor Centre, there are numerous exhibits and an audiovisual theater. Guided tours of the powerhouse, 500 feet (152 m) underground, are available daily from Victoria Day to mid-September from 9:00 A.M. to 6:00 P.M. For information on both dams, contact Box 359, Hudson's Hope, V0C 1V0; (250) 783–5048; fax: (250) 783–9470, or call the toll free number at (888) 333–6667. Admission is by donation.

The **Hudson's Hope Museum** (Box 98, Hudson's Hope, V0C 1V0; 250–783–5735; fax: 250–783–5770; hhmuseum@hhcn.prn.bc.ca;

Trivia
During Saulteaux (pronounced "soh-toh") Pemmican Days near Chetwynd, Indian elders judge horse- and moose-call contests for men, cow-call contests for women, and for the kids—they get to yell their lungs out at donkey- and pig-call contests!

www.hhcn.prn.bc.ca) is housed in a 1942 Hudson's Bay Company store in Heritage Park opposite the Hudson's Hope Tourist Info Booth (10507 105th Avenue, Box 330, Hudson's Hope, V0C IV0; 250–783– 9154 or 783–9901; fax: 250–783–5598). If you're interested in fossils, the museum has an excellent collection including a rare baby ichthyosaur, a prehistoric turtle, and hadrosaur tracks. Also of note is an 11,600-year-old mammoth tusk. The town has adopted a dinosaur called Dudley as its mascot. *St. Peter's Shared Ministry Church,* built in 1938, is next to the Info Centre (which is by the highway near the dam access road). The church is of log construction, very small, and quite beautiful. This highway spot is near where explorer Simon Fraser wintered in 1805.

The pretty, 55-mile (88-km) drive along Highway 29 between Hudson's Hope and Fort St. John follows the *Peace River.* Cast a line for rainbow trout, arctic grayling, Dolly Varden, or northern pike. And keep the camera handy, as the views of the island-stippled Peace River are lovely. The road twists and bends steeply as it approaches Fort St. John.

Should you choose the southern route from Chetwynd—Highway 97— 62 miles (100 km) to Dawson Creek, you'll cross the Pine River at the entrance to the *East Pine Provincial Park,* a pleasant picnic spot, where you can cast for a fish or launch your boat.

But there's yet another side trip to consider before starting the journey north along the Alaska Highway.

A mile or so east of Chetwynd, Highway 29 South leads to *Tumbler Ridge,* developed in the 1980s into the world's largest open-pit coal mine. One mine closed in 2000, and the second is projected to close in 2003, but the town lives on; with housing at Canada's lowest prices, it is set to become a booming tourist/retirement destination. The town once prided itself on having the lowest crime rate in BC and the province's highest average family income.

En route to Tumbler Ridge, you'll pass the turnoff to *Sukunka Falls Provincial Park,* which is 12 miles (21 km) along a forest service road. Stay on the highway and you'll come to *Gwillim Lake Provincial Park* (250–787–3407), located midway between Chetwynd and Tumbler Ridge in the Rocky Mountain foothills. There are excellent camping facilities and miles of wilderness blue-lake shoreline to explore.

Twelve miles (20 km) south of the park—42 miles (68 km) south of

Chetwynd—is the **Bullmoose Mine** (250–242–4702), where tours are offered from mid-June to late August. The town of Tumbler Ridge is 23 miles (37 km) south of the mine, but the jewel of the area is even farther south.

Monkman Provincial Park is a 79,000-acre (32,000-ha) wilderness park, where the 210-foot-high (64-km) **Kinuseo Falls** provides excellent photographic opportunities. In summer jet boats take tourists up the Murray River to visit this unspoiled wonder, which is higher than Niagara Falls. If you don't mind about 30 miles (45 km) of gravel, an industrial road leads from Tumbler Ridge to the falls, where there are trails to a viewing platform and other vantage points. Nearby is the **Kinuseo Falls Provincial Park** (250–787–3407) campground and the **Stone Corral Interpretive Hiking Trail** (4 km return), which leads past scenic lakes to two small caves. Contact the **Tumbler Ridge Visitor Info Centre** on Southgate Road (Box 606, Tumbler Ridge, V0C 2W0; 250–242–4702; fax: 250–242–5159; commerce@pris.bc.ca; www.district.tumblerridge.bc.ca) for information.

A paved road (Highway 52 North) heads 60 miles (98 km) northeast from Tumbler Ridge to Arras, where you rejoin Highway 97, 10 miles (17 km) west of Dawson Creek. Nineteen miles (30 km) along this road there's a pullout at the trailhead of the **Murray Canyon Overlook Interpretive Trail.** This 1-mile (3 km) hike leads to excellent views of the Murray River.

The Alaska Highway: Dawson Creek to Fort Nelson Section

The **Alaska Highway** has its official beginning in **Dawson Creek,** so the popular thing to do there is to have your photo taken at the **Mile Zero Alaska Highway** post. Many of the sites of interest to tourists are found in this general area. The **Dawson Creek Visitor Info Centre** (900 Alaska Avenue, Dawson Creek, V1G 4T6; 250–782–9595; fax: 250–782–9538; dctourin@pris.bc.ca; www.city.dawson-creek.bc.ca) is housed in the **Railway Station Museum.** Throughout the day, the video *The Alaska Highway, 1942–1992* is shown. The **Dawson Creek Art Gallery** is housed in the

Trivia
The Peace River is named for Unijigah (Peace Point), where the Cree and Dunneza peoples smoked peace pipes and drew up an agreement to stop the warring between these two sovereign nations.

renovated annex of a prairie elevator and is situated in a municipal park (NAR Park) in the center of Dawson Creek. On Saturdays, the *Farmers' Market* is in full swing. Ask at the Info Centre about other sites in town: *McQueen Slough* (a waterfowl refuge); the *Walter Wright Pioneer Village* in *Mile Zero Rotary Park*, where you can take a virtual trip back to the 1940s; the *Zip and Dip* at Centennial Pool, where kids can enjoy a swim and a slide; and the local golf course and driving range.

In March 1942 Dawson Creek's population went from about 500 to 10,000 in a few short days when the United States military started arriving in droves. Eight months and three weeks later, the highway was officially opened, an amazing feat, considering that the distance covered was 1,421 miles (2,288 km), and it traversed impossible terrain to its end in Fairbanks, Alaska. At present the Canadian and Yukon governments spend about $40 million annually on its maintenance and reconstruction, and it is now a fully paved highway.

Before heading north you'll find a substantial meal at the *Alaska Café* (250–782–7040), housed in the quaint *Dew Drop Inn* at 10209 Tenth Avenue.

And for a down-on-the-farm place to stay, try *Wildwood Cottage* (Box 220, Pouce Coupe, V0C 2C0; 250–786–5830). Although a little out of town (it's about twenty minutes southwest of Dawson Creek off Highway 2), it's a perfect off-the-beaten-path choice. Situated on a certified organic farm that is both horse and solar powered, the cottage is set very privately in a clearing in the bush on the edge of a ravine by Bissett Creek. Owners Tim and Linda Ewert will hitch up a horse-drawn wagon, or you can walk the five minutes to your door if you wish. Breakfast includes fresh baking from a wood-fired stove, homemade yogurt, and homegrown fruit; it's delivered to the cottage at whatever time you prefer. Farm tours and wagon rides are also available. The cottage sleeps up to six. Double rates are $75 per night or $125 for two nights. Stay a while to fully appreciate this scenic area, where restored buildings from the 1900s and wildlife viewing go hand in hand. For more information on this pioneer community, contact the *Pouce Coupe Visitor Centre* (5006 Forty-ninth Avenue,

Trivia

Back in the early 1800s, the trappers and traders in the Fort St. John area learned to depend on one another for meat, furs, guns, wire for snares, traps, etc. They had, in effect, a kind of unwritten contract. When Fort St. John closed in 1823, the dependent trappers reacted by killing five employees and destroying the fort. This led to the closure of all Upper Peace forts, and much starvation ensued.

Trivia

Box 293, Pouce Coupe, V0C 2C0; 250–786–5555 or, off-season, 250–786–5794; fax: 250–786–5257), open May 15 to September 15.

The city of *Fort St. John* is 45 miles (73 km) north of Dawson Creek. It's the site of the first European settlement on the British Columbia mainland. (It started with twelve men, four women, and five children.) In 1793 Alexander Mackenzie marked it as an excellent fur-trading center during his journey to the coast. There's a monument to him in Centennial Park on 100th Street. Since the first settlement in 1794, the city has occupied six different sites. But it was the *Alaska Highway* (then the Alcan Military Road) that in the early forties caused Fort St. John's great growth spurt. Discovery of oil and gas south of the city in 1951 was the icing on the cake for this Energy Capital of British Columbia. The *Fort St. John Visitor Info Centre* (9923-96 Avenue, Fort St. John, V1J 1K9; 250–785–3033; fax: 250–785–7181; fsjchofcom@awink.com; www.fsjchamber.com) has a wealth of information on this thriving city. The *North Peace Museum* is located right next door. It's housed in a restored schoolhouse, behind a 150-foot-high (46-m) oil derrick. The museum traces the region's development from fur-trapping days to road-building days to oil rich days. Interestingly, although the Peace-Liard Region has only 15 percent of the total farming units in BC, the region contains nearly all (90 percent) of BC's cereal grain and seed crops, 100 percent of canola crops, and 28 percent of all forage crops. For information specific to the *Alaska Highway Parks,* visit the BC Parks District Manager at 150–10003 110th Avenue, Fort St. John, V1J 6M7; (250) 787– 3407; fax: (250) 787–3490.

About 12 miles (20 km) north of Fort St. John, near the junction of Highways 97 and 29, is *Charlie Lake Provincial Park* (fifty-eight sites; 800–689–9025 to reserve). Archaeological findings from caves here show evidence of huge bison having occupied the area. A 10,500-year-old bead

Trivia

Down near Dawson Creek is a village called Pouce Coupe. This means "cut thumb" in French, but the origins of the village's name are vague, ranging from a story of a French voyageur who cut his thumb skinning a buffalo, to that of a Sekanni trapper who lost a digit in a gun accident, to meaning an "abandoned chief's lodge by a deserted beaver dam" in the Beaver language. The real answer, so I hear from local Pouce Coupians, is that it is named after the Puscapi Indians, who inhabited the area when white settlers first arrived. Whatever the origin, the area is rich with rustic views and colorful grain fields.

Trivia

In 1898 a group of gold seekers who were heading for the Klondike were stopped at Fort St. John from continuing their journey by 500 Dunne-za natives. It wasn't until a land treaty with the Indians was promised that the would-be miners were allowed to pass.

Animal Checklist

- ❏ bison
- ❏ black bear
- ❏ caribou
- ❏ coyote
- ❏ deer
- ❏ elk
- ❏ fox
- ❏ grizzly bear

- ❏ lynx
- ❏ moose
- ❏ mountain goat
- ❏ mule deer
- ❏ stone sheep
- ❏ white-tailed deer
- ❏ wolf
- ❏ wolverine

was found here, the oldest evidence of human adornment in North America. You can see a replica on display in the museum.

Between Fort St. John and Fort Nelson, you have only the scenery and the occasional moose or caribou to entertain you for 240 miles (387 km). These long, desolate stretches give the Alaska Highway its mystery and magic and, occasionally, its boredom. After *Wonowon* (at Mile 101 of the Alaska Highway!), the road follows the Blueberry River through densely forested areas as it slowly climbs to 3,600 feet (1,100 m) at *Pink Mountain,* the halfway point between Dawson Creek and Fort Nelson. Services here include *Mae's Kitchen* (Mile 147, Alaska Highway, Box 35, Pink Mountain, V0C 2B0; 250–772–3215; fax: 250–772–5147; mae's_kitchen@ima.connection. com), a restaurant/motel combo, specializing in homemade bread and pastries, and *Pink Mountain Campsite,* Box 73, Mile 143, Pink Mountain, V0C 2B0; phone/fax: 250–772–5133). Here, there's a full-service gas station, a liquor store, hunting and fishing supplies including licenses, a post office, and a convenience store ("the Mall of Pink Mountain"). The campsite is open year-round for camping (if you dare in winter!) and RVs (there's a sani-dump, plug-ins, and a laundry). You'll often see wildlife, mainly moose, on the roadside around here.

A little-known side trip at Mile 147, west on Road 192 for 10 miles (16 km) brings you to a summer road that ascends to a communications tower and lookout at Pink Mountain. When the fireweed is blooming, sometimes at sunrise it actually looks pink. The lowlands to the north and west sides of the mountain are the only areas in the province where you are likely to see wild Plains bison, but this pretty area has another distinctive claim with its high population of rare Arctic butterflies.

The Alaska Highway descends steeply down the Muskwa River Valley into the Beatton River Valley and drops to 1,383 feet (411 m) near *Fort Nelson,* the lowest point on the Alaska Highway. Here long, hot summers and excellent soil provide good growing conditions. It's not unusual to hear of forty-pound cabbages.

But gigantic vegetables aren't the only "biggests" that Fort Nelson has to boast. It's also home to Canada's largest gas-processing plant and a huge plywood/oriented strand-board operation. Despite all the industry there are still quite a few fur trappers in the area, working mostly as their ancestors have done for centuries.

Locals assure me that one of the best meals in town can be found at the *Fort Nelson Flight Centre,* located by the airport. It originally catered only to airline personnel, but word of the scrumptious food hit the airwaves, and the rest is history. Homemade soups, breads, sandwiches, and desserts are enjoyed in a small room just like at home, with the kitchen right there. Coffee is always on, and drinks are located in the refrigerator, from which you can help yourself. Talk to the locals, read a book from the shelf, or play one of the games provided in this laid-back atmosphere.

For those who want to find out more about these offbeat spots and the many hiking areas near Fort Nelson or who want to take tours of the wood-products factories and the gas-processing plant, information is available at the *Fort Nelson Visitor Info Centre,* which is located in the Recreation Centre on the highway at the west end of town. Write Bag Service 399, Fort Nelson, V0C 1R0; or, in winter, phone (250) 774– 2541, ext. 241; fax: (250) 774–6794; in summer, phone (250) 774–6400; fax: (250) 774–6868; ecdev@northernrockies.org; www.northernrockies. org.

Trivia
Just south of Fort St. John, on the Alaska Highway by the Taylor Golf and Country Club, is the World's Largest Golf Ball, which is constructed from an old fuel tank. It measures 42 feet (12.8 m) across and weighs 37 tons.

The Info Centre can lead you to several accommodations in the $65 double range, including the *Ardendale B&B* (Mile 305, Old Alaska Highway, Lot 7645, Box 427, Fort Nelson, V0C 1R0; 250–774–2433; fax: 250–774–2436), a country home where the hosts offer sleigh and wagon rides; and the *Bluebell Inn* (3907 Fiftieth Avenue South, Mile 300, Alaska Highway, Box 931, Fort Nelson, V0C 1R0; 250–774–6961 or, for reservations, 800– 663–5267; fax: 250–774–6983;

bluebell@pris.bc.ca; www.pris.bc.ca/bluebell/), a one-stop motel/RV site/gas-diesel station/ bar/restaurant and convenience store located near the highway.

If you really want to get off the beaten path, visit the **Old Fort.** Getting to the site of the original Fort Nelson is an adventure in itself. You'll need a four-wheel-drive vehicle, though. The trip takes about an hour, and the road is either extremely muddy when wet or very bumpy when dry. It isn't plowed in winter and is often merely a track. To get there take the road to the Helmet Oil Field, just south of the Husky station in Muskwa Heights on the southern outskirts of town. Cross a rickety rail bridge (controlled by a traffic light) and drive until the road forks at a gas-line pumping station called Clarke Lake Central (about twenty minutes). Follow a rough road straight to the Old Fort. In winter access is by an ice bridge across the river. Once there, explore the settlers' first church, now restored, and the rectory and graveyard behind it. I've heard that the only ghost in the Fort Nelson area is the one haunting the basement of this church. A couple of families still live in the vicinity, so respect their private property while you explore.

Fort Nelson to the Yukon Border

As you travel west from Fort Nelson, you'll start to get the feeling of the true north, of its strength, its freedom, and its beauty. There are 326 miles (525 km) of diverse and spectacular scenery ahead of you between Fort Nelson and Watson Lake in the Yukon, so get ready

Recommended Reading - The Northeast

FOR ADULTS:
Peace River Chronicles, by Gordon E. Bowes. Prescott Publishing Company, Vancouver, 1963.

The Alaska Highway in World War II: The U.S. Army of Occupation in Canada's Northwest, by Kenneth Coates and W. R. Morrison. University of Toronto Press, 1992.

The Alaska Highway: A Geographical Discovery, by Thomas and Carole Huber. University Press of Colorado, 2000. A travel log detailing cultural and natural phenomena in the area.

FOR KIDS:
Back to the Cabin, by Ann Blades. Orca Books, 1996. Two boys who don't want to go up to their parent's cabin on a lake south of Prince George end up having an exciting time.

for a little visual ecstasy.

The *Flower Springs Lake Trail* takes you up almost 1,000 feet (300 m) for 3 miles (5 km), hiking through breathtaking scenery along the North Tetsa River, past waterfalls to Flower Springs Lake, looking brilliantly blue in an alpine setting. To get there take the Alaska Highway about 100 miles (160 km) west from Fort Nelson to *Summit Lake Lodge*. About 100 yards past the lodge there's a left turn, which is an access road to a microwave tower. Keep an eye out for moose, mountain caribou, stone sheep, and grizzly bears. Stone Mountain is visible across the valley. Though access by vehicle is restricted, a hike up to the tower will give you a spectacular view of the park.

Either before or after your hike, you may want to stop at the cafe at the highway turnoff where they make wonderful homemade chili and bread. If you have more time and wish to explore *Stone Mountain Provincial Park* (250-787-3407), there's a list of outfitters, available at the Fort Nelson Info Centre, willing to share their knowledge of the park and hoodoo-filled Wokkpash Recreation Area adjoining the southwestern limit of Stone Mountain Park. These hoodoos (pillars caused by erosion), which reach heights of 100 feet (30 m), give the area an otherworldly aura. There are a couple of close-by hoodoos along a short trail just west of the Summit Lake Campground. Ask at the lodge or campground for directions or follow the trails as indicated by the sign across from the entrance to Summit Lake Campground.

Your first vision (the word *view* is too tame) of *Muncho Lake* will leave you speechless. I now have to take a deep breath before turning that special corner when I know a lake so blue-green and clear, surrounded by snow-covered Rocky Mountains at their awe-inspiring best, will be revealed. The jade color comes from reflection and refraction of light on the suspended sediments brought into the lake by glacial melt water, but if you prefer, simply enjoy the beauty unhindered by explanations. Keep your eye out for stone sheep (a southern subspecies of Dall sheep) and woodland caribou, attracted to the salt left on roadsides after winter maintenance.

At Mile 462 of the Alaska Highway, the *Northern Rockies Lodge* is one of the largest log buildings in British Columbia. Sitting right by Muncho

Lake, it has a 45-foot (13-m) stone fireplace that dominates a European-style restaurant. Together with the older **Highland Glen Lodge,** there are a total of forty-five units, open year-round. A campground, RV Park, boat rentals, and other facilities are available. Owners Marianne and Urs Schildknecht will organize complete package holidays whether you're into fishing, photography, or mere sight-seeing. Urs has bush-piloted in the area for more than twenty years; with their own float-planes (Liard Air), the Schildknechts can help you explore a large part of this magnificent area. Write Box 8, Muncho Lake, V0C 1Z0; (250) 776–3481; fax: (250) 776–3482 or (800) 663–5269 for reservations; www.northern-rockies-lodge.com. Lodge prices start at $60.

Ask at any of the lodges or parks in the area about access routes for hiking the **Trail of 42** along the "Old Highway," which runs above the present Alaska Highway along Muncho Lake. You'll soon appreciate the driving (and road-building) skills required to traverse the area fifty years ago.

After leaving Muncho Lake, 16 miles (27 km) on is **Liard River Hot Springs,** another spot worthy of waxing poetic. Not only are the waters intensely hot and soothing, but there are some interesting organisms living here that can be found nowhere else in BC, including the tiny Plains forktail damselfly. There's also a small snail called the hotwater physa, which is unique to these waters. The two pools, Alpha and Beta, are a pleasant stroll along a 760-yard boardwalk (originally built by U.S. servicemen) from the parking lot near the campground. On your walk check the steamy bogs for little lake chub darting about, and several species of orchids, lobelias, cow parsnips, and ostrich ferns. The atmosphere is almost tropical! In fact it's hard to believe that not far from here at Smith River, the province's coldest temperature was recorded in 1947, a chilling -74° F (-58.9° C).

Cold or not, there is nothing quite like a winter stop at Liard River Hot Springs. Not only are there fewer people than in summer, but it's also comical to watch hair turn into spaghetti, as the steam combines with bitter cold air, aging each thread into hoarfrost. The first pool you come to is tiered, with each tier a slightly different temperature, which then runs off in a stream. Take care though, as the waters are so hot—from 100–120° F (38-49° C)—that you can easily become hyperthermic before realizing it. The recommended immersion time is about twenty minutes maximum. The second, deeper, cooler pool is another ten- to fifteen-minute walk through the lush vegetation. Occasionally moose and black bears come to the pools to graze on the aquatic vegetation, so take particular care. A resident park naturalist is a great source of knowledge about the flora and fauna in the area and offers summer hikes. Don't miss the *hanging gardens*, which can be viewed from the boardwalk, just past Alpha pool.

A couple of lodges nearby provide rustic accommodation. *Trapper Ray's Liard Hotsprings Lodge* (Mile 497, Liard River, V1G 4J8; phone/fax: 250–776–7349) is a log building with campground, R.V. park, and attached cafe. It's open year-round, with double-occupation lodge rate approximately $70. *Lower Liard River Lodge* (Mile 496, Alaska Highway, Box 9, Muncho Lake, V0C 1Z0; 250–776–7341; fax: 250–776–7340) provides very friendly service. It's also open year-round and overlooks the Liard River Suspension Bridge. The *Liard River Hot Springs Provincial Park Campground* (250–787–3407) is just east of the 500-mile signpost. Phone (800) 689–9025 for reservations.

The Alaska Highway straddles the BC/Yukon border, passing through Watson Lake and Upper Liard before it meets the Stewart-Cassiar Highway, which we will explore in the next chapter.

PLACES TO STAY IN THE NORTHEAST

DUNSTER
Culp's Farm,
Station Road, Dunster
V0J 1J0; (250) 968–4309.
Stay in antique sheepherder's wagons; $50
including breakfast.
Reservations only.

FORT NELSON
Arendale B&B,
Mile 305, Old Alaska
Highway, Fort Nelson, V0C
1R0; (250) 774–2433.
Country home.

MUNCHO LAKE
Northern Rockies Lodge,
Box 8, V0C 1Z0;
(250) 776–3481 or
(800) 663–5269 for
reservations;

fax: (250) 776–3482;
www.Northern-rockies-lodge.com. European-style
dining too.

Liard River Lodge,
Mile 496,
Alaska Highway,
Box 9, Laird River,
V0C 1Z0; (250) 776–7341;
fax: (250) 776–7340.
RV and tent sites too. Minutes from the famous hot
springs.

PINK MOUNTAIN
Pink Mountain Campsite,
Box 73, Mile 143,
Alaska Highway,
V0C 2B0; phone/fax: (250)
772–5133. Gas, diesel, and
propane available; post
office and store. Cabins.
Open year-round.

POUCE COUPE
Wildwood Cottage,
Box 220, Pouce Coupe,

V0C 2C0; (250) 786–5830.
Private rural cottage bed-and-breakfast.

PRINCE GEORGE
Bed-and-breakfast
toll-free lines:
(877) 562–2626 or
(888) 266–5555.

PLACES TO EAT IN THE NORTHEAST

DAWSON CREEK
Alaska Hotel,
Café and Pub,
10209 Tenth Street,
Dawson Creek,
V1G 3T5; (250) 782–7998;
alaska@neonet.bc.ca.

Fort St. John

Anna's Deli,
9600 93rd Avenue,
Fort St. John, V1J 5Z2;
(250) 785–9741. In the
Totem Mall near the Info
Centre. Serves appetizing
sandwiches, soups,
and full meals.

Liard Hot Springs

Trapper Ray's Liard Hot-
springs Lodge and Café,
Mile 497, Alaska Highway,
Liard River, V1G 4J8;
(250) 776–7349. Open
year-round.

Pink Mountain

Mae's Kitchen,
Box 35, Mile 147,
Alaska Highway,
Pink Mountain,
V0C 2B0; (250) 772–3215.
Homemade bread, pies.

Prince George

Great Wall Restaurant,
2757 Spruce Street and
Highway 97 South;
(250) 563–8128. Canadian
and Chinese cuisine. Open
from 11:00 A.M. to
midnight.

Rosels,
1624 Seventh Avenue,
V2L 3P6; (250) 562–4972.
Corner of Vancouver Street.
Fine dining. Lunch 11:00
A.M. –3:00 P.M.,
dinner from 5:00 P.M.
Reservations recom-
mended.

The Northwest

This huge region, approximately one-third of British Columbia, ranges from the rolling plains of the interior plateau west of Prince George and follows the Yellowhead Highway past myriad fishing lakes and First Nations' villages to the smell of the sea at Prince Rupert. It then heads north along the Stewart–Cassiar Highway, past the stirring Bear Glacier and the Grand Canyon of the Stikine, to the Yukon border.

Vanderhoof

The big-city feel of Prince George is replaced by open country and ranches by the banks of the Nechako River, as the Yellowhead Highway 16 heads to *Vanderhoof,* 60 miles (97 km) west, located close to the geographic center of British Columbia. Vanderhoof, Dutch for "of the farm," grew quickly as a railway town for the Grand Trunk Pacific Railway, but today it's more a gathering-hole for loggers and ranchers, the kind of town where trucks sport bumper stickers such as one I saw declaring BEATEN PATHS ARE FOR BEATEN MEN.

Many travelers rush through Vanderhoof, unaware that on the northern edge of town, the *Vanderhoof Bird Sanctuary,* bordering 3 miles (5 km) of the Nechako River, swarms with migrating birds, notably Canada geese. To find out more contact the Nechako Valley Sporting Association (Box 1077, Vanderhoof, V0J 3A0) or the *Vanderhoof Visitor Info Centre* (2353 Burrard Avenue, Box 126, Vanderhoof, V0J 3A0; 800–752–4094 or 250–567–2124; fax: 250–567–3316; chamber @hwy16.com; onramp.hwy16.com/chamber), located one block north of the highway.

Vanderhoof's history "lives" at the reconstructed *Heritage Village Museum* on the corner of First Street and Highway 16 West (Box 1515, Vanderhoof, V0J 3A0; phone/fax: 250–567–2991; museum@hwy16. com; onramp.hwy16.com/museum). Here costumed waiters in the *OK Hotel and Café* (250–567–2594) serve you as they would have back in the early part of the century. Several hotels and motels line the

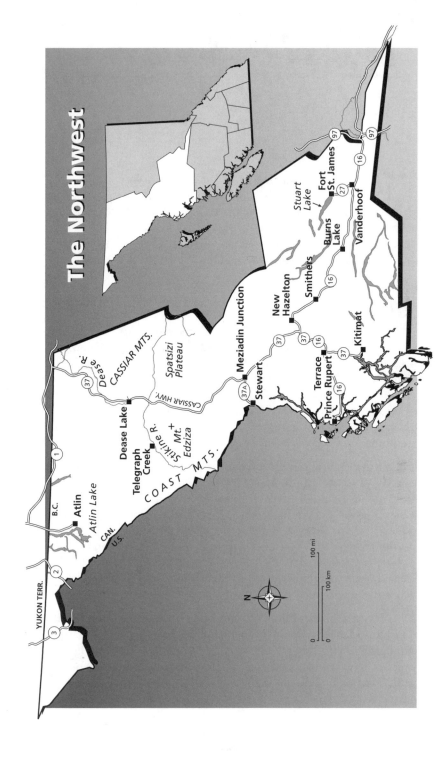

The Northwest

highway strip and beyond, as well as a couple of R.V. Parks and campgrounds. Stay a while and play at the **Tachick Lake Fishing Resort** (Tachick Lake Road, Box 1112, Vanderhoof, V0J 3A0; 250–567–4929; fax: 250–567–5566; tachick@hwy16.com). Cabin rates are $50 to $60 twin, and camping is also available. Here you'll find the **Saddle Bar Lodge,** famous for its (weekends only) gourmet dining. To get there head south from Vanderhoof down the Kenny Dam Road for 15 miles (24 km).

Fort St. James

*H*istoric **Fort St. James** is 34 miles (54 km) north along Highway 27. It's in a "don't miss" area and is the oldest continuously inhabited non-First Nations community west of the Rockies.

Just before entering Fort St. James, visit **Paarens Beach Provincial Park** and, 3 miles (5 km) farther on, **Sowchea Bay Provincial Recreation Area** (Box 2045, 4051 Eighteenth Avenue, Prince George, V2N 2J6; 250–565–6340; fax: 250–565–6940— for both parks), with about thirty-six campsites each on the south shore of Stuart Lake. Take Sowchea Bay Road just before the bridge over the Stuart River. There is no day-use area at Sowchea Bay, but picnic facilities, change houses, a playground, and a log picnic shelter are available at Paarens Beach, located on a long stretch of wide sandy beach. The campsites on the beach all have excellent views across 62-mile-long (100-km) Stuart Lake. Just before the Sowchea Bay Park entrance, on the corner of Heavenor and Sowchea Bay Roads, the **Big Bay Bed and Breakfast** (Box 1849, Fort St. James, V0J 1P0; 250–996–8857; bigbay@fsjames.com) is a new Victorian-style home, with a wheelchair-accessible elevator. Jo Anne and Martial Desrochers run five large guest rooms. Double accommodation ranges from $55, and the hot breakfasts are delicious.

The beach across the road is sandy, and there are plenty of hiking or snow-mobiling/ski trails. The nearby **Antimony Mine** 3-mile (5-km)

Trivia

At the end of Fraser Lake, the Nautley River, at less than half a kilometer, is the shortest river in Canada. It connects Fraser Lake to the Nechako River. Many of the hundreds of trumpeter swans that make Fraser Lake their resting spot during their spring and fall migrations overwinter on the Nautley River.

hiking trail leads to an old mining site, where some old buildings still exist. And for divers there's a *freshwater reef* near Battleship Island, a fortresslike island located 7.5 miles (12 km) from Fort St. James in Stuart Lake.

To get an eagle-eye view of Fort St. James and the surrounding wilderness, do the 3-mile (5-km) hike up *Mount Pope* to T-shaped caves. Inside, the caves are smelly with bat droppings, but from the 4,829-foot (1,472-m) Mount Pope summit, the view of Fort St. James, Stuart Lake, and the snowy Omineca Mountains to the north, is spectacular. The trailhead begins along Stones Bay Road, 3 miles (5 km) from town. It starts out steeply, but there are plenty of viewpoint stops on the way, with a total elevation gain of 2,600 feet (791 m). There's a gazebo on top of the mountain, as well as an old forestry lookout. Allow about five hours for the return trip. A hiking map is available at the *Fort St. James Chamber of Commerce and Visitor Info Centre* (115 Douglas Avenue, Box 1164, Fort St. James, V0J 1P0; 250–996–7023; fax: 250–996–7047; fsjchamb@qlynx.com; www.qlynx.com/biz/chamber.

If you prefer riding to hiking, there are three horses available on Pinchi Road for trail rides. Hans Sturm (phone: N694633 YL Channel) will take you on guided trail rides, on quiet forest trails.

For skiers *Murray Ridge Ski Area* (Box 866, Fort St. James, V0S 1P0; 250–996–8513), twenty minutes north of Fort St. James, has almost 20 miles (30 kms) of downhill runs as well as groomed cross-country ski trails, a T-bar lift, and a lodge with a licensed lounge and a cafeteria. *Whisky Jack Restaurant* (250–996–8828), just past the mill, serves great burgers. To get there take North Road out of town toward Germansen Landing.

The big attraction in Fort St. James is the *Fort St. James National Historic Site* (P.O. Box 1148, Fort St. James, V0J 1P0; 250–996–7191; fax: 250–996–8566; parkscan.harbour.com/fsj/). Here, in an authentic 1896 Hudson's Bay Post, you'll learn about the Carrier Indians (named for their widows who carried the cremated remains of their deceased husbands on their backs until a potlatch could be held). In summer actors become early Hudson's Bay Company officers and Carrier Indians. Chickens and geese run around, and you feel as if you have walked in on a scene from the fur-trading past. "The Fort" is open from 9:00 A.M. to 5:00 P.M. mid-May to the end of September. Admission ranges from $2.00 to $4.00, to a maximum of $12.00 for a family.

Across the road from the fort is the **Nak'azdli Handicraft Shop** (250–996–7368; open seasonally from 9:00 A.M. to 5:00 P.M.). Here an elder's society makes traditional moose-skin crafts and beaded jewelry.

From the fort follow Lakeshore Drive past Cottonwood Park, site of a one-third-scale model of a German Junkers W34 float plane, to one of the oldest Catholic churches in British Columbia. **Our Lady of Good Hope Church** was completed in 1836 by Fr. Blanchet, O.M.I., and was in regular use until 1951. Mass is celebrated on Saturday evenings in summer, but otherwise there is no access to the interior. A graveyard nearby has headstones written in the Carrier syllabics that were developed by another Oblate, Fr. Morice. Behind the church is an old log hut in which Fr. Morice printed the Carrier books and newspapers, which can be seen in the "Old Fort" museum.

Perhaps stay a while in the area, canoe and fish the waterways, ride the trails, or in winter enjoy dog mushing. It's all possible at **Vindsdalur** (Box 1713, Fort St. James, V0J 1P0; 250–996–8384; fax: 250–996–7079; ohm@qlynx.com). Lisi and Marcus Ohm, who have worked and bred Icelandic horses for more than ten years, have built a guest log chalet (three bedrooms, each with its own shower, and a deck overlooking the river) and offer canoe and trail riding trips on their property on the Stuart River.

Gold mining is another part of Fort St. James's history. Pick up some Manson Creek nuggets at **Tannis Gold** (3–264 Douglas Avenue; 250–996–2189). Then head to the **Gourmet Deli** for a healthful, loaded sub before returning south on Highway 27 to the Yellowhead.

Rose Prince

A very special native event is held every summer at Lejac, just east of Fraser Lake. The Rose Prince pilgrimage honors a Carrier woman who attended the Lejac Residential School more than fifty years ago. A kind, gentle woman, who endured curvature of the spine and several family losses, Rose Prince died in 1949 on August 19 (her birthday) from tuberculosis. In 1951, during the transfer of several graves, Rose Prince's casket broke open. It was discovered that her body, which had been buried for more than two years, was perfectly preserved. Other bodies were examined, and all were found to be decaying. There is speculation as to whether Rose Prince will be declared a saint.

Our Lady of Good Hope Church

Fort Fraser, Fraser Lake, and ***Endako*** dot the highway leading to Burns Lake, approximately 100 miles (161 km) west of Prince George. The main employer in the area is Canada's largest molybdenum mine at Endako, but ranching and recreational fishing are also important. A little-known fact about tiny Fort Fraser is that it is the site of the last spike driven when the east–west connection of the Grand Trunk Pacific Railway was made in 1914. Drop in to the ***Last Spike Pub*** (250–690–7433) and ask the locals about the railway history. Nearby, ***Beaumont Provincial Park*** (250–565–6340; 800–689–9025 for reservations) is set on the southeastern sandy shores of Fraser Lake. If you camp here, think back to 1806, when explorer Simon Fraser established historic Fort Fraser on this very spot. Fraser chose the site, originally known as Natleh, for its commanding view of the lake and the summer breezes that kept the bugs at bay. Near Fraser Lake watch for trumpeter swans that nest close by. Stop at the ***Fraser Lake Visitor Info Centre*** (65 Endako Avenue, Box 430, Fraser

Lake, V0J 1S0; 250–699–8844/ 6257; fax: 250–699–6469; fraserlk@flk. auracom. com) to learn more about these beautiful birds whose booming, trumpetlike call is heard around the 300 or so lakes that dot the area. If you're visiting in late fall or early spring, you'll soon realize why Fraser Lake is called The White Swan Capital of the World. The Info Centre is a log building, just off Highway 16, at the east end of the village. Ask here about tours of the **Endako Mine.** The attached museum is an excellent source on the history of the area's earliest inhabitants—from the Carrier people to the early fur traders to the farm settlers—as well as on the history of logging practices and the more recent development of the molybdenum mine. Recreational fishing is very popular in the big lakes as well as in the hundreds of other lakes and rivers in the vicinity. Ask at the **Par 3 Sports in Motion Store** (Box 99, Fraser Lake, V0J 1S0; 250–699–8063; fax: 250–699–8901; par3@flk.auracom. com) in Fraser Lake for information, or else book a fishing guide. **Binta Lake Outfitters** (Box 1092, Fraser Lake, V0J 1S0; 250– 699–6980 or 250–699–6313; fax: 250–699–8989; shoughton@ auracom.com) offers Nechako Country Fishing Adventures. They'll provide seven hours of guided fishing including equipment, transportation, gourmet meals, and, of course, your limit of rainbow or lake trout. If you want to try fly-fishing, they'll provide lessons if necessary. A five-hour hike over groomed trails on Fraser Mountain is also available.

Downtown Fraser Lake's best bet for a tasty lunch is the **Lunch Box Deli** in the Fraser Lake Mall. Its walls are lined with local photography and native art objects.

Another area worth exploring is the east end of François Lake, the Glenannan Tourist Area, which starts about 6 miles (10 km) south of Fraser Lake. It is served by several resorts with the added attraction of the nine-hole **Moly Hills Golf Course** (250–699–7761). One of these resorts, where you shouldn't

Top Annual Events in the Northwest

Tweedsmuir Days, Burns Lake; July; (250) 692-3773

Stuart Lake Fishing Derby, Fort St. James; June; (250) 996-7023

Fort St. James Fall Fair Festival, Fort St. James; August; (250) 996-7023

Kitimat Hill Climb and Car Show, Kitimat; July; (800) 664-6554

Prince Rupert Seafest, Prince Rupert; June; (250) 624-9118 or (800) 667-1994

Cow Bay Days, Prince Rupert; July; (800) 667-1994

Smithers Midsummer Festival, Smithers; June; (250) 847-5072; festival@bvfms.org; www.bvfms.org

Bulkley Valley Exhibition, Smithers; August; (250) 847-5072; fax: (250) 847-3337

Pacific Northwest Music Festival, Terrace; March/April; (250) 635-0131 or (250) 635-5688

Nechako Valley Exhibition, Vanderhoof; August; (250) 567-2124

Stewart/Hyder's International Days, July; (888) 366-5999 or (250) 636-9224; stewhyd cofc@hotmail.com

miss a delicious Swiss meal, is **Stellako Lodge** (phone/fax: 250–699–6695) on the Stellako River, world famous for its fly-fishing. Keen skiers and hikers love the **Fraser Lake–Stuart Lake Pack Trail,** a 28-mile (45-km) link between native villages on the two lakes. At one time it was a Hudson's Bay Company fur-trade route. One more spot you can ask staff at the Info Centre to direct you to is **White Swan Park.** Just north of Highway 16, it has an excellent swimming beach, picnic site, and boat launch.

Lakes District

The area known as the **Lakes District,** with its center at Burns Lake, is another excellent recreation area. In downtown Burns Lake take a drive up **Boer Mountain Road** to a lookout that will give you a panoramic overview of the district. To the south, in **François Lake,** large rainbow trout and char are common. To get to these big fish, take a left just before Burns Lake (Highway 35), passing pretty Tchesinkut Lake (pronounced "te-sink-it"), and drive 15 miles (24 km) south to the ferry landing.

Close to the ferry landing, **Darter's Misty Willows Ranch Bed and Breakfast** (Colleymount Highway, Box 455, Burns Lake, V0J 1E0; phone/fax: 250–695–6573; mdarter@futurenet.bc.ca) has more than 300 acres (122 ha) of aspen groves, rolling meadows, and waterfowl

Bluegrass Ghosts

*G*oats, turkeys, a curious cat, and a dog or two greeted me as I drove into Darter's Misty Willow farm. Before you could sing "Hot Corn, Cold Corn," I was wearing Marie Darter's gumboots and dragging bales of hay to sheep troughs. Later, over roast dinner and excellent wine, Marie reminisced about when she and her late husband, Charlie, added music to their yearly picnics—and the Burns Lake **Bluegrass Country Music**

Festival was born. Marie told of the history of her home, built by Jacob Henkel in 1906. Before the ferry service, settlers across François Lake would signal with fires, and Henkel would row a canoe over to fetch them. That evening I listened as the ferry crunched through the ice, and I imagined I could hear the stomp and twang of a bluegrass banjo beat. Across the lake a brightly glowing fire sent tingles up my spine.

ponds, as well as a lovely view of François Lake. In this 1906-built home, I enjoyed swapping stories beside a grand old woodstove in the big country kitchen with Marie Darter and her neighbors. Bed-and-breakfast rates start at $65 double.

Free ferries leave the north side of the François Lake on the half hour and the south side on the hour. Fourteen paved miles (22 km) south is *Takysie Lake,* where you'll have no trouble filling your creel with rainbow trout. *Likkel's Lakeside Store and Resort* (Box 11, Takysie Lake, V0J 2V0; 250–694–3403; 877–694–3403 toll free; fax: 250–694–3503) has campsites, cabins, a restaurant (popular with the locals after Sunday church), a store, a post office, and a laundromat. You'll also find canoe rentals and pedal boats. Cabins start at $45 double.

Back in Burns Lake (originally called Burnt Lake because of an enormous bush fire), *Process 4 Gallery* (Box 200, 425 Yellowhead 16 and Third Avenue, Burns Lake, V0J 1E0; 250–692–3434 or 888–990–2298; fax: 250–692–3934; www.burns lake.net/process4gallery) sells local art as well as fine art prints, originals, and collectibles by leading artists. All purchases are sold G.S.T. free!) Owner Wayne Brown, who has fished and explored most of the area, reveals readily his good fishing spots. He tells of the *Fulton River spawning grounds,* where the fish are so thick "you can walk across their backs." The best month to see this run is September. The Department of Fisheries and Oceans *Fulton River Salmon Project* (Box 9, Granisle, V0J 1W0; 250–697–2314) is the largest sockeye artificial spawning channel in the world and welcomes visitors. Take the road north from Topley, 32 miles (51 km) west of Burns Lake, for 25 miles (40 km), keeping a watch out for moose, black bears, and bald eagles.

Before heading west, though, stop at the *China Moon* (250–692–7411) in the Lakeview Mall (on the highway opposite Mulvaneys) and enjoy their Subgum Wonton

Relaxing by Red Sand and Kitsumkalum Lakes, hoping to catch sight of the Spirit Bear, the rare kermodei

Cruising the Inside Passage from Prince Rupert to Port Hardy

Shopping in Cow Bay, Prince Rupert

Watching Haisla artists at work in Kitamaat

Driving the Nisga'a circle tour from Terrace

Panning for gold in Telegraph Creek

Chartering a plane to see the crater of Mount Edziza, then continuing on to the Spatzizi Plateau Wilderness Park for an unforgettable sightseeing trip

Renting a boat or canoe to explore the multitude of anchorages in beautiful Atlin Lake

Learning the history of the Tsimshian First Nations people at the Museum of Northern British Columbia in Prince Rupert

Touring the eleven beautifully restored early 1900s buildings in the Vanderhoof Heritage Museum

Fly-fishing for steelhead in the Skeena and Babine Rivers

Soup, loaded with jumbo shrimp, chicken, pork, and vegetables. After eating take a walk along the *Eveneshen Nature Trail*. It starts behind the *Burns Lake Visitor Info Centre* (540 Highway 16 West, Box 339, Burns Lake, V0J 1E0; 250–692–3773; fax: 250–692–3493; bldcoc @cheerful.com), which is on the highway in town. The staff will lead you to the many accommodation options in and around Burns Lake. While at the Info Centre, check out the *Bucket of Blood* beside the *museum*; once a gambling den, the little building earned its gruesome name after a shootout over a game of poker.

A block west of the Info Centre is Babine Road, which leads for 18 miles (30 km) to the Pinkut Creek Project, an artifical salmon spawning channel 30 miles (50 km) north of Burns Lake; it offers good recreational fishing. Burns Lake is also the northern gateway to *Tweedsmuir (North) Provincial Park* (250–847–7320), an untamed wilderness accessible by floatplane, foot, or horseback via the *Alexander MacKenzie Trail*. You can also get there from the Nechako Reservoir (Ootsa and Whitesail Lakes) by jet boat. Ask at the Info Centre for information on guides who can take you into this magnificent, untouched park.

Houston to the Hazeltons

*H*ouston, the self-proclaimed World Steelhead Capital, is 50 miles (81 km) west of Burns Lake. It's the home of the 60-foot-long (18-m), 804-pound (365-kg) *world's largest fly rod,* which is located at the *Visitor Info Centre* (3289 Highway 16, Box 396, Houston, V0J 1Z0; 250–845–7640; fax: 250–845–3682; chamberh@ bulkley.net). This oversized aluminum rod is perhaps a hint at how to catch the steelhead in the Morice and Bulkley Rivers, which run through town. For a good view of the Bulkley, hike the North Side Community Trails, just around the corner from the Info Centre.

Two miles (3 km) west of Houston is a turnoff (Morice Forest Road) to the *Nadina River Project* (250–697–2314). Follow this road past Owen Lake to the Nadina Lake turnoff, then take this road (Tahtsa Road) for 18 miles (30 km) almost to Nadina Lake. Then follow the signs to the artificial sockeye spawning channel. Look for golden eagles in the area. Visitors are welcome, especially in September when the run is at its best.

Thirty miles (49 km) west of Houston is picturesque *Telkwa,* where the

Bulkley River meets the Telkwa. Maps at the museum in the old school-house describe a walking tour of twenty-six historic sites. Accommodation is available at the **Douglas Motel** (Box 291, Telkwa, V0J 2X0; 250–846–5679; fax: 250–846–5656; www.monday.com/douglasmotel), overlooking the green Bulkley River rapids. Double accommodation starts at $75. Telkwa is halfway between Prince George—226 miles (364 km) to the east—and Prince Rupert on the Pacific coast. Tiny Telkwa (population 1,200) has three hidden secrets: **The Crocodile,** (250– 846–9268; open daily and located on the main highway), **Riverside,** and **The Green House,** all first-class restaurants, the latter serving top-notch Chinese food.

Smithers, whose residents have been known to drive the fifteen minutes east to Telkwa to eat out, is at the center of the Bulkley Valley, sitting snugly below the towering 8,600-foot (2,621 m) Hudson Bay Mountain and glacier. As far as recreation goes, Smithers is it. From hiking and hunting to skiing and sledding, just name it, you'll find it in Smithers. The town has eighteen downhill ski runs to choose from, so skiing and snowboarding are the big attractions in winter. Hikes to the Twin Falls and Glacier Gulch are a popular summer activity. Ask for trailhead directions at the **Smithers Visitor Info Centre** (1411 Court Street, Box 2379, Smithers, V0J 2N0; 800–542–6673 or 250–847–5072; fax: 250–847–3337; smicham@bulkley.net; www.bulkley.net/~smicham). There is a wide range of lodgings: On the eastern edge of town is the **Hudson Bay Lodge** (3251 Highway 16 East, Smithers, V0J 2N0; 800–663–5040 for reservations or 250–847–4581; fax: 250–847–4878; reservations @hblodge.com; www.hudsonbaylodge. com); rates for doubles are from $92. Nearer the heart of Smithers is the newer **Stork Nest Inn** (1485 Main Street; Box 2049, Smithers, V0J 2N0; 250–847–3831; fax: 250–847–3852; storknest@bvl.net; www.storknestinn.com), where they serve free breakfasts in a friendly talk-to-the-chef atmosphere; doubles are from $64.50. **Java's,** downtown, is a good bet for lunches and desserts.

If you can find a few days to enjoy the scenic Bulkley Valley, **Berg's Valley & Alpine Tours Bed and Breakfast** (3924 Thirteenth Avenue, Box 3235, Smithers, V0J 2N0; 888–847–5925 or 250–847–5925; fax: 250–847–5945; bvtbb@bulkley.net; www.bbcanada.com/2125.html) runs valley and mountain safari tours, where you can visit historic **Moricetown Canyon,** 20 miles (32 km) west. In fall, fishers armed with gaffs or spears and nets challenge the rushing waters of the Wa Dzun Kwuh (Bulkley River) as it roars through a 50-foot (15-m) chasm. The village has some interesting, original totem poles. Bed-and-breakfast rates at Bergs range from $55 to $69.

An attractive log building houses the **New Hazelton Visitor Info Centre** (4070 Ninth Avenue, New Hazelton, V0J 2J0; 250–842–6071; fax: 250–842–6271), 22 miles (35 km) northwest of Smithers, at the junction of Highways 16 and 62. It's worth a stop to find out what's *off* the highway in this **Totem Pole Capital of the World,** which includes the Hazeltons, 'Ksan Village, and Kispiox.

Head down the Hazelton High Road (Highway 62) and cross the one-lane **Hagwilget Bridge,** suspended like a tightrope high over the Bulkley River. Built in 1931, it replaced a rickety footbridge of poles lashed together with cedar-bark rope, which was used in the past as a trading route by the Gitxsan and Wet' suwet' en ("the people of the lower drainage").

Cross over the bridge, and about 3 miles (5 km) north, where the Skeena and Bulkley Rivers meet, seven communal houses and some fabulous totems make up the **'Ksan Historical Village** (Box 326, Hazelton, V0J 1Y0; 250–842–5544; fax: 250–842–6533; ksan@ksan.org; www.ksan.org). This Gitxsan village has been reconstructed similar in every detail to the village that stood on the site when the first Europeans explored the area some 200 years ago and for millennia before that. Cultural interpreters you through the houses and relate the area's history. The museum houses a collection of items that make up Gitxan material culture, from button blankets to headdresses (both worn by high chiefs) to bentwood books and coppers (valuable possessions). All pieces originate from a 30-mile (50-km) radius of 'Ksan, and some are owned by Gitxsan locals. From October through April 'Ksan Village hosts on-site the Kitanmaax School of Northwest Coast Indian Design, a four-year carving and design program. During the months of July and August, the world renowned 'Ksan Performing Arts Group can be seen. Guided tours are available May through October, but the gift shop and museum are open year-round.

Continue on to Hazelton, sitting like a Western movie set on the banks of the Skeena River. Take time to do a walking tour of this restored pioneer village, which includes a riverboat replica and an original steam donkey. Nine miles (14 km) north, the Kispiox River joins the Skeena. Here you'll find some of the best totems in all of BC. Kispiox's fourteen poles have been moved from their original sites in the village to a spot by the water's edge. Nearby, the **Kispiox Cultural/Information Centre** (Box 25, Kispiox, V0J 1Y0; 250–842–7057; fax: 250–842–5604) sells local arts and crafts; it's open seasonally. About twenty minutes up the Kispiox Valley Road, just before the Rodeo Grounds, the **Sportsman's Kispiox Lodge** (Kispiox Valley Road, Box 252, New Hazelton, V0J 2J0; 250–842–6455; fax: 250–842–6458) is open year-round and has a licensed dining room and lounge. There are also self-contained cabins that sleep five ($125 high season) and lodge rooms ($55 high season). The Kispiox River is famous for its huge—in the thirty-pound (14-kg) range—native steelhead as well as for excellent salmon and trout fishing.

An all-native owned and operated company, **Skeena-Eco Expeditions** (Comp 25, Site K, RR1, Hazelton, V0J 1Y0; 250–842–5248; toll free: 877–842–5911; info@kispioxadventures.com; www.kispioxadventures.com) offers river rafting, jet boat tours, hiking, canoe rental, and fishing trips, all with a cultural tie-in. Try for spring salmon from June to August and steelhead from July to October. (The Stewart-Cassiar Highway section from Kitwanga to the Yukon border will be covered later in this chapter.)

Terrace to Kitimat

Ten miles (16 km) east of Terrace is one of British Columbia's loveliest parks. **Kleanza Creek Provincial Park** (BC Parks, Skeena District, Bag 5000, 3790 Alfred Avenue, Smithers, V0J 2N0; 250–847–7320; fax: 250–847–7659) features cascading waterfalls and a hiking trail to a beautiful view spot at the top of a canyon. *Kleanza* in Gitxsan means "gold," so some people like to try a little panning here. Don't laugh—back in 1934 some lucky panner took out a 6.3-ounce (180-gram) nugget.

Recommended Reading - The Northwest

FOR ADULTS:
Route of the Yellowhead Frontier Series #37 (1980 Heritage House Publishing Co. Ltd.)

Cassiar's Elusive Gold, by Francis E. Caldwell. Trafford Publishing, 2000. An adventure story about a prospector willing to risk his life to find gold. True Northwest history.

Atlin's Gold by Peter Steele. Caitlin Press, Prince George, 1995.

The Cinnamon Mine, Memories of an Alaska Highway Childhood by Ellen Davignon. Studio North, Whitehorse, 1988.

Diary of fort St. James, by Margaret Owen. Owen Enterprises, Box 464, Fort St. James (250–996–8680).

FOR TEENS:
War of the Eagles by Eric Walters. Orca Books, 1998. Set on the west coast of Northern BC. The hero is a Tsimshian native. His best friend, who is a Japanese-Canadian, was interned in BC's interior during World War II.

At the eastern edge of Terrace, Highway 37 leads to **Kitimat,** 36 miles (58 km) south, at the head of Douglas Channel. Kitimat's industry accounts for approximately 10 percent of the province's manufacturing Gross Domestic Product, with the combined value of its industrial products being more than $1 billion. Tours of what keeps Kitimat booming—**Alcan Smelter** (250–639–8259) film and bus tour, one and three-quarter hours; and **Methanex/Pacific Ammonia** (250–639–9292) film and walking tour (no children under twelve, no contact lenses, and no beards)—are provided free of charge. Or if you prefer, the kids can feed salmon hatchlings at the **Kitimat River Fish Hatchery** (250–639–9616) during a forty-five-minute walking tour (wheelchair accessible). Reservations are required for all tours. For information write or phone **Kitimat Chamber of Commerce and Info Centre** (2109 Forest Avenue, Box 214, Kitimat, V8C 2G7; 800–664–6554 or 250– 632–6294; fax: 250–632–4685; kchamber@sno.net; www.sno.net/KCOC/). While there pick up a *Hiking in Kitimat* brochure, which details how to get to the many hiking trails that criss-cross the Kitimat area. One beautiful hike (rated moderate to difficult) is the **Douglas Channel Trail.** Another facility worth touring is **Mike's Wildlife Museum** (phone/fax: 250–632–7083). Children under twelve get in free at this indoor look at BC's wild outdoors.

In town at the **Kitimat Centennial Museum** (293 City Center, V8C 1T6; 250–632–7022; fax: 250–632–8950; kitmuse@sno.net), learn about eulachon trading and the grease trails. Then head over to the Kitimat River, a major spawning ground for eulachon, to see BC's largest Sitka spruce tree. It's more than 500 years old, measures 36.7 feet (11.2 m) around, and is 165 feet (50.32 m) tall. There's apparently enough wood in it to frame nine houses. For campers the nearby **Radley Park Campground** (250–632–8955; fax: 250–632–3668) has fifty-six sites by the river. The **Chalet Restaurant** (852 Tsimshian Boulevard; 250–632–2662) and the **Ol' Keg Pub** (874 Tsimshian Boulevard; 250–632–6920) are both good bets for a tasty meal.

Kitamaat ("people of the snow") **Village,** the home of the Haisla and Henaaksiala people, is 7 miles (11 km) by road from Kitimat. You can see it across Douglas Channel from Hospital Beach near Alcan. Watch for killer whales, eagles, and sea lions as you gaze across to the village, where you can learn about the home of the Hudusdawachdu people in the untouched **Kitlope** ("people of the rocks") **Valley,** an area 60 miles (100 km) southeast of Kitimat. In 1994 this 780,000-acre (317,000-ha) valley was set aside as a protected area to preserve the world's largest intact coastal rain forest. Contact the **Na Na Kila Institute** (130

Owekeno Street, Haisla Resource Centre, Box 1039, Kitamaat Village, V0T 2B0; 250–632–3308; fax: 250–632–3384) for information on Eco-Adventure tours. The recently built **Kawesas Lodge,** a multipurpose 1800-square-foot, post-and-beam building, which can hold up to forty people, will be used to facilitate ecotourism programs by the Na Na Kila Institute. Among the programs to be offered is one on personal growth development using traditional native means.

On the way back to Terrace, the **Mount Layton Hotsprings Resort** (Box 550, Terrace, V8G 4B5; 250–798–2214 or 800–663–3862; fax: 250–798–2478; mountlayton@kermode.net; www.ker mode. net/mountlayton) is near **Lakelse Lake Provincial Park** (Highway 37, Lakelse Lake; 250–798–2277; fax: 250–798–2476 or, in Smithers, 250–847–7320). The park is thick with old-growth giant cedars, hemlock, and Sitka spruce. The public is invited to use the resort's odorless, open-air hot pools and waterslides ($6.75 slides; $4.50 pools, $2.50 for children three to twelve). Double accommodation is in the $80 range, and the sunset views of the snowcapped mountains are wonderful. Cross-country ski trails at **Onion Lake** are just five minutes away.

We're almost back to Terrace. Keep your eyes peeled, as you may catch a glimpse of the rare Kermodei, the elusive and mystical Spirit Bear, a white-colored black bear sometimes seen in the Skeena Valley. When

At Mount Layton Hotsprings Resort by Lakelse Lake Provincial Park, south of Terrace, you'll hear tales about the big-tipping, luggage-lacking "Catholic priests," who were guests there for two weeks in October 1928. They turned out to be none other than Al Capone and three of his henchmen, escaping the heat of their rumrunning in the Prohibition-riddled Chicago.

The Thing

If you're wondering what the large yellow "thing" across from the Terrace Visitor Info Centre is, meet Bertha, the only remaining portable spar pole in the world. This fifty-ton monster has had an up-and-down life as a tree mover. When first unloaded from a flatcar in 1952, it sank 3 feet into the rail-yard mud. After one use it was found to be totally impractical in the Terrace area, so it was parked, never to see service again. Designed to move logs by inserting the cut tree in the iron tube on the top and then attaching cables to lift the logs, Big Bertha was just too huge to move around in the bush; nor would her cables stay taut. So today the huge, bright white elephant exists merely as a curiosity, for tourists to say: "What's that thing?"

two black bears breed, and each of these bears has a double-recessive gene, the result is a Kermodei. It has been chosen as Terrace's municipal symbol. Get your bearings at **Heritage Park** (4011 Sparks Street), where you can tour original log buildings, each depicting a different aspect of pioneer life; a short walk from here takes you to a spot where you can enjoy panoramic views of the Skeena River winding through the city and surrounds. Then check at the **Terrace Visitor Info Centre** (4511 Keith Avenue, Terrace, V8G 1K1; 800–499–1637 or 250–635–2063; fax: 250–635–2573; info@terracetourism.bc.ca; www.terracetourism.bc.ca), where an accommodation book will help you choose a pleasant spot to spend a few days. The staff can also provide a city map and information about hiking. One hike of interest leads round the perimeter of Ferry Island (across the bridge), where a local carver has created about sixty carvings in the trunks of trees—wizards, birds, wolves—there's quite a variety. And don't miss the colorful **Skeena Valley Farmers' Market,** held every Saturday and Wednesday from May to October on Davis Avenue behind George Little Park. This is the largest farmer's market in the northwest.

The Info Centre has information on the **Kitselas Canyon** area, steeped in history, with settlements going back thousands of years. Archaeologists have been involved in digs here since 1968. Petroglyphs, totem poles, and longhouse remnants will hopefully not be allowed to weather away. Obtain permission from the Kitselas Band Council (4562 Queensway Drive, Terrace, V8G 3X6; 250–635–5084; fax: 250–635–5335; kitselas.village@osg.net; www.kitselas.bc.ca) before exploring the area, which is accessible by a walking trail. Plans to develop and restore the area are underway.

But the most spectacular, yet devastating, event in this area happened more than 250 years ago, about one hour north of Terrace toward New Aiyansh. Lava beds, created by a volcanic eruption (Canada's most recent), flowed into the Nass Valley for about 16 miles (25 km) downstream, resulting in an area resembling a **Moonscape.** An amazing 330-foot-high (100-m) cinder cone stands in the spot where the eruption occurred, destroying two native villages and killing perhaps 2,000 people. Find out more about the **Nisga'a Memorial Lava Bed Provincial Park** from BC Parks, Skeena District, Bag 5000, 3790 Alfred Avenue, Smithers, V0J 2N0; (250) 847–7320; fax: (250) 847–7659. A visitor's center, built along the lines of a traditional longhouse, has displays pertaining to the many features and native legends associated with the eruption. Access to the cinder cone is by guided hike only. Call *Hayats-gum Gibuu Tours* (Box 86, Gitwinksihlkw, V0J 3T0; 250–633–2150; hgtours@yahoo.com; www.members.tripod.com/~HGTours/) to see the Nisga'a people's homeland and the volcano that had such a devastating effect on their lives and their land. Hikes are available from Wednesday to Sunday May 1 to September 31 at 10:00 A.M. and 3:00 P.M.

Before heading west to Prince Rupert, stop at the *House of Sim-oi-Ghets* (250–638–1629; fax: 250–635–4622; schristiansen@kitsumkalum. bc.ca), another longhouse-style building, where you can buy traditional west coast First Nations artwork. It's just over the Kalum River west of Terrace on Highway 16 and is run by the Kitsumkalum Indian Band.

Prince Rupert and the Coast

From Terrace there are 91 miles (147 km) of lovely twisting Yellow-head Highway to cover as it follows the Skeena River to Prince Rupert. Drive it by day or you'll miss towering snow-covered peaks, waterfalls, and possibly a bear or two.

Don't miss the *North Pacific Historic Fishing Village* (1889 Skeena Drive, Box 1109, Port Edward, V0V 1G0; 250–628–3538; fax: 250–628–3540; northpac@citytel.net; www.northpacific.org). The turnoff to this 1889-built National Historic Site is about 8 miles (12 km) before Prince Rupert. Students act as guides and storekeepers in this restored cannery (open daily May 15 to September 30 from 9:00 A.M. to 6:00 P.M.) where you can eat in the "messhouse" (The *Salmon House Cafe,* 250–628–3273) and stay in the "bunkhouse" (*The Waterfront Inn,* 250-628-3538). Admission to the village is free, but entrance into the sites to see videos on fishing, the restored canneries, displays on salmon enhancement, and one of the largest collections of model railroads in western Canada costs from $3.00 to $7.50 (children under six are admitted free). Upstairs in the old cannery building (where two cannery cats reign supreme), *MacGregor's Studio* sells local and provincial artwork, books, and gifts.

Prince Rupert is Canada's deepest, ice-free harbor and is a major shipping port. It's the terminus for ferry traffic to Alaska, the Queen Charlotte Islands, and Vancouver Island, and for more than 10,000 years, it has been home to Tsimshian First Nations people. Their culture is depicted in the many totem poles seen throughout the city. Visit the carving sheds near the Court House downtown to watch the creation of

Trivia

It's not often that a city names a street after a living resident, but Terrace is so proud of Dr. Paul Clark, it has done just that. For years the roads around Terrace were the training ground for optometrist Dr. Clark in his pursuit of Olympic Gold. The training paid off, and in 1984 and 1988, he won two gold and eight silver medals in wheelchair racing in the Para-olympics. His fame goes back further though, as it was he who designed the first three-wheeled racing chair. At first it was prohibited from use in races but now is par for the course in wheelchair racing.

these majestic poles.

Back in the eighties I had sailed into Cow Bay. A decade later, I headed straight to the waterfront, keen to see if it had changed. The town used to be called Vickersville, but after a herd of cows was unloaded in 1909, the name Cow Bay stuck. A new cruise-ship terminal has been built, so now, instead of cows, tourists head down the gangplanks. And instead of a dairy, there's fresh seafood for sale. The cow-patch black-and-white hydrants and fuel drums, though, do give you the impression that you're surrounded by a herd of Friesians. To get to Cow Bay from the highway, turn north on Third Avenue East and follow it across the railway line to Cow Bay Road.

"See You Latte" says the reverse of the business card at ***Cowpuccino's Coffee House*** at 25 Cow Bay Road, Prince Rupert, V8J 1A4; (250) 627–1395. For breakfast try a large, fresh-fruit salad and granola loaded up with yogurt, and a choice of Latte, Moocha, or Cowpuccino coffee. It opens early (from 7:00 A.M. daily except Sunday, when it's open from 9:00 A.M.) and will often play foot-tapping Bob Marley music.

Other interesting restaurants in the area include ***Smiles Seafood Café*** (250–624–3072), famous for its halibut, and ***Cow Bay Café*** (250–627–1212), serving a colorful menu of fresh halibut with sun-dried tomato pesto, red Thai chicken curry, and vegetarian moussaka. And you can lose yourself in a library of books as you wait for your meal or watch the fleet come in.

There are accommodations at ***Eagle Bluff Bed and Breakfast*** (201 Cow Bay Road, V8J 1A2; 250–627–4955 or 800–833–1550 [toll free in Canada only]; fax: 250–627–7945; eaglebed@citytel.net; www.citytel.net/eaglebluff), right on the docks overlooking the Yacht Club, perfect for the landlubber with a secret desire to wake up to the sounds and smell of the sea. It was originally a cannery house. Double accommodation with a cozy nautical theme ranges from $55 to $90. Next door and still on the Cow Bay Pier, ***Eco Treks Sea Kayaking Adventures*** (250–624–8311; fax: 250–624–8318; ecotreks@citytel.net; www.citytel.net/ecotreks) offers kayak rentals ($25 per half day, single) and three-hour guided tours of the wildlife-rich local coast ($40 includ-

Canoe and Totem, Prince Rupert

ing introductory lesson). For the more adventurous there are longer trips around the Lucy Islands.

Across from Cowpuccino's on Cow Bay Road, *The Rain Store* (250–627–1002) is full of wet-weather stuff—gumboots with bells attached, umbrellas, rain sticks, and colorful raincoats—which may give you a hint at what to expect from the weather! Above, there's *Opa Sushi* (250– 627–4560)—awesome Japanese food—and *The Loft* (34 Cow Bay Road, Prince Rupert, V8J 1A5; 250–624–6442; fax: 250–627–1309; dspencer@citytel.net), a pottery and art gallery.

If it *should* be raining, visit the **Museum of Northern British Columbia** (100 First Avenue West, Box 669, Prince Rupert, V8J 1A8; 250–624–3207; 800–667–1994; fax: 250–627–8009) in its new quarters at the cedar-beamed **Chatham Village Longhouse.** Exhibits include Tsimshian settlement history and smooth, black argillite carvings. In summer two-hour **archaeological harbor tours** are held. On these you'll see native middens, the Digby Island Finnish fishing village, and Metlakatla Village, considered by many people to be one of the richest archaeological sites in the world. A new tour is the **Pike Island Tour.** Pike Island is an archaeological site specially developed for public education. The tour starts off at the museum with a slide show, then takes you on a boat to the island where you visit the sites, see some petroglyphs, and enjoy a smoked-salmon lunch. The tour runs from 11:00 A.M. to 4:00 P.M. and costs $42.

Also at the museum site (use the same contact address), the **Prince Rupert Info Centre** (250–624–5637 or 800–667–1994; fax: 250–627–8009; prtravel@citytel.net; www.tourismprincerupert.com) has maps for a tour of the city's totem poles; information on the **Fire Museum** (200 First Avenue West; 250–624–2211), where if the firemen aren't out on a call, they'll show you around—ring the buzzer; and information on the **Kwinitsa Station Museum** (Bill Murray Way—named for a longstanding politician, not a comedian), down on the waterfront. This attractive building is one of the last Grand Trunk Pacific railway stations left in BC. Summer hours (June–August) are daily from 9:00 A.M. to noon and 1:00 to 5:00 P.M.

There's an excellent photo view of Prince Rupert from the top of Fifth Avenue West, or you could take a flight-seeing tour of the **Khutzeymateen River Valley,** a protected habitat for one of the highest concentrations of grizzly bears in the world. Contact **Harbour Air** (250–627–1341; fax: 250–627–8307; harbour@harbour-air.com; www.harbour-air.com) or **Inland Air Charters** (Box 592, Prince Rupert, V8J 3R5; 888–624–2577 or 250–624–2577; fax: 250–627–1356; info@inlandair.bc.ca; www.inlandair.bc.ca), two of the companies offering this flight close to the Alaskan border. Flights leave from the seaplane base at Seal Cove. To get there take Sixth Avenue East (off

Trivia

British Columbians have a thing about shoes. Port Hardy had the original "Shoe Tree," and now Prince Rupert has followed suit with its "Shoe Tree II, Home for Lost Soles." In 1994 Crystal Fitzpatrick and her family located a large but dead tree along Highway 16, about 2.5 miles (4 km) east of Prince Rupert. They decorated it with a year's collection of old work boots and children's shoes. Today the tree lives on, as more and more passers-by hang up their old shoes.

McBride Street) and follow the seaplane signs. The cost for the one-hour Khutzeymateen trip from Inland Air is $198. A thirty-five-minute local tour costs $102 per person (minimum three people). Check www. inlandair.bc.ca for an up-to-the-minute live dock camera view of their planes' activities.

The Stewart–Cassiar Highway

We return east to Kitwanga, 138 miles (223 km) from Prince Rupert and join the **Stewart–Cassiar Highway**, which after 454 miles (730 km) joins the Alaska Highway at the Yukon border. Although not as developed as the Alaska Highway, the road is incredibly scenic. Planning your gas and accommodation stops is an essential element to an enjoyable trip up the Cassiar. If you fill up every time you come to a gas station, you should have no problems.

At Kitwanga cross the Skeena River Bridge and turn east, driving slowly along a very narrow loop road to Gitwangak, "place of the rabbits." Here you'll see twelve totems that tell the story of Kitwanga Fort and its defender, the fierce Nekt, who wore a suit of armor made from grizzly skins lined with pitch and slate. Information is available in **St. Paul's Anglican Church** (1893), across the road from the totems. It's one of BC's lovelier old wooden churches.

The **Kitwanga Fort National Historic Site** is 3 miles (5 km) north on Highway 37. Here, back in the 1600s, the Gitwangak people devised a defense system whereby logs were rolled on enemies who tried to attack the fort. Interpretive panels along a trail up to Battle Hill (Ta'awdzep) describe the history (in English, French, and Gitxsanmx). For more information write Fort St. James National Historic Park (Box 1148, Fort St. James, V0J 1P0; 250–996–7191).

Nine miles north of the fort, and appearing on many maps as Kitwancool, is **Gitanyow.** Ask carvers working in the shed near several impressive totem poles to show you Hole in the Ice, believed to be the oldest totem in the world. The original pole was taken down and is in storage, but a new one has been carved and erected. You may have seen some of these poles depicted in paintings by renowned artist Emily Carr, who visited in 1928, and in more recent works by Roy Vickers. The Gitanyow are in the process of com-

Trivia
Gitanyow, on Highway 37, means "place of many people." It was renamed Kitwancool, meaning "place of reduced number of people," after many people were killed by other tribes, then reinstated to its original name.

pleting a historic village project, part of which includes turning the twenty-one *getimgan* (history poles) around to face east, thus restoring the original look of Gitanyow. A museum showcases repatriated artifacts and existing community collections, and future plans are for an interpretive trail, arts, crafts, and interactive displays, as well as a new carving shed. Check out the Web site at www. gitanyowchiefs.bc.ca—it features the Gitanyow totems. For more information contact: Gitanyow Hereditary Chiefs Office, Hu Wilp Society, Box 148, Kitwanga, V0J 2A0; (250) 849–5373; fax: (250) 849–5375; gitanyowchiefs@kermode.net.

The highway follows the shore of Kitwancool Lake and on to Cranberry Junction, where a westerly turn will take you on a logging road 38 miles (61 km) to New Aiyansh and the Nisga'a Memorial Lava Bed Park (covered in the section on Terrace). Fifty-two miles (83 km) north and you're at *Meziadin Junction.* Take a break about 9 miles (14 km) before the junction at the rest area at the south end of the bridge overlooking the Nass River. A few hundred yards north of the bridge, visit the *Meziadin Fish Ladder.* Information signs give the ladder's history. It's interesting and well worth a stop, especially in July and August, when the chinook are on their homeward spawning run. Don't be surprised to see a thirty-pound (13.5 kg) salmon leaping into the air in an effort to navigate the ladder. Close to the junction, camping facilities at the *Meziadin Lake Provincial Park* (250–847–7320; sixty-two sites), 96 miles (155 km) north of Kitwanga, are excellent. Fish, launch your boat, swim in the cool lake, and rest before the long road ahead.

Side Trip to Stewart

Highway 37 forks at Meziadin Junction, and Highway 37A (the Glacier Highway) travels 40 miles (65 km) to *Stewart,* at the head of Portland Canal. It passes the magnificent *Bear Glacier,* 16 miles (25 km) from Meziadin Junction, just beyond the Strohn Creek Bridge. Here, even on hot days, you can feel the cool air flowing off the glacier. It's a fantastic sight, with the glacier so opalescent and blue that it glows at night. Along the 40 miles (65 km) to Stewart, you'll see more than twenty glaciers amid towering, craggy mountains. This road is definitely one of the most spectacular in North America.

Stewart and its American sister, Hyder, are frontier towns with a history of hard-rock gold, silver, and copper mining, but with such spectacular natural beauty, tourism is fast becoming a mainstay. The area is also valued as a movie backdrop (*Bear Island, The Thing, Iceman,* and *Leaving Normal*). By 1910 Stewart's population was booming at 10,000;

today it's just a little more than 400. Around morning teatime you'll find a good percentage of the population at **Rainey Mountain Bakery and Deli** (250–636–2777) when the steaming aroma of delicious donuts and pastries wafts from within.

Seaport Limousine (516 Railway, Box 217, Stewart, V0T 1W0; 250–636–2622; fax: 250–636–2633) provides bus service to Terrace and will also take you into the glacier country for a breathtaking trip through the steep Salmon River Valley. Colorful commentary of the valley's interesting history and characters adds to the tour as you travel past alpine meadows, bears, eagles, spawning salmon, and the spectacular **Salmon Glacier.** From mid-July through early September, with the arrival of the spawning salmon, the **Fish Creek Wildlife Observation Site** (one of the few bear-viewing areas in the world that you can drive to) allows visitors to see grizzly and black bears as they fish for chum and pink salmon in the shallow waters of the Fish and Marx creeks below. The site, operated by the U.S. Forest Service (250–636–2367), is a day-use area only. To get there, follow a well-maintained gravel road (Salmon River Road) through Hyder and continue 3 miles (5 km) north. The parking area is on the left, past the Fish Creek Bridge. To cut down on congestion, owners of larger vehicles are advised to use the shuttle vans from Hyder and Stewart. Contact Seaport Limousine in Stewart (250–636–2622) or the Grandview Inn in Hyder (250–636–9174). For more information, drop into the **Historical Society Museum** and **Stewart/Hyder International Chamber of Commerce Information Centre** (225 Fifth Avenue, Box 306, Stewart, V0T 1W0; 888–366–5999 or 250–636–9224; fax: 250–636–2199; stewhydcofc@ hotmail.com; www.stewartcofc.bc.ca). The friendly staff will sell you a *Salmon Glacier Self-Guided Auto Tour* pamphlet to show you the way. They'll also reveal the good hiking and fishing spots in the area. If you're camping, the **Rainey Creek Campground** (250–636–2537; fax: 250–636–2668; off-season: 888–366–5999) on Eighth Avenue borders a salmon stream. It's just a few minutes walk to the shops and a mile or so from Hyder, Alaska, where you can get into the "spirit" of things at the **Glacier Inn** bar and earn an I'VE BEEN HYDERIZED certificate. While there, you may as well continue to follow tradition and sign a dollar bill, which you then add to the multitude already on the wall of the inn. Nothing's too serious in this friendly little ghost town.

The Grand Canyon of the Stikine

From Meziadin Junction the Stewart–Cassiar follows the Bell Irving River to Bell II, 57 miles (92 km) north. From Bell II you cross several creeks, then skirt Kinaskan, Tatogga, and Eddontenajon Lakes on the way to Iskut and the Grand Canyon of the Stikine. With so much dusty road to cover, and so many logging trucks, you're advised to drive cautiously.

On Eddontenajon Lake, about 2 miles (3 km) before Iskut, **Red Goat Lodge** (Box 101, Iskut, V0J 1K0; 888–RED–GOAT/733–4628 for reservations; phone/fax: 250–234–3261) is open year-round. The $85 double rate includes a full breakfast. There are also cabins and bunk rooms available, as well as a campground with hot showers and a laundry. It's perfectly positioned for hiking, canoeing, and fishing, with **Spatsizi Plateau Wilderness Park** to the east and **Mount Edziza Park,** with its 900,000-year-old crater surrounded by thirty small lava and cinder cones, to the west. Phone (250) 847–7320 for information on both provincial parks. Another recommended place to stay is **Bear Paw Ranch** (Box 69, Iskut, V0J 1K0; 250–234–3005; bearpaw@room42.com; www.room42.com/wilderness), 5 miles (8 km) north of Iskut in beautiful surroundings. Soak in the outdoor hot tub, take a package tour into the scenic wilderness, or simply cozy up around the fireplace with either hotel or cabin accommodation. For those who want to rough it, there's a tipi too. High-season hotel rates start at $85, and cabins, complete with a wood-fired sauna, start at $60.

When you reach Dease Lake, accommodation is limited. The **Northway Motor Inn and Restaurant** (Box 158, Dease Lake, V0C 1L0; 250–771–5341; fax: 250–771–5342) is about it.

Dease Lake should be renamed Halfway, as it's halfway between Seattle and Anchorage and halfway between Whitehorse and Smithers. It's also 52 miles (83 km) north of Iskut, at the junction of the 74-mile (119-km) rough and winding but spectacularly scenic road to **Telegraph Creek.** Leave your trailer in Dease; then check at the **Dease Lake and Tahltan District Chamber of Commerce** (Box 338, Dease Lake, V0C 1L0; 250–771–3900) for information and road conditions. At about 50 miles (80 km) west, the road starts to twist and roller-coast along narrow canyons, with rock walls almost 1,000 feet (300 m) high, past fish camps and lava beds along the Stikine River, till it reaches Telegraph Creek.

Accommodation here is limited, but you'll find everything you need (including free Internet access) at the original Hudson's Bay Company store, now the **Stikine RiverSong Cafe, Lodge & General Store** (Stikine Avenue, Box 47, Telegraph Creek, V0J 2W0; 250–235–3196; fax: 250–235–3194; stikine.riversong@kermode.net; www.stikineriversong. com). Double accommodation units are from $55. Talk to Dan Pakula at the lodge about a four-day boat trip down the Lower Stikine to Wrangell, Alaska. Shorter trips are available also, notably one to the breathtaking Lower Grand Canyon of the Stikine. For paddlers, Dan can also arrange canoe rentals and back hauls from Wrangell, thus cutting down on trip costs, as well as simplifying customs paperwork in Wrangell. The Web site gives all the details. If you have any doubts about driving the road to Telegraph Creek, staff at the lodge are a good source of information.

North to the Yukon Border

The road north from Dease Lake follows the pretty lake and river of the same name. A couple of rest areas at scenic spots, and good char and grayling fishing, make for a pleasant trip. At the Cassiar Junction you can pick up souvenirs at *Jade City Store* (Box A8, Jade City, Cassiar, V0C 1E0; 250–636–2593). Buy raw jade and gold, gold nugget jewelry, semiprecious stones such as rhodonite and bloodstone, and gifts such as paintings done on jade. You can also watch jade being cut. Continue north through the Kaska Dene First Nation village of Good Hope Lake for 20 miles (33 km) to one of the prettiest campsites I've ever stayed in, *Boya Lake Provincial Park* (250–847–7320). The forty-five sites, set beside a turquoise lake, are a boater's and photographer's joy. The clarity and rich color of the lake result from light reflecting from the bottom, which is composed of marl, a mixture of silt and coarse shell fragments.

At Boya Lake, the *60th Parallel* (the Yukon border) is 50 miles (80 km) north, and the Alaska Highway is 2 miles (3 km) farther on. Since we left the Yellowhead, we've covered many a dusty mile, but there's still one little gem hidden way up in the far-northwestern corner.

Atlin is 290 miles (460 km) from the junction of the Alaska and Stewart–Cassiar Highways. The turnoff is at Jakes Corner, 52 miles (84 km) southeast of Whitehorse. Although Highway 7 is mostly gravel, the 60-mile (98-km) scenic trip along Little Atlin Lake and Atlin Lake, with the stunning, snow-clad Coast Mountains towering splendidly over them, is nothing short of magnificent. In the past it was a thriving gold rush town. Now its streets are paved with creativity, and there's a certain spirituality.

A good starting point for a tour of Atlin is the *Atlin Historical Museum* (Box 111, Atlin, V0W 1A0; phone/fax: 250–651–7522), on the corner of Third and Trainor Streets in a little 1902 schoolhouse. In summer museum staff members conduct walking tours of the town and the historic, elegantly restored **MV *Tarahne*.** In 1928 it took wealthy tourists on round-the-island cruises, but since 1936 it has lain idle on the shores of Atlin Lake. It's now the site of an annual Tea Party held the first weekend of July, when period-costumed hostesses serve delicious refreshments.

A delightfully rustic place to stay can be found at the **Atlin Inn & Kirkwood Cottages** (Box 377, Atlin, V0W 1A0; 250–651–7546; fax: 250–651–7500; atlininn@atlin.net; 800–68–ATLIN/28546 for reservations) on Lake Street. The eighteen hotel rooms and eight cozy cottages occupy a downtown spot on the lakeshore, where, until the Depression, the three-story White Pass Hotel sat so majestically. Inn rooms in high season are in the $84 double range, and cabins run $94 double, with much reduced rates in winter. The fully licensed **Atlin Inn Lakeshore Restaurant** has recently been added and offers great views over the lake.

If you prefer bed-and-breakfast accommodation, try **Quilts & Comforts Bed & Breakfast** (Box 59, Atlin, V0W 1A0; 250–651–0007; 800–836–1818; quiltsandcomforts@clarkmail.com; www.quiltsand comforts.com). Word has it that the breakfasts are amazing, the quilts (some available for purchase) beautiful, and the view stunning. Afternoon tea, available to the public, is served in the garden. There's also **The Anderson House** bed-and-breakfast (Box 253, Atlin, V0W 1A0; 877–651–7473; 250–651–7473; fax: 250–651–7656); **Tundra Bed & Breakfast** (Box 45, Atlin, V0W 1A0; 250–651–7551; tundra@atlin.net); and **Win's Place** (Box 1, Atlin, V0W 1A0; 250–651–7490; 867–668–3653; fax: 250–651–7550). The latter is a restored, Victorian-style lakefront home built in the early 1900s in Discovery, a gold rush town that a century ago thrived about 5 miles (8 km) from Atlin. The historic cottage has been restored to classy accommodation that sleeps four. Privacy is the key, with home-baked goods supplied for guests to cook their own breakfast.

Log cabins are available from **Sidka Tours** (Box 368, Atlin, V0W 1A0; 250–651–7691), which also rents kayaks and canoes and offers guided tours. **Brewery Bay Chalet** (Box 349, Atlin, V0W 1A0; 250–651–0040; fax: 250–651–0041; brewerybay@brewerybay.com; www.brewerybay. com) offers self-contained two-bedroom units on the lake. The barbecue and hot tub are a welcome addition. **Atlin Lake Houseboat Tours** (Box 381 Atlin, V0W 1A0, 250–651–0030; peterputter@telus.net) at Brewery Bay Marina offers sight-seeing and dinner cruises.

The **Atlin Centre** (Box 207 Atlin, V0W 1A0; 800–651–8882 or phone/ fax: 250–651–7659; atlinart@netcom.ca; www.atlinart.com) offers something entirely different. Overlooking the largest natural lake in BC (Atlin is from *ahtlah,* meaning "big lake" in the Taku River Tlingit people's language), guests here are given the choice of either art or adventure. ***Atlin Quest*** is a series of ten-day wilderness adventure vacations, including hiking and canoeing ($1,800). ***Atlin Art*** offers creative retreats; ten days costs $980 and three weeks $1,400, tuition and accommodation included. The center operates from June to September.

One of the coolest things to do in Atlin is to pan for gold—legally and with hope! East of town, on Spruce Creek, there's a "Keep all you find" panning claim, to which the friendly staff at the ***Atlin Visitor Centre*** (Box 365, Atlin, V0W 1A0; phone/fax: 250–651–7522) at Trainer and Third Streets will direct you; they'll also direct you to the artists and outfitters who make this wild but exquisite part of British Columbia their home. Further information on Atlin can be found at www.atlin.net.

Trivia
The lowest temperature ever recorded in British Columbia is -74° F (-58.9° C) at Smith River (in the northwest corner) in 1947.

And to finish your exploration in this utopian northwestern corner, take a guided raft trip on the Tatshenshini and Alsek Rivers with ***Tatshenshini Expediting*** (1602 Alder Street, Whitehorse, Yukon, Y1A 3W8; 867–633–2742; fax: 867–633–6184; tatexp@polarcom.com; www.tatshenshiniyukon.com). Prices range from $100 per person for a one-day trip on the Upper Tatshenshini River to $2,500 for an eleven-day Tatshenshini/Alsek expedition. (Special group rates are available.) You'll pass through three United Nations World Heritage Sites: ***Kluane National Park*** in the Yukon; ***Tatshenshini–Alsek Wilderness Park*** in the most remote corner of BC; and Alaska's ***Glacier Bay National Park.*** You can expect to be overwhelmed as you pass by huge icebergs thunderously calving off Alsek Glacier, and the gigantic peaks of the St. Elias Mountains, which include BC's highest peak, the 15,300-foot (4,663-m) Mount Fairweather. You'll end your journey in Alaska where the Alsek meets the Pacific's pounding surf at Dry Bay, and from here, fly by charter to Whitehorse in the Yukon.

The final adventure in our BC journey takes place on the magical Queen Charlotte Islands, as the eagle flies, about 400 miles (640 km) south of Dry Bay.

PLACES TO EAT IN THE NORTHWEST

BURNS LAKE
China Moon;
(250) 692–7411.
In the Lakeview Mall.

KITIMAT
Chalet Restaurant,
852 Tsimshian Boulevard,
V8C 1T5; (250) 632–2662.
Moderately priced meals.
Motel accommodation also.

PRINCE RUPERT
Cowpuccino's Coffee
House, 25 Cow Bay Road,
V8J 1A4; (250) 627–1395.
Light and healthful.

Cow Bay Café,
205 Cow Bay Road,
Prince Rupert, V8J 1A2;
(250) 627–1212.
Fresh halibut on the
waterfront.

TELKWA
The Crocodile,
Highway 16, Telkwa, V0J
2X0; (250) 846–9268.

VANDERHOOF
OK Café;
(250) 567–2594. Located
in Vanderhoof's Heritage
Village Museum.

PLACES TO STAY IN THE NORTHWEST

ATLIN
Atlin Inn & Kirkwood
Cottages, Box 377, Atlin,
V0W 1A0;
(800) 68–ATLIN; atlin-
inn@atlin.net.
On Lake Street. New fully
licensed restaurant also.

BURNS LAKE
Darter's Misty Willows
Ranch Bed and Breakfast,
Colleymount Highway, Box
455, Burns Lake, V0J 1E0;
phone/fax: (250)
695–6573;
mdarter@futurenet.bc.ca.

FORT ST. JAMES
Big Bay Bed and Breakfast,
Box 1849, V0J 1P0;
(250) 996–8857.

ISKUT
Bear Paw Ranch,
Box 69, Iskut, V0J 1K0;
(250) 234–3005;
www.room42.com/
wilderness.

Red Goat Lodge,
Box 101, Iskut, V0J 1K0;
(888) RED–GOAT
(733–4628) for
reservations; phone/fax:
(250) 234–3261.

PRINCE RUPERT
Eagle Bluff Bed
and Breakfast, 201 Cow Bay
Road, Prince Rupert,
V8J 1A2;
(250) 627–4955 or
(800) 833–1550;
www.citytel.net/eaglebluff.

SMITHERS
Berg's Valley & Alpine Tours
Bed and Breakfast,
3924 13th Avenue, Box
3235, Smithers, V0J 2N0;
(888) 847–5925 or
(250) 847–5925;
www.bbcanada.com/
2125.html.

TERRACE
Mount Layton Hotsprings
Resort, Box 550, Terrace,
V8G 4B5; (250) 798–2214
or, in Canada,
(800) 663–3862;
www.kermode.net/
mount layton.

The Queen Charlotte Islands/ Haida Gwaii

Tell any Canadian that you're trekking around British Columbia, and the first question is inevitably: "Have you been to the Charlottes?" Canadians think of them much as a new mother does her baby. They're precious. When a drifter took a chain saw to a beloved golden spruce tree near Port Clements, not only were residents horrified at the destruction, the whole country was in an uproar.

I had dreamed for years of visiting these misty, mysterious islands, known for 10,000 years to their outspoken native inhabitants as *Haida Gwaii* ("Islands of the People"). Their appeal lies in the mythology and artistry surrounding the Haida culture, combined with their isolation and stormy, rugged loveliness.

Consisting of two main islands, the more populated Graham in the north and Moresby in the south, four smaller islands, and about 150 teeny specks of islands, Haida Gwaii stretches like an elongated, curved triangle for 166 miles (251 km) from Langara Island in the northwest to Kunghit in the southeast. The remote southern part of Moresby is entirely Gwaii Haanas National Park Reserve, an area cherished by wilderness adventurers and the Haida people, who make up about one-sixth of the population of 6,000.

We begin our journey with an eight-hour sailing across a sometimes boisterous Hecate Strait on a BC ferry trip from Prince Rupert to Skidegate, a few minutes from Queen Charlotte City on Graham Island. Vehicle reservations (888–223–3779 or 250–386–3431) are required, as there are only four to six sailings per week from each port in summer and three in winter. BC Ferries' Web site (www.bcferries.bc.ca) lists fares and schedules and allows on-line reservations. (As a general guide, in summer expect to pay about $25 one-way per person—$16.75 for seniors (residents of BC only) and teens, $12.50 for children five to eleven—and $93.00 per regular-height vehicle, with an extra $40–$46

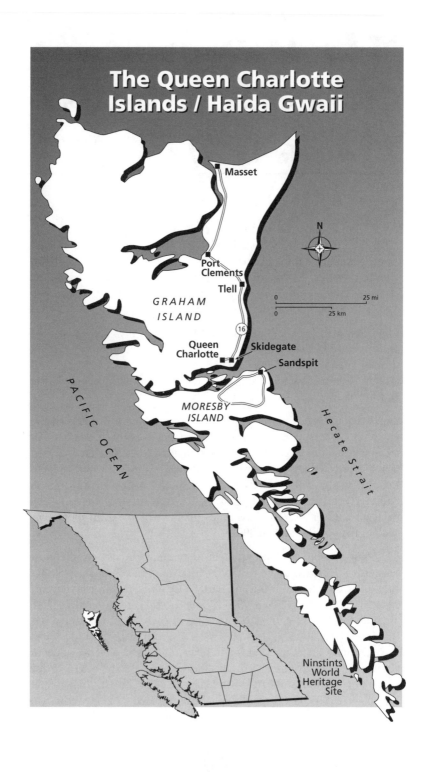

The Queen Charlotte
Islands / Haida Gwaii

Masset

N

Port
Clements

Tlell

GRAHAM
ISLAND

16

Queen
Charlotte

Skidegate

Sandspit

MORESBY
ISLAND

PACIFIC OCEAN

Hecate Strait

0   25 mi
0   25 km

Ninstints
World
Heritage
Site

if you want an overnight cabin.) From Sandspit, 3 miles (5 km) from Queen Charlotte City, a paved road (Highway 16 and still the Yellowhead) leads to Masset and clam-filled northern beaches, or alternatively, a twenty-five-minute ferry ride runs south to Alliford Bay, 8 miles (13 km) from the village of Sandspit on Moresby Island, gateway to the Gwaii Haanas National Park Reserve and UNESCO World Heritage Site, Ninstints.

Queen Charlotte City

Queen Charlotte City is the administrative center for the islands. Don't be fooled by the word *city,* though. It's about as laid-back as a city can be. You'll see what I mean if you start with a 6:30 A.M. coffee at *Lam's Café* on Wharf Street (250–559–4204). Previously called Margaret's, this little gem of a restaurant has been around for about fifty years and has that homey help-yourself-to-the-coffee friendly feel about it. Don't come after 2:45 P.M., though, as the owners, Melissa and Lam, close up early. I tried the hamburger and seafood chowder lunch special for $6.50, which was excellent. There's also a variety of delicious-sounding crab items on the menu and some newly added Chinese specials.

Author's Top Ten Picks on the Queen Charlotte Islands
Haida Gwaii Museum at Skidegate, with its ancient totems
More ancient totems at Ninstints—a spiritual odyssey
Bird-watching at Delkatla Wildlife Sanctuary, north of Masset
Kayaking at Hot Springs Island
Hiking to the blowhole near Tow Hill
Golfing at Dixon Entrance Golf and Country Club
Crystal Cabin Gallery Rock and Gem Gift Shop
Hiking to the Pesuta shipwreck in Naikoon Provincial Park
Camping at Rennell Sound on the wild west coast
Joining in the fun at Logger Sports Day in Sandspit

Across the road, the *Sea Raven Motel and Restaurant* (Box 519, Queen Charlotte City, V0T 1S0; toll free in BC or Alberta. 800–665–9606 or 250–559–4423; fax: 250–559–8617; info@searaven.com; www.searaven. com), *Joy's Island Jewellers* (Box 337, Queen Charlotte, V0T 1S0; 250–559–8890; fax: 250–559–8896; joys@qcislands.net; www.qcislands. net/joys) sells Haida-carved argillite, gold, and silver, woven cedar baskets, button blankets, trade beads, and other souvenirs such as T-shirts, local books, and jewelry. Farther along the main street at *Rainbows Gallery* (3201 Third Avenue, Box 489, Queen Charlotte, V0T 1S0; 250–559–8420; fax: 250–559–8430; rainbows@qcislands.net; www. gcislands.net/rainbows), there's a large selection of Haida art, including antique Native heritage crafts and collectibles, books, carved gold, and the famous black argillite, a soft slate found only on Slatechuck Mountain, west of Queen Charlotte City, and reserved exclusively for the Haida.

A quick look in at *Hanging by a Fibre* (250) 559–4463, a clothing store/cappuccino bar with unusual Queen Charlotte–theme T-shirts, then on to *Meegans Store* (*The Best Little Lure House in the Charlottes;* 250–559–4428), where they have tide tables and hand out "lurist" information (if you're here for the wild steelhead or trophy halibut), and I was ready to explore this Canadian Galápagos.

Before heading off though, get up-to-date information at the *Queen Charlotte Visitor Info Centre* (3220 Wharf Street, Box 819, Queen Charlotte City, V0T 1S0; 250–559–8316; fax: 250–559–8952; info@ qcinfo.com; www.qcinfo.com), open May 1 to September 30, 10:00 A.M. to 7:00 P.M., or at the airport in Sandspit (250–637–5362) from 9:00 A.M. to 5:00 P.M.

Less than a mile north of the ferry landing, at the blue "M" sign on Highway 16 at Second Beach, is the Haida Gwaii Watchmen Office (Box

Some Facts on the Gray Whale: *Eschrichtius Robustus*

*L*ook out to Hecate Strait during late spring and keep your eyes peeled for the blotchy back of a gray whale. Besides their gray color, sometimes mottled orange and white with barnacles and whale lice, grays are distinguished by the lack of a dorsal fin. They can be quite active and are often seen spyhopping and breaching.

Unlike the killer whale, which has teeth, the gray whale mainly feeds by straining its food through baleen, which is made of about 150 fringed, overlapping keratin plates hanging like fine hairs from the roof of the mouth on each side of the upper jaw. When feeding, the whale rolls on its side on the ocean bottom and draws sediment into its mouth. (You can tell if it's a left or right feeder by checking the barnacles and scratches!) It closes its mouth, then water and sediment

get pushed through the baleen, which traps the food near the huge tongue and is then swallowed. While migrating, the gray will feed at the surface on small fish and shrimplike mysids. Once it reaches the Arctic, it will consume its main prey, gammarid amphipods. The adult gray whale can grow to a length of 50 feet (15 m) and weigh up to 36 tons (33,000 kg). Calves are born approximately 16 feet (5 m) long and weigh about 0.8 tons (700 kg), but after suckling 200 liters of milk (53 percent fat!) daily, by the time they are ready for the 12,000-mile (19,500-km) round trip between the northern feeding grounds in the Beaufort, Bering, and Chukchi Seas and the southern breeding grounds in Baja California and off the Korean coast, they'll have doubled in weight.

THE QUEEN CHARLOTTE ISLANDS/HAIDA GWAII

609, Skidegate, Haida Gwaii, V0T 1S0; 250–559–8225; fax: 250–559– 8693) where you'll get information on the ancient villages in South Moresby. Next door lie totems and *Loo Taa* ("Wave Eater"), a 50-foot (15-m) cedar dugout canoe, whose carving was overseen by the famous Haida artist Bill Reid. Traditional techniques were used in this Expo 1986 commission, which was paddled home from Vancouver when the fair ended. In true Haida style a great potlatch celebration greeted its arrival.

Next door *The Haida Gwaii Museum* at Qay'llnagaay (Box 1373, Skidegate, V0T 1S1; 250–559–4643; fax: 250–559–4662; muse@qcislands.net; www.chin.gc.ca/haida) has a collection as eclectic as the people of the Charlottes. Magnificently displayed totem poles, two from Tanu (the ancestral home of many of Skidegate's residents) and two from Skedans, are this 10,000-square-foot (929-sq.-m), cedar post-and-beam building's most distinctive features. Other displays include fossils, Haida art, hands-on discovery boxes (island nature themes), endemic birds and mammals, and the world's largest argillite collection. An outdoor viewing deck extending to the tip of Qaykun Point offers an excellent observation area for birds, seals, sea lions, killer whales, and the gray whales that migrate in spring. You'll also find historic photos of Mexico Tom (the area's first rancher) and a seismometer, a reminder that the strongest earthquake (8.1) ever recorded in Canada occurred on Aug 22, 1949, off the west coast of Graham Island. The shaking was so severe along the Queen Charlotte Fault (Canada's equivalent of the San Andreas Fault)—the boundary between the Pacific and North American Plates, which runs underwater along the west coast of the Queen Charlotte Islands—that cows were knocked off their feet! The museum is open daily in summer. Off-season it varies, so phone for information. The museum gift shop has an excellent selection of Haida art, crafts and books. But there's expansion in the air.

The Qay'llnagaay Heritage Centre Society (250–559–7709) recently commissioned the carving of six poles on Second Beach; they were raised in June 2001. This event heralded the beginning of the construction of a 68,000-square-foot (6,3217-sq-m) facility that will incorpo-

Masset Harbour Days, Masset; May; (250) 626–3995; www.massetbc.com

Logger Sports Day, Sandspit; June; (250) 637–5362; www.sandspitci.com

Skidegate Days, Skidegate; June; (250) 559–4496

Hospital Day, Queen Charlotte City; July; (250) 559–8316; www.qcinfo.com

Tlell Fall Fair, Tlell; August; (250) 557–4468

Canada Day Celebrations, Port Clements; July; (250) 557–4295; portclem@gcislands.net

rate the existing museum. Aimed at preserving and celebrating Haida culture, the facility will eventually include an expanded museum, an interpretive center, the Bill Reid Teaching Centre, a performing arts theater, and a canoe center, plus a hotel and restaurant.

Before heading north make sure to stop at the Skidegate Band office on the highway to see the tall *Dogfish Pole,* also created by Bill Reid. Just north of Skidegate look for *Balance Rock,* a strange phenomenon left on the beach thousands of years ago by moving glaciers. From late April to June, a plume of rainbowed mist rising out of the water may enhance the scene, as a gray whale pauses to feed on its Mexico-to-Alaska migration.

Graham Island Central

Tlell is becoming noted for its community of artists. The first studio you pass driving north on Highway 16 (peacefully hidden on the beach, but there's a sign) is *Bottle and Jug Works* (250–559–4756). John and Jennifer Davis, teachers who arrived on these isolated islands in 1965, named the studio for their two previous dogs. They create bowls and other interesting, functional pottery.

North of the post office on Highway 16 in Tlell, follow the "**A**" signs left onto Wiggins Road and right onto Richardson. Tucked away, just a minute from the highway, are a few little treasures. At one, the *Crystal Cabin Gallery Rock and Gem Gift Shop* (778A Richardson Road, Box

The Dawn Watch

I had just driven off the ferry from Prince Rupert and was now between Skidegate and Tlell. A delicate first blush of sunrise added sheen to views across Hecate Strait. I quietly unlocked my Pentax, eager to capture the magic. I looked up. A lone bald eagle eyed me inquisitively from a stark conifer. Exhilarated, I clicked, hoping I wouldn't destroy the dawn's serenity. As I drove off, huge wings spread out above me. A few hundred yards on,

another rose-tinted seascape had me reaching for my camera. As if reading my mind, the brown-black body and radiant white head swooped, sharp talons finding a tall gray snag above me. Again, the golden-brown eyes pierced me intensely. I felt like an intruder, but furtively stole another image. Mysteriously, the eagle followed my journey, continuing to sear my soul with its glare, as together, we kept this lonely vigil.

88, Tlell, V0T 1Y0; phone/fax: 250– 557–4383; goldngem@island.net), French-born Dutes Dutheil creates fabulous gold and silver gemstone jewelry. His wife, Laura, makes fiber-art-sculpture spirit dolls, intricately embroidered and beaded amulets, and incredible talking sticks—6 feet long and hand-beaded with crystals. Her spirit dolls have spellbinding stories associated with them. From Copper Woman to Medicine Woman and Jade Woman, they're all unique, all beautiful. Hidden inside there may be a stick of sage, a crystal—something special to the doll. You'll also find here one of the island's largest Haida argillite collections, both small and large pieces. Talented native artists work with Laura, designing and creating blankets and clothing sold exclusively in the store. The gift shop also sells fossils, crystals, and Island Scenic Stone, a local stone surreally embedded with natural scenes. Open hours are 9:00 A.M. to 6:00 P.M. year-round and 9:00 A.M. to 8:00 P.M. July and August; all major credit cards are accepted.

Across the road is **Sitka Studio** (Box 460, Queen Charlotte City, V0T 1S0; 250–557–4386; fax: 250–557–4241). Barbara Small and artist Noel Wotten sell exceptional artwork, batiks, bird's-eye yellow cedar boxes, and Haida art, plus quality chocolate and organic coffee beans.

Recommended Reading - The Queen Charlotte Islands

A Guide to the Queen Charlotte Islands, by Neil G. Carey. Grasshopper Books, March 1998. A must for travelers to the Queen Charlottes.

Haida Gwaii: The Queen Charlotte Islands, by Dennis Horwood and Tom Parkin. Heritage House, May 2000.

The Beloved Island, by Kathleen Dalzell. Harbour Publishing, October 1998.

Islands at the Edge: Preserving the Queen Charlotte Islands Wilderness, Islands Protection Society. Vancouver: Douglas and McIntyre, 1984.

Ninstints: Haida World Heritage Site, by George F. MacDonald. Vancouver: UBC Press, 1984.

FOR CHILDREN:

The Raven Steals the Light, by Robert Bringhurst and Bill Reid (Illustrator). University of Washington Press, 1996. Ages four to eight. Adults will enjoy this book too—anyone with an interest in native legends will.

Myths and Legends of Haida Indians of the Northwest: The Children of the Raven, by Martine Reid. Bellerophon Books, June 1988. Ages nine to twelve.

Upstairs there's a large selection of books and artists' supplies.

They also rent out a fully equipped, two-story cottage. *Sitka Lodging* (250–557–4386/4241) overlooks geese, ducks, and wild swans by the Tlell River. Don't leave without asking Noel to show you his unique tree house, which is the butt of an enormous burled spruce tree, roofed with cedar shakes and a droopy copper peak, looking a little like a giant guard-cockatoo. Some people might say it's more like the butt of an enormous joke. It's furnished with chain-saw-hewn chairs, and the story goes that the famous Canadian author/artist/filmmaker James Houston had a hand in it. If you're lucky, as I was, you'll find some of Houston's original work in Sitka Studio.

Tlell has been the site of fish camps, farms, and artists' hideouts. The spread-out community, 22 miles (36 km) north of Skidegate, also has some intriguing places to stay.

Austrian-born Cacilia Honisch runs *Cacilia's B&B* (Box 3, Tlell, V0T 1Y0; phone/fax: 250–557–4664; ceebysea@qcislands.net; www.qc islands.net/ceebysea). There's loads of space to spread out in and elegant double bedrooms from $60 double. *Rustic* (the toilet-roll holders are driftwood and the shower-stall floor is pebbled) and *beachy* (the dunes are right outside) are key words. You never know who you might meet sitting on the driftwood/macramé barstools. You may even get to join in the weekly tai chi exercises. The B&B is easy to find—heading north on Highway 16, turn right after the 2 KM TO NAIKOON PARK sign, 25 miles (40 km) north of the Skidegate ferry dock.

Just north of Tlell, near the *Misty Meadows Campsite* at the southern tip of *Naikoon Provincial Park* (BC Parks Skeena District, 3790 Alfred Avenue, Bag 5000, Smithers, V0J 2N0; 250–557–4390 local or 250–847–7320; fax: 250–847–7659), a 3-mile (5-km) trail beginning at the Tlell River Bridge leads along the north shore of the river and through the forest to Hecate Strait and the 1928 *Pesuta* shipwreck. Do the hike on an outgoing tide, as the river comes up to the dune cliffs on high tides.

Trivia

The famous golden spruce that drew tourists to the Port Clements area before it was destroyed in 1997 was 165 feet (50 m) tall, was more than 300 years old, and had uniquely golden-colored needles.

If you keep walking, it's another 52 miles (84 km) to *Rose Point* (or "Naikoon," as it was called by the Haida), the most northerly spot in the Charlottes.

As one local commented: Why would anyone want to do that? It's total wilderness hiking, with no drinking water, nothing but rugged beach scenery, Sitka blacktail deer, tufted puffins, possibly even a few wild cows

Sitka Lodging burled tree house

(although it's a while since they've been seen), and a few streams to ford. Tide tables and a lot of common sense are necessary items, especially considering how the surf can pound against the 400-foot (120-m) cliffs just north of Cape Ball. There's some respite, though, with three rustic wilderness shelters en route, off the beach, but open one end for the wind to whistle through! You must register and have permission from the park office to hike this dramatic East Beach Trail, in this unspoiled 179,490-acre (72,640-ha), boggy, wild tract.

From Tlell the highway crosses the island for 13 miles (21 km) northwest to **Port Clements,** home to loggers and purse seiner fishers on Masset Inlet. The famous **Golden Spruce,** a feature of Haida mythology that was sadly destroyed in an act of madness in 1997, was its claim to fame. There's still a piece of history left in the area, though—the beginnings of an ancient 50-foot (15-m) **Haida dugout canoe.** Follow the signs into Port Clements, staying on Bayview Drive heading toward

Juskatla. The road quickly deteriorates and becomes a private, industrial logging road, so you must first get permission from Weyerhaeuser at their office in Juskatla (250–557–6810), open Monday to Friday 8:00 A.M. to 4:30 P.M., drive with headlights on, expect a logging truck on every corner, pull over and stop when you do see one, and obey all speed limits and posted signs. The canoe is in its original site on the east side of the road. Look for the trail sign 8 miles (13 km) south of Port Clements. The Ministry of Forests in Queen Charlotte City (250–559–6200) can also help with logging road usage.

This gravel road from Port Clements makes for an exciting circle tour. It follows the Mamin and Yakoun Rivers south across a couple of bridges to the *Marie Lake Fish Hatchery,* 25 miles (40 km) south of Port Clements. The program is run by the Old Massett Village Council (Box 189, Masset, V0T 1M0; 250–626–5655) and is designed to enhance chinook stocks in the Yakoun River. A short walk from the 40Q bridge on the Yakoun River (renowned for its steelhead fishing) there's a campsite called *Papa John's* (picnic tables, but no toilets or water), popular with fishing fanatics.

When you see sign 23S, you're at the turnoff to Rennell Sound. Other than by boat, it's the only way to get to the rugged west coast. The road passes the turnoff to Yakoun Lake, and near the end there's a very steep hill (24 percent grade for 1 km!), with an appropriate STEEP HILL sign. This is followed by an equally appropriate NO SHIT sign. BC Forest Service operates *Rennell Sound Forestry Recreation campsites.* Picnic tables, pit toilets, and fire pits, plus a pounding surf and miles of empty beaches, add to the appeal of these rustic wilderness campsites. A yearly camping permit is $27.00 (this is good for all forestry campsites in BC); seniors $22.00; a single-night fee is $8.00.

> ## Trivia
>
> *The islands that make up the Queen Charlotte archipelago have developed in isolation from the rest of the province. They were spared the effects of the ice age that covered the rest of British Columbia up to 15,000 years ago.*

Back at the junction the main logging road continues south from the Yakoun River Bridge for 14 miles (22 km) to Queen Charlotte City, ending on dust-free (yes!) paved roads. You may wish to do the circle clockwise, starting in Queen Charlotte City at *Hooterville,* a squatter community of weather-beaten float homes at the west end of town.

It's but 25 miles (40 km) from Queen Charlotte City to Rennell Sound. Consider doing a twenty-minute hike to *Yakoun Lake.* You'll pass old-growth, absolutely enormous Sitka spruce (Haida Giants!) en route to

THE QUEEN CHARLOTTE ISLANDS/HAIDA GWAII

WORTH SEEING/DOING ON THE QUEEN CHARLOTTE ISLANDS

Go bird-watching north of Masset at Delkatla Wildlife Sanctuary.

Do an artisan tour of Haida and non-Haida studios.

Sail or kayak around the islands.

Take a helicopter sight-seeing trip from the Sandspit airport.

this pristine lake, enhanced by views of Mount Stapleton, Mount Needham, and Delta Dome. Watch for the YAKOUN LAKE TRAIL sign, after turning south off Rennell Sound Road. There's a pebbly beach to be enjoyed when you get there.

Graham Island North

M asset, 25 miles (40 km) due north of Port Clements on Highway 16, has until recently been a Canadian Forces Base. Here you're at Western "Mile Zero" for the Yellowhead Highway (Highway 16), and here I discovered a superb place for a meal. *Restaurant Sandpiper,* at 2062 Collison Avenue (250–626–3672), run by Thi Hai and Fritz Engelhard, is one of those unexpected treats you sometimes stumble on in the most out-of-the-way places. With Haida prints gracing the walls to add local flavor, I enjoyed an evening special: a delicate lemon-chicken vegetable soup followed by Potatoes William, Fillo Purse (stuffed with peppers and onion) and Steak and Prawns Marsellaise, and completed by sinfully rich chocolate mousse cake all for $17.95, the equal of any big-city haute cuisine. The poached halibut with shrimp sauce is a winner with seafood lovers. The restaurant is near the Royal Canadian Mounted Police station and is open every day except Sunday.

Old Massett (different spelling, and sometimes called Haida) is the largest Haida village in the Charlottes and stands on the site of three ancient Haida town sites. To get there from Masset, travel west on Collison Avenue and turn right at the beach. The village is about a mile along and is spread out parallel to the beach on two main streets, Raven and Eagle.

The first thing you'll notice is the number of totems in the village. Some are erected outside homes, one outside St. John's Anglican Church (carved in 1969 by talented Haida artist Robert Davidson), and in the ball field there are replicas of two that stood in the old village of Yan. Two Reg Davidson poles stand in front of *Haida Arts and Jewellery* (250–626–5560). Behind a frontal house painting of Raven and Eagle, Sarah Hillis sells Haida art and souvenirs, including large argillite carvings, painted cedar-bark woven hats and baskets, and painted drums and paddles.

Before leaving Masset, visit the *Delkatla Wildlife Sanctuary* (Box 246, Masset, V0T 1M0; admin@birdsanctuary.org; www.birdsanctuary.org),

Haida Arts and Jewellery, Old Massett

where trails and three viewing platforms make it easy to spot some of the rust-colored sandhill cranes and white trumpeter swans that stop over during the spring and fall migration in this diverse marsh ecosystem. More than one hundred and forty species have been identified, including great blue herons, pied-billed grebes, peregrine falcons, hairy woodpeckers, and sandpipers. Trails start from points along Trumpeter Drive on the west side of the bridge, where the streets are named, delightfully, Brant, Widgeon, Pintail, Swan, and Teal. For many generations of Haida the area was a favorite waterfowl hunting area. A military settlement in the sixties brought about change, and in 1964 a causeway was built across the mouth of the Delkatla Sanctuary, thus blocking the tidal flow. In 1995, after years of lobbying and fund-raising by the Delkatla Wildlife Sanctuary Society, a $1 million restoration plan began, culminating in the construction of a 108-foot (33-m) bridge. Once again, tidal waters returned to Delkatla.

For more information on the northern section of the Queen Charlotte Islands, contact **Masset Visitor Info Centre** (Box 68, Masset, V0T 1M0; 250–626–3982 or 888–352–9292; 250–626–3955 in winter; fax: 250–626–3956; visitorinfo@massetbc.com; www.massetbc.com). When visiting the village office check out the world's largest blue heron sculpture, carved with a chainsaw out of yellow cedar by Haida carver Dick Bellis and Austrian-born Wilffred Penker.

On a cool fall day, I drove northeast from the Delkatla Wildlife Sanctuary past "The Elephant Pen," as some locals refer to the Canadian Forces Base signal station, and past one of the world's most remote (and Canada's most northwesterly) golf courses. The **Dixon Entrance Golf and Country Club** (Box 990, Masset, V0T 1M0; 250–626–3500 or 250–626–3735) works on an honor system. It's 2.5 miles (4 km) past Masset—just follow the signs. Set in the dunes, it has grass greens, great views, and lots of deer. I was soon at Graham Island's northern coastline looking across 37 miles (60 km) of Dixon Entrance waters at soft pinkish-gray shapes. I was looking at Alaska.

It seemed fitting then that I should stay at the **Alaska View Lodge Bed and Breakfast** (12291 Tow Hill Road, Box 227, Masset, Queen Charlotte Island, V0T 1M0; 250–626–3333 or 800–661–0019; fax: 250–626–3303; info@alaskaviewlodge.com; www. alaskaviewlodge. com). It's directly on South Beach on Tow Hill Road, 7.6 miles (12.291 km—hence the prop-

Your Personal Birder's Checklist

*M*any rare birds have been seen at Delkatla—during the Christmas Bird Count of 1985 the only Canadian sightings of the cattle egret and the least sandpiper were made. Use this checklist of birds seen annually at Delkatla for your personal sightings:

American Coot ❑ American Pipit ❑ American Robin ❑ American Widgeon ❑ Bald Eagle ❑ Barn Swallow ❑ Belted Kingfisher ❑ Black Oystercatcher ❑ Black-bellied Plover ❑ Bufflehead ❑ Canada Goose ❑ Cedar Waxwing ❑ Chestnut-backed Chickadee ❑ Common Goldeneye ❑ Common Merganser ❑ Common Raven ❑ Common Snipe ❑ Dark-eyed Junco ❑ Dunlin ❑ Fox Sparrow ❑ Glaucous-winged Gull ❑ Golden-crowned Kinglet ❑ Great Blue Heron ❑ Greater Scaup ❑ Greater Yellowlegs ❑ Green-winged Teal ❑ Hairy Woodpecker ❑

Hermit Thrush ❑ Herring Gull ❑ Killdeer ❑ Least Sandpiper ❑ Long-billed Dowitcher ❑ Mallard ❑ Mew Gull ❑ Northern Saw-whet Owl ❑ Northwestern Crow ❑ Orange-crowned Warbler ❑ Pacific Golden Plover ❑ Pacific-slope Flycatcher ❑ Peregrine Falcon ❑ Pine Grosbeak ❑ Pine Siskin ❑ Pintail ❑ Red Crossbill ❑ Red-Tailed Hawk ❑ Red-breasted Sapsucker ❑ Rufous Hummingbird ❑ Sandhill Crane ❑ Semipalmated Plover ❑ Sharp-shinned Hawk ❑ Short-billed Dowitcher ❑ Song Sparrow ❑ Starling ❑ Steller's Jay ❑ Swainson's Thrush ❑ Thayer's Gull ❑ Townsend's Warbler ❑ Tree Swallow ❑ Trumpeter Swan ❑ Varied Thrush ❑ Western Sandpiper ❑ Winter Wren ❑

Rare Bird Sightings: Bar-tailed Godwit ❑ Brambling ❑ Cattle Egret ❑ Smith's Longspur ❑ Tufted Duck ❑ Wood Sandpiper ❑

erty numbers) from the Masset Causeway. Eliane and Charly Feller's hospitality is unparalleled. Fabulous Swiss antique furniture, views of Prince of Wales Island, and scrumptious breakfasts make this a memorable retreat. Some of Eliane's unique, esoteric collages are displayed on the walls. There's great beachcombing—you may even pick up agates or those elusive, delicious razor clams. Whales, eagles, and, occasionally, northern lights add to this special experience. The lodge is open year-round, with double rates ranging from $70, including breakfast. There's also a guest house ($90 double in summer), in which each room has an en-suite bathroom and large shower, with a deck overlooking South Beach.

From Alaska View Lodge it's just a short drive on gravel road east to **Tow Hill.** Park just before the Hiellen River bridge and follow the map directions (on a bulletin board) to the boardwalks leading to the top of this 358-foot (109-m) basalt cliff. From here enjoy the great view of the Coast Mountains (on a clear day) and North Beach, which seems to run forever. Nearby is a trail to a **blowhole,** all that remains of a whale that was turned to stone in a famous Haida legend.

Moresby Island

There are only 62 miles (100 km) of paved roads separating Masset in the north from Skidegate in the south, from where the MV *Kwuna* (250–559–4485), a small car and passenger ferry, travels to Moresby Island and the magic of Gwaii Haanas. The crossing time to Alliford Bay is about twenty minutes; the round-trip fare (approximately $22 for a car and two adults in peak season) is paid on the Skidegate side. From Alliford Bay the road hugs the ocean for 8 miles (13 km) to the little village of Sandspit and the island's main airport. If you intend to drive farther afield along any of Moresby's back roads, phone *J. S. Jones Sandspit Ltd.* (250–637–5323), or drop in to their office on the road into Sandspit (just before the baseball field and the Lions Community Hall) to find out about road traffic and conditions. This is strongly recommended.

To explore Moresby by road, do a *circle tour* (allow approximately three hours) heading southwest from Alliford Bay. Those traveling on foot should keep in mind that there is no phone at the southern ferry terminal, so if you intend to go into Sandspit, arrange a taxi (*Bruce's*

THE QUEEN CHARLOTTE ISLANDS/HAIDA GWAII

Taxi, 250–637–5655) beforehand to meet you on the other side. Another choice is to rent a vehicle from Budget Car and Truck Rental (Box 133 Sandspit, V0T 1T0; 250–637–2330; 800–577–3228; fax: 250–637–2355; budgetqc@island.net). From the ferry turn right, sticking to the coast road for 6 miles (10 km) to South Bay. You're onto active logging roads now, so abide by the rules stressed in the Port Clements section. At South Bay, the road heads south for 4.5 miles (7 km) to the Moresby Road turnoff, which leads to a well-maintained campsite at Mosquito Lake (eleven units, boat launch, picnic site, and excellent trout fishing) and a major chum and coho enhancement facility on Pallant Creek; it then follows the creek to Cumshewa Inlet. This is as close as you can drive to Gwaii Haanas—from here to the southern tip of the national park, transportation is possible only by air or water.

So unless you are here to kayak, head back to the South Bay Main, passing western hemlock and Sitka spruce forests near the shores of Skidegate Lake. The road follows the Copper River to Copper Bay, Sandspit, and back to the ferry at Alliford Bay. If you have the time, take another side trip—14 miles (23 km) from South Bay Main—to the campsites at *Gray Bay* on Moresby's east coast. The road is not recommended for two-wheel-drive vehicles, but phone the Moresby Island Management Commission (250–637–2466) or the Sandspit/ North Moresby Chamber of Commerce/Visitor Info Centre (Box 148, Sandspit, V0T 1T0; 250–637–5362; fax: 250–637–2326; office@sandspitqci.com; www.sandspitqci.com) to get more up-to-the-minute information on these delightful areas on Moresby Island. You'll find the Info Center at the Sandspit Airport.

Golfers don't have to go far from the airport to enjoy a round of golf at *Willows Golf Course* (250–637–2388; fax: 250–637–2288), a 6,154-yarder complete with bar and grill. It's open from 11:00 A.M. to 11:00 P.M.

While at the airport take a look inside the terminal at the 14-foot dugout canoe *BiJaBoJi* used by Sandspit's Betty Carey in a gutsy west coast trip with her son Gene in 1962. Since the mid-fifties, Betty and Neil Carey have had a love affair with the Charlottes, which can be shared in Neil's famous *Guide to the Queen Charlotte Islands.* For thirty years they lived and explored from Puffin Cove on Moresby's remote west coast; today home is on the seafront in Sandspit. They're avid collectors of anything nautical or recyclable and are recipients of the prestigous CleanWorld Award.

If there's one fair not to miss in Sandspit, it's the annual *Logger Sports Day* held at the baseball field in June. You'll see record-setting pole climbs, ax throws, speed sawing, and birling at its best when hulking loggers dance like cats on fire trying to spin a log and dump their opponent into the freezing water. King and Queen Logger Trophies go to the male and female loggers with the highest aggregate scores. You'll need a hearty home-cooked meal after all that fun. Right in the heart of Sandspit on Shingle Bay, Monte Cobbs at the licensed *Eagle's View—Orange Roof Restaurant* (250–637–2217; fax: 250–637–5619) can come up with the goods and more.

Close by to the Eagle's View and still on the seafront in Sandspit, there are a couple of cozy bed-and-breakfasts. The *Seaport Bed and Breakfast* (371 Alliford Bay Road, Box 206, Sandspit, V0T 1T0; 250–637–5698; fax: 250–637–5697) is different in that it has separate private accommodations from its hosts, with a self-serve hot breakfast. A complete kitchen and laundry—and plenty of lawn on which to clean out your kayak—makes it an ideal base for Gwaii Haanas explorers. Rates are $40 double.

But if it's the ghosts of Nan Sdins (Ninstints), Skedans, and Tanu and the magic of Gwaii Haanas that you've been patiently waiting for, you need water or air transport. Too many tourists come to the islands expecting to immediately see ancient totems and wilderness, only to be disappointed that so much of it is inaccessible by road. For environmental concerns limits are set on the number of tourists allowed to experience the beauty of Gwaii Haanas each year. You should first talk to staff at Gwaii Haanas National Park Reserve (Department QCO, Box 37, Queen Charlotte, V0T 1S0; 250–559–8818; fax: 250–559–8366; gwaiicom@qcislands.net; parkscan.harbour.com/gwaii/) for permits and general park information. Independent travelers must abide by a reservation system (800–HELLO BC [435–5622] or from outside North America 250–387–1642 to register) and participate in a mandatory orientation held seasonally at either the Sandspit Airport at 11:00 A.M. or in Queen Charlotte City at 8:00 A.M. and 7:30 P.M. Registration fees (partially refundable if you cancel in time) are $15 per adult or $60 per group. There's also a user fee (collected at the orientation) for visitors more than seventeen years old—$10 per day for up to five days or $60 for up to two weeks. A seasonal user fee is $80. For those traveling on a loose schedule, there are six extra spaces available daily on a "first come" basis.

Commercial tour operators authorized to take you there can help cut the red tape. *Moresby Explorers* (Box 109, Sandspit, V0T 1T0; 250–637–2215 or 800–806–7633; doug@moresbyexplorers.com; www. moresbyexplorers.com) is a Sandspit-based business owned and operated by a lifetime local. Doug Gould will take you on day trips to nearby Louise and Hot Springs Islands or on three- and four-day excursions to the hallowed, abandoned village of Ninstints in Anthony Island Provincial Park, a World Heritage Site on the remote and rugged southern part of the island. If you're experienced, try a kayak rental, ranging from $210 single per week, which includes transportation to the Moresby Explorers Float Camp in Crescent Inlet. Check the Web page for tour and rental information and start planning for a wilderness experience unique in its combination of beauty, solitude, Haida Culture, and spirituality.

PLACES TO STAY ON THE QUEEN CHARLOTTE ISLANDS

MASSET
Alaska View Lodge Bed and Breakfast, Tow Hill Road, 8 miles (12 km) from the Masset Causeway; Box 227, QCI, V0T 1M0; (250) 626–3333 or (800) 661–0019; info@alaskaviewlodge.com. Double $70 . Guest house $90, double in summer.

Copper Beech House, 1590 Delkatla, Box 97, V0T IM0; (250) 626–5441; www.copperbeechhouse. com. David Phillips runs an off-beat laid-back B&B establishment year-round, and as well, serves gourmet dinners by arrangement (bring your own bottle) using produce from his own garden.

QUEEN CHARLOTTE CITY
Gwaii Eco Tours and Lodging, 604 First Avenue, Box 249, Queen Charlotte, Haida Gwaii, V0T 1S0; 877–559–8333 or 250–559–8333; gwaiieco@haidagwaii.net; www.gwaiiecotours.com. Double from $86.25 including taxes; two-night minimum. Land and sea day trips and multi-day interpretive spiritual tours offered. Garden and forest setting with ocean view and outdoor hot tub.

Sea Raven Motel,
3301 3rd Avenue, Box 519
QCC, V0T 1S0; (250)
559–4423 or (800)
665–9606;
fax: (250) 559–8617.
Modern; overlooks
Bearskin Bay. $70 double.

ROSE HARBOUR
Gwaii Haanas Guest House
and Kayaks, Box 578,
Rose Harbour, Gwaii
Haanas, Haida Gwaii,
V0T 1S0; (250) 559–8638;
by radiophone (April to
October): ask your operator
for a BC Telus operator,
then for a Marine Radio-
phone Operator: Vessel:
South Moresby, Number:
N–159009, Channel:
Cape St-James 24;
mailbox2001@
gwaiihaanas.com; www.
gwaiihaanas.com. Open
May 1 to September 30. $95
per person per day includes
three meals. Weekly, group,
and children's discounts
available. Family-owned
extreme wilderness accom-
modation on the north
shore of Kunghit Island.
Kayak rentals, inflatable
boat excursions, and tours.
Accessible only by boat or
floatplane (ranging from
$125 to $275 one-way from
Queen Charlotte City,
depending on group size
and day traveled).

SANDSPIT
Seaport Bed and Breakfast,
371 Alliford Bay Road,
Box 206, V0T 1T0;
(250) 637–5698.
$40 double. Home-baked
goodies placed in
your fridge.

TLELL
Cacilia's Bed & Breakfast,
Box 3, V0T 1Y0;
phone/fax:
(250) 557–4664. Rustic,
beachy. $60 double.

Sitka Lodging,
Box 460, QCC, V0T 1S0;
(250) 557–4386/4241.
Very private cottage on
Tlell River. $75.

**PLACES TO EAT ON THE
QUEEN CHARLOTTE ISLANDS**

MASSET
Daddy Cool's Pub and Grill,
Collison Avenue, V0T 1M0;
(250) 626–3210

Restaurant Sandpiper,
2062 Collison Avenue, V0T
1M0; (250) 626–3672.
Haute cuisine!

QUEEN CHARLOTTE CITY
Lam's Café,
Wharf Street; (250)
559–4204. Opens 6:30 A.M.
Delicious crab and Chinese
specialties.

Keenanii's Kitchen,
237 Highway 33;
(250) 559–8347.
Authentic Haida cuisine.

Oceana Chinese and
Continental Restaurant,
3119 Third Avenue, V0T
1S0; (250) 559–8683. Great
ice creams, yogurt, and
sherbet.

SANDSPIT
Sandspit Inn Restaurant;
(250) 637–5334. At the
airport; accommodation
also (800–666–1107).

Eagle's View-Orange Roof
Restaurant; (250)
637–2217.

TLELL
Tlell River House, Beitush
Road; (250) 557–4211.
Accommodation also.

Index

INDEX

INDEX

INDEX

INDEX

INDEX

INDEX

INDEX

INDEX

INDEX

About the Author

As an enthusiastic traveler to many of the world's lesser known places, and with a sailing circumnavigation under her belt, Tricia Timmermans is well qualified to uncover British Columbia's unique destinations. Australian by birth, she is a qualified teacher and photojournalist. She has lived in some of Canada's more remote areas, from Baffin Island to the Yukon, and presently·resides in Victoria, BC, where she is a photographer and travel writer.

Help Us Keep This Guide Up to Date

Every effort has been made by the author and editors to make this guide as accurate and useful as possible. Many things, however, can change after a guide is published—establishments close; phone numbers, E-mail addresses, and Web site URLs change; and facilities come under new management.

We would love to hear from you concerning your experiences with this guide and how you feel it could be improved and kept up to date. While we may not be able to respond to all comments and suggestions, we'll take them to heart, and we'll also make certain to share them with the author. Please send your comments and suggestions to the following address:

The Globe Pequot Press
Reader Response/Editorial Department
P.O. Box 480
Guilford, CT 06437

You may also E-mail us at editorial@globe-pequot.com, or contact the author at photo-j@shaw.ca; www.photo-j.com.

Thanks for your input, and happy travels!